THE GREATER WAR
1912–1923

General Editor

ROBERT GERWARTH

Paramilitarism in the Balkans

The Cases of Yugoslavia, Bulgaria, and Albania, 1917–1924

DMITAR TASIĆ

OXFORD
UNIVERSITY PRESS

OXFORD
UNIVERSITY PRESS

Great Clarendon Street, Oxford, OX2 6DP,
United Kingdom

Oxford University Press is a department of the University of Oxford.
It furthers the University's objective of excellence in research, scholarship,
and education by publishing worldwide. Oxford is a registered trade mark of
Oxford University Press in the UK and in certain other countries

© Dmitar Tasić 2020

The moral rights of the author have been asserted

First Edition published in 2020

Impression: 1

Published in the United States of America by Oxford University Press
198 Madison Avenue, New York, NY 10016, United States of America

British Library Cataloguing in Publication Data
Data available

Library of Congress Control Number: 2019957895

ISBN 978-0-19-885832-4

Printed and bound by
CPI Group (UK) Ltd, Croydon, CR0 4YY

For Tanja and Magdalena

Acknowledgements

When, nearly two decades ago, I began my career as a researcher at the Belgrade's Military History Institute (Vojnoistorijski Institute), Milan Terzić, my friend and colleague, often knew to point out how being a historian means you are involved in collective activity. What happened afterwards clearly confirmed his stand, not only through collaborative work on several collections of documents and thematic volumes, but also through everyday activities at the Institute as well as in the editorial board of Military History Review (Vojnoistorijski glasnik). This book is not different, actually it represents yet another confirmation of his stand, but this time on a much wider, international scale.

This exciting and fulfilling journey began during the work on my master thesis dedicated to the military rule in Old and South Serbia, that is areas of Sanjak, Macedonia and Kosovo and Metohija right after the First World War. Already during the archival research and frequent talks with my mentor Ljubodrag Dimić, as well as with Đorđe Stanković and Mira Radojević from the History Department at the Philosophical Faculty University of Belgrade, it became clear that there is much more to it and that involvement of the different paramilitary groups and organizations in Yugoslav state after the Great War demanded study of its own. How and in what form it wasn't clear at the moment, but one thing was sure, the idea was there, and it just needed the right spark. While I was in the middle of my PhD studies in 2011, I was invited to conference *War, Revolution, Civil War: Eastern Europe 1917–1923* organized by the University College Dublin Center for War Studies. There, beside John Paul Newman who I knew from Belgrade and who was acquainted with my work, I met other fellows of the Center and its director Robert Gerwarth. It was the time when his and John Horne's project on paramilitary violence in Europe after the First World War was finalized in collective volume under the title *War in Peace: Paramilitary Violence in Europe after the Great War*, published by Oxford University Press as part of the book series *The Greater War*. Following year, in 2013, I got the chance to translate the book for Serbian publisher *Arhipelag* and in the same time I was acquainted with Robert Gerwarth's work on his book *The Vanquished: Why the First World War Failed to End, 1917–1923*. Slowly but surely what was once just an idea started to shape up as a potential project. After consultations with Robert Gerwarth it was agreed to focus not only on Yugoslav state but to make it as comparative study of paramilitarism in Albania, Bulgaria and Kingdom of Serbs, Croats and Slovenes. Chronological boundaries 1917–1924 roughly coincided with those of Gerwarth's and Horne's study (1917–1923) with small difference in terms of major historical events. Here, 1917 was taken as year in which happened Toplica Uprising (uprising against Bulgarian and Austro-Hungarian occupation in Serbia) marked by extremely bloody and violent encounter of old adversaries—Serbian, Bulgarian and Albanian paramilitaries and irregulars—while 1924 was taken because during that year in Albania happened final coup d'état which ended period of post-Great War instability in that Balkan country marked by series of coups and countercoups.

However, not before the successful outcome of the 2014 Government of Ireland Postdoctoral Fellowship call this project was initiated. This prestigious fellowship gave me a privilege to come to UCD Center for War Studies and join vibrant community of researchers gathered around two prominent centers for war studies—one at UCD and the other at Trinity College Dublin—and Centre for European and Eurasian Studies at Maynooth University. Two years between 2014 and 2016 were filled with research as well as with frequent seminar series, workshops, and conferences during which I had opportunity to listen to leading experts in the filed. I equally benefited from opportunity, not only to listen to comments and questions of John Horne, Allan Kramer, Robert Gerwarth, William Mulligan and John Paul Newman, but also to enjoy their company in less formal occasions. Special place in this story belongs to group of "Dubliners"—former and current members of both centers for war studies as well as members of the UCD School of History. I am immensely grateful for the opportunity to work and cooperate with Mercedes Peñalba Sotorrio, Maria Falina, Susan Grant, Matteo Millan, Stuart Aveyard, Jennifer Wellington, Judith Devlin, Conor Mulvagh, Franziska Zaugg, Tomas Balkelis, Julia Eichenberg, Ugur Ümit Üngor, Tamir Libel, Sean Brady, Mahon Murphy, Alex Dowdall, and Fergus Robson. Special thanks belongs to Suzanne D'Arcy, our Research Administrator, whose expertise helped us greatly in dealing with everyday administrative challenges.

Important part of the research process were visits to archives and libraries in Belgrade, Skopje, Sofia, Tirana, Prokuplje and Bitola. Research in Belgrade was conducted in Archive of Yugoslavia and Military Archive where my special thanks goes to kind ladies at their reading rooms: Ivana Božović, Jelena Kovačević, Marina Đukić, Tamara Ivanović, Ljiljana Spaić as well as to archivist Marijana Mraović. From the National Library of Serbia, I am grateful to Nenad Idrizović, Ljubomir Branković, Nemanja Kalezić, Dragana Milunović, Maša Miloradović, Srđan Tadić and Uroš Žugić. Srđan Mićić and Vladan Jovanović from the Institute of Recent History of Serbia as well as Danilo Šarenac from the Institute of Contemporary History shared my enthusiasm and helped me immensely with their knowledge and literature. My stays in Skopje proved to be very useful and fruitful. I am in particular grateful to my colleagues Nikola Žežov from the Philosophical Faculty and Makedonka Mitrova, Katerina Todorovska and Isamedin Azizi from the Institute of National History of Northern Macedonia who helped me with useful advices and directions. Research stays in Sofia were especially rewarding primarily because of abundance of documents and literature related to that troublesome period of Bulgarian history. I am eternally grateful to my friend and colleague Marijana Stamova, who not only eased my ways through administration process at Archives State Agency but also introduced me to her colleagues from the Institute of Balkanology. The same can be said for Snezhana Radoeva, Todor Petrov, Stancho Stanchev and Yordan Baev from the Military History Section at the Military Academy "G. S. Rakovski". That particular group of friends and colleagues with whom I have collaborated for years provided me not only with literature from their incredibly rich library collections but also with kindness and support. Thanks to them I was able to meet Alexander Grebenarov, head of the Macedonian Scientific Institute—independent institution dedicated to preserve memory of IMRO, its history and members. During my later stays in Sofia, when I already left Dublin, I was able to continue with my research on para-militaries thanks to the help of Diana Mishkova, Rumen Avramov, Dimitar Dimov and Sylvia Stancheva from the Center for Advanced Studies where I stayed as fellow for six month in 2017. There I was also able to meet colleague Dimitar Mitev from the Institute of Recent History as well as cohort of young historians from the Sofia University "St. Clement of Ohrid" Martin Valkov, Dimitar Grigorov, and Petar Dobrev. Frequent meetings in the aftermath of Sofia's numerous seminar lectures and presentations provided me with plenty of opportunities to discuss with them various aspects of the Balkan paramilitarism throughout the 20th century.

I am also grateful to my current employer, Philosophical Faculty of the University Hradec Kralove, that is, its History Department and its head Jiří Hutečka for providing me opportunity to work in a stimulating environment and for enabling me to finalize work on my research and monograph manuscript within separate project. I also have to mention support I received from Eduardo Fonseca Garcia De Oliveira, Georgi Dimitrov, Tamara Scheer, Tetsuya Sahara, Catherine Horel, Nadine Akhund—Lange, Erwin Schmidl, Effie Paschalidou, Harold Raugh, Mark Kramer, Gia Caglioti, Olindo de Napoli, Vanni D'Allessio, Jovo Miladinović, Ivan Laković, Isa Blumi, Toomas Hiio, Javier Rodrigo, Miguel Alonso, Milan Sovilj, Milić Milićević, Božica Slavković, Frederic Guelton, André Rakoto, Saša Stanojević, Spyros Tsoutsoumpis, Pavlina Springerova, Iva Vukušić, Roberto Trajkovski, Zvezdan Marković, Blaž Torkar, Maja Božić, Árpád Hornyák, Özcan Gençer, James Horncastle, Jan-Phillipe Pomplun, Naoimh O'Connor, Tadgh O'Hannrachain.

Some of the illustrations in this book are courtesy of my friend Zoran Živković, a passionate collector of old photos. He was kind enough to allow me to present several valuable pieces from his collections and in that way enrich the books content.

Special thanks goes to friend and colleague John Dayton from Rochester Institute of Technology in Dubai, another important international collaborator in this enterprise on paramilitarism, for finding time to correct and comment my attempts to write in English. His knowledge of history of the Balkans, local lan-guages and understanding of Balkan ways in general proved to be of crucial importance in adjusting my style and ways of expression to somewhat different readership which doesn't have problems with definite and indefinite articles.

Robert Gerwarth kept a close look all the time. His involvement was crucial throughout the process, and, despite numerous obligations, he always find the way to check on progress, to comment, to encourage and recommend, and to be patient when work on other projects kept me away from my paramilitaries. For that I owe him eternal gratitude.

To be an author for the Oxford University Press represents a real honor. The whole process went smoothly and for that special thanks goes to Stephanie Ireland, Cathryn Steele, Lucy Hyde, Balasubramanian Shanmugasundaram and Matthew Williams.

Finally, I will use this opportunity to express my special gratitude to my wife Tanja and our daughter Magdalena for their important role in this process. It was especially visible in those days when I was faced with the choice between continuing my career in Serbia and accepting IRC fellowship. Although later it meant an academic life filled with uncertainty and struggle for permanent positions, when both of them simply said, "You should do it", I knew I was on the right way. This book I dedicate to them, in the loving memory of nineteen years filled with love, support and understanding.

Dmitar Tasić
Hradec Kralove, Autumn 2019

Table of Contents

List of Illustrations

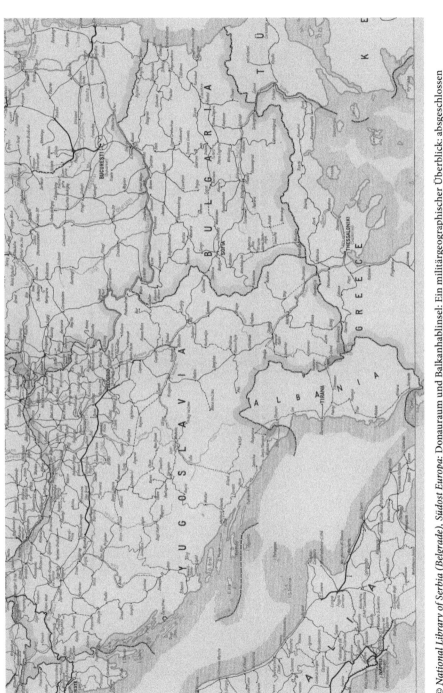

© *National Library of Serbia (Belgrade), Südost Europa: Donauraum und Balkanhalbinsel: Ein militärgeographischer Überblick: abgeschlossen 15 Mary 1940. – [Berlin]: Generalstab des Heeres, 1940 (Kp III 2627)*

Introduction: Balkan Paramilitaries – Undemobilized Combatants

One of the notable features marking the end of the Great War in Europe and its immediate aftermath was intensive paramilitary organizing followed by equally intensive paramilitary violence. All over Europe, from Finland in the north to the Balkans in the south, paramilitary movements and formations sprang up like mushrooms after the rain. A great number of European states witnessed this regardless of their post-war status—whether they were on victorious or losing side or they appeared as successor states of old empires that vanished in the course of the first global conflict. Here, the paramilitarism appeared in turbulent political circumstances where newly established national states often had to either struggle against revolutionary threats coming from the East as in Finland, Estonia, Latvia, Lithuania, and Poland, or, as in Germany, Austria, and Hungary where defeat and a subsequent 'culture of defeat' actually acted as a mobilizing factor for all those having difficulties in accepting new realities. Even the winning states France and Great Britain witnessed the emergence of numerous paramilitaries, whether as a result of concerns of certain political groups that their recently achieved victory might be endangered, as in France, or intensive usage of different paramilitary formations as a way to suppress separatist tendencies, as during the Irish War of Independence 1919–1921. The latter was also known as the Tan War named after the *Black and Tans*—the notorious and extremely brutal British paramilitary formation.[1] In this sense, the Balkans represented no exception. As in contemporary Europe after the Great War, the paramilitarism in the Balkans can be defined as 'military or quasi-military organizations and practices that either expanded or replaced the activities of conventional military formations.'[2] As a rule, paramilitarism and paramilitary culture in general were followed by paramilitary violence which was manifested in several different ways, whether against regular forces, rival paramilitaries or against the civilian population supporting rival groups. Furthermore, paramilitarism in the Balkans, as elsewhere in

---

[1] For an analysis of paramilitary violence in Europe 1917–1923, see: In Robert Gerwarth, John Horn (eds.), *War in Peace: Paramilitary Violence in Europe after the Great War*, (Oxford andNew York: Oxford University Press, 2012).

[2] Robert Gerwarth and John Horn, 'Paramilitarism in Europe after the Great War; An Introduction'. In Robert Gerwarth, John Horn, (eds.) *War in Peace; Paramilitary Violence in Europe after the Great War*, (Oxford: Oxford University Press, 2012), 1–18, here 1.

Paramilitarism in the Balkans: The Cases of Yugoslavia, Bulgaria, and Albania, 1917–1924. Dmitar Tasić,
Oxford University Press (2020). © Dmitar Tasić.
DOI: 10.1093/oso/9780198858324.001.0001

Europe, had its roots in the state's incapacity to function normally, in weak state institutions, in a legal vacuum, in corrupt political and dysfunctional security systems. In such cases paramilitaries often served as auxiliary force in an effort to impose state authority or acted directly against it.[3] Rather than being restricted solely to concrete paramilitary groups or movements, paramilitarism and paramilitary violence in the Balkans, as elsewhere, can be associated with the actions of conventional military and police formations as well. In terms of specific ways of warfare, rules of engagement, behaviour and manifestations like brutality, anger, and, reprisals, the conventional military and police formations often did not differ from paramilitaries and in that sense a particular situation had been created, which can be considered as the state of paramilitarism.[4]

However, the existence of a strong paramilitary 'culture' in the Balkans in the period of 1917–1924 has somewhat different origins and paths from the same phenomenon so widely present in the Europe of the same period[5] While paramilitarism in most of post-Great War European states was the product of violence of the First World War and brutalization which societies of both victorious and defeated countries went through, paramilitarism in the Balkans was closely connected with the already existing traditions originating from the period of armed struggle against the Ottoman rule, and state and nation building projects of the late 19th and early 20th century.[6] Paramilitary traditions here were so strong that in all subsequent crises and military conflicts in the Balkans, i.e. the Second World War and Wars of Yugoslav Succession during the 1990's, the legacy of paramilitarism remained alive and present.

During the Second World War in Yugoslavia, Albania, Bulgaria, and Greece all factions relied on their own traditions of paramilitarism in organizing their struggle. A common feature was that the struggle against occupiers in all four above-mentioned countries was waged simultaneously with brutal civil wars and violence. On one side there were local Communist parties and on the other their nationalist or royalist rivals, often collaborators. The stake was post-war rule and change or preservation of the existing political system. Even if they tried to distance themselves from their opponents and their political agendas, attitudes, values, symbols, dynamics and way of operating and organizing, they acted in pretty much similar fashions.

---

[3] Robert Gerwarth and John Horn, 'Paramilitarism in Europe after the Great War; An Introduction'. In Robert Gerwarth, John Horn, (eds.) *War in Peace; Paramilitary Violence in Europe after the Great War*, (Oxford: Oxford University Press, 2012), 1–18. here: p. 1.

[4] Anne Dolan, 'The British Culture of Paramilitary Violence in the Irish War for Independence'. In Robert Gerwarth, John Horn (eds.), *War in Peace: Paramilitary Violence in Europe after the Great War*, (Oxford and New York: Oxford University Press, 2012), 200–15, here 209.

[5] For the analysis of paramilitary violence in the Balkans 1917–1923, see: John Paul Newman, 'The Origins, Attributes, and Legacies of Paramilitary Violence in the Balkans'. In Gerwarth, Robert, John Horn (eds.), *War in Peace; Paramilitary Violence in Europe after the Great War*, (Oxsford: Oxford University Press, 2012), 145–62.

[6] See: Mark Biondich, *The Balkans: Revolution, War, and Political Violence since 1878* (Oxford: Oxford University Press, 2011).

During the wars that marked the collapse of Yugoslav state in the 1990's, within an entirely different political and ideological context, the bearers and activists of paramilitarism and perpetrators of paramilitary violence invoked the memory and traditions of paramilitaries of previous epochs through personal identifications, iconography, symbols, and organization. Like their predecessors, they represented mismatched groups of nationalists, patriots, enthusiasts, trained professionals and inspired amateurs. However, the active participation of a significant number of different types of criminals, from petty criminals, common burglars to drug-traffickers, was the novelty. In some cases they took over the leadership of different paramilitary groups or even formed their own. Some of them ventured onto the path of war crimes, often combined with different criminal activities, while the others went in pursuit of obscure political agendas, in most cases followed by violent acts like kidnapping or physical elimination. For most of them the invocation of patriotic vocabulary, paramilitary traditions and visual identity represented a convenient cover-up for various criminal acts aimed only for the purpose of rapid and enormous enrichment. Modern paramilitarism and paramilitary violence in the Balkans reached its climax with the assassination of Serbian Prime Minister Zoran Đinđić on 12 March 2003. The assassination was organized and executed in the joint action of one criminal organization and the leadership and part of the rank-and-file of controversial paramilitary *Unit for Special Operation* (*Jedinica za specijalne operacije*—JSO) which, although officially a part of the Serbian Ministry of Interior, was rogue in action.

Regardless of the actual historical, political and ideological context, Balkan paramilitarism proved to be very adaptable. One can notice the existence of a pattern in which paramilitarism steps in whenever the state institutions are weak or fall into a period of crisis. Different political factions sometimes used paramilitaries in on-going political or armed conflicts. However, in most instances the paramilitaries entered into these arrangements with their own calculations and expectations. In both situations the paramilitaries were practically investing their valuable assets such as armed and disciplined force, experience, organization, etc, for the purpose of fulfilling their own political agenda.

This study is focused on the part of the Balkans closely associated with the Ottoman Empire and its political, administrative, cultural, religious, and military legacies. Here, in the southern parts of the Kingdom of Serbs, Croats and Slovenes as well as in Bulgaria and Albania, existed common traditions of paramilitary organizing.

Some of the main features of paramilitarism in the Balkans 1917–1924 are as follows:

1. Intensive political engagement.

This feature is visible in paramilitaries' open support of different parties and influential groups in pursuing their agendas. In addition, paramilitary organizations and movements from one country were often supporting political parties, movements and groups in another in view of the fact that certain parts of their political programs coincided.

2. Strong inclination towards guerrilla warfare.

Guerrilla warfare or small war represented the integral part of the warfare culture of the Balkans paramilitaries. Basically, their initial involvement in action on the territory of the Ottoman Empire influenced all of their subsequent engagements. Although reluctantly, in certain cases the regular army and police relied on their 'services' both in times of war and peace. Their experiences and examples in some instances led to the official introduction of the doctrine of guerrilla warfare and creation of units for special operations within regular army and police.

3. Personal allegiances rather than organizational or institutional ones.

From their beginnings the Balkan paramilitaries were led by strong and often charismatic figures. Their influence over their followers caused the creation of special ties and personal allegiances. Sudden changes or disruptions of these ties often led to drastic shifts of career paths of some paramilitaries and had deep effect not only on their own future but the future of the organization they belonged to.

4. Active participation in armed conflicts, political crisis, coups, etc.

This aspect of paramilitarism often went along with the intensive political engagement, mostly in cases where additional arguments and assets were needed in imposing political or ideological agendas or suppressing those of the rival organizations or states. In almost all crises that occurred in the Balkans during the period under investigation, the participation of paramilitaries represented an integral part.

5. Arrival of new bearers of paramilitarism and paramilitary violence.

After the end of the Great War most of the Balkans witnessed the return of those individuals who fought on the Bolshevik side during the Russian revolutions and Civil war, as well as the arrival of their opponents from the ranks of 'White' Russians who were forced to leave their country for various reasons. Their experiences and ideological affiliations continued to develop and were transferred to the next generations, leading towards prolonged conflicts in new political and geographical surroundings.

6. Violence as an integral part of paramilitarism.

Although violence per se represents an integral part of war conflicts and of a great number of political crises, in the Balkan context levels and manifestations of paramilitary violence were additionally spiced by prolonged rivalries, revisionism, religious differences, imported ideologies (such as communism), specific cultures and traditions of warfare, personal animosities, and overall political and economical instability.

7. Reoccurring in identical or similar shapes despite the changes in ideological and political context.

Despite the development and changes of ideological, religious, international, political and economical context in the Balkans after 1924, paramilitarism appeared again on a massive scale during the Second World War and among all warring sides. It was interconnected and somewhat mixed with phenomena such as resistance and collaboration, and it represented a model for the organization of post-war resistance against the establishing of communist regimes in Yugoslavia, Albania, Romania and Bulgaria. The most drastic example of this feature was the renewal of paramilitarism during the violent dissolution of Yugoslavia in the 1990's, where the legacy of 'classical paramilitarism' was misused by different players, thus contributing to the appearance of invented traditions, which, apart from visual identity, did not have any type of connection with paramilitaries of the past.

This study is focused on the period between 1917 and 1924; however, in many sections it will go beyond this chronological framework in an attempt to present the origins and pre-modern manifestations of paramilitarism as well as its legacies and contemporary manifestations. The year of 1917 was taken as the initial year of this chronological framework due to the fact that the Toplica Uprising took place that year when, in the course of the Great War, in the south-eastern Serbian region of Toplica, the local Serbian population rebelled against Bulgarian and Austro-Hungarian occupation authorities. Although the popular narrative tends to represent the Toplica Uprising as 'the only uprising in occupied Europe during the Great War,' in this particular case its paramilitary component is the main reason why this event has been given such importance. The uprising itself was a unique occasion when different traditional Balkan paramilitary groups (Serbian, Bulgarian and Albanian) encountered each other. In addition, this was the year when thousands of miles to the north, in the Russian Empire, almost simultaneously, the series of revolutionary events began. They drastically influenced and changed the existing world order, and Europe's political and ideological image. In the following years, participants from the ranks of both sides would return to or arrive in the Balkans carrying a clear intention to continue their struggles. This intention, together with their experiences and ideological setting, contributed to the appearance of new levels and intensity of paramilitary organizing and violence. On the other hand, 1924 is taken as the year in which the *coup d'état* in Albania happened. This coup was the last in the series of similar turbulent events that marked the post-Great War period in the Balkans in which different paramilitaries, as a rule, played a crucial part. During this period Albania, Bulgaria and the Kingdom of Serbs, Croats and Slovenes, despite expressed desires to establish themselves as modern, legally and economically regulated states, continued to rely on or to tolerate paramilitaries.

Unlike their comrades-in-arms from regular armies, most of the Albanian, Bulgarian and Serbian (Yugoslav) paramilitaries remained under arms after the end of the Great War. They showed to be extremely adaptable to new circumstances. In no time they continued with their actions, simultaneously maintaining organizational structures and adapting political and ideological agendas. Old rivalries continued and it looked like they were waging their own, almost private, war against each other. Soon, newcomers who brought their own rivalries and differences to the Balkans joined them. First were thousands of Russians, both civilian and military, who objected to the establishment of the Bolshevik dictatorship and who were ready and willing to continue the struggle. Second were ex-revolutionaries and returnees from Russia among whom many were eager to spread new ideas and initiate a struggle for their fulfilment in their respective countries. In the years to follow both groups would make significant contributions to the continuation of conflicts and prolongation of crises.

These 'undemobilized combatants' and their actions in the period 1917–1924, as well as personal destinies and life trajectories, represent the main topic of this book.

I
Origins

The modern notion of paramilitarism in the Balkans was preceded by abundant warfare experience and authentic military tradition primarily shaped during the centuries of life under the Ottoman rule. For several hundreds of years, faced with the overwhelming military power of the Ottomans, small Balkan nations were forced to resort primarily to guerrilla warfare.

Another factor that made it possible to use these methods for centuries was the Balkan mountain habitat and its unique geographic position between Europe and Asia with important routes running from Central Europe towards the Eastern Mediterranean and the Middle East. The mountain habitat itself caused the evolution of a specific mentality or culture widely present in isolated, poor, infertile, and road less mountainous regions. The Serbian geographer Jovan Cvijić in his studies classified the population of Europe's Southeast, that is their psychological types, according to their natural environment. He particularly highlighted the 'Dinaric type' characterized by national pride, honour, sense of justice, love of freedom, warrior spirit, solidarity, patriarchal order etc. His 'Dinaroids' basically were Serbs who lived in the Dinaric mountain chain (regions of Montenegro, Bosnia and Herzegovina, Dalmatia), from which they spread to other, in this case lower, fertile and more civilized regions.[1] However, these features can easily be extended to other dwellers of Balkan mountainous areas such as Macedonia, Kosovo and Metohija, Northern Albania, Epirus, Mt. Balkan and the Rhodope mountains. In this predominantly cattle-breeding, almost semi-nomadic culture, the mountain was considered as place of protection or refuge, a natural fortress. As Ulf Brunnbauer mentions in his study, mountains have a specific meaning in the process of nation building in South-eastern Europe:

> "Mountains serve as cultural landscapes that inspire collective commemoration of the heroic past of the nation. They are sites where resistance against foreign intruders is most commonly located...Mountains become both metonyms of the nation and metaphors of its characteristics."[2]

---

[1] Jovan Cvijić, *O balkanskim psihološkim tipovima* (Beograd: Prosveta, 2014). However, his crowning work is the study *Balkan Peninsula* (Balkansko poluostrvo) which although written, among other things, to support Yugoslav/Serbian claims after the Great War represents the results of long and extensive empirical research.

[2] Ulf Brunnbauer, '"Bold and Pure Highlanders" Mountains and National imagination in the Balkans', In Predrag J. Marković, Tetsuya Sahara, Momčilo Pavlović (eds), *Guerrilla in the Balkans/*

Paramilitarism in the Balkans: The Cases of Yugoslavia, Bulgaria, and Albania, 1917–1924. Dmitar Tasić, Oxford University Press (2020). © Dmitar Tasić.
DOI: 10.1093/oso/9780198858324.001.0001

Ottoman policies of Islamization and assimilation were, among other things, followed with brutality and different kinds of violence that unavoidably led to the emergence of armed resistance, which occurred in two ways. One was by joining and assisting other armies that waged war against the Ottomans, like Austrians, Venetians or Russians. The other way was waging guerrilla warfare with small bands of *hajduks* or *kleftes*.[3] However, in many instances it was difficult to distinguish freedom fighters with clear political motivation from simple brigands or cattle rustlers motivated only by the wish to make profits. It was almost impossible to make a clear distinction between these two phenomena, which often served for mutual justification. After all, in this sense the Balkans is not unique. This kind of lifestyle and economic activities was typical for many other cultures—especially in borderlands of neighbouring empires or where religiously confronted communities used to coexist—Spain in the time of Reconquista, the Baltic during the German crusades or borderlands of Russian and the Ottoman Empires in the Caucasus and Central Asia.

The first to recognize the potential of the Balkan fighters for guerrilla warfare were the Austrians. Within the organization of *Military Border* (Militärgrenze), at first envisaged as an obstacle for further Ottoman advancements and conquests, organized Balkan fighters (primarily Serbs and Croats) constituted a valuable military asset. For their service under arms, soldiers of the *Military Border* were exempted from all usual taxes and contributions and were allowed to keep their traditional institutions and church. However, troops of the *Military Border* were not used only in war against the Ottomans. During the 17th and 18th centuries these forces participated in numerous wars which Habsburgs waged against other European powers. From some 48,000 soldiers within 13 regiments in peacetime, the number of so called 'border men' (*graničari* in Serbo-Croat) during war campaigns sometimes reached 100,000.[4] Members of the *Border Troops* were well known for their special inclination to guerrilla warfare or *Small war*. As members of light units of infantry and cavalry they used to disturb enemy communications, interrupt supply lines, attack headquarters, capture couriers etc.; similar to the Cossacks in Imperial Russia.[5] However, this had contributed to enormous demographic strain and losses. Compared to other parts of the Habsburg Empire where the ratio between soldiers and civilians was 1: 64, in the *Military Border* it was 1:7.[6]

Gerila na Balkanu, (Belgrade: Institut za savremenu istoriju; Tokyo: Meiji University, 2007), 31–56, here 50. See also: Ulf Brunnbauer, Robert Pichler, 'Mountains as "lieux de mémoire". Highland values and the nation-building in the Balkans', *Balkanologie* 6 (1–2), 2002, pp. 77–100.

[3] A. Yu. Timofeyev, 'Serbskie chetniki nakanune i v hode Balkanskih voin: social'nii fenomen, nacional'naya tradiciya i voennaya taktika' In *Modernizaciya vs. voina—Chelovek na Balkanah nakanune i vo vremya Balkanskih voin (1912–1913)*, (Moskva: 2012), 102–22.
[4] Petar Tomac, *Vojna istorija* (Beograd: VIZ JNA, 1959) 604–11.
[5] P. Tomac, *Vojna istorija*, 698 and 711.   [6] P. Tomac, *Vojna istorija*, 611.

At the same time in Serbian lands under Ottoman rule a different kind of development occurred. During the 18th century in these areas, more precisely the Belgrade region or *pashalik*, Ottomans accepted establishment of limited local autonomy that eventually allowed undisturbed economical development and the creation of local militias, which often assisted Ottoman regular forces in their struggle against different outlaws. However, crises that became more frequent by the end of the 18th century led to the appearance of several local administrators or *pashas* who rebelled against the Ottoman central administration. In Belgrade *pashalik* the rebellion or mutiny was followed by a wave of violence against local Christians who responded with a counter-wave of resistance and subsequent uprising in 1804. During this uprising against the Ottomans, the majority of leading Serbian figures possessed substantial military experience originating from years of fighting against the Ottomans. Some of them in earlier period of their life used to be *hajduks* or members of the Austrian *Freikorps*, or in several cases both.[7] Following the same pattern, among the Greek insurgents from 1821 the leading figures were the so-called *kleftes*—irregular fighters of whom many prior to the uprising used to be simple brigands. The second were the *armatoloi* or Christian militia organized by the Ottomans for the purpose of guarding communications and bridges.

A similar thing happened during the uprising against Ottoman rule in Bosnia and Herzegovina in 1875, which was introduction to the Great Eastern Crisis of 1875–1878. This uprising demonstrated the importance of guerrilla warfare as a means of resisting a superior opponent. Successful guerrilla warfare performed by Bosnian Serbs in 1875 led to Serbian and Montenegrin entry into the war the following year. After Russian intervention and the response of other Great Powers at the Berlin Congress in 1878, Serbia and Montenegro were granted formal independence from Ottoman rule, as well as substantial territorial enlargements.[8]

However, the modern notion of paramilitary organizing in the Balkans is closely related to the intensive political, educational and military engagement of Balkan Christian states (Bulgaria, Greece and Serbia) in Ottoman Macedonia. It reached its climax at the beginning of the 20th century and was followed by the subsequent participation of paramilitaries in the Balkan Wars 1912–1913, as well as in the Great War.

Intensive Bulgarian efforts to strengthen its positions in Ottoman Macedonia, which began after the creation of the Bulgarian autocephalous church or the Exarchate and especially after the creation of the autonomous Bulgarian state, had already begun in the last decades of the 19th century. The creation of the Exarchate and establishment of its church infrastructure in the 1870's was followed by the establishment of Bulgarian education institutions both in the

---

[7] *Istorija srpskog naroda.V-1*, (Beograd: SKZ, 1994) 70–2.
[8] *Istorija srpskog naroda.V-1*, (Beograd: SKZ, 1994) 510–18.

territories of autonomous Bulgaria and the Ottoman Empire. Thus, the Bulgarian influence within the Ottoman Empire has extended from religious to educational. Creation of the *Internal Macedonian and Adrianople Revolutionary Organization* (IMARO) in 1893, and the *Supreme Macedonian Committee* in 1895 marked the beginning of a new stage of armed struggle with the ultimate goal of acquiring full political autonomy for Ottoman regions of Macedonia and Adrianople.[9] According to the head of the Bulgarian Exarchate, Exarch Iosif, revolutionary organizations had an educational role as well:

> "Revolutionary organizations should be educators of Bulgarians in Macedonia in a spirit of liberty and readiness for struggle without necessarily throwing them into dangerous actions."[10]

In order to respond to the rise of Bulgarian influence in Ottoman Macedonia, Greeks and Serbs began with similar activities. By copying Bulgarian methodology Serbian action was implemented on two fronts. The first one was education through organizing Serbian schools while the second was military organizing or so-called *chetnik* action. The second was supposed to assist the first.[11]

Although already during the 1880's and 1890's Belgrade had tried to increase its presence in Macedonian affairs, primarily through propaganda and education, private initiatives were constantly blocked by hesitation and the non-existence of a consistent state policy towards the Ottoman Empire and in particular the Macedonian Question. With respect to Serbian action in Macedonia, changes would occur after the turbulent events in 1903 and overthrow of the Obrenović dynasty. The action itself was preceded by formation of the organization called the Serbian Committee in 1903. At first, it was merely a private initiative of several intellectuals, politicians, officers and entrepreneurs. The idea was to imitate the Bulgarian example by sending small units of *chetniks* across the border with the task of organizing inhabitants of pro-Serbian areas and villages in Ottoman Macedonia and to oppose *komitaji* bands from the rival IMARO as the main agents of the same activity on the Bulgarian side. After initial failure this initiative got official support of the special board of the Serbian Ministry of Foreign Affairs. The change was visible in their approach. Beside enthusiasts among those designated to go across the border there were also young officers and NCO's whose

---

[9] On this see: Nadine Lange-Akhund, *The Macedonian Question 1893–1908, from Western Sources* (Boulder: East European Monographs, 1998).

[10] Simeon Radev, *Ranni spomeni* (Sofia: Strelec 1994) 211.

[11] Further readings: Stanislav Krakov, *Plamen četništva*, (Beograd: Vreme 1930); Vasilije Trbić, *Memoari*, I i II, (Beograd: Kultura 1996); Ilija Trifunović Birčanin, *Trnovitim stazama*, (Beograd, 1933); Vladimir Ilić, 'Učešće srpskih komita u Kumanovskoj operaciji 1912. godine', In *Vojnoistorijski glasnik*, 1–3/1992, 197–217; Vladimir Ilić, *Srpska četnička akcija 1903–1912*, (Beograd: Ecolibri Beograd 2006).

engagement contributed considerably to the military training and preparation of *chetniks*.[12]

In following years two groups or organizations distinguished themselves in intensifying of *chetnik* action as well in rise of their political influence. First group consisted of officers-conspirators led by Dragutin Dimitrijević Apis. In years after the 1903 *coup d'etat* and assassination of Serbian Royal couple officers-conspirators became intensively involved in Serbian political life. Austro-Hungarian annexation of Bosnia and Herzegovina 1908 was turning point for drastic change of Serbian foreign policy which until the 1903 and *coup d'etat* was closely connected to Austro-Hungarian Empire. Simultaneously, as a result of general discontent over the annexation of Bosnia and Herzegovina, in 1908 civilian activists— intellectuals, politicians and entrepreneurs have formed second group, that is, patriotic association *National Defence* (Narodna odbrana). This organization has sponsored intelligence, guerrilla and political actions in 'still non-liberated regions' like Macedonia and Bosnia and Herzegovina. In 1911 officers-conspirators together with some civilians finally formed secret organization *Unification or Death* (Ujedinjenje ili smrt) better known as *The Black Hand* (Crna ruka). They saw themselves as destined to perform unification of all south Slavs. Title of their unofficial newspaper—*Piedmont* clearly demonstrated political agenda.[13]

The most important event from the period of struggle for Macedonia was the *Illinden Uprising* (St. Elias) on 2 August 1903. It represented a set of IMARO activities aimed at the liberation of Macedonia in light of the failure of Sultan Abdul Hamid's regime to implement reforms in Ottoman Macedonia, and the indifference of the European powers. It happened after a series of clashes with the Ottoman army and police forces. The most serious one was the so-called 'Revolt' of Djoumala Bala in Pirin Macedonia in October-November 1902.[14] Despite the level of Ottoman reprisals during the revolt, IMARO continued with preparations for the general uprising in Macedonia. Numerous diversions of railway communications and bomb explosions preceded the uprising. The centre was the small town of Kruševo in Monastir *vilayet*. Insurgents managed to assemble some 25,000 fighters but despite initial successes they failed to spread insurgency to the other parts of Macedonia. On August 12, the Ottoman army sacked Kruševo thus

---

[12] Vladimir Ilić, 'Učešće srpskih komita u Kumanovskoj operaciji 1912. godine', In *Vojnoistorijski glasnik*, 1–3/1992. 200.

[13] Ya. V. Vishnyakov 'Balkanskie voini 1912-1913.gg i organizaciya "Chernaya ruka"', in: *Modernizaciya vs. voina—Chelovek na Balkanah nakanune i vo vremya Balkanskih voin (1912–1913)*, (Moskva 2012) 269–91.

[14] Nadine Lange-Akhund, *The Macedonian Question 1893–1908, from Western Sources* (Boulder: East European Monographs, 1998) 113–18. Around 400 fighters of the Supreme Committee fought some 32 clashes with Ottoman troops of some 14 battalions and 30 guns between October and 18 November. The Supreme Committee had some 80 dead and 40 taken prisoner. While *komitaji* were forced to seek refuge in Bulgaria, the Ottoman army conducted punitive expedition against 28 villages in that area. Villages were burned down, women raped, old people tortured and massacred. Some 3000 people escaped to Bulgaria.

ending the so-called 'Kruševo republic'. Remaining insurgents continued with guerrilla resistance until October when the insurgency was finally over.[15] However, the insurgency resulted in intervention of European powers, drawing their attention to the Macedonian Question and implementation of necessary reforms through provisions of the Mürzsteg Agreement.[16] The next phase of activities of Bulgarian, Serbian and Greek paramilitaries lasted until 1908 and the Young Turk revolution. There were no open uprisings; however, their encounters (Bulgarian-Serb and Bulgarian-Greek) and with Ottoman Gendarmerie and army continued to be intensive, with losses on both sides. After the Young Turk revolution, the new regime announced changes leading towards the modernization of the Ottoman state and the equality of its citizens.

On the other hand, the Young Turk policy of *Ottomanization* challenged the Albanian national movement—another formidable actor that stepped again onto the political scene after a period which looked like hibernation during the reign of Sultan Abdul Hamid II (1876–1908). He personally favoured Albanians, often saying that his empire relied on Albanians and Arabs, or referring to Albanians as his iron barrier in the Balkans.[17] Albanians were exempted from conscription and were allowed to bear firearms. Now, under the Young Turks, the Albanians were, as everyone else, subjected to census, taxation and compulsory military service. Growing dissatisfaction among Albanians led to a series of uprisings from 1909 until 1912.[18] In a way, the Young Turks did not realize the extent to which Albanian national sentiment had grown meanwhile.[19] However, most of the Albanians, especially those of the north, saw themselves as constituent part of an empire 'based upon re-energised Islamism' rather than 'revived Ottomanism based upon order and progress through centralization'.[20] Thus, in June 1909 Ottoman regular troops under the command of Djavid-pasha were sent to fight rebels under the leadership of Isa Boletini. Faced with resistance regular troops were forced to withdraw. Not even passing of the new *Law on bands*, forbidding further carrying of arms and announcing punishments to family members of everyone participating in activities of the bands, helped to crush Albanian resistance.[21] In March 1910 another armed rebellion was initiated in Kosovo against new taxes. The rebels

---

[15] Nadine Lange-Akhund, *The Macedonian Question 1893–1908*, 118–30. During the insurgency Ottoman troops destroyed 201 villages with 12,400 houses, while 4,694 people died in battles, 70,835 became homeless and 30,000 sought refuge in Bulgaria.

[16] Nadine Lange-Akhund, *The Macedonian Question 1893–1908*, 135–45.

[17] Bernd J. Fischer, 'The Balkan Wars and Creation of Albanian Independence'. In, James Pettifer and Tom Buchanan (eds) *War in the Balkans; Conflict and Diplomacy before World War I*. (London: I.B. Tauris 2016) 102–14, here 105–6. The Sultan's personal guard consisted of Albanians as did the majority of security forces in the Ottoman capital. Abdul Hamid personally spoke some Albanian.

[18] Miranda Vickers, *The Albanians: a modern history* (London: Tauris, 1995) 62–5.

[19] Miranda Vickers, *The Albanians: a modern history*, p. 60.

[20] Bernd J. Fischer, 'The Balkan Wars and Creation of Albanian Independence', p.110.

[21] Stavro Skendi, *The Albanian National Awakening 1878–1912*, (Princeton, NJ, Princeton University Press, 1967) 392–5.

quickly gained control over the main centres and managed to inflict serious causalities on Ottoman regulars led by Shefquet Turgut-pasha in the battle of Kačanik. However, with new troops, the Ottomans won the battle of Crnoljeva and after implementing harsh measures, the rebellion was quelled. After Kosovo, in July, Shefquet Turgut-pasha proceeded in the direction of Shkodra demanding surrender of weapons, the conduction of a census and conscription of all young males. From Shkodra he proceeded to Salonika, passing through Miriditë and Debar and conducting the same procedure.[22]

Another rebellion broke out in the same region in March 1911. Again, it was Shefquet Turgut-pasha who was called to quell the rebellion. After Russian and Austro-Hungarian interventions an amnesty was proclaimed in June 1911 on the occasion of Sultan Mehmed V Reshad's visit to Kosovo.[23]

Following year another insurrection broke out, again under the leadership of Isa Bolletini. In short time insurgents managed to take Peć and Đakovica. Albanians demanded that Albania should be located within one single villayet, with schools in the Albanian language, as well as in the Latin alphabet; local administration should be Albanian; military service in peacetime would be served within Albania. By using the fact that the Ottoman state was at war with Italy, insurrection spread very fast, with numerous Albanians deserting regular forces. Negotiations started by the end of July. They resulted in the resignation of the Ottoman government and dissolving of the Parliament. After failing to reach an agreement the insurgents took Skopje and after that pressure the Young Turks agreed upon the terms in mid-August.[24] These events showed how deeply certain traditions and habits were embedded and how difficult it was to eradicate them. Thanks to that, Albanians figured as an independent political actor in the following years.

Participation of Balkan Paramilitaries in the Balkan Wars and the Great War

Thanks to the existence of organized armed movements, which operated on the territories of Ottoman Empire, the Balkan Christian states could count on the services of numerous irregulars.

By 1912 Serbian irregulars or *chetniks* represented a respectable force whose services the Serbian army could count on. However, their participation in the Balkan Wars and their total number has not been extensively researched. The

---

[22] S. Skendi, *The Albanian National Awakening*, 405–6.
[23] S. Skendi, *The Albanian National Awakening*, 411–20.
[24] S. Skendi, *The Albanian National Awakening*, 427–37.

total number of *chetniks*, which fought in the ranks of Serbian army, varied between 2,000 and 4,000 members grouped in 10 *chetnik* detachments.

Who were members of these detachments?

Beside officers and NCO's of the Serbian army and members of the Gendarmerie and Border Troops, there were individuals inspired by national ideas, such as university and high school students, volunteers from Austro-Hungarian Empire and Montenegro, Macedonian refugees and seasonal workers in Serbia, as well as local Macedonian peasants.

For example, on the eve of the First Balkan War in Captain Pavle Blažarić's detachment the overwhelming majority of *chetniks* were members of the Serbian Border Troops. Being commander of a border section, at the first sign of war Blažarić had just gathered his subordinates and strengthened them with a certain number of volunteers. Their experience came from previous engagements with Albanian and Sanjak brigands and it made them ideal for irregular or guerrilla warfare. The detachment under the command of Captain Blažarić counted some 200 members.[25]

His colleague Captain Božin Simić did the same. Unlike Blažarić, Simić was the officer responsible for three border sections of the Serbian army's intelligence department. However, the situation in his detachment was identical.[26]

For example, in detachment under the command of Captain Vojislav Tankosić there were also some Muslim volunteers, mostly from Bosnia and Herzegovina.[27] The later assassin of the Habsburg heir to the throne in Sarajevo, Gavrilo Princip, also tried to enlist in Tankosić's detachment but was refused by Tankosić himself due to poor physical constitution and health.[28]

On the other hand, in detachment under the command of prominent *chetnik* leader Major Vojin Popović, better known as Vojvoda Vuk, among its 1,300 members, beside the above mentioned volunteers majority were local Macedonians.[29] A similar situation existed in other detachments operating in Ottoman Macedonia, like in detachment under the command of Vasilije Trbić. Due to the

---

[25] Božica B. Mladenović and Miroslav D. Pešić,'Prvi balkanski rat u memoarma Pavla Blažarića' in: *Prvi balkanski rat 1912/1913. godine: društveni i civilizacijski smisao*, knj. 1, (Niš: Filozofski fakultet Niš, 2013) 287–300, here 292.

[26] Milić Milićević, 'Četnička akcija neposredno pre objave i tokom prvih dana srpsko-turskog rata 1912. godine'. In *Prvi balkanski rat 1912/1913. godine: društveni i civilizacijski smisao. Knj. 1*, (Niš: Filozofski fakultet, 2013), 221–34, here 231.

[27] Jovana D. Šaljić, 'Muslimani u oslobođenju Srbije 1912/1913: od mita do stvarnosti'. In *Prvi balkanski rat 1912/1913. godine: društveni i civilizacijski smisao Knj. 1* (Niš: Filozofski fakultet, 2013), 325–39, here 328.

[28] Gavrilo Princip, *Princip o sebi* (Zagreb: Jugoslovenska knjiga, 1926) 11 and 19; Dobrosav Jevđević, *Sarajevski zaverenici, Vidovdan 1914.*, (Beograd: Familet, 2002) 14; Vojislav Bogićević, *Sarajevski atentat. Stenogram Glavne rasprave protiv Gavrila Principa i drugova*, (Sarajevo: Državni arhiv NR Bosne i Hercegovine) 61.

[29] Vladimir Ilić, 'Učešće srpskih komita u Kumanovskoj operaciji 1912. godine', In *Vojnoistorijski glasnik* 1–3/1992,197–217, here 203.

influx of locals, in just several days the strength of his detachment grew from 30 to 200 *chetniks*.[30]

The main task of *chetnik* detachments was to perform reconnaissance missions or to create diversions in the enemy rear. However, in the days that followed, *chetnik* detachments were also assigned the task to disarm civilian population, mainly in the Kosovo region where local Albanians traditionally possessed huge quantities of light infantry armament. In their actions they acted differently, mainly according to the personalities of their commander. While detachment of Vojislav Tankosić was responsible for many violent acts (pillage, arsons, beatings and liquidations) both during initial fighting's and subsequent disarming campaign, detachment under command of Sreten Vukosavljević (another Black Hand member) acted reasonably, respecting both civilians and their properties, avoiding necessary loss of lives. In the case of Vasilije Trbić and his detachments, initial successes were compromised by several atrocities committed during punitive campaign. Because of his brutality Tankosić and his *chetniks* earned terrifying reputation. His methods quickly became known as 'Tankosić methods' and they were responsible for enormous success in disarming campaign in Kosovo region.[31]

Bulgarians, like others, decided to use the experience of battle-hardened *komitaji* fighters of the IMRO. Several hundreds of them were gathered in so-called Guerrilla Detachments under the command of a specially formed Headquarters. *Komitaji* leaders were promoted to officers and NCO ranks which gave the whole enterprise a strict military appearance.[32] The majority of common members were experienced IMRO fighters from the ranks of Macedonian émigrés residing in Bulgaria. However, unlike the Serbian case where officers and NCO's of *chetnik* detachments rarely originated from Macedonia, officers and NCO's from Bulgarian Guerrilla Detachments were Macedonians by blood. Guerrilla Detachments were divided into platoons with the main task of performing reconnaissance missions in front of the advancing army. Still, because the main actions of the Bulgarian army were executed in Thrace, guerrilla platoons could not be used to as full an extent as they would be in Macedonia. Nevertheless, cooperation between the IMRO and army was achieved.[33] On the other hand, not all of the *komitajis* joined Guerrilla Detachments. A certain number decided to fight in Macedonia in a way and on territories familiar to them. They proved to be very useful for reconnaissance missions and diversions in the Ottoman rear.[34]

---

[30] Vasilije Trbić, *Memoari. II*, (Beograd: Kultura 1996) 6.

[31] Dmitar Tasić, 'Repeating Phenomenon: Balkan Wars and Irregulars'. In Catherine Horel (ed), *Les guerres balkaniques (1912-1913): conflits, enjeux, mémoires* (Bruxelles: Peter Lang, 2014), 25–36, here 33–5.

[32] Dimitre Minchev, *Participation of the Population of Macedonia in the First World War: 1914-1918*, (Sofia: Voenno Izdatelstvo, 2004) 53.

[33] D. Minchev, *Participation of the Population of Macedonia in the First World War 1914-1918*, 53.

[34] Georgi Pophristov, *Revolyutsionnata borba v' bitolskiya okr'g*, (Sofia: NS OF, 1953) 100–1.

In the Greek army operating in the Balkan Wars there were several different irregular units commonly named *Volunteer Scouts units*. Many of them were experienced guerrilla fighters from the time of the Greek Macedonian struggle (1903–1908) or were the members of the *Pan-Hellenic Organization*. This organization was formed in 1909 and consisted of some 100 officers and NCO's of the Greek regular army operating in Macedonia and Thrace. Greek irregular units during Balkan Wars varied in strength. In total, there were 77 units of Cretan scouts with 3,556 men, 9 Epirotan units with 446 men and 9 Macedonian units with 211 men. In addition, there were another 1,812 volunteer scouts from other Greek regions.[35]

Interestingly, among Greek irregular units there was one which clearly distinguished itself. The commander of this unit was Riccioti Garibaldi—the son of Giuseppe Garibaldi. It had some 2,300 volunteers of Greek origin and Philhellenes from different parts of the world, and they were, for obvious reasons, called the 'Redshirts'.[36] Among Balkan allies Greeks had the largest number of irregulars.

Even after the changes in the organization of armed forces that occurred during the 19th century, Ottoman armies traditionally relied on auxiliary irregular troops. In most instances those were tribal or clan contingents from the Empire's borderlands, like Crimean Tatars in the 17th and 18th centuries and Circassians in the 19th. Irregulars were commonly named *bashibozluk*. In the Balkans most of the *bashibozluk* bands came from the Albanian clans. However, the rising of the Albanian national conscience, which began in the last decades of the 19th century, led to the disruption of their traditional relations with the Ottoman state and military. Moreover, after the disappointment with the policies of the Young Turk regime, several consecutive Albanian insurgencies forced Ottoman central authorities to wage serious military campaigns.[37] The last one happened in spring 1912 and when the Balkan allies in October of the same year declared war against the Ottoman Empire, Albanians found themselves in an unusual and strange position; they were supposed to defend authorities which they had rebelled against just a couple of months before. Instead of defending the Ottomans they resolved to defend their own territories, but this brought them again into the same ranks with the Ottoman regular army. Although they put up serious resistance in several initial clashes against Serbian irregulars and regulars, Albanian resistance was too weak to stop the advance of the Serbian army. The crucial moment was the Ottoman defeat in the battle of Kumanovo (23–24 October 1912), after which the mass desertion of Albanian irregulars began.

---

[35] *A Concise History of the Balkan Wars 1912–1913*, (Athens: Army History Directorate 1998) 17.
[36] *A Concise History of the Balkan Wars 1912–1913*, 17.
[37] Further readings: Peter Bartl, *Albanci Albanci, od srednjeg veka do danas* (Beograd: CLIO, 2002) 124–38; Stavro Skendi, *The Albanian National Awakening 1878–1912*, (Princeton, NJ, Princeton University Press, 1967); Miranda Vickers, *The Albanians: a modern history* (London: Tauris, 1995).

The overall number of Albanian irregulars that participated in the First Balkan War cannot be precisely determined; however, good illustration is the initial battle against Serbian troops at place called Merdare (15–19 October 1912) where three to four battalions of regular Ottoman army were strengthened with 5,000–6,000 Albanian irregulars.[38]

During the short Second Balkan War in the summer of 1913 both sides continued to use their paramilitaries. Fighting was characterized by the existence of determined front and rear lines so the usage of the paramilitaries was more conventional. However, during their surprise night attack at the opening of the fighting on 29/30 June 1913 against Serbian sentries and patrols Bulgarians did use their *komitaji* fighters. In most instances their actions were successful, but they could not influence the outcome of the opening battle on the river Bregalnica.[39]

After the wars, according to the peace signed in Bucharest in 1913, the Balkan Peninsula was divided into two parties—victorious and satisfied Greece, Montenegro, and Serbia; and defeated and deeply unsatisfied Bulgaria and the Ottoman Empire. Nevertheless, the picture was not black and white. The subsequent interference of the Great Powers contributed to the additional complication of inner-Balkan relations. Greece was awarded the largest territorial gains, while the appearance of the Albanian state, which resulted from direct Austro-Hungarian interference, deprived Serbia of a sea outlet on the Adriatic coast, while Montenegro was, due to international pressure and sea blockade, forced to withdraw from Shkodra for which it had paid tremendous losses.[40] Defeated Bulgaria and the Ottomans were counting on some new moments in the future that would grant them opportunity for a re-match. The outbreak of the Great War in 1914 was an introduction to such developments. Thus, in practical terms, the Great War became just an extension of the Balkan Wars.

During the Great War both sides in the Balkan war theatre continued to use paramilitaries as auxiliary units.[41] One purpose was to use them against their enemies while another was the enforcement of occupation regimes. Following previous experiences in initial stages of war, Serbian supreme command organized four detachments of 2,250 *chetniks* in total. *Black Hand* interference in the military planning and misconducts of *chetnik* detachments led by *Black Hand* prominent members during the Balkan Wars, caused Serbian Supreme Command

---

[38] Ljubomir Marić, 'Moravska divizija II poziva u ratu 1912. i 1913. godine', In *Ratnik* IV/1924, p. 32.

[39] Milutin Lazarević, *Drugi Balkanski rat*, (Beograd: Vojno delo 1955).

[40] *Prvi Balkanski rat 1912–1913: (Operacije crnogorske vojske)*, (Beograd: Istorijski institut Jugoslovenske narodne armije, 1960) 63 and 408. From 35,600 mobilized Montenegrin soldiers in the course of the First Balkan War, 2,836 were listed as killed in action while 6,602 were listed as wounded. The overwhelming majority of these casualties was suffered during the siege of Shkodra.

[41] See: Dmitar Tasić: 'Warfare 1914–1918 (South East Europe)'. In: *1914-1918-online. International Encyclopedia of the First World War*, Daniel, Ute...[et al.] (eds.), (Berlin: Freie Universität Berlin), 2014-10-08. DOI: http://dx.doi.org/10.15463/ie1418.10366.

to issue detailed instructions for their usage with clear criteria for the enlistment of people in these detachments. Only *chetniks* from 'previous wars' could be considered for this kind of service, as well as volunteers and conscripts who had volunteered for such a service.[42] 'Guerrilla' warfare supposed to be their main way of action. However, to avoid previous experiences of disobedience and lack of coordination, these detachments should remain in permanent connection with their army group commanders. In case of successful Serbian offensive *chetnik* detachments would serve as embryos for 'insurgency in areas populated by Serbs'. On the other hand, if Austro-Hungarians proved to be successful, *chetnik* detachments would remain in enemy rear where they would constantly act against enemy communications, signals, logistics and commands and simultaneously organize local insurgents.[43] In both cases the most reliable *chetniks* should be taken for special '*terrorist groups* which would perform assassinations of senior enemy commanders, as well as to use every possible means to spread terror and panic in enemy ranks'.[44] How successful *chetniks* have been in respect to these principles is not a subject of this study however, it should be noted that these instructions were followed.[45]

The first one to experience the efficiency of the Serbian paramilitaries were the Austro-Hungarians. Confusion that Serbian *chetniks* have caused in Austro-Hungarian rear manifested how unprepared traditional European armies were for this particular kind of warfare and how brutal their answer was. *Chetniks* overall appearance, which was half military-half civilian, additionally contributed to specific blurring of traditional boundaries between soldiers and civilians. In this manner, Austro-Hungarians made their own contribution in reviving the existing myth of *franc-tireurs*. As in the German case on the Western front, amongst the Austro-Hungarian troops invading Serbia 1914, there existed a strong fear of civilians acting as combatants.[46] Fear from these faceless fighters made every civilian a potential fighter and therefore a legitimate target. In some cases, it is

[42] Živko Pavlović, *Bitka na Jadru avgusta 1914. godine*, (Beograd: Grafički zavod 'Makarije', 1924) Annexes: Disposition of *chetnik* detachments for the war against Austria-Hungary 1914; and Instruction for the implementation of *chetnik* action in war against Austria-Hungary 1914.
[43] Ž. Pavlović, *Bitka na Jadru*, Instruction for the implementation of *chetnik* action in war against Austria-Hungary 1914.
[44] Ž. Pavlović, *Bitka na Jadru*, Instruction for the implementation of *chetnik* action in war against Austria-Hungary 1914.
[45] *Chetnik* actions in Austro-Hungarian rear in 1914 were actually very successful causing huge fear and insecurity among enemy forces. However, these actions in combination with already existing anti-Serbian propaganda became an excuse for manifested brutality and war crimes against civilian population in West Serbia. Other tasks, like reconnaissance or attempts to instigate uprising among Bosnian Serbs proved to be utter failure. First one because of lack of modern signal equipment, while second was prevented by large scale counter-insurgency measures conducted by the Austro-Hungarians in Bosnia and Herzegovina, like massive internment of representatives of Serbian elites, mobilization of service-able Serbian population and sending them to fight elsewhere and favoring local Muslims by enlisting them in auxiliary security forces.
[46] John Horn and Alan Kramer, *German Atrocities 1914, A History of Denial* (New Haven: Yale University Press; 2001) 149–50.

said that Austro-Hungarian commanders stimulated this fear in order to manipulate their own soldiers.[47]

In Austro-Hungarian reports from 1914, it was said that Serbian *chetniks* managed to disrupt communications and supply lines, slow the advance and affect the morale of Austro-Hungarian troops.[48] *Chetniks* actions combined with an already overheated atmosphere due to anti-Serbian propaganda caused constant fear among Austro-Hungarian forces. For that reason, these actions often caused severe reprisals against Serbian civilian populations.[49]

As it was the case in the Balkan Wars, the Bulgarians also relied on the services of some 500 IMRO *komitajis*, yet again organized in Guerrilla Detachments. As in the Serbian case, their main task was reconnaissance and creating diversions.[50] However, being an independent political movement, IMRO has already carried out several independent operations against Serbian troops and infrastructure in Macedonia during 1914 and 1915. The best known was the *Attack on Good Friday* which took place on 20 March 1915, when some 1,500 *komitajis*, in an attempt to destroy the railroad near Valandovo, inflicted serious causalities on Serbian troops protecting the railway and bridge.[51] This action, as some others before, was financed by Austro-Hungarian Empire through its military attaché in Sofia.[52]

After the Serbian and Montenegrin defeat in 1915, and consequent withdrawal across Albania, most of the Serbian paramilitaries were grouped in a *Volunteer Detachment* assigned to participate in conventional warfare. Due to the heavy causalties during the battle for Kajmakčalan Mountain in summer 1916, its remaining members were dispersed among regular troops.

The Austro-Hungarian military also relied on paramilitaries in capacity of irregular troops. These troops consisted of Albanian clansmen, mostly from northern Albania and Kosovo. After 1916 and stabilization of a front line, Albanian volunteers proved to be very useful in the rough conditions of Albania where Austro-Hungarian regular troops suffered from the adverse effects of the local climate and malaria.[53] Following the Serbian defeat in autumn 1915, the Austro-Hungarians authorities an organized occupation regime in Serbia

---

[47] R.A. Reiss, *Report upon the Atrocities committed by the Austro-Hungarian Army during the first Invasion of Serbia*, (London: Simpkin, Marshall, Hamilton, Kent&Co, 1916) 144.

[48] John Schindler, 'Disaster on the Drina; The Austro-Hungarian army in Serbia 1914'. In *War in History* 9/2, 2002, 159–95, here 165, 169, 173, 178, 183, 185.

[49] Ferenz Pollman, 'Austro-Hungarian atrocities against Serbians during WWI (Šabac, 17 August 1914)'. In: *Prvi svetski rat i Balkan—90 godina kasnije: tematski zbornik radova*, (Beograd: Institut za strategijska istraživanja 2010)135–41.

[50] D. Minchev, *Participation of population of Macedonia in the First World War*, 51–6.

[51] Further readings: Ljubomir Marić, 'Valandovski zločin i njegove žrtve', In *Ratnik* IV (1930), 19–31; and Dragiša I. Kecojević, *Valandovski pokolj 20. marta 1915*, (Skoplje, D. Kecojević 2005).

[52] D. Minchev, *Participation of the population of Macedonia in WWI*, p. 52.

[53] Ferenc Pollman, 'Albanian irregulars in the Austro-Hungarian army during World War I'. In Raugh, Harold E. Jr (ed): *Regular and Irregular Warfare: Experiences of Historical and Contemporary Armed Conflicts* (Belgrade: Institute for Strategic Research 2012) 63–8.

officially labelled as *k.u.k. Militärgeneralgouvernement Serbien*. Bulgarians, however, considered their own occupied areas (Macedonia and South Serbia) as already annexed to their fatherland while the locals were considered to be Bulgarians. Measures in the Austro-Hungarian zone included taking hostages, requisition, internment, press censorship, martial law, changes in school curricula, banning of the Cyrillic alphabet, and giving privileges to friendly minorities—such as Sanjak Muslims and Albanians.[54] Bulgaria also implemented a thorough policy of denationalization of the Serbian population in South Serbia and Macedonia through complete ban of Serbian institutions, introduction of the Bulgarian language and alphabet, changes of personal names, replacement of Serbian teachers and priests with Bulgarian, etc. Harsh occupation regimes enforced by Austro-Hungarian Empire and Bulgaria in Serbia and Montenegro facilitated the emergence of armed resistance. It was manifested through actions like ambushes of small groups of insurgents against the army and police patrols or forage units, like in Montenegro, or open massive uprising such as that which happened in the Toplica region of Southern Serbia in 1917.[55] Both individual actions as well as uprising caused severe reprisals against the insurgents and civilian population.

Almost immediately after the withdrawal of the Serbian and capitulation of the Montenegrin army and the introduction of occupation regimes in both occupation zones, armed individuals as well as smaller groups started to appear. Initially they were without leadership and organizational unity. Those were Serbian and Montenegrin soldiers who somehow, for different reasons, remained in the country.[56] Meanwhile, the Serbian Supreme command became aware of the existing potential for irregular warfare. In order to prepare a mass uprising for the purpose of assisting the Allied advance after the expected breakthrough on the Macedonian front, in September 1916 they sent to Serbia Kosta Milovanović-Pećanac, a reserve officer and experienced *chetnik*. By the end of February 1917 uprisings broke out in the Toplica region in southeast Serbia in the Bulgarian occupied zone as well as in the southern part of the Austro-Hungarian occupied zone. During the quelling of the rebellion by the end of March 1917 thousands of civilians fell as victims of extremely brutal anti-insurgency measures. Despite the repressive measures and defeat most of the insurgents continued their struggle, waging a guerrilla campaign against occupiers. This proved extremely valuable when the actual Allied offensive began in mid-September 1918.[57]

---

[54] Tamara Scheer, 'Forces and Force. Austria-Hungary's occupation regime in Serbia during the First World War' in *Prvi svetski rat i Balkan—90 godina kasnije: tematski zbornik radova* (Beograd: Institut za strategijska istraživanja 2010), 161–79.

[55] Further readings: Andrej Mitrović *Ustaničke borbe u Srbiji: 1916–1918*, (Beograd: SKZ, 1987).

[56] A. Mitrović, *Ustaničke borbe u Srbiji*, 133–49.

[57] Frédéric le Moal, *La Serbie: du martyre à la victoire, 1914–1918*, (Paris: Saint-Cloud, 2008) 128.

The Balkans after the Great War

When the Allies finally launched the offensive on the Macedonian front in mid September 1918, they certainly did not expect such a sudden collapse of Bulgaria or the series of turbulent events that followed. Bulgarian troops fought well, and on the Dojran section of the front they even managed to repel combined British and Greek attacks, inflicting serious causalities on their adversaries. However, in the section of Dobro Polje, the combined French and Serbian onslaught led to a successful breakthrough of Bulgarian lines. In just a couple of days Bulgarian and German units were in full retreat. Bulgarian soldiers were already demoralized by constant shortages in provisions while news from home about similar developments just added new burdens. While retreating, some of them even resolved to undertake revolutionary action against King Ferdinand's regime. The rebellion was suppressed, however, and Bulgaria signed an armistice, becoming the first country of the Central Powers to leave the war.[58] The Bulgarian defeat suddenly opened ways for Allied forces to advance towards undefended Constantinople to the east, as well as toward Romania—their isolated ally across the Danube.

In Albania, the Austro-Hungarian troops began to retreat following the Bulgarian disaster at Dobro Polje. In a short time one occupation was replaced with another as Austro-Hungarian troops were swapped with Allied contingents from France, Italy and Serbia, creating new garrisons from Korça in the south to Shkodra in the north. From the Albanian standpoint, one occupation was merely replaced with yet another. Italian, French, British and Serbian contingents took control over the most important towns; demarcation lines were drawn dividing 'spheres of influence', and different combinations aimed at the division of Albania started to appear. The following years of Albanian history would be marked by intensive efforts of different and often conflicted political groups and individuals over a single issue—restoring and establishing an independent Albanian nation-state.[59]

In 1918 Bulgaria suffered their second consecutive defeat, which was in collective memory considered the *Second national catastrophe*. The first one came after the defeat in the Second Balkan War in 1913, and it actually represented the turning point in modern Bulgarian history. As a result of this defeat Bulgarian policy started to depart from its traditional ally and protector, the Russian Empire and to approach Austro-Hungarian Empire. The loss of Macedonia, that focal point of Bulgarian national aspirations, its territories, important towns like

[58] Hall, Richard: 'War in the Balkans'. In: 1914–1918-online. International Encyclopedia of the First World War, Daniel...[et al.](eds.) (Berlin:Freie Universität Berlin) 2014-10-08. DOI: http://dx.doi.org/10.15463/ie1418.10163.
[59] On Albania see: Peter Bartl, *Albanci, od srednjeg veka do danas* (Beograd: CLIO, 2002) 124–38; Stavro Skendi, *The Albanian National Awakening 1878–1912*, (Princeton, NJ, Princeton University Press, 1967); Miranda Vickers, *The Albanians: a modern history* (London: Tauris, 1995).

Monastir (Bitola), Ohrid, Prilep, Veles, Kilkis and Salonika, meant that in every future crisis in the Balkans Bulgaria would be tempted to join those forces offering the return of land so long coveted. That was the main reason why in 1915 Bulgaria entered the war on the side of the Central Powers.[60] Now, after the defeat in the Great War, Bulgaria not only had to withdraw from the territories it had occupied but could expect additional territorial losses.[61] The defeat led to the loss of Thrace in favour of Greece and three border towns and surrounding areas in favor of the newly created Kingdom of Serbs, Croats and Slovenes.[62]

After the Bulgarians signed the armistice and stepped out from the war, the Serbian troops, as part of the Allied forces, spearheaded a further advance towards the north. Additional German and Austro-Hungarian troops arriving from Ukraine and the Italian front were not capable of stopping Allied advancement. In addition, after the Bulgarian expulsion, the Ottoman Empire became extremely vulnerable. Allied troops were now able to start advancing towards Constantinople. The same day the Serbian capital Belgrade was liberated, 30 October, another armistice was signed.[63] This time it was in Mudros, where the representatives of the Ottoman Empire signed an armistice after their capital became endangered by an unexpected British advance from the Macedonian front.[64] A couple of days later Serbian troops stepped onto Austro-Hungarian soil.

While Austro-Hungarian Empire was passing through collapse, in the Balkans, as elsewhere throughout the empire, different local national councils started to organize some kind of provisional authority.[65] After a failed attempt to organize South Slav lands under Habsburg rule, a new State of Slovenes, Croats and Serbs was proclaimed in the Croatian capital of Zagreb on 28 October 1918. The declaration announced the breaking of all ties with Austro-Hungarian Empire. However, the new state was in turmoil, incapable of organizing its institutions; primarily, the armed forces. This proved to be difficult if not impossible mostly because former Austro-Hungarian soldiers just wanted to return to their homes after four years of war. Many of them were already hiding after desertion or organizing themselves in small bands of the so-called *Green Cadre*. At that particular moment the main danger for the prospect of unification was the Italian advance towards Slovenia, Istria and the Dalmatian coast because Italy, being an Allied country, was entitled to implement stipulations of the armistice with Austro-Hungarian Empire, as well as those of the secret London Treaty, which

[60] Richard J. Crampton, *Bulgaria*, (Oxford and New York: Oxford University Press, 2007) 204.
[61] R.J. Crampton, *Bulgaria*, 218.   [62] R.J. Crampton, *Bulgaria*, 219 and 222.
[63] Andrej Mitrović, *Serbia's Great War: 1914–1918*, (London: Hurst&Company, 2007) 320.
[64] Ulrich Trumpener, 'Turkey's War', in: *The Oxford illustrated History of the First World War*, Hew Strachan (ed.), (Oxford: Oxford University Press, 2014) 90.
[65] Steven K. Pavlowitch, *A History of the Balkans 1804–1945*, (New York and London: Longman, 1999) 220.

allowed it to occupy a part of the Austro-Hungarian territories.[66] Politicians from
Zagreb turned to Belgrade and Serbia, as representatives of Vojvodina (formerly
southern Hungary), Montenegro, and Bosnia and Herzegovina had already
done.[67] On 1 December 1918, after delegates from Zagreb presented declaration
to the Serbian Prince Regent Alexander Karađorđević, expressing their wish to
enter into state union with Serbia, a new state Kingdom of Serbs, Croats and
Slovenes was officially proclaimed. Subjects of this new state, apart from its politicians and social elites, were not aware of its creation. It was news that needed to
be communicated to them.[68]

The outcome of the Great War introduced a rather new balance in the Balkans,
which was yet to be confirmed and regulated more precisely at the Paris Peace
Conference. Firstly, there were new states like Albania and the Kingdom of Serbs,
Croats and Slovenes. Then, there were the old ones, enlarged like Romania and
Greece or diminished like Bulgaria and the Ottoman Empire. They all had several
things in common. They were all exhausted and they were all facing new challenges, such as administration over new population and territories or continuation of war efforts. The Kingdom of Serbs, Croats and Slovenes and Romania
were clear victors with territorial gains whose protection and security demanded
insurance from the Great Powers as well as establishment of new military-
political alliances. Greece and its attempt to fulfil The Grand Idea would make it a
'loser in victory,' while Bulgaria represented a typical example of the 'loser in
defeat'.[69] The peace process initiated on Paris Peace Conference was followed by a
series of crises that in the Balkans would be over by 1924 with the creation of a
stable Albanian government.[70] Clashes on the Yugoslav-Austrian and Yugoslav-
Albanian borders, revolution in Hungary and the subsequent Romanian invasion
of Hungary, Yugoslav-Italian tensions, the Greek landing and invasion of Asia
Minor followed by defeat and massive exodus of Greek populations, together
with *coup d'états* in Bulgaria and Albania represented the most important events
of that turbulent period. On top of that, during this period each one of these
countries experienced internal political and economical crises.

Within the new Yugoslav state framework, former Austro-Hungarian lands
experienced a closer encounter with the 'traditional' Balkans. They entered into

---

[66] Steven K. Pavlowitch, *A History of the Balkans 1804–1945*, (New York and London: Longman,
1999) 223.

[67] On 25 November in Novi Sad representatives of local communities (mainly Serbian) in the
regions of Srem, Bačka and Banat gathered and officially proclaimed unification of these areas with
the Kingdom of Serbia, see Andrej Mitrović, *Serbia's Great War*, p. 324.

On 28 November in Podgorica, Montenegro, the Grand National Assembly voted in favor of unification of Serbia and Montenegro and the deposition of Petrović dynasty, see Steven K. Pavlowitch,
A History of the Balkans 1804–1945, 223.

[68] Steven K. Pavlowitch, *A History of the Balkans 1804–1945*, 224.

[69] Steven K. Pavlowitch, *A History of the Balkans 1804–1945*, 230.

[70] Charles and Barbara Jelavich, *The Establishment of Balkan National States 1804–1920* (Seattle;
London: University of Washington Press, 1977) 298.

this encounter with a legacy and memory of a vanished empire that was visible and alive in art, culture, politics, and everyday life. At the same time, it also meant their industrial, infrastructural, organizational and cultural supremacy over the southern parts of the kingdom.

Turbulent events that started in 1917 in Russia echoed in the Balkans even during the Great War. The first group to face new political attitudes were Serbian officers sent to Russia to organize volunteer units consisted of former members of Austro-Hungarian armed forces who became prisoners of war (POWs).[71] Slogans demanding peace and land influenced many of them to leave the ranks of volunteers either to remain in the camps and return to their homes after the war or to join the ranks of the revolutionaries. The same thing happened among soldiers of the Russian contingent on the Macedonian front.[72] In total, more than 15,000 Russians arrived there during 1916 and 1917, adding their contribution to the diversity of Allied forces in the Balkans.[73] They participated in fighting along with other Allied forces, suffering heavy casualties, up to the time of the revolutionary events in Russia, when the Allied command proclaimed the Russians as 'unreliable'. On those grounds the entire Russian contingent was removed from the front line.[74]

After the war two new streams of former combatants started to arrive in the Balkans (as almost everywhere else in Europe). The first were defeated anti-revolutionaries from different armies and groups that had tried to fight against the revolution in Russia. The most homogenous and therefore the most ardent group was General Wrangel's *Army of South Russia*, which started to arrive in Bulgaria and the Kingdom of Serbs, Croats and Slovenes after the Bolsheviks had inflicted the final blow on the Crimea in the autumn of 1920.

The second were ex-revolutionaries, whose arrival brought new ideas as well as experience in their implementation. Their appearance and the echo of revolutionary events in Russia, Hungary, and Germany alarmed authorities into paying more attention to the threat labelled as the 'export of revolution'.

Furthermore, there were already functioning organizations or movements with or without (para)military structures and political goals. Some of them already had paramilitary structure and rules of engagement, while the others slowly

---

[71] Milan Micić, *Srpsko dobrovoljačko pitanje u Velikom ratu: (1918–1914)*, (Novo Miloševo: Banatski kulturni centar; Beograd: RTS, 2014),113–15.

[72] Denis Aleksandrovič Maljcev, 'Ruske jedinice u Francuskoj i na Solunskom frontu tokom Prvog svetskog rata'. In *Prvi svetski rat i balkanski čvor: Zbornik radova*, (Beograd: Institut za savremenu istoriju, 2014) 477–88, here 486–7.

[73] On Salonika or Macedonian front Allied forces consisted of French, British, Serbian, Italian, Greek, and Russian troops. French troops were from France, Senegal, Algeria, Morocco and Indochina, while British troops were from the British Isles and India. A small Albanian contingent also fought on the allied side.

[74] D. A. Maljcev, 'Ruske jedinice u Francuskoj i na Solunskom frontu tokom Prvog svetskog rata', 488.

started turning to paramilitary organizing. The typical example was the Internal Macedonian Revolutionary Organization (IMRO), which after a very short stand-still continued its struggle.[75]

Immediately after the Great War, IMRO looked rather different from the organization of the same name at the time of its establishment and most intense functioning. It was more 'in exile' than 'internal'; it was Macedonian only because of the origins of its members. In reality, they had spent most of their life in Bulgaria, while its 'revolutionary' aspect in time dissolved in the organization's convenient cohabitation with the Bulgarian state. In the course of time this support created mutual dependence where the organization depended on state resources and support (armament, ammunition, finances, etc.) and the state depended on the organization's armed forces in moments of showdown with its political opponents.

The other organization was the Kosovo Committee. It promoted an ambitious Albanian national agenda aimed at the creation of Great Albania—a state that would include and unite all territories in the Balkans inhabited by Albanians. The organization was founded in the North Albanian town of Shkodra in November 1918 and had initially been named the *Committee for the Defence of Kosovo*. The founders of the organization were the influential Kosovar Albanians Hasan Prishtina, Bayram Curr, Salli Mallica, Sotir Peci and others and their goals were the protection of the Albanian borders and Albanian interests in the forthcoming Paris Peace Conference. Immediately after the Great War the Committee called on Kosovar Albanians to start an uprising, which would enable fulfilment of an ultimate goal—the unification of Kosovo with Albania.[76] The Committee became very influential in all Yugoslav territories inhabited by Albanians, as well as in Albania, where it exerted a strong influence on Albanian politics and everyday life.[77]

Another thing that has marked post-Great War years in the Balkans was the appearance of several remarkable political figures whose actions affected to a great extent the developments and dynamics in their respective countries and whose career trajectories were closely connected with the existing paramilitaries and their organizations. In Albania it was Ahmed-bey Zogu. His personality and political attitudes had been shaped by his family legacy, the complexity of Albanian historical and political developments, his engagement in turbulent events that marked the beginning of 20th century and Albania's exit from the

[75] Decho Dobrinov, 'Todor Aleksandrov i v'zstanovanieto na VMRO sled p'rvata svetovna vojna (1918-1924 g.)'. In *100 godini V'treshna makedono-odrinska revolucionna organizaciya*, (Sofia, Makedonski nauchen institut, 1994), 145–56.

[76] Đorđe Borozan, *Velika Albanija, porijeklo, ideje, praksa*, (Beograd: Vojnoistorijski institut Vojske Jugoslavije, 1995) 75.

[77] Further readings: Ljubodrag Dimić and Đorđe Borozan, (eds), *Jugoslovenska država i Albanci. Tom 1* (Beograd: Službeni list SRJ; Arhiv Jugoslavije; Vojno-istorijski institut, 1998).

Ottoman state framework. Beside continuous engagement with paramilitaries and militias both as allies and adversaries, Zogu's ascent to power was marked by a rivalry of short duration with Fan Noli, another remarkable political figure whose ambitious plans for reforms and the overall transformation of Albanian society did not correspond with its harsh realities. Although both of them were striving to achieve stability and lay the foundation for a prosperous Albania, at the end of the day Zogu's adaptability as a clan chieftain proved to be more efficient than Nolli's Harvard degree.[78]

The defeat suffered by Bulgaria contributed to serious political changes visible in the rise of the Bulgarian Agrarian National Union (BANU) and its charismatic leader Alexander Stamboliyski. However, old political structures, the army and especially the IMRO were constantly blocking efforts of Stamboliyski intended to improve Bulgarian positions in international relations as well as to reform and stabilize the economy.[79] In the end, despite a parliament majority and huge support among Bulgarian peasantry, BANU could not execute control over the important state institutions such as the police and army. Above mentioned forces proved to be stronger than the legitimately chosen government. In the subsequent *coup d'état* Stamboliyski was brutally murdered while pre-1918 parties seized all power. Their most trusted ally—IMRO—began a rampage by sending new bands to Yugoslav Macedonia and entering into a series of internal clashes in which many members lost their lives. IMRO also took control over the Pirin Macedonia or Petrich region, making it a 'state within the state'.[80]

Certainly, after the recently concluded global war everyone awaited peace settlements. The victorious expected awards and compensations in war reparations and new territories, while the defeated knew that these could only happen at their expense. At the beginning of 1919 all eyes were directed towards Paris where the Peace Conference commenced its work. Its outcomes and subsequent peace accords had a huge impact on the future of the Balkans. However, the situation was extremely complicated, considering the changes in international relations that had occurred during the Great War. In the Balkans, the biggest change was the appearance of a Yugoslav state that encompassed the Kingdoms of Serbia and Montenegro and former Austro-Hungarian provinces: Slovenia, Croatia, Bosnia

---

[78] Further readings: Robert C. Austin, *Founding a Balkan State; Albanian Experiment with Democracy, 1920-1925* (Toronto: University of Toronto Press, 2012); and Bernd J. Fischer, *King Zog and the Struggle for Stability in Albania*, (Tirana: Albanian Institute for International Studies, 2012).

[79] Further readings: Vasil Vasilev, *Pravitelstvo na BZNS, VMRO i B'lgaro-Yugoslavskite otnosheniya,* (Sofia: BAN, 1991); Veselin Yaanchev, *Armiya, obshtestven red i vatreshna sigurnost mezhdu voynite i sled tyaah: 1913-1915, 1918-1923* (Sofia: Universitetsko izdatelstvo 'Sv. Kliment Ohridski', 2014); John D. Bell, *Peasants in Power: Alexander Stamboliiski and the Bulgarian Agrarian National Union 1899-1923*, (Princeton: Princeton University Press, 1977).

[80] Dimitar Tyulekov, *Obrecheno rodolyubie. VMRO v Pirinsko 1919-1934* (Blagoevgrad: Univ. Izd. 'Neofit Rilski', 2001), http://www.promacedonia.org/dt/index.html [last checked on 4 November 2016]

and Herzegovina, and Vojvodina (South Hungary).[81] Despite the fact that from December 1914 the unification of South Slavs had been a publicly proclaimed war aim of Serbia, Italy for entering the war on the side of the Entente was rewarded by stipulations of the secret London Treaty of 1915, which promised Italy huge Austro-Hungarian territories in Slovenia, Croatia, Istria and Dalmatia. However, Italy's poor performance during the war and the fact that after the breakthrough on the Macedonian front Serbian and Allied troops managed to penetrate deep into territories of the collapsing Austro-Hungarian Empire and successfully occupy most of the above mentioned provinces made it possible to recognize the creation of Yugoslav state as a fait accompli, despite strong Italian objections. After the recognition, the new state needed to determine and secure its borders, and to sign peace accords with the defeated countries, which was done during 1919. According to the peace treaty signed at Neuilly on 27 November 1919, Bulgaria lost its sea outlet in Thrace in favour of Greece, parts of Dobruja in favour of Romania, and the towns of Strumica, Caribrod and Bosilegrad in favour of the newly formed Yugoslav state. Bulgaria had to reduce its armed forces to 20,000 professionals as well as to pay war reparations. Most importantly, the Bulgarian *Second national catastrophe* deprived it of all gains earned in the Balkan wars, especially one that generations of Bulgarians had coveted—Macedonia. Bulgarian Prime Minister Stamboliyski did not hide his resentment of the peace stipulations—according to his words, the peace conditions were hard and unjust, especially in terms of territorial cessations and their inability to resolve Balkan issues. However, Bulgaria would ensure the fulfilling of its obligation.[82]

Although the world war was over, a new period of conflicts and crisis (this time local and of low intensity) began to appear on the horizon.

---

[81] Parts of Margaret MacMillan's book *Peacemakers. The Paris Conference of 1919 and Its Attempt to End War*, (London: John Murray, 2002) related to the Balkans present a somewhat simplified interpretation of events in the Balkans, territorial issues and their echoes at the Paris conference. However, some conclusions, although under strong influence of the turbulent events from the 1990's, openly challenge existing descriptions of Yugoslavia as a 'creation of Versailles'.

[82] Vasil Vasilev, *Pravitelstvo na BZNS, VMRO i B'lgaro-Yugoslavskite otnosheniya*, (Sofia: BAN, 1991), 39.

II

Demobilization vs. Mobilization

While Bulgarian emissaries and Allied representatives were signing the armistice in Salonika on 29 September 1918, on the outskirts of Bulgarian capital patched-together forces of Bulgarian Army Cadets, German troops and *komitajis* of the Internal Macedonian Revolutionary Organization (IMRO) were preparing for a counterattack against mutinous Bulgarian soldiers. This incident was named the Radomir or Soldiers or Vladaya Rebellion, marked the end of Bulgarian participation in the Great War, yet it announced turbulent events in the succeeding years in Bulgaria. Dissatisfied soldiers who deserted their units after heavy fighting during the final Allied offensive on the Macedonian front were led by Rayko Daskalov, one of the top officials of the Bulgarian Agrarian National Union (BANU)—a political party whose activities in the following years would leave a lasting trace in Bulgarian political life.[1] Soldiers' anger was directed towards those they considered responsible for their ordeals during the years of deprivation and fighting in the trenches of the Macedonian front. Although of short duration, this rebellion was not different from other soldiers' uprisings in the defeated countries of the Central Powers at the end of or immediately after the Great War. Their dissatisfaction opened a small window of opportunity for BANU to make an attempt to end the Bulgarian 'old regime'. At that moment Daskalov and leader of the BANU and future Prime Minister Alexander Stamboliyski had just been released from imprisonment where they had spent most of the time during Bulgaria's Great War adventure.[2] They ended up there because of their strong opposition to official circles and their policies of entering the war on the side of Central Powers. With the approval and knowledge of Stamboliyski, Daskalov seized the leadership over the mutineers and led them on the Bulgarian capital. The day after, on 30 October, the mutiny or revolution was crushed. However, it announced a period of deep political divisions within Bulgarian society, divisions marked by political instability and extreme violence. Nevertheless, despite success in quelling the

---

[1] On BANU see: *B'lgarskiyat zemedelski naroden s'yuz 1899–1944*, (Sofia: Fond Detelina, 1999); Vasil Vasilev, *Pravitelstvo na BZNS, VMRO i B'lgaro-Yugoslavskite otnosheniya*, (Sofia: BAN, 1991); John D. Bell, *Peasants in Power: Alexander Stamboliiski and the Bulgarian Agrarian National Union 1899–1923*, (Princeton: Princeton University Press, 1977).

[2] On Stamboliyski see: John D. Bell, *Peasants in Power: Alexander Stamboliiski and the Bulgarian Agrarian National Union 1899–1923*, (Princeton: Princeton University Press, 1977); Richard J. Crampton, *Aleksandur Stamboliiski: Bulgaria*, (Chicago: University of Chicago Press and Haus Publishing, 2009); On Daskalov see: Dimitrina Petrova, *D-r Rajko Daskalov (1886–1923): politik i drzhavnik reformator*, (Stara Zagora: Znanie, 1995).

Paramilitarism in the Balkans: The Cases of Yugoslavia, Bulgaria, and Albania, 1917–1924. Dmitar Tasić,
Oxford University Press (2020). © Dmitar Tasić.
DOI: 10.1093/oso/9780198858324.001.0001

rebellion, in the following days King Ferdinand of Bulgaria had to abdicate. His son Boris assumed the throne at the age of twenty-four as Boris III, Tsar of Bulgaria.[3]

The Radomir Rebellion in a way announced future developments, marked by the rise to power of BANU and its leader Alexander Stamboliyski. At the same time the rise of BANU was followed by crisis within the old political parties. IMRO, unlike other players on Bulgarian political scene, was ready to adjust to new conditions and continue with its fight for Macedonia.[4] With new leadership embodied in General Alexander Protogerov, Todor Alexandrov and Petar Chaulev, IMRO decided, despite the Bulgarian defeat, to continue the struggle for the unification of Macedonia and Bulgaria. Technical preparations for the renewal of IMRO activities were conducted in the office of the 11th Macedonian Division in the Bulgarian capital.[5] The office was at 22 Gurko Street and was the unofficial headquarters of the organization. IMRO had inherited substantial quantities of the Macedonian Division's armament after this unit was disbanded, as well as large sums of money.[6]

However, what was about to come would cause deeper divisions within Bulgarian society. Bulgaria was about to suffer new territorial losses, war reparations and the reduction of its armed forces. Humiliated and occupied by the Allies, Bulgaria was obligated to reduce its army, which meant that many officers and NCO's would be forced to leave their commissions. This process began even before Bulgaria had signed the peace treaty. By the end of 1919, many units of the Bulgarian regular army were already disbanded, with their officers and NCO's discharged, reducing overall composition of the army to 3,436 officers and 46,852 privates.[7] As a result of these events many officers joined the *Military* or *Officers League*, initially a secret organization of discharged and active officers.

---

[3] Hall, Richard 'War in the Balkans'. In: 1914–1918-online. International Encyclopedia of the First World War, Daniel...[et al.](eds.) (Berlin: Freie Universität Berlin) 2014–10–08. **DOI**: http://dx.doi.org/10.15463/ie1418.10163.

[4] While the history of the IMRO before the Balkan Wars has been subject of different studies in both Bulgaria and former Yugoslavia/Macedonia, the post-Great War history of the organization can be assessed by analyzing different monographs, articles, and memoirs whose subject is closely related with leading political figures of the movement as well as contemporary historical events and processes; see: Zoran Todorovski, *Todor Aleksandrov*, (Skopje: Makavej; Državen arhiv na Republika Makedonija, 2014); Kostadin Paleshutski, *Makedonskoto osvoboditelno dvizhenie sled P'rvata svetovna vojna: (1918-1924)* (Sofia: BAN, 1993); ibid, *Makedonskoto osvoboditelno dvizhenie 1924–1934*, (Sofia: Akademichno izdatelstvo 'Prof. Marin Drinov', 1998).

[5] The 11th Macedonian division of the Bulgarian armed forces was comprised solely of conscripts of Macedonian origin that were already residing in Bulgaria or had escaped to Bulgaria to avoid being conscripted into the Serbian army. Many IMRO members or supporters of the organization's cause fought within its ranks during the Great War.

[6] Decho Dobrinov, 'Todor Aleksandrov i v'zstanovanieto na VMRO sled p'rvata svetovna vojna (1918-1924 g.)'. In *100 godini V'treshna makedono-odrinska revolucionna organizaciya*, (Sofia, Makedonski nauchen institut, 1994), 145–56.

[7] Military Archive Belgrade (Vojni arhiv –VA), Collection 4/3 Command of the Third Army District, r. 4/3, b. 54, f. 13, d. 12/185, Ministry of Army and Navy to the Command of the Third Army

During August 1919, while serving in the Burgas garrison, Petar Shandanov, an officer in the Bulgarian army, member of the IMRO and war veteran, was approached by one of his colleagues, who said:

"I have to tell you something extremely confidential, which I hope if you dis-agree, will remain secret forever like we never spoke about it', I said that he could rely on my officer's honour. Then he continued to explain that in almost all major garrisons a secret officer's league had been created, whose main task is to include intelligent and pro-active officers, who in the beginning would join in the concealing of weaponry which, at that moment, the Allied special commis-sion was already collecting. The second task of the Military League was to take care of the national upbringing of the people, which immediately after the entry into the war went astray in relation to the national question due to the extremely demagogic and devastating agitation of the leftist parties. Apart from that, the League wanted to struggle for the improvement of material situation of military servicemen, because at that time officers were poorly paid."[8]

Basically, that is how the *Military* or *Officers League* was created and what were its ideological foundations and rationale. However, this type of self-organizing was not a novelty within the Bulgarian officers' corps. The Bulgarian armed forces had already undertaken an attempt to create a secret officers' organization after the 'First National Catastrophe' or defeat in the Second Balkan War in 1913. The jus-tification was almost identical—the interests of the fatherland should be above the interests of political parties. In order to achieve that, the officers should have the final word in relation to future military alliances and choosing the right moment to enter or exit a war. Additional demands included: upbringing of the nation in a patriotic spirit, strengthening of the army and navy, restricting the activities of radical groups and press, and the annihilation of socialism in the school system. With these ends in view the organization even sent threatening letters to the opposition parties. Unlike in 1919, when there was no official response, in 1914 the Bulgarian state reacted instantly by dismantling the organ-ization structure that 'was creating a schism within the army and represented danger for the country's internal and foreign security'. Some of the organization's prominent figures were given new posts away from the capital while circular instructions of the Ministry of Defence were dispatched saying that there were indications that among the officers corps a tendency to create military associ-ations similar to those in Greece and Serbia.[9] Already by the end of March 1914

District, confidential no. 39150 from 13 October 1919, Report of the Delegate of the Supreme Command from Sofia, confidential no. 43949 from 12 October 1919.

[8] Petar Shandanov, *Bogatstvo mi e svobodata; Spomeni*, (Sofia: Izdatelstvo 'Gutenberg', 2010), 76.
[9] Practically simultaneously, Serbia went through a major political crisis marked by the so-called 'Struggle for Supremacy'. Basically, representatives of the army, i.e. members of the organization

during a Parliament session, the Minister of Defence assured Members of the Parliament that the *Officer's League* was not operating—omitting to add 'any more'.[10]

In the months that followed the secret conversation between Petar Shandanov and his colleague, the newly established *Military League* managed to stash a substantial amount of weapons for future use. Although the Allies, during their occupation of Bulgaria, performed bit by bit a somewhat 'forceful demobilization' by disbanding whole army units, requisitioning armament and ammunition and storing it under strict control, former army members and IMRO activists kept operating in a spirit of expectation of new actions and showdowns. In their case two consecutive Bulgarian war defeats, followed by huge human and territorial losses, contributed to the creation of a 'culture of defeat' which actually became a strong mobilizing factor. It has significantly influenced contemporary revisionist claims throughout Bulgarian society, mostly among supporters of the old regime. Because of that, the new government led by BANU in fact never managed to perform the complete demobilization of Bulgarian society despite the proclaimed goals. Organizations like the *Military League* and IMRO never stepped out from the 'state of war'. It looked for them as if war actually continued, while previous events and defeats were just episodes and battles in an on-going conflict. For these postwar unofficial centres of power in Bulgaria it was only the enemy who changed. Unlike in previous years when their enemies were Ottomans, Greeks and Serbs, in the years immediately after the Great War an enemy existed within their own society as well. From their perspective those were representatives of the leftist parties, i.e. both wings of the socialist party—'narrow' and 'broad'—i.e. future communists and social democrats, as well as BANU. The latter came into an extremely difficult position because they were to sign a peace agreement that came as a result of policies the agrarians had not supported or contributed to. In addition, the extent of Bulgarian territorial losses and war reparations were yet to be determined.

Cooperation between the army and IMRO had a long history. In previous decades a substantial number of Macedonians joined the Bulgarian Army, maintaining organization membership and continuing to support its efforts. Likewise, Bulgarian officers and NCO's of Macedonian origin participated in *komitaji* action, the Balkan Wars, and the Great War as well. Needless to say, this kind of interaction in the past facilitated networking and the creation of political alliances in post-Great War Bulgaria.

Unification or Death, better known as the *Black Hand*, demanded that army officials have supremacy over the civilian in newly liberated territories of Macedonia, Sanjak, and Kosovo and Metohija. They felt that temporary military rule had to be imposed on these lands. Conflict was so deep and serious that it caused a parliamentary crisis, resignation of the cabinet, serious discord among officers and the 'quiet' abdication of old King Peter Karađorđević who handed over his royal prerogatives to Prince Alexander, making him Prince Regent. On this see: Andrej Mitrović, *Serbia's Great War: 1914–1918*, (London: Hurst&Company, 2007) 24.

[10] Veselin Yaanchev, *Armiya, obshtestven red i vatreshna sigurnost mezhdu voynite i sled tyaah: 1913–1915, 1918–1923* (Sofia: Universitetsko izdatelstvo 'Sv. Kliment Ohridski', 2014), 35–9.

Maybe the best and obvious example was General Alexander Protogerov, one of the IMRO leaders and a career officer with rich experience from previous wars. He served as brigade commander during the Balkan Wars, and divisional commander and Head of the Occupation District during the Great War.[11] Another example is Colonel Petar D'rvingov who initially participated in the Gornya Dzhoumaya and Ilinden Uprising in 1903. As the closest associate of General Protogerov later on, he was Chief of Staff of the Macedonian Volunteer Corps during the Balkan Wars, as well as Chief of Staff of the 11th Macedonian Division and the Chief of Staff of the Occupation District during the Great War.

Albania was a new Balkan country that obtained independence after the Balkan Wars of 1912–1913. In the course of the Great War Albania was occupied both by the Entente and Central Powers, thus temporarily losing its independence. Following its pro-Albanian and pro-Muslim policies, Austro-Hungarian authorities enlisted some 8,000 Albanians into the ranks of the Bosnian Gendarmerie and the 14th Corps of Ottoman Army fighting on the Eastern front.[12] During the Great War Albanians also served as auxiliary forces to Austro-Hungarian and Bulgarian occupation regimes in Serbia and Montenegro.[13] Also, as a result of chaotic changes that occurred in Albania during 1915, the Albanian magnate Esad-pasha Toptani (ca. 1863, Tirana—14 June 1920, Paris, France) was forced to leave the country, following the columns of his Serbian allies who were retreating from their homeland after the successful offensive of a joint German, Austro-Hungarian and Bulgarian force. Esad-pasha left Albania with some 2,500 supporters. At that moment his hopes lay in the Entente and a potential successful breakthrough on the Macedonian Front.

However, due to another 'mobilization' that was taking place in Albania in the aftermath of the Great War, Esad-pasha's prospects for return to his homeland looked highly unlikely. What was going on in Albania was a widely popular 'mobilization' of Albanians aimed at the restoration of their independence. With the end of the war practically nothing changed for common Albanians since their country remained under occupation. The Italians and, to a lesser extent, the French arrived instead of the defeated Austro-Hungarians. They spread their troops from Korça in the south up to the Shkodra in the north. At the same time Serbs/Yugoslavs deployed their troops on the provisional borderline. Various Albanian political actors like local magnates, landlords, national workers, clan chieftains and others began a series of meetings envisaged as a prelude to the final

[11] Dimitre Minchev, *Participation of the Population of Macedonia in the First World War: 1914–1918*, (Sofia: Voenno Izdatelstvo, 2004).

[12] Milan Ristović, 'Occupation during and after the War (South East Europe)'. In *1914–1918-online. International Encyclopedia of the First World War*, Daniel, Ute...[et al.] (eds.), (Berlin: Freie Universität Berlin), 2014-10-08. DOI: http://dx.doi.org/10.15463/ie1418.10481.

[13] Ferenz Pollman, 'Albanian irregulars in the Austro-Hungarian army during World War I'. In Raugh, Harold E. Jr (ed): *Regular and Irregular Warfare: Experiences of Historical and Contemporary Armed Conflicts* (Belgrade: Institute for Strategic Research 2012) 63–8.

liberation of their homeland. This was possible only after forcing Italian occupiers to leave the country, as well as Yugoslav troops to retreat from the provisional borderline defined by the Allies on the eve of the breakthrough on the Macedonian front. The final meeting took place in January 1920, better known as the Congress of Lushnjë, where the *Committee for National Defence of Albania* was founded. There, Albanian leaders reached a consensus over the future of their state. Interestingly, they decided that Albania would remain a monarchy, but instead of a sovereign there was Regency comprised of prominent members of all Albanian religious communities. Soon, this group proved to be more powerful than the provisional government established in Durres under Italian sponsorship. By March they successfully organized elections and established the new government in Tirana. Under the command of Ahmed-bey Zogu, the young but capable chieftain of the Mati clan, Albanians slowly created the embryo of an armed force of some 5,000 men. By August, actions of Albanian irregulars forced Italian troops to disband most of the garrisons throughout Albania and to concentrate their troops in the port of Vlora. Strong pressure from the Albanians combined with ill-advised political moves of the Italian government and combat fatigue and leftist agitation among Italian soldiers led to the first Albanian victory and expulsion of the Italians from Albanian soil. Needless to say, this became possible thanks to the existence of a strong culture of bearing arms among Albanians. Because of that, the number of irregulars was always considerably higher than the number of regular forces. These clan militias would play an important role in future internal Albanian disputes and political crises.[14] However, once they expelled foreign invaders the Albanians entered a period of internal clashes. The extent of political instability in Albania is visible from the fact that between 1920 and 1922 the cabinet was changed seven times, before Ahmed-bey Zogu resumed position of Prime Minister in 1923 and managed to hold it for one year.

An intensive course of events after the successful breakthrough on the Macedonian Front led to creation of the new state—the Kingdom of the Serbs, Croats, and Slovenes. At the time of its proclamation, it hardly looked like a state. Newly liberated and devastated Serbia and Montenegro were united with parts of dissolved Austro-Hungarian Empire: Slovenia, Croatia, Bosnia and Herzegovina, Dalmatia, and southern Hungary. A great migration of nations and individuals was on the move—soldiers, internees, deserters and POW's were all returning to their homes, or wished to do so.

Interestingly, in the Serbian case the first ones to be relieved of their duty or in a certain sense to be 'demobilized' were its paramilitaries or irregulars. After initial battles during the breakthrough on the Macedonian Front, *chetniks* from the

---

[14] Bernd J. Fischer, *King Zog and the Struggle for Stability in Albania*, (Tirana: Albanian Institute for International Studies, 2012), 21.

detachment of Jovan Babunski were granted unlimited leave of absence. On 1 November the Serbian Supreme Command issued an order saying:

"Since the detachment under command of Jovan Babunski managed to accomplish the task for which it was formed, and since the houses of all of his *chetniks* have been pillaged and damaged with all moveable properties destroyed, I order this detachment to be disbanded and all of its *chetniks* to be relieved from service and allowed to return to their homes on unlimited absence."[15]

At that moment they belonged to the only remaining irregular detachment in the Serbian army. Most of its members were simple Macedonian peasants and for them, in normal circumstances, this order would mean the real end of the war. However, the future had rather different plans both for them and their leader.

While one group of irregulars/paramilitaries was allowed to go home and continue life in peace, the others were grouping *en masse*. After the successful breakthrough in Macedonia in mid-September, Serbian and French forces, during their advance to the north, received reports on numerous encounters between Serbian insurgents and retreating German and Austro-Hungarian troops. This series of events was actually what the Serbian Supreme Command initially planned to achieve when, in September 1916, they decided to send the experienced *chetnik* leader Kosta Milovanović-Pećanac back to Serbia. After being briefed and trained for this endeavour, a French airplane infiltrated him into the South Serbian region of Toplica in an adventurous manner. His task was to prepare and organize an insurgency that would help the planned Allied advance after a successful offensive.[16] He personally suggested this area because he was familiar with its population and geography. At that moment Serbia was divided between occupation authorities of the Austro-Hungarian Military General Governorate (*Militärgeneralgouvernement*) and the Bulgarian Military Inspectorate of Morava. Upon arrival, he managed to get in contact with numerous associates from the period of Serbian *chetnik* action in Macedonia as well as with other soldiers and officers who, for various reasons, remained in Serbia and did not retreat with the main body of the Serbian army. Whether they lost their units, were wounded at the time and were incapable of walking, or simply disliked the prospects of marching over the Albanian mountains, and managed to avoid capture, they represented a valuable and highly motivated military asset. In addition, Pećanac encountered a group of determined and battle-hardened Montenegrin officers who refused to surrender after the Montenegrin capitulation in early 1916 and who wanted to continue fighting. Their intention

---

[15] *Veliki rat Srbije za oslobođenje i ujedinjenje Srba, Hrvata i Slovenaca 1914–1918*, (Beograd: Glavni đeneralštab 1937) XXX, 658.

[16] Dmitar Tasić: 'Pecanac, Kosta'. *1914–1918-online. International Encyclopedia of the First World War*, Daniel, Ute … [et al.] (eds.), (Berlin: Freie Universität Berlin), 2014-10-08. DOI: http://dx.doi.org/10.15463/ie1418.10112.

was to march across occupied Serbia in the direction of Romania where they would eventually join the Russian army. Pećanac managed to persuade them to join and help him in his enterprise. With their support he started to create an organization and prepare a massive uprising. Beside already active policies of denationalization marked by the banning of the Serbian Cyrillic alphabet, closure of Serbian schools, killing and internment of members of intellectual and spiritual elites, introducing new curricula, bringing in Bulgarian teachers and priests etc,[17] both Austro-Hungarian and Bulgarian occupation authorities also realized that there was a certain number of Serbian and Montenegrin soldiers who did not withdraw with the bulk of the Serbian army but decided to return to their homes. When the occupiers initiated search for them it automatically increased the prospects of a massive armed rebellion.[18]

In addition, a specific measure of Bulgarian occupation authorities, the planning of conscription of Serbian youth, as well as an expressed wish for fighting among some over-zealous Serbian leaders, like Kosta Vojinović, led to somewhat different developments. Although Pećanac was against a premature uprising it actually happened in winter 1917, on 26 February, after the Bulgarian decision to initiate conscription of Serbian youth. Although unwillingly, Pećanac joined the mainstream and together with the above-mentioned people became one of the leaders of the Toplica Uprising.[19] In couple of weeks insurgents managed to liberate several small towns and vast territories in both the Austro-Hungarian and Bulgarian occupation zones. Despite initial successes insurgents faced a joint counteroffensive of Bulgarian and Austro-Hungarian forces. Beside already present occupation forces both of them engaged irregular troops like bands of *komitaji's* and Albanian irregulars to quell the rebellion. The Bulgarians authorized Colonel Alexander Protogerov to be in charge of this operation, with his Chief of Staff, Lieutenant Colonel Petar D'rvingov. Protogerov was one of the leaders of IMRO and one of its most active members, which actually meant that IMRO deeply influenced the whole enterprise.[20] By the end of March the insurgency was quelled with extreme brutality. Thousands of civilians were brutally tortured and murdered while their villages were burnt down. Some of the leaders of the insurgency, like Kosta Vojinović, were killed during the quelling or in subsequent sweeps. On the other hand, Kosta Milovanović-Pećanac managed to escape all pursuits. In one moment. in order to draw enemy attention from the Toplica region, his *chetniks*, in one audacious raid, sacked the small Bulgarian border

[17] Milan Ristović: 'Occupation during and after the War (South East Europe)'. In *1914–1918-online. International Encyclopedia of the First World War*, Daniel, Ute…[et al.] (eds.), (Berlin: Freie Universität Berlin), 2014–10–08. **DOI:** http://dx.doi.org/10.15463/ie1418.10481.

[18] Andrej Mitrović, *Serbia's Great War: 1914–1918*, (London: Hurst&Company, 2007) 245.

[19] On the Toplica Uprising as well as on armed resistance in occupied Serbia during the Great War see: Andrej Mitrović, *Ustaničke borbe u Srbiji: 1916–1918*, (Beograd: SKZ, 1987).

[20] Milovan Pisari, 'Gušenje Topličkog ustanka: VMRO na čelu represije'. In *Vojnoistorijski glasnik 2* (2011), 28–41.

Друго ослобођење М-ра Високих Дечана 29. септ. 1918

Кључ Лавре Високих Дечана прима Војвода Коста Пећанац
од аустријског чиновника.

Fig. 1. Kosta Pećanac receives keys of Serbian monastery Dečani from Austro-Hungarian official, Kosovo and Metohija, 29 November 1918.

After the breakthrough of Macedonian front in mid September 1918 Kosta Milovanović-Pećanac managed to activate his guerrillas, who after the failure of Toplica Uprising in 1917 were mostly hiding and avoiding confrontation. This time their actions proved to be very successful because they created chaos in enemy rear, disrupting their lines of supply, taking numerous prisoners and liberating villages and towns. Here we see how Kosta Milovanović-Pećanac receives keys of one of the most important holy places in Kosovo and Metohija, monastery Visoki Dečani, in whose vicinity Pećanac was born and where Albanian outlaws killed his parents making him an orphan and forcing him to move to Serbia and later on to join chetniks movement. Symbolically, this moment meant closing of a circle in his extremely turbulent life.

© National Library of Serbia (Belgrade), Postcard, Second liberation of monastery Dečani on 29 September 1918: voivoda Kosta Pećanac receives keys from Austrian official – Prokuplje [1936] (RG 1159/28)

town of Bosilegrad not far from the capital of Sofia, causing huge unrest.[21] Meanwhile, instead of regular Bulgarian troops, bands of IMRO *komitajis* were used to hunt down the remaining insurgents. Their vast experience of guerrilla warfare obtained during years of IMRO action in Ottoman Macedonia proved to be a winning combination. New severe measures were introduced as well. If someone was proven an associate to insurgents or maintained some kind of connection with them, he or she would be shot on the spot, house burnt down, property seized, and family interned. This led to efficient quelling of the uprising with just a few leaders and their bands remained active.[22]

---

[21] On events in Bosilegrad, see: *Pogrom't v Bosilegradsko 16–17 may 1917. g*, (Kyustendil: Faber, 2016).

[22] Martin Vulkov and Dimitar Grigorov, 'The Toplice Uprising'. In *The First World War and its impact on the Balkans and Eurasia, 17–18 September 2013*, Sofia University, PAPERS, 5. http://www.viaevrasia.com/documents/D.Grigorov%20M.Valkov%20THE%20TOPLICE%20UPRISING%20.pdf [Last time checked 13 April 2016]

Finally, in autumn 1918, after the successful breakthrough on the Macedonian Front Kosta Milovanović-Pećanac organized a successful guerrilla action. After the failure of Toplica Uprising he spent most of the time in mountainous regions between Kosovo and Metohija, Sanjak and northern Montenegro with a handful of his *chetniks*. When in the first days of October 1918 Pećanac heard about the Allied offensive, he decided to put the original plan into action and activate his *chetniks*. In the first actions they interrupted all road communications in the above-mentioned regions, which practically paralyzed movement of enemy troops, disrupted the chain of command, and caused panic. In a very short period *chetniks* managed to capture 12,000 enemy soldiers and some 324 officers. Since they did not have the capability to keep POW's they just disarmed them and let them go. Most of the captured soldiers claimed to be 'of Yugoslav origin', stating, 'they would wait at their homes' for the arrival of Serbian troops. Meanwhile, Pećanac managed to establish contact with advancing Allied troops. He then turned his attention towards the town of Peć in the Kosovo and Metohija region where in several clashes from 10 to 13 October he managed to liberate the town and surrounding villages, taking some 2,000 Austro-Hungarians as POWs. He ended his campaign there with a photo of the official surrender of the nearby medieval Serbian monastery Dečani that had been occupied by Austro-Hungarians. Tall and proud, in full *chetnik* gear, Pećanac was photographed while accepting the keys of the old monastery from a humble Austro-Hungarian officer of Czech origin in the presence of several Serbian Orthodox clergymen. For him this moment represented the peak of his career and something of a reversal of fortune because he was born in the nearby village of Dečani, but as a young boy was forced to flee to Serbia after his father was killed in a dispute with local Albanians. From Peć he dispatched orders to all insurgent bands in Montenegro, Herzegovina, Sanjak and Western Serbia to initiate a wide-scale offensive against the retreating enemy. He reported:

"So far the results of the insurgency are as follows: Plav, Gusinje, Andrijevica, Rožaj, Berane, Bijelo Polje i Kolašin are taken after fighting the enemy. There are some 3,000 German and Austrian POW's, but many more were killed because Germans used to fight bitterly, not wanting to surrender to *komitaji* bands."

After a short break and recovery, on 23 October 1918 he directed his forces towards northern Montenegro hoping to instigate a similar response in 'Bosnia, Herzegovina, Western Montenegro, and Dalmatia.'[23]

However, despite successes in clashes with the enemy, Pećanac's further engagement caused controversies which eventually led to his own 'demobilization'.

---

[23] *Veliki rat Srbije za oslobođenje i ujedinjenje Srba, Hrvata i Slovenaca 1914–1918*, (Beograd: Glavni đeneralštab 1937) XXX, 334–7. Pećanac's report to Serbian Supreme Command.

New Colours in the Balkan Palette
of Paramilitarism

Whites

The Russian revolutions and the subsequent civil war by their influence and significance went beyond the territories of the world's largest land empire. The fact that the revolutions occurred in the midst of the Great War contributed even more to the spreading of their influence. The appearance of a new state with a drastically different ideological and political system was followed by turbulent and fundamental changes marked, among other things, by widespread terror and violence. Many people, it is said some 2,000,000 citizens of the Russian Empire, willingly or unwillingly decided to leave their homeland because of the revolution and civil war, thus becoming the largest political emigration in the period between the two world wars.[24]

Russian émigrés or refugees[25] left Russia in three major waves. The first one was immediately after the October revolution in 1917. The second one happened in March 1920, after the Bolshevik forces defeated General Denikin and his *Volunteer Army* that led to evacuation of the port Novorosiysk. The third and final wave occurred in November 1920, after another defeat, this time of Denikin's successor, General Wrangel, and his *Army of Southern Russia* in Crimea, which led to subsequent evacuation towards Constantinople.[26] In the first years, as long as hope for return existed, the majority of Russian émigrés continued to live in countries closest to their homeland like Finland, Estonia, Latvia, Lithuania, Poland, Czechoslovakia, Germany, Bulgaria, Yugoslavia and China (Manchuria).[27]

Around 200,000 Russian émigrés arrived in the Balkans in 1919–1920.[28] The overwhelming majority settled down in two of the Balkan countries—the Kingdom of Serbs, Croats and Slovenes and Bulgaria.

The new Yugoslav state continued the traditional Serbian (also Montenegrin) policy towards Russia. This policy came about as a result of strong traditional political, cultural and religious ties between the two nations. Especially important were: Russian political support of Serbia and Montenegro in the days before the outbreak of the Great War; Russo-Serbian wartime cooperation; Russian military

---

[24] Miroslav Jovanović, *Doseljavanje ruskih izbeglica u Kraljevinu SHS 1919–1924*, (Beograd: Stubovi kulture, 1996), 25.

[25] Although these two terms have the same meaning, in the Soviet Union the term emigrants was practically equal with 'enemies of the Soviet Union'—M. Jovanović, *Doseljavanje ruskih izbeglica u Kraljevinu SHS 1919–1924*, 26.

[26] Miroslav Jovanović, *Doseljavanje ruskih izbeglica u Kraljevinu SHS 1919–1924*, (Beograd: Stubovi kulture, 1996), 29; and Bruno Bagni, 'Lemnos, l'île aux Cosaques'. In *Cahiers du Monde russe*, Vol. 50, No. 1, *Écrits personnels. Russie XVIIIe-XXe siècles*, (Janvier-mars 2009), 187–230.

[27] M. Jovanović, *Doseljavanje ruskih izbeglica u Kraljevinu SHS 1919–1924*, 24.

[28] Miroslav Jovanović, *Ruska emigracija na Balkanu (1920–1940)* (Beograd: Čigoja, 2006), 12.

support; Russian political and diplomatic support of the Serbian war program (with unification of South Slavs as the main Serbian war aim); and finally Russian support of the Serbian government and army after the defeat in 1915 and subsequent exile, i.e. during the most difficult period for the Serbian state in the course of the Great War. In addition, after the turbulent events of 1917 Serbia openly supported the anti-Bolshevik side in the Russian civil war. After the withdrawal of the Serbian ambassador from Moscow in July 1918 and the breaking of diplomatic relations in March 1919, now Kingdom of Serbs, Croats and Slovenes was the only country to officially recognize the 'All-Russian Provisional Government' of Admiral Kolchak in April 1919 and to exchange top-level diplomatic representatives. Following its policy, the Serbian government even refused to engage its own forces, which were organized in Russia from the Austro-Hungarian POW's of South Slav origin, in fighting against the Bolsheviks. Even the thought that Serbian and Russian soldiers might confront each other on the field of battle (no matter their ideological affiliation) was inconceivable for the Serbian political elite.[29]

On the other hand, the Bulgarian position was somewhat different since Bulgaria was fighting on the side of the Central Powers. Bulgarian and Russian soldiers clashed on several occasions, such as in the Dobruja campaign 1916 and in fighting on the Macedonian front in 1916-1917. In addition, Bulgaria was one of the co-signees of the Brest-Litovsk Treaty in spring 1918. However, on 29 September after the successful allied offensive on the Macedonian Front Bulgaria was the first among the Central powers to exit the war. At that moment Bulgaria as the defeated side could only wait, hoping it would have the opportunity to improve its international position before the signing of the peace treaty. And this opportunity appeared when General Denikin, in need for weapons for his forces, addressed the Bulgarian government (with full knowledge and support of the command of the Allied occupation forces in Bulgaria). Their agreement not only provided some 50,000 rifles, 25,000,000 rounds and 8 guns with 25,000 grenades to Denikin's South Russian army but also initiated negotiations that, following the Greek example, should have resulted in deployment of one or two Bulgarian divisions in South Russia in order to assist Denikin's forces. However, despite the active involvement of General Saraffov, one of several Bulgarian generals that had joined the Russian Imperial Army, and had been fighting on the side of the Entente during the Great War, negotiations over the question of a Bulgarian expeditionary corps did not bring any results.[30]

Meanwhile, the above-mentioned waves of Russian émigrés started to arrive in the Kingdom of Serbs, Croats and Slovenes and in Bulgaria. In the Yugoslav case,

[29] M. Jovanović, *Ruska emigacija na Balkanu*, 43–4.
[30] Lyudmil Spasov, *Vrangelovata armija v B'lgariya 1919–1923* (Sofia: Univerzitetsko izdatelstvo Sv. Kliment Ohridski, 1999),11–17.

the first larger groups started to arrive in mid February 1920 from Odessa. Those groups consisted of supporters of General Denikin and came in through Salonika. Evacuation of the port of Novorosiysk brought new groups to the Kingdom of Serbs, Croats and Slovenes. In a couple of months, from March to June, the number of Russian émigrés reached 8,000.

What was their composition?

Beside individuals, several organized groups arrived in the Kingdom of Serbs, Croats and Slovenes as well, such as the cadets and teaching staff of three cadet corps—Odessa, Kiyev and Polotsk. There were also two female schools, 'Mariinskiy Donskoy Institute' and 'Charkhov Institute.' The general attitude of Yugoslav authorities towards Russian émigrés was clearly visible in the case of the state funeral arranged for the founder of the *Volunteer Army*, General Alekseyev, who died in October 1918, and whose family brought his remains to the Kingdom of Serbs, Croats and Slovenes, refusing to leave them in Soviet Russia. His remains were buried in Belgrade with full honours.[31]

After the defeat of Denikin's forces in the Odessa region on 8 February 1920, new Russian refugees started to arrive at the Bulgarian port of Varna. By 26 February, 6,756 of them hade arrived and by 15 March their overall number reached 8,000. Out of them 2,000 continued their journey to the Kingdom of Serbs, Croats and Slovenes, while the rest was either dispersed throughout the Bulgarian interior or remained in Varna.[32]

Meanwhile, the majority of Denikin's forces were evacuated to Crimea where Denikin handed over his command to General Baron Petar Nikolayevitch Wrangel. However, a new and final offensive of Soviet forces in early November 1920 inflicted the decisive blow to General Wrangel forces. After the Red Army managed to end the fighting on several other fronts, including the war against Poland in 1919–1920, it was able to fully concentrate its forces against the only remaining enemy. After suffering several defeats, around 150,000 of Wrangel's soldiers and civilians withdrew towards the Crimean ports. In just three days General Wrangel managed to organize and execute their evacuation to Constantinople. For their protectors, the French, the major problem was General Wrangel's wish to maintain the military structure of his forces in order to continue fighting against the Bolsheviks sometime in the future. Because of that, and also because of a radically changed situation in international relations wherein many countries had either already recognized the Soviet regime or entered into serious relations with it, the military part of the Russian emigration was exposed to different kind of pressures including total suspension of support in order to persuade them to agree to demilitarization. The French offered General Wrangel and his army three possibilities:

---

[31] M. Jovanović, *Doseljavanje ruskih izbeglica u Kraljevinu SHS 1919–1924*, 111–15.
[32] L. Spasov, *Vrangelovata armiya v B'lgariya*, 25.

1. To return to Soviet Russia
2. To emigrate to Brazil and Peru
3. To live from their own income.

Wrangel refused the offer and entered into direct negotiations with the Kingdom of Serbs, Croats and Slovenes, Bulgaria, and Hungary. Meanwhile, suffering from lack of provisions and on the edge of famine, some of his men decided to accept the French offer. Around 3,500 returned to Soviet Russia, some 3,000 went to Brazil, several hundreds joined the French Foreign Legion, while several thousands decided to leave military service and accept civilian status. Those who decided to return to Soviet Russia were greeted with a bitter fate; the same happened with the group headed to Brazil.[33]

Already during the evacuation of Crimea 21,343 of refugees went directly to Kingdom of Serbs, Croats and Slovenes, without stopping in Constantinople. At the same time Bulgaria decided to accept only 4,170.[34] When in November 1920 the French decided to address the Bulgarians, asking them to accept 10,000 Russians, Prime Minister Stamboliyski was willing to grant this request for several reasons:

1. France was the key for Bulgarian entrance into League of Nations;
2. France was important for solving the question of Thrace and a Bulgarian sea outlet on the Aegean;
3. France was important for the release of Bulgarian POW's.

At the same time, on 10 December 1920, the Soviets offered Bulgarians to establishment of diplomatic and friendly relations in order to counterbalance the 'anti-Soviet League of Nations.' Since Bulgaria failed in fulfilling the French request, on 16 December French representatives voted against Bulgarian admittance to the League of Nations.[35] However, the more important question was what the destiny of Wrangel's army would be.[36] In spring 1921, after negotiations with Yugoslav representatives, it was agreed that the Kingdom of Serbs, Croats and Slovenes would accept 12,000 of Wrangel's soldiers, of whom 9,000 would be engaged in road construction while 3,000 would be hired as border guards.[37] Beside in Border Troops significant number of 'White' Russians was accepted in Gendarmerie

[33] M. Jovanović, *Doseljavanje ruskih izbeglica u Kraljevinu SHS 1919–1924*, 148–9.
[34] M. Jovanović, *Ruska emigacija na Balkanu*, 143.
[35] Cvetana Kyoseva, *B'lgariya i ruskata emigraciya: (20-te—50-te godini na XX v.)* (Sofia: Mezhdunar. Cent'r po problemite na malcinstvata i kulturnite vzaimodejstviya, 2002), 32–4.
[36] On international efforts related to expatriation of Russian refugees in the wider Black sea area, see: Martin Housden, 'White Russians Crossing the Black Sea: Fridtjof Nansen, Constantinople and the First Modern Repatriation of Refugees Displaced by Civil Conflict, 1922-23' In *The Slavonic and East European Review*, Vol. 88, No. 3 (July 2010), 495–524.
[37] M. Jovanović, *Doseljavanje ruskih izbeglica u Kraljevinu SHS 1919–1924*, 151–6.

and their names often appeared among awarded or deceased Gendarmes during the 1920's.[38] Apart of technical difficulties there was no objection to their arrival primarily because there was no international political interference over the issue of 'White' Russians, simply because the Kingdom of Serbs, Croats and Slovenes did not recognize Soviet Russia and did not establish any kind of relations with it (political, economical, cultural). Actually, Yugoslavs were only careful not to provoke an Italian reaction, and after the Italian ambassador in Belgrade expressed his concern they avoided sending 'White' Russians to Dalmatia. In Bulgaria, because the new Bulgarian regime actually established some kind of relations with Soviet Russia and because the local Communist Party had huge political influence, every action of the Bulgarian government in relation to 'White' Russians encountered objections. However, in order to avoid such developments Bulgarian authorities managed to prolong evacuation until November 1921 and divide emigrants into smaller contingents. In the end, it turned out that Bulgaria actually accepted a larger number of 'White' Russian soldiers than the Kingdom of Serbs, Croats and Slovenes—around 21,000.[39] Meanwhile, the Bulgarian Chief of Staff, General Topaldzhikov signed an agreement with Russian military leadership aimed at maintaining the military structure of Wrangel's force. According to the agreement it was allowed to keep 20 rifles per 1,000 men. Also, officers were allowed to keep their revolvers and sabres. This agreement was enforced despite Allied pressures to completely disarm Russian soldiers. Justification for this measure lay in the Neuilly peace accords, however, their disarmament proved to be quite unsuccessful, enabling the Russians to keep their military structure alive.[40]

General Wrangel and his Headquarters left Constantinople on 26 February 1922 and after several days arrived in the Kingdom of Serbs, Croats and Slovenes, in the small town of Sremski Karlovci where they established new Headquarters. Local press followed his arrival with huge interest. The last group of Russian soldiers left Gallipoli in May 1923. From 1,300 of that group, 1,000 decided to remain in the Kingdom of Serbs, Croats and Slovenes, while 300 continued their journey to Hungary.[41] In addition, during the same period many 'White' Russians came to the Kingdom of Serbs, Croats and Slovenes and Bulgaria individually. The two last organized groups that arrived in the Kingdom of Serbs, Croats and Slovenes were the 367 cadets of *Chabarovsk Cadet Corps* who came in 1924 all the way from Shanghai. They settled down in the small town of Bileća in Herzegovina

---

[38] For example one of two Gendarmes killed in an action on 15 July 1924, when famous *kachak* leader Azem Bejta was finally killed, was acting gendarme Victor Abakumoff who 'sacrificed his life on the altar of his brotherly country [...] in which after fleeing Russia from communists he had found warm hospitality and eternal rest'—*Žandarmerijski kalendar* 1928, 280.

[39] M. Jovanović, *Ruska emigracija na Balkanu*, 131.

[40] Cvetana Kyoseva, *B'lgariya i ruskata emigraciya (20-te—50-te godini na XX v.)*, 40–1.

[41] M. Jovanović, *Doseljavanje ruskih izbeglica u Kraljevinu SHS 1919-1924*, 148–9.

where they joined the already operating *River Don Cadet Corps*. The second group arrived in May 1928 when around 440 refuges decided to leave Constantinople due to the worsening of the political climate regarding the refugees in Turkey.[42]

In the years that followed the status of Russian émigrés in Kingdom of Serbs, Croats and Slovenes and Bulgaria began to change. In the Kingdom of Serbs, Croats and Slovenes they found friendly surroundings. The fact that the Kingdom of Serbs, Croats and Slovenes did not recognize Soviet Russia made it possible for Russian émigrés to fully enjoy hospitality by keeping their military, educational and religious institutions. In Bulgaria however, Russian emigration became the object in a complex political game. Being in the unfavourable position of loser in the previous war, Bulgaria experienced plenty of political pressures both from Western allies and Soviet Russia. In order to strengthen its own position the agrarian regime had to introduce unpopular measures targeting the Russian community, which led to their gradual alienation.

Both Yugoslav and Bulgarian societies in general benefited greatly from the arrival of Russian émigrés, especially from those who were scholars, scientists, architects and artists. Some professions, however, could not be practiced in exile primarily because of language issues, like civil servants and lawyers. Although predominantly military in composition, Russian emigration was basically intellectual—from 17,138 émigrés in the Kingdom of Serbs, Croats and Slovenes in 1922, 2,722 (12.4 per cent) had a university degree and 9,519 (61.5 per cent) had a high school degree. Out of 6,775 Russian émigrés registered at the Constantinople Labour Bureau (April 1920 to January 1921) 70 per cent were fluent in at least one foreign language. In order to adapt and survive, many officers, civil servants, and lawyers became tutors, chauffeurs, and butlers, while civil engineers and architects became simple craftsmen. For example, thanks to the diligence and thoroughness of several Russian imperial officers (even Generals) who were contracted to conduct cataloguing of the Yugoslav Military Archive their inventories are still in use. And while in the Soviet Union revolution made it possible for a simple shoemaker like Lazar Moyseyevich Kaganovich to become Mayor of Moscow, Minister and finally General, several former imperial generals in the Kingdom of Serbs, Croats and Slovenes opened shoe repair and shoe-making workshops.[43] In Sofia alone five Russian libraries were operating during the 1920's, while in the whole of Bulgaria there were eight Russian high schools. Thanks to the efforts of several Russian scholars a Balkan Middle East Institute was established in Sofia with the single aim of helping Russian students to finish their higher education. According to the records of *Union for the Return to the Fatherland*—Sovnarod (Союз за завръщане въ родината) out of 27,000 Russian

---

[42] M. Jovanović, *Doseljavanje ruskih izbeglica u Kraljevinu SHS 1919–1924*, 158–9.
[43] M. Jovanović, *Ruska emigacija na Balkanu*, 178–92.

émigrés residing in Bulgaria in March–April 1923 some 2,000 were physicians, engineers, lawyers, professors, agronomists etc.[44]

Both in the Kingdom of Serbs, Croats and Slovenes and Bulgaria the main objections against the presence of Russian émigrés came from local communist parties. However, due to the banning of the Communist Party of Yugoslavia in 1921, communists could not influence or endanger the position of Russian emigration there. In contrast, in Bulgaria communists actually managed to continuously hamper the position of Russian émigrés. Although many of Russians who used to wear uniforms adapted to new circumstances and life as civilians, there was still a considerable number of Russian ex-military men ready to continue the anti-Bolshevik struggle.

Reds

The Yugoslav writer Miroslav Krleža described his first encounter with future Yugoslav leader Josip Broz Tito after his return from Russia in 1920:

"I remember very well that among labourers in Zagreb you could hear the story of one labourer under the name Broz, who arrived from Russia, in an Astrakhan-style fur hat on which you could still notice traces of the red star he used to wear in Russia"[45]

The story of Josip Broz Tito and his journey back from Russia did not differ from that of thousands other returnees, mostly former Austro-Hungarian POW's. When in 1917 two revolutions happened in Russia, initiating Russia's exit from the Great War, there was a somewhat substantial number of POW's from Central Powers armies in Russian captivity. It is said that during the Great War there were 2,333,328 POW's in imperial Russia of whom 167,082 were Germans, 50,000 Ottomans, 200 Bulgarians and 2,104,146 Austro-Hungarians. The estimated number of Austro-Hungarians of South Slav origin was at least 10 per cent, i.e. around 200,000.[46] Many of them died in captivity due to the hardships caused by insufficient provisions, diseases, or extreme climate conditions. Josip Broz Tito noticed that while he was in camp in the small town of Kungur near the Ural mountains, from 1916-1917 (after being wounded and captured during fighting in the Carpathian campaign) many inmates—Hungarians, Slovaks, Romanians

---

[44] Doncho Daskalov, 'Byalata ruska emigratciya v' B'lgariya mezhdu dvete svetovni voiyni' In *Voennoistoricheski sbornik*, 1/1990, 56–75, here 67 and 72.

[45] Vladimir Dedijer, *Novi prilozi za biografiju Josipa Broza Tita. 1*, (Zagreb: Mladost, 1980), 87.

[46] Goran Miloradović, *Karantin za ideje; Logori za izolaciju 'sumnjivih elemenata' u Kraljevini Srba, Hrvata i Slovenaca: 1919–1922*, (Beograd: Institut za savremenu istoriju, 2004), 165.

and other Austro-Hungarians—died from cold and insufficient food provisions despite regular shipments of Swedish and US Red Crosses.[47]

After being released from captivity the long journey home began for many of them, no matter whether they tried to reach their countries or decided to join revolutionaries, thus contributing to the incredible diversity of Bolshevik forces at that moment. The vastness of the Russian state was another factor that contributed to a prolonged process of repatriation. Civil war and its side effects actually made it very difficult, if not impossible, for some of them to return to their homes by using usual and logical routes. Many Central and Southeast Europeans, instead of going directly through Ukraine and Poland, for example, were forced to use alternative routes that added incredible mileage to their already long journeys. Particularly hard and time-consuming was the route across Siberia to the Russian Far East and the port of Vladivostok or various Chinese ports. On all the usual routes that went straight towards the West via Baltic States, Poland, and Germany or Southwest via Ukraine, Czechoslovakia, Hungary and Romania returnees were occasionally detained either for questioning or for medical reasons. Also, the question arose of what the term 'home' meant for returnees after the end of Great War, i.e. the dissolution of old empires and appearance of new state entities on the map of Central and Southeast Europe. Unlike others, Tito managed to escape his POW camp already in 1917 and reach St. Petersburg where he participated in the so-called July demonstrations against the Provisional Government. He was arrested and sent back to the camps. However, he again decided to escape, but this time in the opposite direction. In the Siberian town of Omsk in 1918 he joined the Red Guard. However, his unit was defeated in clashes with troops of Admiral Kolchak. Tito fled to the steppes where he joined Kirgiz nomads and stayed with them for more than a year. After the defeat of White forces in Siberia he returned to Omsk in the autumn of 1919 where he married Pelagiya Belousova with whom he had already been in a relationship during his first stay there. In January 1920 they moved to St. Petersburg from where, after three weeks, they began the journey back to the Kingdom of Serbs, Croats and Slovenes. In the border town of Narva they went through the first quarantine. One of their fellow inmates was Jaroslav Hašek, Czechoslovakian writer, author of the famous anti-war satire *The Good Soldier Švejk*. From Narva they sailed to the German harbour of Stettin where they were divided according to their nationalities. From there, they travelled to Kingdom of Serbs, Croats and Slovenes by train. On Yugoslav border they again went through quarantine. Finally, they entered the Kingdom of Serbs, Croats and Slovenes in the autumn of 1920.[48]

How complicated the issue of repatriation of now-former POW's from Russia was is visible from the fact that the League of Nations, on its first assembly in

---

[47] V. Dedijer, *Novi prilozi za biografiju Josipa Broza Tita 1*, 65.
[48] V. Dedijer, *Novi prilozi za biografiju Josipa Broza Tita 1*, 65–72.

April 1920, decided to appoint renowned Norwegian geographer and explorer Fridtjof Nansen as *High Commissioner for Refugees and Relief Work in Russia* for the purpose of repatriation of former POW's whose number was estimated at over a half a million. He needed more than two and a half years to complete his mission and submit a report in September 1922 saying that thanks to the effort of his mission 427,886 representatives of 12 nations from 26 countries were repatriated from Russia.[49]

Another group worth mentioning were former Austro-Hungarian soldiers of South Slav origin in Italian captivity as well as Serbian and Montenegrin soldiers in German, Bulgarian and Austro-Hungarian captivity. By the beginning of 1920 some 26,000 of total 40,000 former Austro-Hungarian POW's of Yugoslav origin returned from Italian captivity, meaning that 14,000 of them had actually died there.[50] From nearly 220,000 Serbian POW's during the Great War, 154,000 were in camps in Austro-Hungarian Empire, 38,000 in Bulgaria and 30,000 in Germany. In 1919 some 160,000 survivors returned back to Serbia.[51]

As for international participants of the Bolshevik revolution, it is estimated that in the ranks of the Red Army in March of 1919 there were some 30-35,000 combatants from the former armies of the Central Powers. If we continue with the above-mentioned proportion of 10 per cent than there were probably 3,000 to 3,500 Yugoslavs among them. Not necessarily all of them were 'Bolsheviks', for example, in 1920 among 2,412 fighters in the Red Army's Yugoslav detachment deployed in Kazakhstan there were only 49 party members and 133 party member aspirants.[52]

An undetermined number of Bulgarians also participated in the Russian revolution and civil war. They came from several groups. Some of them were already there, like members of the Bulgarian minority in Bessarabia. Others were seasonal workers, gardeners, students, cadets, and administrative workers in different departments. For example, within the Russian Imperial Army there were 13 generals of Bulgarian nationality and even more officers of lower rank. Also, there were Bulgarian POW's. Like other international participants of the Russian revolution and subsequent civil war, Bulgarians fought either within regular units of the Red Army or different international units. For example, during the summer of 1918, a special international detachment under the command of Stoyan Dzhorov, 'prominent Bulgarian internationalist,' was deployed in Dagestan with the task to fight remaining groups of 'Whites'. In his detachment there were around 400

---

[49] G. Miloradović, *Karantin za ideje; Logori za izolaciju 'sumnjivih elemenata' u Kraljevini SHS,* 115.
[50] G. Miloradović, *Karantin za ideje; Logori za izolaciju 'sumnjivih elemenata' u Kraljevini SHS,* 143.
[51] Stanislav Sretenović and Danilo Šarenac (eds.), 'Srpski zarobljenici Centralnih sila' In *Leksikon Prvog svetskog rata u Srbiji,* (Beograd: Institut za savremenu istoriju; Društvo istoričara Srbije 'Stojan Novaković', 2015), 388–91.
[52] G. Miloradović, *Karantin za ideje; Logori za izolaciju 'sumnjivih elemenata' u Kraljevini SHS,* 165–6.

fighters: 100 Bulgarians, 100 Hungarians, and several groups of 50-70 Yugoslav, Austrian, Romanian and other internationalists. As in the Yugoslav case, not all of the Bulgarians were members of the party—either Bolshevik or Bulgarian 'narrow' socialist. For example, legendary Red Army commander Yoriy Pehlivanov was not a party member. Beside those who were already in Russia several groups of Bulgarian 'narrow' socialist secretly went from Bulgaria to Soviet Russia from the end of 1918 onwards. To do so, they used several 'channels' like Varna—Odessa or Varna—Sevastopol. When they started to return to Bulgaria after their engagement in revolutionary events they brought new experiences and skills.[53]

No matter whether they returned to their countries with or without ambitions to implement their experiences and continue revolutionary struggle, they encountered suspicion and mistrust. For the newly founded Yugoslav state and its authorities, news of the revolutionary events in Germany, Bavaria and Hungary[54] was disturbing enough. The arrival of participants of revolutionary events aroused suspicion of their intentions because the true danger did not lie in their numbers but in the fact that they were considered as sleeper cells for the intended revolution in the Kingdom of Serbs, Croats and Slovenes. Already during 1919 the first steps were taken in order to regulate the eventual treatment of returnees. Their ideology was described as the 'lethal virus of Bolshevism', so accordingly a system of quarantine detention or internment camps had to be established.[55] However, during 1919, besides the expected arrival of returnees from Russia, already present promulgators of socialism or socialist ideology and their proclamations caused additional uneasiness among tenuously established Yugoslav authorities. The combination of social unrest, existing deserters from the former Austro-Hungarian army—the so-called 'Green Cadre', ideologies of anti-unification movements and parties, and socialist addresses directed towards the soldiers of the Serbian army, the only existing reliable armed forces, calling them to 'turn their weapons against the loan sharks, capitalists and bandit Alexander [Serbian/Yugoslav Prince Regent] who keeps sending you to the slaughterhouse...' led to establishment of the first internment camps in the interior of the country. It is unknown how many socialists, former Russian and Austro-Hungarian POW's, deserters and other suspects were actually detained in camps like Belgrade, Smederevo, Mostar, Klis, Petrovaradin, Požarevac, Valjevo, Livno, and the island of Žirje, near the Dalmatian town of Šibenik.[56]

---

[53] Panayotov, Panayot, *B'lgaro savetski otnosheniya i vr'zki: 1917–1923* (Sofia: Darzhavno izdatelstvo nauka i izkustvo, 1982), 122–51.

[54] On the course of the revolutions in East Central Europe see: Robert Gerwarth, *The Vanquished: Why the First World War Failed to End 1917–1923* (London: Allen Lane, 2016).

[55] G. Miloradović, *Karantin za ideje; Logori za izolaciju 'sumnjivih elemenata' u Kraljevini SHS*, 99–101.

[56] G. Miloradović, *Karantin za ideje; Logori za izolaciju 'sumnjivih elemenata' u Kraljevini SHS*, 99–101.

As for the returnees from Soviet Russia (and Italian captivity), whether they were international members of the Red Army or had just remained stranded in the Russian vastness, different sort of camps were designed. They did not have any kind of official name but were designed as 'reception camps' with the purpose of reception, isolation, control, process of identification and hearings (interrogations), as well as health control and disinfection. Most of the camps were located in places where international land and maritime routes entered Yugoslav territory, such as in Subotica, Maribor, Ljubljana, and the port of Dubrovnik. Upon arrival returnees would spend between two or three weeks passing through a combination of security and sanitary measures and lengthy questioning about their involvement in events in Russia. Police investigators were especially keen to discover members of the communist party. Sometimes they were successful for the simple reason that they managed to find hidden party credentials, which returnees needed for the establishment of contact with existing party structures.

The exact number of returnees was never precisely determined. However, the only figure that can illustrate this process was the number of people who passed through four of the above-mentioned camps. During their period of operation (1919 till 1922) it is estimated that some 57,000 returnees passed through these camps. However, the overall number is probably much higher since at least a similar number arrived before and after the camps were fully operational.[57] Among them, a substantial number represented followers of Bolshevik ideology.

On top of that, it happened that in several countries, upon their return, returnees realized that their adversaries from the Russian Civil War, the so-called 'White' Russians were already there or they were in the process of settling as refugees after their final defeat in Crimea. This was especially visible in the Balkans where these groups and their attitudes and actions contributed largely to the continuation of the existing rivalry in a new political context. For some of the returnees the first thing they would see and the first people they would encounter after arriving in the Kingdom of Serbs, Croats and Slovenes were former members of General Wrangel's army now in the service of the Yugoslav state as border guards.

In the years that followed in Bulgaria, and to a lesser extent in the Kingdom of Serbs, Croats and Slovenes, numerous incidents and political crises occurred in which former adversaries on the battlefield clashed again. In a way, due to these encounters, the Russian Civil War actually had a prolonged effect in the Balkans.

While the Kingdom of Serbs, Croats and Slovenes did not recognize Soviet Russia as a state, nor had it established diplomatic relations with Moscow, Bulgaria, under the regime of Alexander Stamboliyski, had a somewhat benevolent policy towards the Bolsheviks. For example, Stamboliyski and his regime made several pro-Soviet gestures during 1920, like preventing a group of

[57] G. Miloradović, *Karantin za ideje; Logori za izolaciju 'sumnjivih elemenata' u Kraljevini SHS*, 221–66.

volunteers led by German Staff officer Count Norman to go via Bulgaria to assist anti-Bolshevik forces or refusing the French diplomatic representative in Sofia when he requested Bulgaria to send weapons to Poland during the war against the Soviets.[58]

The Yugoslav communist party was initially named the Socialist Labour Party of Yugoslavia (communist) (Socijalistička radnička partija Jugoslavije (komunista)). It was founded in 1919 by the unification of social-democrat parties of Serbia, Bosnia and Herzegovina, Dalmatia and the majority of the social-democrat party's membership from Slovenia and Croatia. After initial soul-searching because of different factions within the party, in 1920 the party adopted Bolshevik policies, and changed its name to the Communist Party of Yugoslavia (KPJ). That, together with numerous strikes, election success and widespread support (it became the fourth most powerful party by number of votes—200,000 in elections for the Constitutional Assembly in 1920 which secured it 59 out of 415 seats in the parliament) resulted in a reaction by state authorities. In December, the Ministry of the Interior issued the famous decree called *Announcement* (*Obznana* in Serbian) placing a ban, until the proclamation of the new Constitution, on all activities in spreading communist propaganda. It also banned communist papers and their social clubs. All weapons had to be registered under threat of imprisonment. During the work of the Constitutional Assembly all public gatherings were prohibited. Special military courts would prosecute everyone who would raise their weapons against state authorities. All foreigners involved in these activities would be deported, civil servants fired and student members of communist organization would be deprived of school allowances. However, when in 1921, on 28 June, Spasoje Stejić—a war veteran and member of the KPJ—threw a grenade at the Prince Regent's carriage (without hurting him) and when Alija Alijagić—a member of the revolutionary group *Red Justice*—killed Milorad Drašković, Minister of the Interior and creator of the *Announcement,* the state immediately reacted. A special *Law for the protection of public safety and public order in the state* was passed that completely banned KPJ. Its parliamentary mandates were cancelled and its remnant forced to go underground, making it too weak to perform any revolutionary activity.[59]

Bulgarian Communists, for their part, contributed to the intensity of Bulgarian political life in the period after the Great War. With 21,557 members in 582 local organizations, the Bulgarian Communist Party at the end of 1919 represented a respectable force on the Bulgarian political scene.[60] The Party's decision to embrace Bolshevik revolutionary methods and doctrine resulted in an unsuccessful attempt

[58] P. Panayotov, *B'lgaro savetski otnosheniya i vr'zki: 1917–1923*, 155.
[59] Branko Petranović, *Jugoslavije 1918–1988. 1*, (Beograd: Nolit, 1988), 111–13.
[60] Veselin Yaanchev, *Armiya, obshtestven red i vatreshna sigurnost mezhdu voynite i sled tyaah: 1913–1915, 1918–1923* (Sofia: Universitetsko izdatelstvo 'Sv. Kliment Ohridski', 2014), 148.

at socialist revolution in September 1923. For that purpose, since their congress in 1919, Bulgarian communists were carefully building a (para)military structure within the party through so-called *Illegal Military Organization*.[61] The basic unit of the organization was 'triplet'. 'Triplets' were associated with the existing party structure. Each regional and district party committee, both in towns and country-side was associated with one 'triplet'. In larger towns 'triplets' were associated to party section as well. During 1921 several party members were secretly sent to Soviet Russia for military training. They also started to recruit active and reserve officers and NCO's which in March 1922 finally led to the creation of the *People's Union of Reserve Officers and NCO's* (Narodniya soyuz na zapasanite oficeri i podoficeri—NSZOP).[62] The Communist (para)military organization was not based exclusively on party membership but tried to attract different groups of sympathizers.

Thus, in all three above-mentioned states: Albania, Bulgaria and the Kingdom of Serbs, Croats and Slovenes, the initial post-Great War years proved to be prom-ising for different paramilitaries and their movements. Depending on the polit-ical context and how particular 'culture' manifested in each country, whether it was 'culture of victory' or 'culture of defeat' in three countries in question hap-pened specific wave of partial or complete mobilizations or remobilizations. No matter if they were old, like Bulgarian *komitajis*, Serbian *chetniks* or Albanian *kachaks* or new one, such as communists and 'White' Russians, they were all able to maintain their presence and structures and continue operating. In the Bulgarian case 'culture of defeat' proved to be main incentive for the creation of legal and illegal organizations of former officers—once proud and elite members of society now discharged and forced to struggle for existence in defeated country on a verge of economic collapse as tutors, chauffeurs or hotel valets. Their energy and frustrations would be fully expressed in near future.

Some of the paramilitaries, like IMRO *komitajis* and Albanian *kachaks* became an important factor both in internal political organization and among anti-Yugoslav emigration. Others, like communists and 'White' Russians, depending on local context, established cooperation or entered into conflict with existing paramilitaries and their political representatives, thus contributing to the com-plexity of existing rivalries. Rivalry between communists and 'White' Russians, at least within the Yugoslav context, continued for several decades, reaching its climax during the violent years of the Second World War.

---

[61] Veselin Yaanchev, *Armiyaata, obshtestven red i vatreshna sigurnost mezhdu voynite i sled tyaah*, 208.

[62] Slavi Chak'rov, 'Voennata organizatsiya i podgotovkata na septemvrijskoto v'stanie 1923. g'. In *Septemviyskoto v'stanie 1923 godina—voennite deiystviya*, (Sofia: Ministerstvo na narodnata otbrana, 1973), 9–45.

III
Balkan Borderlands

The post-Great War years in the Balkans, more precisely in the three states at the centre of this study: Albania, Bulgaria and Yugoslavia (Kingdom of Serbs, Croats and Slovenes), were marked by overall political and economic instability. Even before the war, these regions had been underdeveloped compared to Central Europe, especially those parts which until 1912 belonged to the Ottoman state. Furthermore, what contributed to additional economical exhaustion and caused huge demographic strain apart from the Great War were the two Balkan Wars, fought in 1912–1913, as well as several subsequent smaller insurgencies and incidents. In practical terms, a state of war in most of the Balkans had already been in effect from October 1912 and the beginning of the First Balkan War, almost two years before the outbreak of the Great War in 1914. If we take into consideration the prolonged engagement of armed forces after the official end of war in November 1918 and their subsequent participation in numerous military and security operations, border clashes and incidents, quelling of rebellions, and counterinsurgency operations, then the actual end of war arrived in 1920—in total there were some eight years of a state of war or something that resembled it.

In terms of security especially sensitive areas were Sanjak, Kosovo and Metohija and the former Ottoman Macedonia. Ottoman Macedonia, interestingly, never existed as an entity under that name.[1] In its full extent Ottoman Macedonia consisted of three *vilayets* or provinces. The first one, Salonika *vilayet*, was the central and largest part; the second was Kosovo *vilayet* lying to the north all the way to the border with Serbia, while the third—Monastir *vilayet*—was in the southwest encompassing parts of today's Albania as well.[2] In the autumn of 1918 parts of these territories were reclaimed by Serbia and they entered the new Yugoslav state as an integral part of the Kingdom of Serbia. These areas are also known as Vardar Macedonia although that name never entered official use. Sensitive in the same way were the parts of Macedonia that belonged to Bulgaria, better known as Pirin Macedonia—named after the mountain in that area. A similar situation existed in the mountainous parts of Albania. Both in Pirin Macedonia and North Albania traditions of paramilitary organizing and activities existed, and both remained

---

[1] Nadine Lange-Akhund, 'Nationalisme et terrorisme en Macédoine vers 1900'.In *Balkanologie*, Vol IV, no. 2 (2000), 1–11, here 2.

[2] Nadine Lange-Akhund, *The Macedonian Question 1893–1908, from Western Sources* (Boulder: East European Monographs, 1998), 13.

Paramilitarism in the Balkans: The Cases of Yugoslavia, Bulgaria, and Albania, 1917–1924. Dmitar Tasić, Oxford University Press (2020). © Dmitar Tasić.
DOI: 10.1093/oso/9780198858324.001.0001

remote from the central authorities in every possible respect, to the extent that local paramilitaries in certain moments acted as a 'state within a state'.[3] The third part of Macedonia, the one which belonged to Greece, became known as Aegean Macedonia, however it was never actually recognized under that name in Greece. These territories could be named the 'Balkan border lands' using a similar approach as in Omer Bartov and Eric D. Weitz's edited volume. Here, 'border-lands' are defined as 'spaces-in-between, where identities are often malleable and control of the territory and population is subject to dispute'.[4] This definition certainly applies to the Kingdom of Serbs, Croats and Slovenes (its southern parts), Bulgaria and Albania, primarily in those stretches of land which until 1913 belonged to the Ottoman Empire.

County	km²	Ser/Cro.	Albanians	Turks	Vlachs	Total
Berane (San.)	987	23,561	275	19	–	23,684
B. Polje (San.)	1,215	26,136	8	1	–	26,147
Bitola (Mk.)	5,803	134,535	19,209	18,007	4,425	180,732
Bregalnica (Mk.)	4,956	72,764	71	29,011	1,197	104,347
Zvečan	1,810	20,679	42,275	5,180	88	70,137
Kosovo (Kos.)	4,046	47,229	108,541	10,619	178	171,285
Kumanovo (Mk.)	3,556	111,682	25,097	6,813	299	147,184
Metohija (Kos.)	1,997	17,761	70,409	1,430	61	90,080
Ohrid (Kos.)	1,956	48,460	11,448	7,506	1,597	69,211
Pljevlja (San)	1,293	26,723	16	40	4	26,798
Prizren (Kos.)	2,216	28,179	57,216	10,681	74	96,781
Prijepolje (San.)	1,760	41,962	–	341	–	42,322
Raška (San.)	2,828	69,944	1,944	145	64	72,365
Skoplje (Mk.)	3,475	21,551	862	13,980	543	145,880
Tetovo (Mk)	3,609	53,668	48,399	14,547	70	117,179
Tikveš (Mk)	4,210	73,210	34	17,338	882	92,435
Total	45,717	878,625	416,977	148,019	9,585	1,476,747

Kos.—Kosovo and Metohija

Mk.—Macedonia

San.—Sanjak

County	Orthodox	Catholics	Muslims	Jews	Greek-Catholic and Lutherans	Total
Berane (San.)	14,970	71	8,822	1	–; –	23,684
B. Polje (San.)	12,022	19	14,105	–	–; 1	26,147
Bitola (Mk.)	134,939	338	42,689	2,643	60; 63	180,732

[3] Peter Bartl, *Albanci, od srednjeg veka do danas* (Beograd: CLIO, 2002) 188–9; Dimitar Tyulekov, *Obrecheno rodolyubie. VMRO v Pirinsko 1919–1934* (Blagoevgrad: Univ. Izd. 'Neofit Rilski', 2001), http://www.promacedonia.org/dt/index.html [last checked on 4 November 2016]

[4] Omer Bartov and Eric D. Weitz (eds.), *Shatterzone of Empires: Coexistence and Violence in the German, Habsburg, Russian and Ottoman Borderlands* (Bloomington: Indiana University Press: 2013), 1.

Bregalnica (Mk.)	71,484	117	32,084	491	1; 170	104,347
Zvečan (Kos.)	19,288	533	50,205	104	5; 2	70,137
Kosovo (Kos.)	42,935	3,664	124,336	322	5; 23	171,285
Kumanovo (Mk.)	112,071	50	35,017	18	3; 25	147,184
Metohija (Kos.)	16,247	8,227	65,581	–	9; 16	90,080
Ohrid (Kos.)	44,761	406	23,997	10	4; 33	69,211
Pljevlja (San)	17,306	134	9,356	2	–; –	26,798
Prizren (Kos.)	14,482	3,359	78,906	1	7; 26	96,781
Prijepolje (San.)	24,570	27	17,719	–	–; 6	42,322
Raška (San.)	28,723	51	43,361	225	1; 4	72,365
Skoplje (Mk.)	75,498	1,012	67,376	1,872	31; 91	145,880
Tetovo (Mk.)	47,009	139	70,021	–	–; 8	117,179
Tikveš (Mk.)	62,973	159	27,906	13	666; 718	92,435

Final results of the census from 31 January 1921.[5]

Kos.—Kosovo and Metohija

Mk.—Macedonia

San.—Sanjak

Several factors contributed to the continuation of instability in these regions. Some of them were inherited from the Ottomans, others appeared as novelties. Ethnical and religious diversity was certainly one of the most important. In sense of ethnicity these territories were populated by Bulgarians, Turks, Slavic Muslims, Albanians, Serbs, Montenegrins, Macedonians, Jews, Vlachs, Roma, Greeks, etc. In a religious sense the situation was additionally complicated. For example, Albanians were divided between Greek Orthodox, Roman Catholics, Muslims and Bektashis (Sufi order). Before the Great War, the Macedonian Orthodox population was divided between jurisdictions of the Bulgarian Exarchate and the Ecumenical Patriarchate. After the Great War these territories belonged to the jurisdiction of the renewed Serbian Orthodox Patriarchate.

According to the Ottoman census from 1905–06, the three *vilayets* of Ottoman Macedonia counted 2,879,634 inhabitants. Around 50 per cent were Slavs, 25 per cent Turks, while Greeks accounted for 10 per cent. The rest were minorities like Vlachs, Gypsies and Jews.[6]

Creation of the Yugoslav state brought in new subjects like Croats, Slovenes, Germans and Bosnian Muslims, raising existing diversity to a completely new level. The results of the first census in the Kingdom of Serbs, Croats and Slovenes in 1921 showed that of 1,476,747 inhabitants of 'Old and South Serbia'—the unofficial name of 16 counties in the regions of Sanjak, Macedonia and Kosovo

---

[5] See: V. Jovanović, *Jugoslovenska država i Južna Srbija*, p. 46. taken from *Final results of the census from 31 January 1921*, Sarajevo 1932, pp. 86–122.

[6] Nadine Lange-Akhund, *The Macedonian Question 1893-1908, from Western Sources* (Boulder: East European Monographs, 1998) 13 and 24.

and Metohija—734,164 were males and 740,396 females. Some 59.5 per cent were Serbs/Croats, 28.2 per cent Albanians, 10 per cent Turks, 0.6 per cent Vlachs, 0.03 per cent Slovenes, 0.01 per cent Germans etc.[7] Some 76.3 per cent of the total population of the Yugoslav part of the 'Balkan border lands' lived in rural areas. Although there were no nationally homogeneous areas, Muslim villages were dominant in plains while Christian ones dominated in mountainous areas.[8] Both rural and urban settlements, no matter if they were Christian or Muslim, were characterised by disorder, poor hygiene and poor living conditions. People used to sleep on floors on sheepskins or mattings, often alongside their cattle in the same premises. Bad diet habits and living conditions stimulated the widespread presence of different diseases such as tuberculosis or endemic malaria, the latter especially in areas known for rice cultivation. As for the 'Balkan borderlands' the appearance of new state borders after the Great War in what used to be integrated political and economical spaces created visible and traumatic changes. Most of the traditional administrative and economical centres from the Ottoman times lost their significance and influence. Bitola or Monastir, which used to be the centre of the Ottoman administration, became just another border town. By 1921, because of the combined effects of destruction during the Great War and changes in the economical-political surroundings it had lost 41.2 per cent of its pre-Balkan War population.[9] The same thing happened with Debar/Dibra which used to be a very important station on the ancient road from Durres towards Salonika, and whose Albanian inhabitants exerted huge economical and political influence all the way to Constantinople. Interruption of traditional trading routes and the fact that the town was given to the Yugoslav kingdom while its hinterland remained in Albania significantly contributed to Debar's decay.[10]

The fact that during the period of the Yugoslav kingdom (1918–1941) Macedonians were not recognized as a nation represents a separate issue. They were considered as a constituent part of the Serbian ethnic community.[11] Needless to say, Bulgarians, and Greeks as well, did not recognize Macedonians as a separate entity, but as a constituent part of their own nations.

---

[7] Vladan Jovanović, *Jugoslovenska država i Južna Srbija 1918–1929 (Makedonija, Sandžak i Kosovo i Metohija u Kraljevini SHS)*, (Beograd: INIS, 2002), 45. The total population of 'Old and South Serbia' was smaller than the population of Ottoman Macedonia. Ottoman Macedonia had 96.400 km² while 'Old and South Serbia' had 45.717 km². The difference comes from the fact that Aegean Macedonia consisted of much of the Salonika *vilayet* which belonged to Greece.

[8] V. Jovanović, *Jugoslovenska država i Južna Srbija*, 56.

[9] V. Jovanović, *Jugoslovenska država i Južna Srbija*, 49.

[10] Milosav Jelić 'U mrtvome gradu'. In *Letopis Juga*, (Beograd, 1930).

[11] On the place of Macedonia within the mid-war Yugoslav state see: Vladan Jovanović, *Jugoslovenska država i Južna Srbija 1918–1929 (Makedonija, Sandžak i Kosovo i Metohija u Kraljevini SHS)*, (Beograd: INIS, 2002); Vladan Jovanović, *Vardarska banovina 1929–1941*, (Beograd: INIS, 2011); and Vladan Jovanović, *Slike jedne neuspele integracije: Kosovo, Makedonija, Srbija, Jugoslavija*, (Beograd: Fabrika knjiga; Peščanik, 2014).

Initial Usage of Paramilitaries in the Kingdom of Serbs, Croats and Slovenes, and Controversies that Occurred

When in the summer of 1918 the Allied command on Macedonian front decided to start preparations for the final offensive, from the Serbian point of view this was not merely a military operation. In case of a successful offensive Serbian and Allied troops would enter the territories which, although before the war used to be within the Serbian constitutional and territorial framework, were now devastated and insecure. Already before the final breakthrough on the Macedonian front the Serbian Ministry of the Interior initiated preparations for the renewal of civil and police authorities in the territories which would be liberated first, i.e. Macedonia, south Serbia, Kosovo and Metohija, and Sanjak. The aim was to avoid creation of an atmosphere of overall insecurity after the Allied armies passed through these areas. Insecurity would be primarily manifested in incidents that might endanger the personal safety of Serbian citizens as well as their private properties. Political instability and economic devastation together with religious and national intolerance, as well as the presence of Allied forces from Greece, Italy, France, Great Britain and their respective colonies (Morocco, Senegal, Algeria, French Indochina, India) could create an inflammable situation where even the smallest incident could have long-lasting and devastating effects. So, following the pace of the Allied advance during September and October 1918 Serbian civil and police authorities were returning to their communities, districts and counties.[12] At the same time local Montenegrin authorities self-organized and returned to their positions throughout the counties of the old kingdom. However, the number of police and civil servants was far from sufficient. In order to impose order several army units were placed under the command of local authorities. Somehow, even that was insufficient to provide security for everyone.

During the first months of functioning of the renewed Serbian (and Montenegrin) authorities several issues appeared:

– Cases of pillaging committed by various perpetrators, including Allied troops;
– Raids of Albanian cattle-rustlers in western Macedonia;
– Presence of huge amounts of firearms, especially among local Albanians;
– Final status of the renewed Montenegrin authorities.

The most challenging proved to be the attitudes of the Albanian population who were in a state of shock after the sudden and complete defeat of their sponsors from the Central Powers. However, the fact that on 1 December in Belgrade a

---

[12] Dmitar Tasić, *Rat posle rata, Vojska Kraljevine Srba, Hrvata i Slovenaca na Kosovu i Metohiji i u Makedoniji: 1918–1920*, (Beograd: Utopija, 2008), 22.

new state was proclaimed under the name of the Kingdom of Serbs, Croats and Slovenes and that Serbian and Allied troops were deployed practically everywhere did not prevent the initiation of intensive agitation in favour of unification of Macedonian and Kosovar territories with a renewed Albanian state. Agitation was followed by different incidents like shootings and assaults on police stations and community centres, as well as sabotages. After several clashes with army forces designated to conduct a campaign of disarmament of Albanians from Kosovo and Metohija regions, the situation there temporarily settled down. However, desperate times call for desperate measures—beside regular army and police forces there were several cases of usage of paramilitary or irregular forces either with autonomy in action or as auxiliary forces.

The first challenge for the renewed but unstable authorities in the Kingdom of Serbs, Croats and Slovenes was an open rebellion that broke out at the beginning of 1919 in Plav and Gusinje—small Montenegrin towns on the border with Kosovo and Metohija.[13] Here, in just several years, numerous cycles of inter-ethnic violence and retaliation occurred.

The local Muslim majority was not overwhelmed by the fact that the end of the Great War brought them again under Montenegrin rule. After the Balkan Wars of 1912–1913 the territory of Montenegro expanded, encompassing this area as well. The short Montenegrin rule was marked, among other things, by cases of forceful conversion of local Muslims to Christianity. The collapse of the Montenegrin state in the course of the Great War in January 1916, and the Austro-Hungarian occupation that followed, meant that local Muslims became free to return to their old faith, but also to do some other things. Now, after the defeat of the Central Powers they were in fear of potential retaliation from the local Montenegrin Vasojević clan with whom they had centuries-old disputes which now had a different dimension after three years of occupation and the favouring one religious group against the other, a repeated practice of Austro-Hungarian occupation authorities throughout the region. Another reason for open rebellion was the fear that local Muslim magnates would lose influence among locals as well as traditional ties with Shkodra, an important town in Northern Albania. On 9 February, rebels started advancing towards the town of Peć, simultaneously blocking one infantry company of Serbian troops, which was stationed in Plav. The sheer number of rebels, which went up to 5,000, and the fact that Albanian clansmen from north Albania joined to help, demanded an immediate reaction. Although rebel envoys tried to assure local Serbian commanders that their action was strictly directed against Montenegrins and their renewed authorities, it was still a huge challenge for fragile state authorities. Because the strength of local army troops was not sufficient for serious actions, local commanders had to rely on the assistance of

[13] Dmitar Tasić, *Rat posle rata, Vojska Kraljevine Srba, Hrvata i Slovenaca na Kosovu i Metohiji i u Makedoniji: 1918–1920*, (Beograd: Utopija, 2008), 92.

local volunteers from Kosovo and Metohija as well as on former members of Montenegrin armed forces from the Vasojević clan, whose clansmen meanwhile organized themselves under the command of their former officers. Although motivated and self-organized according to Montenegrin military standards, they represented a real threat for the local Muslim and Albanian population and especially for their property because pillaging was an integral part of their culture of warfare. After failing to reach a peaceful solution, Serbian troops strengthened with volunteers started advancing from Peć in the direction of Plav and Gusinje. Volunteers (local Serbs, Montenegrins, and even some Albanians) proved to be extremely unreliable and undisciplined, while artillery fire and the presence of regular troops were the only things capable of securing the advance. In addition, in a couple of days these forces were joined by some 1,200 poorly-armed but well organized Montenegrins and they continued pushing further on together.[14] On 20 February, one Serbian and one Montenegrin infantry company with machine guns and artillery advanced on enemy positions around the town of Plav, defended by some 1,500 rebels. Once more, the artillery fire proved to be the crucial factor. After several rounds the rebels deserted their position in panic and fled in the direction of Shkodra, many of them with their families fearing possible retaliation, especially by the irregulars. In order to prevent looting and pillaging most of the Montenegrins and volunteers were dispersed in surrounding Montenegrin villages and forbidden to enter Plav and Gusinje.[15]

For the representatives of the Serbian military it became obvious that, even during the quelling of the rebellion, certain measures were most urgent. According to their analyses, beside strict control of Muslim magnates and introduction of a ban of bearing weapons for Montenegrins, the only measures which would lead to consolidation of the overall situation was strong, fair and responsible police authority, together with firm assurances of freedom, personal safety, and state assistance for those damaged during the course of events. The whole affair did not pass without Allied interference. Both the British and French sent envoys to assess the extent of violence committed, especially against local civilians.[16]

The quelling of the rebellion in Plav and Gusinje was one of the first incidents which clearly demonstrated overall instability in the region, the weaknesses of the new authorities, and the unreliability of any kind of paramilitaries.

Almost simultaneously another event took place, which again demonstrated the difficulties that go hand-in-hand with the engagement of paramilitaries. After the end of his combat engagements in late 1918 and early 1919, the famous

[14] Ljubodrag Dimić and Đorđe Borozan, (eds), *Jugoslovenska država i Albanci. Tom 1* (Beograd: Službeni list SRJ; Arhiv Jugoslavije; Vojno-istorijski institut, 1998), 247–56.
[15] Dmitar Tasić, *Rat posle rata, Vojska Kraljevine Srba, Hrvata i Slovenaca na Kosovu i Metohiji i u Makedoniji: 1918–1920,* (Beograd: Utopija, 2008), 95.
[16] Ljubodrag Dimić and Đorđe Borozan, (eds), *Jugoslovenska država i Albanci. Tom 1* (Beograd: Službeni list SRJ; Arhiv Jugoslavije; Vojno-istorijski institut, 1998), 261–7.

chetnik leader Kosta Milovanović—Pećanac remained in the service of local Serbian command in the town of Peć. Insecurity in the Kosovo and Metohija region together with his previous merits somehow prolonged his self-proclaimed status of 'Commandant of the Rebel Troops'. In terms of their final status Pećanac and his comrades found themselves in the 'no man's land' because fundamentally they were irregulars. Nevertheless, because he was a reserve officer as well, in the following months Pećanac, in cooperation with the Army and Gendarmerie, continued to operate successfully in different actions such as guarding the mines and road communications or seizure of weapons in local Albanian villages.[17]

Problems started to emerge when Pećanac stepped out of his unclear and undefined 'jurisdiction', in a wish to protect some of his comrades who, for different reasons, ended up in prison. In order to protect them he officially addressed several county and district executives appealing for his comrades. In his letters sealed by a unique seal, he presented himself as 'Commandant of Rebel Troops', referred to his own and his comrades' merits, the importance of their achievements etc. First to react was the Ministry of the Interior which demanded that Pećanac be warned 'not to interfere in affairs outside of his jurisdiction'.[18] The Ministry of the Army and Navy reacted similarly, issuing an order with a final warning to Pećanac to avoid interfering with the activities of police and civil authorities, and forbidding him further use of pretentious titles and other actions that were not in accordance with his status of reserve officer, military ethos and military service regulations.[19]

In addition, the Minister of the Army and Navy issued a separate order forbidding further engagement of Pećanac and his comrades, as well as regular security checks of his and his comrades' conduct with emphasis on potential acts of disloyalty.[20] Nevertheless, Pećanac and his comrades remained in service until October 1919 when local military authorities asked their dismissal because there was no need for their services, especially as his engagement was not legally regulated.

In general, this demonstrated how paramilitaries had very restricted manoeuvring space if the state demonstrated ambition to regulate everyday life in troubled areas. In this particular case, Pećanac and his comrade's valour on the field of battle was compromised by their tendency to show-off and pretend to be very important so that civil authorities would turn a blind eye to their potential misconduct.

[17] Dmitar Tasić, 'Između slave i optužbe – Kosta Milovanović Pećanac 1919'. In *Istorija 20. veka*, 2/2007, 2007, 119–24, here 121.
[18] VA, r. 4/3, b. 56, f. 11, d. 10/5, Request of the Ministry of Internal affairs to the Ministry of Army and Navy, confidential no. 3976 from 28 May 1919, forwarded report of the Toplica county office, confidential no. 68 from 14 May 1919.
[19] VA, r. 4/3, b.56, f. 11, d. 10/5, Order of the Ministry of Army and Navy to the Commander of Third Army District, confidential no. 26539 from 7 June 1919.
[20] VA, r. 4/3, b.56, f. 11, d. 10/1, Order of the Ministry of Army and Navy to the Commander of Third Army District, confidential no. 26539 from 7 June 1919.

While previous examples demonstrate what the situation in Yugoslav areas inhabited by Albanians was like, the Yugoslav part of Macedonia had already witnessed a slow renewal of IMRO *komitaji* action. In fact, the action itself was not that intensive so much as the Yugoslav security forces were actually insufficient. Because of the need for additional forces already in 1919, the local army command in Skopje decided to engage Serbian *chetnik* veterans. In his memoirs, one of the former *chetnik* champions, Vasilije Trbić, mentioned how both he and Jovan Babunski, another *chetnik* champion and his close friend, were invited once more to gather their comrades and, as commanders of so-called 'flying detachments', conduct a thorough neutralization of IMRO activities. They would be equipped and paid by the army and they would have unrestricted authority to act and punish in their own way all those who were acting against the state. At one moment Trbić asked General Miloš Vasić, Commander of the Third Army District:

> "'Under which legal provisions we are supposed to act?' He said that there is no such law but we would be turning a blind eye. I have categorically refused General Vasić's proposal, saying that I cannot be someone above the law... I refuse to wage guerrilla warfare in Serbia; if our state has a need to organize our bands in Albania, Bulgaria or Greece I am ready to act instantly..."[21]

Opposite to Trbić, Jovan Babunski accepted the offer of General Vasić and in a short time managed to gather most of his comrades.

Who was Jovan Babunski and who were the members of his detachment?

As for the most of the prominent figures among Serbian paramilitaries, the story of Jovan Babunski began more than 20 years earlier when young Jovan from Martolci, a small village near the town of Veles, being an ardent supporter of the Serbian cause in Macedonia, accepted an offer to finish his education in Serbia. After attending the School for Teachers, he returned to Macedonia as one. However, this kind of engagement was not challenging enough, and he decided to change his pencil and blackboard for a rapid-firing rifle and uncertain destiny as a *chetnik* leader or *voivoda*. Babunski actively participated in Serbian *chetnik* action in Macedonia from 1903–1912 where, together with other Serbian *chetnik* leaders such as Vasilije Trbić, Jovan Dolgač, Krsta Kovačević, Kosta Pećanac, Vojin Popović and others, he fought in numerous clashes against rival IMRO *komitajis* and Ottoman regular troops. Also, Babunski and his *chetniks* fought in both Balkan Wars (1912–1913), as well as the Great War. In the fall of 1915 after the joint German, Austro-Hungarian and Bulgarian offensive, Babunski and his detachment were defending positions in Macedonia. Unlike the majority of Serbian forces, which experienced ordeals during the withdrawal across Albania,

---

[21] Vasilije Trbić, *Memoari. II*, (Beograd: Kultura 1996)146.

Babunski managed to withdraw directly to Greece with some 250 members of his detachment. On the newly established Macedonian front he placed his detachment under the French command where he actively participated in many actions. Babunski and his *chetniks* were mostly responsible for reconnaissance missions. During one of these they managed to capture the crew of a German patrol boat on Prespa Lake and for that act Babunski was awarded the highest French and Serbian decorations.[22] Together with his *chetniks*, of whom the majority were simple Macedonian peasants—veterans from the above-mentioned years—he participated in the breakthrough on the Salonika front in September 1918 where he fought on the left flank of the advancing Allied forces. At the beginning of November Babunski and his detachment were relieved from their duty.

Insufficient Army and Gendarmerie forces provided a perfect opportunity for the IMRO to increase its presence and propaganda in Macedonia. Right after the war the organization renewed its activities through infiltration of *komitaji* bands across the border. This unstable situation in Macedonia at the beginning of 1919 forced new Yugoslav military authorities to summon Babunski and his detachment. Babunski accepted this invitation gladly and in a very short time, together with another prominent *chetnik* commander and his close associate, Krsta Kovačević, he started patrolling troubled districts with some 200 *chetniks*, neutralizing IMRO actions. Special credit was assigned for the payment of his *chetniks*, as well as authorization for the local army garrisons and posts to issue necessary ammunition and provisions for his detachment.[23] However, although he had verbal authorization from the local army commander, objections made by Vasilije Trbić proved justified. Despite the fact that the activities of Babunski and his detachment had been successful in term of eradication of IMRO infrastructure, after complaints made by the civil authorities, Babunski and his detachment were dismissed because of brutal misconduct. Being an old-school *chetnik* Babunski simply continued to do what he used to do back in the Ottoman times—apply different kinds of violence against members and supporters of rival organizations. However, it seems that he was unaware of the fact that in the newly created Yugoslav state, former opponents became equal citizens with rights that had to be respected— something that in the 'old times' was unimaginable.

Nevertheless, after the dismissal of his detachment the IMRO continued with its agenda, leaving no alternatives to Yugoslav military authorities but to reconsider their previous decision and summon Babunski once more in September 1919. This time he was introduced to 'rules of engagement' forbidding him to implement brutal methods. He again answered the call of the state and did what

[22] V. Trbić, *Memoari. II*, 147.
[23] Dmitar Tasić, 'Leteći odred Jovana Babunskog u sprečavanju komitske akcije VMRO 1919. godine'. In *Vojnoistorijski glasnik* 1–2/2006, 79–92, here 81.

he knew best. He would patrol and visit villages of IMRO supporters where he would gather the locals, talk to them and dismantle the local organization's structure. But when IMRO supporters noticed this unusual change in his behaviour they commented: 'there is something which restrains Babunski just to preach like a bishop'.[24] That was too much for him and his reputation—after hearing these comments he returned to one village capturing several local IMRO activists whom he had known for a quite long. Soon after, they were all reported as missing and to all questions made by the police related to their whereabouts Babunski answered that immediately after they had been captured and interrogated, he had released them from captivity. Since they were nowhere to be found it became obvious that he had executed them. Because of this action he was again dismissed in late autumn 1919. He returned to his home in the Macedonian town of Veles where he settled with his family after the war.

The life story of Jovan Babunski represents one of the typical illustrations of Balkan paramilitaries' way of thinking, readiness for personal sacrifice, attitudes towards life and death, and perspective on their own role and importance. The aftermath of this story corroborates this claim even further. It happened that during the last days of his activities Babunski suffered a leg injury that started to display complications. In the winter of 1920, his comrade Vasilije Trbić paid him a visit

Fig. 2. Veterans from flying detachment of Jovan Babunski.
During the 1930's former members of the Jovan Babunski's flying detachment were given probably the last chance to dress up and bring out their decorations. Most of them were simple Macedonian peasants who after the end of their service continued to live in hard conditions of Macedonian countryside marked by uncertainty and everyday struggle. (Voivoda Mihailo Josifović, standing on the left; Zarije Jaćimović, standing on the right; Petruš Đorđević, upper left; Vasilije Kostić, lower left; Stojan Ristić, upper right; Pano Arsić, lower right)

[24] D. Tasić, 'Leteći odred Jovana Babunskog', 86.

when he was already lying in bed. Trbić reprimanded him for not taking care of his wound and that he should immediately go to see a doctor in Belgrade. However, Babunski answered that he could not go there because he was sub-poenaed to Belgrade for a parliamentary inquiry caused by his criminal acts. He refused to go although gangrene was at an advanced stage. For Babunski the pros-pect of investigation of his misconduct after so many sacrifices he had made for the Serbian cause was unimaginable. He decided to stay at home although some leading figures from Belgrade political life strongly suggested that he appear in front of the parliamentary committee. He died in February 1920.[25] He was buried with honours as a national hero. The public was deprived of the truth about his last days.[26]

Several years after his death one of the Yugoslav veteran associations from the Great War, *Association of the Reserve Officers and Warriors* (Udruženje rezervnih oficira i ratnika) paid a final tribute to Jovan Babunski, their former member and national hero, by consecrating a monument in Veles in October 1924—a large granite pyramid with the names of Babunski and *Association of Reserve Officers and Warriors*.[27] The monument represented a clear reminder and even a warning to all those doubting or denying the Serbian and Yugoslav character of Macedonia. However, the extent of animosity that existed between Serbians and Bulgarians and especially their *chetniks* and *komitajis* was clearly illustrated in April 1941 when Yugoslavia after the attack of the Axes was dismembered and occupied. The new Bulgarian occupation authorities in Macedonia systematically destroyed all monuments commemorating the Serbian presence in the region—using the same pattern they had already implemented during the Great War. After arriving in Veles, Bulgarian soldiers exhumed Babunski's remains and threw them into the waters of the river Vardar.[28]

However, even this example did not restrain Yugoslav authorities in the south from engaging paramilitaries. In the following years *chetniks* continued to be engaged occasionally, though under the command and control of the Gendarmerie. On top of that, in 1923 Yugoslav Macedonia witnessed the formation of a com-pletely new paramilitary organization—again aimed against the IMRO but at the same time conceived as a useful tool in preserving the domination of the Radical Party. Initially called *Organization against Bulgarian Bandits*, by the end of the 1920's it became known as *People's Self-Defence*. It was an organization with con-siderable territorial dispersion and manpower.

[25] V. Trbić, *Memoari. II*,132.
[26] *Spomenica Jovana S. Babunskog,* (S.l., Udruženje rezervnih oficira i obveznika činovničkog reda, Beograd 1921).
[27] John Paul Newman, *Yugoslavia in the Shadow of War. Veterans and the Limits of State Building 1903–1945* (Cambridge: Cambridge University Press, 2015), 63 and 89.
[28] V. Trbić, *Memoari. II*, 147.

Bulgaria and Paramilitarism: Weak State vs. Strong Movements

As one of the defeated Central Powers in the Great War, Bulgaria entered 1919 with grim prospects. The Entente forces occupied the country, once-proud armed forces were facing drastic diminution, and new territorial losses were inevitable; the economy was devastated, while the arrival of around 100,000 refugees from Macedonia, Dobruja and Eastern Thrace overburdened the already exhausted and bankrupted state. It looked like the bloody quelling of the Radomir Rebellion in the last days of September 1918, when some 3,000 mutineers were killed in follow-up operations, announced future political developments.[29] A new political reality was presented by the gradual ascent to power of the Bulgarian Agrarian National Union (BANU), a party representing the interests of the Bulgarian countryside, which during previous years had voiced strong criticism of governmental policies that had eventually led country into two consecutive war defeats and huge human, territorial and material losses. However, at the beginning, BANU or the agrarians found themselves almost alone against both the political left and right, the military and IMRO. In the following years Bulgarian society was marked by weakness of state institutions like the army, police and judiciary and by rapid paramilitarization. During this, in a way, 'golden age' of Bulgarian paramilitarism, several distinctive paramilitary organizations were formed besides the already existing IMRO. The creation of the *Military League*, the communist *Illegal Military Organization*, and the paramilitary organization of Russian émigrés have already been described. This part of the study will deal with how IMRO adapted to the new circumstances and how a new paramilitary organization—agrarian *Orange Guard*—was created as an agrarian answer to new Bulgarian political realities.

After the Great War, the IMRO continued to function following the old consti-tution. The last elections for the organization's Central Committee were held in 1911. At that time it consisted of Hristo Chernopeev, Todor Alexandrov and Petar Chaulev. Alexander Protogerov, at that moment Colonel, was elected as a reserve member. Because Chernopeev had been killed on the Macedonian front Protogerov succeeded him after the war.[30] Basic technical preparations for the renewal of the organization's activities were carried out in the IMRO unofficial headquarters, in the office of the 11th Macedonian Division at 22 Gurko Street in Sofia. The IMRO had inherited a significant part of the division's armament, as well as large sums of money.[31] The fact that after the Bulgarian surrender the

---

[29] Robert Gerwarth, *The Vanquished: Why the First World War Failed to End 1917–1923* (London: Allen Lane, 2016), 112–14.

[30] Krasimir Karakachanov, *VMRO—100 godini borba za Makedoniya*, (Sofia: VMRO-SMD, 1994), 34 and 44.

[31] Decho Dobrinov, 'Todor Aleksandrov i v'zstanovanieto na VMRO sled p'rvata svetovna vojna (1918–1924 g.)'. In *100 godini V'treshna makedono-odrinska revolucionna organizaciya*, (Sofia, Makedonski nauchen institut, 1994), 145–56.

Serbian army was not allowed to enter Bulgarian territory in many ways helped the IMRO maintain its field infrastructure intact and relatively quickly to consolidate its ranks. The organization's main asset was a considerable number of experienced and battle hardened *komitajis*, which, despite the fact that most of them had been in some kind of military engagement since the beginning of the 20th century, were ready to continue with their struggle. The overwhelming majority of *komitajis* were of Macedonian origin. They were recruited mostly from the ranks of Macedonian emigration in Bulgaria. Their career paths followed several patterns. Usually after finishing Exarchate schools in Macedonia, some of them would continue their education in Bulgaria (like prominent IMRO leaders Goce Delchev and Nikola Karev). Many found employment in civil service as clerks, policemen, security guards, etc, and thus permanently tied themselves to Bulgaria, while others chose the fate of migrant labourers working on seasonal jobs, occasionally returning to Macedonia. Both represented an inexhaustible reservoir for recruitment of new *komitajis*.

The importance of Macedonian emigrants increased over time so before, during and after the Balkan Wars and Great War, they became an important factor on the Bulgarian political scene. Macedonians living in Bulgaria were organized into so-called *fraternities*. Fraternities used to gather people of same regional origin, like fraternities from the towns of Štip, Strumica, Ohrid, Tetovo, Skopje, Serres, Kilkis (Kukuš), Veles, Kavadarci, etc[32] Macedonian Fraternities would periodically assemble and discuss important questions, thus presenting legal cover for IMRO actions.

The leadership of the Macedonian emigrants in Bulgaria quickly consolidated their ranks and less than a month after the Bulgarian exit from the war, on 22 November 1918, they managed to organize a congress of Macedonian Fraternities. At the same time, the new Central Committee of IMRO began to operate. Todor Alexandrov undertook practical activity—organization of work on the ground both in matters of personnel and material. Thanks to the diligence of Todor Alexandrov and his 'Provisional Instructions', during 1919 the IMRO established its basically illegal or parallel organization in Pirin Macedonia (Petrich County) or as they used to call it 'the part of Macedonia under Bulgarian rule'. Throughout Petrich County local militia and *chete* were organized for the protection of villages from banditry and contraband as well as for assisting in protection of state borders; regional *voivode* were appointed and administrative bodies elected. With the administrative role they also assumed a legal or judiciary role for all kinds of transgressions including murder. Whatever they could not decide would be left to the official state authorities, but only after the consent of regional *voivode*. All acts related to religious affairs, except 'abductions of maidens', were subjected to the church tribunals. Thus, the foundations for future *komitaji's* 'state within the state'

32 V. Trbić, *Memoari. II*, 129.

in Petrich County were laid.[33] Even after decades, memories of IMRO rule are still very much alive among the people from these areas.

Elaboration of strategies and tactics, the constitution of the IMRO, and rules and directions of revolutionary activity were under the authority of Alexander Protogerov.[34] He presented the view that the IMRO should assume part of the activities and tasks which were previously performed by activists of the Exarchate—IMRO revolutionaries were to become simultaneously priests and teachers.[35] Fostering of Bulgarian spirit was to be achieved by revolutionary and legal means: by guerrilla actions and assassinations of Yugoslav government officials and sabotage on government buildings, but also in participation in the public political life of the invading countries (Greece and the Kingdom of Serbs, Croats and Slovenes) as well as appealing to international institutions to meet the clauses of the peace treaties in relation to the protection of national minorities.[36]

Autumn of 1919 was marked by anticipation of the results of the Peace Conference. The Macedonian emigration in Bulgaria had been working feverishly to prepare possible variant courses of action—depending on the outcome of the conference.[37] In early October 1919 the *Congress of Macedonian Fraternities* was held in Sofia. The aim of the congress was to overcome the schism that existed in the organization.[38] In total over 500 delegates from all over Bulgaria worked four days with important issues relating to the life of Macedonian emigration in Bulgaria, as well as ways to exit the current crisis.[39] The Congress decided to send a delegation to the Paris Peace Conference which would convey the wishes of the Macedonian population. IMRO would use all legal means to reach its goal, and if the conference did not meet the demands, it would commence with a 'desperate struggle'.[40]

The level of changes that had occurred within the organization after the Great War was visible from an event that happened precisely at the time of the *Congress*

---

[33] Dimitar Tyulekov *Obrecheno rodolyubie. VMRO v Pirinsko 1919–1934* (Blagoevgrad: Univ. Izd. 'Neofit Rilski', 2001), http://www.promacedonia.org/dt/dt1_1.html [last checked on 12 November 2016]

[34] In his memoirs later IMRO leader Ivan Mikhailov tries to diminish the roles of the other two Central Committee members–Petar Chaulev and General Alexander Protogerov. The main reason for this attitude lies in the special animositiy he felt against Protogerov because of his alleged role in the later assassination of Mikhailov's mentor Todor Alexandrov, see Ivan Mikhailov, *Spomeni II, Osvoboditelna borba 1919–1924* (Louvain, 1965), 22.

[35] D. Dobrinov, 'Todor Alexandrov i v'zstanovanieto na VMRO', 146.

[36] D. Dobrinov, 'Todor Alexandrov i v'zstanovanieto na VMRO', 147.

[37] VA, r. 4/3, b. 54, f. 12, d. 12/150, Report of the delegate of Supreme command in Sofia to the command of Third army district, confidential no. 590 number of telegram 959 from 3 September 1919.

[38] VA, r. 4/3. b. 57, f. 4, d. 7/11, Transcript of the invitation to the Macedonian emigration from Neutral commision toward the overcoming of the schism; see also Zoran Todorovski, *Avtonomističkata VMRO na Todor Aleksandrov 1919–1924,* (Skopje: Makavej, 2013) 42–5.

[39] VA, r. 4/3, b. 54, f. 12, d. 12/168, Report of the Ministry of Army and Navy to the delegate of Supreme command in Sofia, confidential no. 39 353 from 19 October 1919.

[40] VA, r. 4/3, b. 54, f. 12, d. 12/168, Report of the delegate of Supreme command in Sofia to the command of Third army district, number of telegram 1150 from 5 October 1919.

of Macedonian Fraternities when a number of disgruntled *komitaji voivode* tried to get in touch with the authorized representatives of the Kingdom of Serbs, Croats and Slovenes in Sofia. These were *voivode* Milan Kyurlukov, Petar Dyosha, Pavle Hristov and Petar Chaulev. All four were known and respected members of the IMRO. Kyurlukov headed the Centre in Prilep, and Chaulev, besides his membership in the Central Committee, headed the Centre in Ohrid. On that occasion, according to military intelligence sources, they expressed an attitude that further fighting was pointless and that they wanted peacefully to influence the Macedonians to be reconciled to become equal subjects of the great Yugoslavia. This group felt that the autonomy of Macedonia once and for all would neutralize the rivalries of the Balkan states and would bring lasting peace to the Balkans.[41] They expressed the absurdity of the earlier ways of fighting because the fight against Serbia was lost, while in the Yugoslav framework Macedonia could finally be able to find the conditions for cultural and economic development. They also asked for a full pardon and safety of life.[42]

The motive of the group in presenting such a proposal to the Yugoslav authorities cannot be determined with certainty. Was their break with the organization feinted as a method for 'testing the pulse' of the Yugoslav authorities over the issue of Macedonia? Maybe it was fatigue? Or was a true change in the mind-set of renowned *voivode* caused by disappointment because of the strong ties of IMRO and Bulgarian official and unofficial circles, forcing them to find a better calculation in cooperation with the authorities of the Kingdom of Serbs, Croats and Slovenes? This idea was not realized because sources show that a year later in Tirana one of the signatories of the agreement between the IMRO and the Kosovo Committee was Pavle Hristov, and that Kyurlukov and Chaulev continued with *komitaji* raids in the following years.

According to reports from the end of 1919, huge and numerous contradictions existed within the IMRO. Although the idea of an autonomous Macedonia was pointed out as the goal, three different factions could be identified. The first was in favour of an independent Macedonia outside any Balkan state. Another, smaller group was in favour of Macedonia entering the Yugoslav state on confederate principles. However, a third group was uncompromising, and also the best organized. Their goal was to fight to the end with propaganda activities and strong pressure on public opinion in Western countries in order to achieve a change in the provisions of the peace treaties. Leaders and representatives of this group were Protogerov, Alexandrov, D'rvingov, Tatarchev and others. These were people who had committed a series of war crimes in occupied Serbia in the period

---

[41] VA, r. 4/3, b. 54, f. 13, d. 12/178, Report of the trustee of delegate of Supreme command in Sofia.

[42] VA, r. 4/3, b. 54, f. 13, d. 12/193, Report of the Ministry of Army and Navy to the command of Third army district, confidential no. 39 930 from 30 October 1919, forwarded report of the delegate of Supreme command, confidential no. 708 (no date).

1915–1918 while serving in the Bulgarian occupation authorities.[43] All above mentioned represented an indication of future schism within the organization which eventually resulted in bloody consequences.

In the practical, paramilitary, component of its activity the IMRO continued to rely on its already proven organizational structure, methods and rules of engagement. The basic unit of *komitajis*, and Balkan paramilitaries in general, was the *cheta* which literally means company or band.[44] It did not possess precise composition and strength and it seldom exceeded ten or twenty members. In his memoirs Ivan Mikhailov gave a vivid description of what the *cheta* and its significance were actually:

> "As during the Turkish rule, the illegal *cheta* would inspire fighting spirit and take care of the people's interests. It was the best agitator against the enslaver. *Voivods* used to advise locals on issues of education, hygiene, economy.
>
> Especially at the beginning, the IMRO couldn't show up without *chetas*, because they were seen as symbols of struggle and they encompassed hope for a better tomorrow with all risks taken into consideration…It was the best solution for those forced to flee from an unbearable regime."[45]

The head of a *cheta* was known as *voivoda*. *Voivodas* were appointed according to the territorial principle of the organization and preferably operated in areas known to them or from which they originated. Sometimes their nickname clearly testified this principle, like Simeon Kochanski, Velichko Skopski and others.[46]

During the Ottoman rule IMRO organization was based on the existence of regional and village bands or *chete*. Regionals were composed of experienced *komitajis* while the village bands consisted of armed peasants. Peasants were provided with weapons after a collective declaration and consent to join the organization. An important motivating factor for individuals and entire villages to join the IMRO, in addition to faith in its political goals and affiliation with Exarchate church organizations, was existential fear, because treachery and defection were

[43] VA, r. 4/3, b. 54, f. 13, d. 12/221, Report of the delegate of government and Supreme Command in Sofia to the command of Third Army District, confidential no. 862 from 24 December 1919.

[44] In the Serbian language the expression četovanje (*chetovanye*) has been for centuries used for 'conducting guerrilla warfare'.

[45] Ivan Mikhailov, *Spomeni II, Osvoboditelna borba 1919–1924* (Louvain, 1965), 160–1.

[46] K. Karakachanov. *VMRO–100 godini borba za Makedoniya*, 47–9. Overview of the famous *voivode* and the areas in which they operated: Carevo Selo: Stefan Karadzha and Haralampiye Zlatanov; Kočani: Pancho Mikhailov and Dimitar Medarov; Kratovo: Pano Grigorov, Todosiye Hadzhijata and Todor Alexandrov; Štip: Ivan Krstev, Hadzhi Grigor Hadzhikimov; Kumanovo: Krsto Lazarov and Cvetan Spasov; Skopje: Lazar Velkov, Velichko Velyanov, Spiro Kitanchev; Kriva Palanka: Stoyan Lekov-Caro; Veles: Gosho Cholakov, Nikola Panov, Iliya Kushev, Stefan Petkov-Sirketo, Nikola Gulev; Strumica: V'ndev Georgi; Maleš: Efrem Chuchkov, Boris Tsekov, Eftim Tsekov; Radoviš: Hristo Simeonov, Nikola Vasilev, Lazar Klonkov; Tikveš: Stoyan Antov, Atanas Kalchev, Ivan Iliev; Gevgelija: Ichko Dimitrov, Stojan Mandalov; Kruševo: Lyubomir Vesov.

punished with cruel execution in the presence of the entire village population. Regional bands were supposed to roam throughout their designated area, controlling organizations in villages, keeping contact with the organization's leadership, and occasionally returning to Bulgaria to rest. However, after the Great War, the circumstances changed. The field Organization of IMRO was shattered despite the infiltrated bands so that it was primarily based on the actions of regional bands and prominent individuals.

In the territory of the Kingdom of Serbs, Croats and Slovenes *chete* were infiltrated in secrecy, usually at night, with the active or passive support of Bulgarian border units. The old channels for insertion of *chete*, used so often in Ottoman times, were operating efficiently after the Great War as well. Pathless mountains, experienced guides and lack of a sufficient number of border guards and gendarmes greatly facilitated the work of *komitajis*. The main *komitaji* centres were located in the Bulgarian border towns of Kyustendil, Gornya Dzhumaya (todays Blagoevgrad), Nevrokop (todays Gotse Delchev) and Petrich.

Komitajis, and especially their *voivode*, paid great attention to their external appearance and armament. Earlier, in the days before and during the First World War, *komitajis* would be easily identified by the long hears and beards, Bulgarian caps, cockades, daggers, rifles of the Austrian model *Mannlicher* 8 mm, Russian 7.62 mm *Mosin-Nagant* revolvers, hand grenades of the *Odrin* model, bandoliers and binoculars. Binoculars were a particular sign of recognition of the *voivode*. Bandoliers, which *komitajis* used to wear for practical reasons because they were guerrilla fighters without logistics, in time became their distinctive feature. Later, after the First World War, *komitajis* often had to replace their half peasant-half military appearance with more practical solutions. They resorted to disguise, starting to wear Serbian folk hats and folk costumes or Gendarmerie and military uniforms; they also shortened the barrels of their rifles to make them easier to hide, or rejected the impressive revolver lanyard, known from many *komitajis* photos from the period before the Great War. Automatic weapons did not come into use primarily due to the size and heavy weight of the first models. For the survival of their bands their mobility was of primary importance. On the ground they used to take minimum amounts of food, again because of mobility, which meant that the peasants were obliged to supply bands residing in their village or passing through.

While the IMRO was in full renewal, BANU and its leader Alexander Stamboliyski began to cope with the harsh realities of Bulgarian political life. The first Bulgarian government led by agrarians and their charismatic leader actually represented coalition with so-called 'old parties' or parties that had led Bulgaria through the period of recently ended wars. Since agrarians could not find common grounds with socialists and communists they addressed 'old parties' which did not hesitate to accept the possibility of continuing to rule. This government, through no fault of its own, became responsible for the signing and implementation of the

Neuilly peace accords in November 1919. In a situation heated up by the fact that Bulgaria was about to pay reparations, to reduce its army to 20,000, and make huge territorial concessions, normal functioning of the state institution was questioned. The economic situation additionally contributed to the creation of overall instability. Bulgaria was in the middle of inflation, which brought devaluation of wages. Some basic commodities became very expensive and very difficult, if not impossible, to find. In such a situation communists and socialists agreed to organize general strike, partly because they wanted to turn attention to the hardships into which the ordinary working class had fallen. Their choice was the well-organized and important union of transportation, responsible for the functioning of the state railway and telegraph services. An additional problem was the fact that Prime Minister Stamboliyski was abroad, actually in Paris where he was supposed to sign the peace treaty.[47]

A general strike in the above-related services represented a serious threat to the normal functioning of the whole country, and some provisions for this kind of situation already existed. It was also a test of how the new government would react. The state was authorized to intervene through an action called militarization of the railways and telegraph. This simply meant that soldiers would be brought in to take over the control of trains, depots, railway stations, and telegraph posts. Also, the missing number of workers for normal functioning of the railway system would be acquired through mobilization of reservists—in this particular case those would be some of the people already on strike. If they failed or refused to answer to mobilization, they would face consequences like eviction from state-owned housing, cancellation of their food ration cards and prosecution before military courts. However, because the process of disarmament and reducing of Bulgarian armed forces was already underway there were not enough soldiers trained to take over the railroads. In order to address this issue after failure to reach any kind of agreement with the union, the two agrarian ministers responsible for negotiations decided to use BANU's infrastructure and membership. For decades the basic units of BANU organization were so-called 'associations' (druzhbi) which encompassed BANU supporters organized on territorial principles. Ministers went on a tour all over Bulgaria visiting BANU *druzhbi*, choosing able-bodied men and organizing them in units of the *Orange Guard* under the command of their local leaders. They were supposed to wait for the call and immediately to take control of towns if the government became endangered. At that moment they more resembled party militia armed only with clubs organized to control and secure party rallies than a classical paramilitary formation.[48]

[47] John D. Bell, *Peasants in Power: Alexander Stamboliiski and the Bulgarian Agrarian National Union 1899–1923*, (Princeton: Princeton University Press, 1977), 147–8.
[48] John D. Bell, *Peasants in Power. Alexander Stamboliyski and the Bulgarian Agrarian National Union*, 149.

Their first action happened when the Bulgarian Communist Party decided to organize mass protests on 24 December 1919. Agrarians reacted by summoning 10,000 members of the *Orange Guard* onto Sofia streets. Only several smaller communist gatherings were reported, the majority was too afraid to go out on the streets because of the massive presence of agrarian guardsmen. And while this was a typical example of intimidation of political opponents, the general strike of transport workers that began on 28 December put the government to the real test. However, this time socialists joined communists. In response, on 31 December, the government decided to militarize the railways. The *Orange Guard* was summoned to strengthen the army, and by 5 January the strike had collapsed. In the following general elections held in March BANU won a majority of seats in parliament and was able to form its own government.[49]

In a later parliamentary debate Stamboliyski, while addressing the representatives of leftist parties, explained the reasons and causes for the creation of the *Orange Guard*:

"Are your proletarian and bureaucratic unions state institutions? Are your clubs, your 'people's halls', your groups state institutions? Who gave them right to conceal weapons, to demolish bridges, to throw bombs, to terrorize government's workers?...Against your organization the Agrarian Union will oppose its own..."[50]

This successful engagement of the *Orange Guard* during social unrest provided BANU with some assurance for the future. The character of the *Orange Guard* had certain specifics compared to its contemporaries in the region. Although arbitrarily characterized as a paramilitary formation, in its initial phase it was very different from other paramilitary organizations. As already said, in the beginning it was more like a party militia, but without firearms, with duties related to security and assistance to official institutions when they were not able to perform their duties—like during strikes, etc. Unlike Serbian *chetniks* or IMRO *komitajis*, and to a certain extent Albanian *kachaks*, the *Orange Guard* was not associated with the legacies of Balkan guerrilla fighters. Also, if we compare the *Orange Guard* with similar organizations elsewhere, for example the Italian fascist *squadristi* or the Organization of Yugoslav Nationalists (ORJUNA),[51] the differences

---

[49] John D. Bell, *Peasants in Power. Alexander Stamboliyski and the Bulgarian Agrarian National Union*, 150–3.

[50] Cited from John D. Bell, *Peasants in Power. Alexander Stamboliyski and the Bulgarian Agrarian National Union*, 149.

[51] ORJUNA, a paramilitary organization founded in 1921 in the Dalmatian town of Split. It was marked by distinctive anti-Italian sentiments because of Italian territorial aspiration towards the Yugoslav Adriatic shores. It has adopted a pro-violence vocabulary glorifying figures like Gavrilo Princip (assassin of the Austro-Hungarian heir to the throne in 1914) or the years of the Great War since they led to the creation of Yugoslavia. The main targets of ORJUNA attacks were communists, members of the Croatian Peasant Party, and former Austro-Hungarian officers. See: John Paul

appear to be even greater. In their ascent to power agrarians certainly resolved on a certain level of violence; however, they did not habitually point out its importance as Italian fascists or members of ORJUNA did. They actually came to power after general elections, and by following and respecting democratic procedures, not by causing a major political crisis in the country. The only similarity would be related to agrarian plans for the establishment of a peasant dictatorship through a major transformation of Bulgaria from a parliamentary to a corporate state. Since this turn of events never happened, we cannot say if this change would have caused serious resistance or what the role of *Orange Guard* in enforcing of agrarian political agenda would have been. In addition, although at a certain point after entering into conflict with almost every actor on the Bulgarian political scene, the leadership of the BANU decided to arm and additionally 'militarize' the *Orange Guard* in order to secure its position, the dynamics of the political events that followed practically prevented it. The coup of 9 June 1923 almost completely wiped out the legacy of BANU rule, including the *Orange Guard*.

Albania: Paramilitarism or Pre-militarism?

The appearance of an independent Albanian state, as a consequence of the combination of two parallel processes, the rise of Albanian national consciousness and international intervention during the Balkan Wars of 1912–1913, was also deeply influenced by the specific characteristics of Albanian society at the beginning of the 20th century. However, no matter how homogenous Albania appeared, its society was extremely diverse. The Albanian south was characterized by the existence of urban communities of traders and craftsmen, well connected and wealthy, however, without substantial political influence. The Albanian north was inhabited by mountainous clans, extremely poor but well armed, whose influence often exceeded clan territories because they were ready to sell their rifles to the highest bidder. In between there was an area administered by a class of landlords or beys, who were the legacy of the Ottoman rule over Albania. Beys ruled over the masses of tenants and clients and their voice and political influence, thanks to that, was much stronger than their sheer number. Another aspect of the diversity of Albanian society was religion. In the Albanian north, communities of Muslims and Roman Catholics dwelled side-by-side, living a life ruled by the strict norms of the unwritten medieval Code or Canon of Leka Dukagjini.[52] The Code insisted

---

Newman, 'The Origins, Attributes, and Legacies of Paramilitary Violence in the Balkans'. In Gerwarth, Robert, John Horn (eds.), *War in Peace; Paramilitary Violence in Europe after the Great War*, (Oxford: Oxford University Press, 2012), 145–62, here 158.

[52] Leka Dukagjini (1410–1481) was an Albanian medieval ruler of whose existence beside the fact that he fought against the Ottomans together with Skanderbeg we know very little. His association

on defence of individual honour by all means and vendetta was its main feature. The beys, as well as most of the population in central Albania, were Sunni Muslims, while in the south lived a considerable number of Orthodox Christians. Another group were Bektashi, members of the Sufi order with a strong inclination towards Shia mysticism. Although in a political sense a considerable number of Albanians lived in the neighbouring Yugoslav areas of Montenegro, Kosovo and Metohija, and western Macedonia, they shared common identities with their compatriots in Albania. Montenegrin and Kosovar Albanians were predominantly Sunni Muslims with smaller Roman Catholic communities, and they also lived under the strict norms of Leka Dukagjini's Canon, while Albanians from western Macedonia appeared more like their compatriots from central Albania. One thing, which used to attract attention of anyone encountering Albanians at the turn of the 19th into the 20th century, was their affection towards firearms, which in a practical sense was an integral part of their attire. A combination of the norms of the above-mentioned Canon of Leka Dukagjini, which allowed all necessary means for protection of an individual's honour, and the privileged status the Albanians enjoyed during the reign of Sultan Abdul Hamid II (1878–1908) resulted in a situation in which almost all Albanians of age possessed and bore firearms. Mountain clansmen were inclined to rifles, preferably the latest models, while those living in urban areas preferred revolvers for more practical reasons. Thanks to that, the Ottomans were able to raise huge numbers of Albanian irregulars, especially among north Albanian and Kosovar clansmen, and use them as auxiliary troops or *bashibozluk*. However, whoever dared to limit their traditional rights in respect or possessing and bearing firearms, like the Young Turks after 1908, Serbs after the Balkan Wars 1912–1913, and Yugoslavs after 1918, would encounter fearsome resistance embodied in massive uprisings or actions of individual outlaws or *kachaks*. However, it cannot be said that Albanian society was inclined to paramilitarism as were its neighbours Serbia, Bulgaria and Greece. The main reason was its backwardness and specific position within the broader context of the Ottoman state and its internal dynamics. Another reason was that Albanian neighbours passed through certain stages of social and political developments whose main features were the breaking of ties with Ottoman heritage and the introduction of Western customs and social, political, legal, and cultural institutions. In that sense Albania can be primarily compared with Montenegro, which through its recent history shared many similarities with Albanian society with respect to clan structure, rule of customary law, blood feuds, and culture of bearing firearms. In this sense their religious differences—Montenegrins as Greek Orthodox Christians and Albanians either as Muslims or Roman Catholic Christians did not play an important role. Overemphasized masculinity connected with constant fear of

with the above-mentioned code or Kanun in Albania is not completely clear—Robert Elsie, *A Biographical Dictionary of Albanian History*, (London; New York: B. Tauris, 2013), 126.

Fig. 3. North Albanian clansman.

Harsh environment, clan society, endemic poverty, life arranged by the unwritten medieval Code or Canon of Leka Dukagjini and favourable position of Albanians during the rule of Abdul Hamid II, when they were exempted from conscription but given right to bare firearms, created unique culture epitomised in respect of honour by all means and vicious circles of blood feuds. Combination of poverty and strong affection to fire arms meant that north Albanian clansmen, both Muslim and Roman Catholic, in the early 1920's could offer their services to higher bidder among confronted Albanian factions.

Bibliographical information: https://www.europeana.eu/portal/en/record/9200291/bildarchivaustria_at_Preview_4814466.html?q=albanian#dcId=1563906555999&p=27

© Austrian National Library (Vienna), Albanian leader, WK1/ALB063/17543

losing honour, however, was a common feature of both Montenegrin and Albanian cultures, a kind which can be found in similar, primarily mountain or isolated communities like those in the islands of Sicily, Sardinia, Corsica, Crete or throughout the Caucasus. Although their culture of warfare was closely connected to their social order, which insisted on blood ties even within the structures of their armed formations, it can rather be characterized as pre-military instead of paramilitary. In Montenegrin case it is most visible because even though being *de facto* independent from Ottoman rule throughout its modern history, Montenegro was not able to introduce modern military institutions like other Balkan Christian states: Serbia, Bulgaria or Greece. Although it had compulsory military service, the Montenegrin army was nothing more than a militia organized according to its territorial and clan structure. Even though well armed with modern means of warfare, and led by educated officers,[53] Montenegro entered the period of wars in 1912–1918 with armed forces of the militia type. Modern principles of unquestioning subordination and following orders could never have been introduced in the Montenegrin army. An officer's reputation depended on his valour, not on his rank or position in the hierarchy. Beating of soldiers by their superiors was unimaginable both among Albanians and Montenegrins. According to their codes even a slap in the face demanded satisfaction in blood. As in the case of Montenegrins, among Albanians, especially their northern mountain clans, a similar order existed, which enabled raising considerable contingents of irregulars whose composition followed clan affiliations and long-lasting, almost ancient, allegiances to their clan chieftains. However, chieftains were expected to lead their men by example. Both Montenegrins and Albanian militias were known for their endurance and ability to 'march on an empty stomach'. As other militias elsewhere, when inspired and motivated they could perform miracles in combat, but also when defeated their withdrawals often turned into panicked flight.

When after 1908 the Young Turks introduced conscription and compulsory military service, those strongly opposed were northern and Kosovar Albanians. Among other things, this was the reason for their mutinous behaviour in the period 1909–1912 that caused a considerable engagement of Ottoman regular troops. However, when in autumn 1912 the Balkan allies declared war on the Ottoman state, Albanians rallied once more in defence of their homeland—once again following their traditional ways, as irregular troops. The Ottoman defeat and the subsequent birth of the Albanian independent state in 1913 did not change much with respect to the culture of warfare and military institutions.

A clear illustration of how strong and deep-rooted was the affection towards firearms, even among those Albanians who should have represented the elite and progressive part of their society, was an attempted assassination of at that time Prime Minister Ahmed Zogu on 24 February 1924, and the follow-up events. While Zogu was about to join a parliamentary session, a certain Beqir Walteri, a member of the nationalist-revolutionary organization *Bashkimi* (Unification),[54]

---

[53] Thanks to the generous support of the Russian Empire by the beginning of 20th century the Army of Montenegro was armed with modern repeating rifles, machine guns, and rapid-firing artillery. Unlike soldiers of contemporary armies in Europe each Montenegrin soldier, besides a rifle, was armed with a revolver as well, which provided him a huge advantage in close combat during the wars of 1912–1918.

[54] *Bashkimi* was founded in 1922 by Avni Rustemi, a young nationalist responsible for the assassination of Esad-pasha Toptani in Paris two years earlier. *Bashkimi* was organized as an association of primarily young students who saw assassination as a natural means of removal of everyone considered the enemy of Albania.—Bernd J. Fischer, *King Zog and the Struggle for Stability in Albania*, (Tirana: Albanian Institute for International Studies, 2012), 60.

fired several shots at the Prime Minister while he was on the stairs of the parliament, wounding him twice. However, Zogu was able to enter the parliamentary chamber where he was surrounded by a party of his supporters and was examined by the physician present, while others entered into a gunfight with the assassin, who barricaded himself in a nearby bathroom. Member of the Parliament Eqrem-bey Vlora said in his memoirs that bloodshed was imminent because the MPs from the confronted conservative and democrat blocs were heavily armed with revolvers and that only the soberness of the wounded Zogu and several other politicians saved the day.[55] Another prominent figure, Fan Noli, claimed he was virtually the only one among those present without a firearm.[56]

In 1924, one of the prominent leaders of the IMRO, Peter Chaulev, after spending several years in Albania, and shortly before he lost his life in internal IMRO disputes, wrote and published a short account based on his personal experiences with Albania and the Albanians. Among many of his observations several clearly stand out:

"1. An Albanian is not used to military service;
2. An Albanian has not paid his taxes for centuries;
3. An Albanian (as Muslim) could not reconcile with the fact that he had to serve a Christian king;

...

6. An Albanian could not reconcile with the new law obliging him to take the rifle off his shoulder."[57]

It is needless to say how important were weapons for the enforcement of traditional customs and maintaining of personal safety in general. However, it came with a price. The above-mentioned blood feuds and violence arising from them represented one of the major obstacles for the modernization of Albanian society and the introduction of a legal state. The death toll that was bleeding the male population, crippling an already primitive economy and the functioning of everyday life, was huge and never precisely determined. One of Zogu's goals was to regulate this important segment of Albanian tradition. And actually, he did it, but with limited success. In order to win the loyalty of northern clansmen Zogu entered into negotiations with them using traditional means of bribery and privileges. The loyalty of northern clans was always achieved through their chieftains. Zogu made an agreement with them, giving them regular payments and promoting them into the rank

---

[55] Ekrem-beg Vlora, *Sekavanjata ot životot. Tom II*, (1921–1925) (Skopje: Fondacija Otvoreno opštestvo, 2015), 206–9.

[56] Cited from: Robert C. Austin, *Founding a Balkan State; Albanian Experiment with Democracy, 1920–1925* (Toronto: University of Toronto Press, 2012), 39.

[57] Petar Chaulev, *Skipniya*, (Carigrad': Tip. L. Babok' i S-v'ya Galata, ul Kamondo 8, 1924) 7–8; cited in: Katerina Todorovska, *Petar Čaulev*, (Skopje: Univerzitet 'Sv. Kiril i Metodij', Filozofski fakultet, 2014), 226.

of Colonel of the Albanian army. Chieftains were perfectly acquainted with this way of 'communication' often used in the past by Austrians, Serbs and Montenegrins. Chieftains were obliged to maintain a certain number of irregulars at the disposal of the government as auxiliary troops. This agreement was achieved in traditional ways through personal relations between Zogu and northern chieftains and through the traditional Albanian sacred oath or *besa*.[58] Chieftains were not acquainted with the concept of loyalty to the state; for them Zogu's title of Minister of the Interior did not have any importance. They pledged an oath to him as chieftain of the Mati clan. Following the existing pre-state pattern Zogu as well became personally responsible for arbitration in cases of future disputes among clansmen.[59]

Another measure Zogu implemented was a major disarmament of the civilian population. It was a risky and bold measure whose failure could cost him dearly. And while he managed to pacify the south and lowlands by collecting some 35,000 pieces of firearms, the northern mountain clans refused to participate, which actually resulted in their alienation from Zogu. Some of them even joined the camp of his adversaries. Only his diplomatic skills prevented one of the first attempts to depose him that occurred in February 1923.[60] After he dodged this bullet his reputation among northern clans grew because he showed himself to be heroic against overwhelming odds. Needless to say, Zogu, following his sense for practical politics and knowledge of Albania's peculiarities, did not disarm militia of his own Mati clan. The main reason was his need to have a reliable force on his disposal since he realized very early that in the turbulent Albanian circumstances the possession of reliable and well-armed forces was sometimes the only thing that stood between staying in power and the complete loss of it. Zogu's introduction of a regular army could not substitute for the existing large contingences of irregular troops. The regular army was to small and its modernization and development was often neglected primarily because of the financial difficulties which the Albanian state had fallen into after the Great War. The same can be said for the Gendarmerie whose members often proved extremely unreliable. For these reasons, until his final return to power in 1924, Zogu was forced to play a very difficult and intensive political game.

Chetniks in the Post-Black Hand Era

Unlike *komitajis* of the IMRO who already in 1919 were continuing with activities aimed at renewing their action and presence in parts of Macedonia 'occupied' by

---

[58] Isa Blumi, 'An Honorable Break from *Besa*: Reorienting Violence in the Late Ottoman Mediterranean' In *European Journal of Turkish Studies* 18 (2014), *(Hi)stories of Honor in Ottoman Society*, 1–19, here 11–12.

[59] Bernd J. Fischer, *King Zog and the Struggle for Stability in Albania*, 35.

[60] Bernd J. Fischer, *King Zog and the Struggle for Stability in Albania*, 36.

the Greeks and Serbs, the position of Serbian *chetniks* in the new post-Great War circumstances was rather different. Initially, immediately after the Great War some of them participated in several actions and were given authority to enforce the law in troublesome areas. However, they lost any kind of autonomy of action, something they were very proud of in the recent past. After the Great War they usually operated together with or as an integral part of security forces, namely the Gendarmerie.

From 1921 onwards *chetniks'* main role started to move slowly towards the field of commemorations and celebrations rather than combat. They were grouped in the *Association of Chetniks for the Freedom and Honour of the Fatherland* (Udruženje četnika za slobodu i čast otadžbine). As other veteran associations they embraced official Yugoslav agenda of 'one nation in three tribes'—Serbs, Croats and Slovenes. Contrary to the Bulgarian and Albanian cases where old organizations and their paramilitary structures, after a period of consolidation and adaptation of their political agenda, continued with their activities, in the Kingdom of Serbs, Croats and Slovenes the remaining paramilitaries were seen as a 'necessary evil' and state and military authorities resorted to their services reluctantly. Several exceptions have already been mentioned. Apart from the occasional usage of *chetnik* veterans in actions against IMRO *komitajis* during the 1920's in Macedonia, their largest engagement was to take part in an attempted incursion of emigrants from the Bulgarian Agrarian National Union (BANU) in 1924 and 1925. A large number of Serbian *chetniks* led by Kosta Milovanović—Pećanac, together with dissidents from the federalist wing of the IMRO, was supposed to assist the agrarians its returning to power in Bulgaria after the 1923 June *coup d'état* in which BANU had lost its power and their Prime Minister and leader Alexander Stamboliyski had been brutally murdered. However, this plan was never put into action.[61]

The main reason for such an attitude of the state authorities lay in the recent history of the movement. From the official institutions' point of view Serbian paramilitaries were always seen as closely connected with the *Black Hand* due to the fact that many *Black Hand* members were active in the organizing and activities of paramilitary structures in Ottoman Macedonia in the period 1903–1908, as well as before and during the period of wars of 1912–1918. For example, during the Balkan Wars of 1912–1913 the majority of commanders of *chetnik* detachments were members of the *Black Hand* like Sreten Vukosavljević, Božin Simić, Vojislav Tankosić, Vojin Popović—Vojvoda Vuk etc. A similar thing happened during the Great War. In the period between the Balkan Wars and the outbreak of the Great War, with overall numbers varying between 2,000 and 4,000, along with determined leadership and strong personal relations and allegiances, *chetnik*

[60] Srđan Mićić, 'Kraljevina Srba, Hrvata i Slovenaca i planiranje državnog udara u Bugarskoj 1923–1925', In *Vojnoistorijski glasnik*, 1/2014, 203–32, here 211–19.

structures and their membership were considered a valuable asset on the side of the *Black Hand* which could actually endanger the existing order and lead to a new overthrow and introduction of a military dictatorship. However, the paramilitaries' main advocate and organizer, the *Black Hand*, was annihilated in 1917. The organization was accused of plotting to assassinate Prince Regent Alexander and Prime Minister Nikola Pašić, to overthrow the Government and to sign a separate peace with Austro-Hungarian Empire. From 2 April till 23 May 1917, in a staged trial, the leader of the *Black Hand*, Colonel Dragutin Dimitrijević Apis, and two prominent members: Ljubomir Vulović and Rade Malobabić—the latter participated in the organization of the Sarajevo assassination in 1914—were sentenced to death and executed by a firing squad. Nine others were sentenced to prison. In total, in the course of this final showdown with the *Black Hand* more than 100 Serbian officers passed through some kind of investigation.[62] The fact that in the course of the Great War some prominent and very violent figures from the *Black Hand* had already lost their lives, like Vojislav Tankosić in 1915, or Vojin Popović in 1916, probably eased the final showdown with the organization.

As for the Serbian paramilitaries, at the moment of the Salonika trial against the *Black Hand,* the *chetnik* detachment of Jovan Babunski with some 250 *chetniks* was actually the only remaining irregular detachment in the Serbian army, with all other former *chetniks* being already dispersed among regular troops.

Toplica Uprising 1917: Cornerstone of Post-Great War Chetnik Identity

After the war, *chetniks,* as a veterans' association, besides commemorating and celebrating important events and people from the period of *Wars for Liberation and Unification* (1912–1918), were particularly keen on commemorating the Toplica Uprising from 1917, which in a way represented a central event in the history of *chetniks* endeavours from their establishment in 1903.[63] Together with the Macedonian struggle of 1903–1912, the Toplica Uprising can be considered as one of two cornerstones in *chetniks* tradition and memory culture. Although the Toplica Uprising was limited to parts of South Serbia, the fact that the region of Toplica represented the most diverse Serbian region made it the epitome of Serbian eternal striving for freedom. Due to the colonization process, through which this region had passed since 1878 and the end of Ottoman rule, by the beginning of the Balkan Wars, the region of Toplica was populated by the representatives of almost all regions populated by Serbs—Montenegro, Herzegovina,

---

[62] Andrej Mitrović, *Serbia's Great War: 1914–1918*, (London: Hurst&Company, 2007), 182–3.
[63] John Paul Newman, *Yugoslavia in the Shadow of War. Veterans and the Limits of State Building 1903–1945* (Cambridge: Cambridge University Press, 2015), 104.

Kosovo and Metohija, Sanjak, east and central Serbia, Šumadija and even Vojvodina. In addition, constant border clashes with brigands and irregulars from the Kosovar Albanians contributed to the emergence of a specific 'border-lands culture' so often found in similar regions worldwide. Toplica was also known as the homeland of the elite 2nd Infantry Regiment, better known as the 'Iron Regiment'—the most decorated unit in the Serbian army in all three wars in which it has participated.[64]

How strong was the memory of Toplica Uprising became clearly visible when on 9 September 1934, on the central square of Prokuplje, the administrative centre of Toplica, a monument dedicated to all residents of the Toplica region fallen in previous wars was consecrated. Unlike in other Serbian towns where after the Great War monuments dedicated to the fallen had an almost identical pattern representing the simple Serbian soldier as liberator and victor of the Great War, in Prokuplje the plinth is occupied by two figures charging together—one was a regular Serbian soldier while the other was a typical *chetnik* or insurgent of the Toplica Uprising. How important this event was is attested by the fact that around 40,000 people filled the streets of Prokuplje, at that time a small town with only 6,000 inhabitants. War veterans and participants of the Toplica Uprising were all there together with Kosta Milovanović—Pećanac, one of its surviving leaders. The presence of King Alexander and Patriarch Varnava, the head of the Serbian Orthodox Church, gave the whole endeavour a special touch.[65] Interestingly, this commemoration and consecration of the monument was the last official duty of King Alexander on Yugoslav soil. Exactly one month later, on 9 October 1934, in Marseilles, France, he fell as a victim of assassination organized and executed by Croatian *ustashe* and the IMRO.

A part of the participants and leaders of the Toplica Uprising, such as Kosta Milovanović Pećanac, were also veterans of Serbian *chetnik* action in Macedonia. Again, one of the reasons for emphasizing the importance of the Toplica Uprising and its special place in *chetniks'* memory culture was the participation and role in quelling the uprising of some of the Serbian *chetniks'* archenemies. IMRO leaders like General Protogerov and Colonel D'rvingov, at that time officers of the Bulgarian regular army, were specially assigned to quell the rebellion, while entire bands of IMRO *komitajis* led by prominent leaders or *voivods* like Tane Nikolov were brought in to do the same. In that sense, the Toplica Uprising and encounter with old adversaries represented for Serbian *chetniks* just another act in an

---

[64] Dragan R. Lekić (ed), *Drugi pešadijski puk 'Knjaz Mihailo'—Gvozdeni puk u oslobodilačkim ratovima: 1912-1918*, (Prokuplje: Istorijski arhiv Toplice, 2014); and Radoje Lekić, *Toplički vitezovi—nosioci Karađorđeve zvezde sa mačevima iz Topličkog okruga*, (Prokuplje: Biblioteka Narodnog muzeja Toplice u Prokuplju, 2013).

[65] Saša Stanojević, 'U slavu Gvozdenog puka – svečanosti povodom otkrivanja spomenika Topličanima palim u Oslobodilačkim ratovima i žrtvama Topličkog ustanka u Prokuplju 1934'. In Dragan R. Lekić (ed), *Drugi pešadijski puk 'Knjaz Mihailo'-Gvozdeni puk u oslobodilačkim ratovima 1912-1918*, (Prokuplje: Istorijski arhiv Toplice, 2014), 151–9.

ongoing conflict and rivalry. Together with the participation of another known adversary—Albanian irregulars, at that time in Austro-Hungarian service—this encounter of different irregulars and paramilitaries represented a conflict within the conflict. The fact that *komitajis* and their leaders managed to avoid punishment for their crimes perpetrated against the civilian population during the quelling of the Toplica Uprising, and subsequent fighting elsewhere in Serbia and Macedonia, acted as a mobilizing factor for Serbian *chetniks* to continue with their engagement after the Great War. It is needless to say how challenging was this continuation of the conflict for the establishment of any kind of order in the Yugoslav south. The *Chetniks'* specific *esprit de corps* primarily based on the principle of self-sacrifice for the greater good (in this case the national idea) continued to exist throughout the 1920's and was manifested in occasional engagement in actions against the old rivals from the IMRO. Already in 1920 there were several smaller *chetnik* detachments in Macedonia operating as an auxiliary or temporary Gendarmerie. Members and leaders of these detachments were *chetnik* veterans like *voivods* Krsta Kovačević, Mina Stanković, Milan Stevanović, Boža Đurić, Vojvoda Bogdan, and Rista Petrović. In one moment there were six detachments with some 162 *chetniks*.[66]

However, what distinguished *chetniks* from other veteran associations in the Kingdom of Serbs, Croats and Slovenes was the strong influence of their leaders even in the post-war context. This feature was one of the most recognizable during the years of classic *chetnik* action of 1903–1912, as well as the war years of 1912–1918. Names like Vojislav Tankosić, Vojin Popović (better known as Vojvoda Vuk) or Jovan Babunski and their exploits became legendary and they were considered national heroes even during their lifetime. Their premature deaths (Tankosić in 1915, Popović in 1916 and Babunski in 1920) additionally contributed to their popularity. Although during the war *chetniks* used to be part of the more complex enterprise, which actually influenced their autonomy because they had to operate within the existing military planning, still their allegiances were more closely connected with the personalities of their leaders than anything else. Legendary *chetnik* leaders or *vojvode* who had survived, like Kosta Milovanović-Pećanac, Ilija Trifunović-Birčanin or Puniša Račić, continued to have strong personal influence over the activities of the *Chetnik Association* throughout the mid-war period.[67] At the same time their *chetnik* background and ethos marked their activities on the Yugoslav political scene. In some cases, it led to violent and bloody outcomes with deep repercussions on future political developments. Best known is the incident from 1928 when the Member of Parliament

---

[66] VA, r. 4/3, b. 60, f. 2, d. 6/9, Report of the Minister of Army and Navy to the Comander of Third army district, Confidential no. 15285 from 1. 9. 1920.
[67] John Paul Newman, *Yugoslavia in the Shadow of War. Veterans and the Limits of State Building 1903–1945* (Cambridge: Cambridge University Press, 2015), 104.

and former *chetnik* Puniša Račić, during a fiery parliamentary dispute, in an attempt to 'restore the honour of the Serbian war veteran' pulled out his gun and fired shots at the representatives of the Croat Peasant Party, killing several of their prominent members including party leader Stjepan Radić. This incident led to the abolishment of the constitution and introduction of the Royal dictatorship of King Alexander Karađorđević on 6 January 1929.

The end of the Great War and slow but certain introduction of the new order in all three countries marked a short break in activities of their respective paramilitaries. Orientation and adjustment to new realities lasted very short or was conducted on the way. Majority of those who have been active from the beginning of the century and who have survived war years 1912–1918 remained active and were preparing for the continuation of struggle. While in Kingdom of Serbs, Croats and Slovenes they were considered as necessary evil doomed to slowly exist only in the form of veterans' associations, in Albanian struggle for the postwar consolidation of their young country paramilitaries from northern mountainous clans played prominent role. In Bulgaria however, ruling agrarians created completely new paramilitary organization simply because they realised that despite wining majority in the elections they weren't capable to impose monopoly of violence only through drastically reduced army and police. Although majority of above-mentioned paramilitaries were members of already existing organisations and movements that used to operate since the Ottoman times, creation of the agrarian *Orange Guard* showed how the Balkans were not immune to changes that were happening all over Europe and how the Balkans didn't differ from the rest of Europe in terms of appearance of new, reliable and motivated mass paramilitary organisation created on completely new rationale. In the case of agrarians in Bulgaria, similar to cases of communists and Russian émigrés, we can observe how implementation of genuine ideological and political programme demanded to be supported by creation of respectable paramilitary organisation. Unlike the traditional Balkan paramilitaries whose existence is inseparable from to nation and state building projects of the late 19th and early 20th century and who after the Great War were still deeply influenced by the 'blood and soil' concepts, agrarians and their communist counterparts had something different in mind, that is, they were concerned with the wellbeing of particular social class.

In years to come Serbian *chetniks*, IMRO *komitaji's*, north Albanian clansmen, guardsmen of the *Orange Guard* as well as members of the paramilitary organisations of Bulgarian communists and Russian émigrés played important role in their countries respectively either acting directly against the state authority or as state assistant in imposing it. Needles to say that almost by the rule their engagement was burdened both by old and new rivalries, political and ideological confrontations, and uncontrolled violence.

IV
New Context + Traditional
Methods = Unexpected Outcomes

When the newly founded Kingdom of Serbs, Croats and Slovenes entered the struggle for international recognition, one of the challenges it faced was the recurring Macedonian Question. In the past, during several decades, this question had seriously threatened the integrity of the Ottoman Empire. Occasionally it entered the focus of the Great Powers of the time and imposed itself as an integral part of a larger and more complex Eastern Question—'a diplomatic problem posed in the nineteenth and early twentieth century by the disintegration of Ottoman Empire, centering on the context for control over former Ottoman territories'.[1] However, although the Lausanne Treaty 1923 marked the end of the Eastern Question, the Macedonian Question continued to be present in international and especially inter-Balkan relations. It remained 'on the table' in very complex Yugoslav-Bulgarian and Greco-Bulgarian relations throughout the 20th century. The creation of an autonomous Macedonian federal unit within the renewed Yugoslav state and recognition of the Macedonian nation after 1945, combined with the Cold War international context and logic, just added new flavour to the complex issue that was already complicating inter-Balkan relations. The Macedonian Question outlived all the turbulent changes during the period of the Cold War and violent dissolution of the Yugoslav state during the 1990's, maintaining its prominent place in complex inter-Balkan relations in the twenty-first century as well.[2]

---

[1] Encyclopedia Britannica, Eastern question https://www.britannica.com/event/Eastern-Question [last checked 23 November 2016].

[2] On different aspects (and different perspectives) of the Macedonian Question see: Nadine Lange—Akhund, *The Macedonian Question 1893–1908, from Western Sources* (Boulder: East European Monographs, 1998).; Kostadin Paleshutski, *Makedonskiyat v'pros v burzhoazna Jugoslaviya 1918–1941*, (Sofia: BAN, 1983); K. Paleshutski, *Yugoslavskata komunisticheska partiya i makedonskiyat v'pros, 1919–1945*, (Sofia: BAN, 1985); Ivan Katardžiev, *Makedonsko nacionalno pitanje 1919–1930*, (Zagreb: Globus, 1983); Nikola Žežov, *Makedonskoto prašanje vo jugoslovensko-bugarskite diplomatski odnosi (1918–1941)* (Skopje: Univerzitet 'Sv. Kiril i Metodij', 2008); Nadežda Cvetkovska, *Makedonskoto prašanje vo jugoslovenskiot paralament među dvete svetski vojni*, (Skopje: Institut za nacionalna istorija, 2000); Andrew Rossos, *Macedonia and the Macedonians: A History*, (Stanford: Hoover Institution Press, Stanford University, 2008) (ch. 8–14); R.P. Grishina (ed.), *Makedoniya—Problemy istorii i kul'tury*, (Moskva: Institut slavyanovedeniya, Rossiyskaya Akademiya Nauk, 1999); *Makedonija vo dvaesettiot vekot*, (Skopje, Institut za nacionalna istorija, 2003); *Makedonskiot identitet niz istorijata*, (Skopje, Institut za nacionalna istorija, 2003); 'Dimitrios Returns: Macedonia and the Balkan Question in the Shadow of History'. In: *World Policy Journal*, Vol. 10, No. 2 (Summer, 1993), 67–71.

Paramilitarism in the Balkans: The Cases of Yugoslavia, Bulgaria, and Albania, 1917–1924. Dmitar Tasić,
Oxford University Press (2020). © Dmitar Tasić.
DOI: 10.1093/oso/9780198858324.001.0001

Initially, among other things, the Macedonian Question was the issue of division of the territory of Ottoman Macedonia between Serbia, Greece and Bulgaria. By the end of the 19th century each of the aforementioned Balkan nation-states initiated its own 'Macedonian struggle' which, in its infancy, resembled more of a missionary than a military endeavour. Through different cultural and relief associations such as the Bulgarian *St. Cyril and Methodius Committee*, Serbian *St. Sava Society* and Greek *National Society*, three Balkan Christian nations tried to expand their influence and spread national propaganda while simultaneously denying the existence of a separate and authentic Macedonian Slav nation. Cultural and humanitarian actions were backed by historical, ethnographic, and linguistic proofs and claims. However, when they all added a military aspect to the enterprise by sending armed bands across the border, 'its ideological character predisposed it to political violence.'[3]

Although the outcomes of the Balkan Wars 1912–1913 and the First World War in essence sanctioned the division of Macedonia, the Macedonian Question remained very much alive. Although defeated, the Bulgarians hoped that, with respect to the questions of Macedonia and Thrace, the Wilsonian principle of 'national self determination' would be applied at the Paris Peace Conference. However, the Allies supported the position of the delegation of the Kingdom of Serbs, Croats and Slovenes that the Macedonian Question was resolved[4] Allied support to the Yugoslavs resulted in a modification of attitudes, doctrines and ways of operating of official and unofficial Bulgarian circles. The Internal Macedonian Revolutionary Organization (IMRO) continued to be the most active player in this complicated game.

The other huge issue that troubled the Kingdom of Serbs, Croats and Slovenes was the complex question of Albanian national emancipation. The problem was that after the final end of Ottoman rule over the Balkans, some of former Ottoman territories populated by Albanians ended up as integral parts of Serbia, Greece and Montenegro. Despite the fact that the same wars marked the foundation of the independent Albanian state, an already awakened Albanian national movement could not be reconciled with the fact that their compatriots living in western Macedonia, Montenegro and Kosovo and Metohija had become subjects of two foreign nations. On the other hand, from the Serbian and Montenegrin perspectives, the Balkan wars were seen as 'Wars for Liberation and Unification' after which the ancient territories of 'Old and South Serbia', i. e. Sanjak, Macedonia, Kosovo and Metohija were liberated from 'five centuries of the Ottoman yoke'. These lands represented the 'core of Serbian medieval statehood,' recollecting its most glorious days marked by the rule of Tsar Stefan Dušan (1331–1355) from

---

[3] Mark Biondich, *The Balkans: Revolution, War, and Political Violence since 1878* (Oxford: Oxford University Press, 2011) 68–9.

[4] Čedomir Popov, *Od Versaja do Danciga* (Beograd: Službeni list SRJ, 1995) 137.

the Serbian Nemanjić dinasty. However, strong Serbian and Montenegrin euphoria after the Balkan Wars of 1912-1913 was interrupted by the harsh reality on the ground. Simultaneous resistance coming from Kosovar Albanians and the pro-Bulgarian-oriented inhabitants of Macedonia challenged Serbian and Montenegrin rule to a great extent. The outbreak of the Great War and the Serbian and Montenegrin defeat in late 1915 returned some hope to the Albanians and IMRO supporters that previous territorial divisions could be annulled. But, in September 1918 their hopes were shattered, this time by the Allied artillery barrage that announced the breakthrough on the Macedonian front. What followed was swift Allied victory and renewal of Serbian and Montenegrin rule, though slightly transformed due to the creation of the Yugoslav state. However, the issues remained the same. After a short standstill, already during 1919 IMRO *komitajis* started to return to Macedonia, while traditional Albanian outlaw *kachaks*, this time as agents of the Kosovo Committee, started to emerge in Kosovo and Metohija. These two organizations and their paramilitary structures represented the number-one issue for security in the Yugoslav south. They were natural allies because their aspirations did not overlap and in the initial years after the Great War the effects of their actions had been increased by the weakness of the Yugoslav security apparatus—Army, Gendarmerie and Border Troops—as well as by numerous moves of the main political players on the ground.

Border service, i. e. border security, was within the jurisdiction of Border Troops. They acted as an autonomous, special and professional military formation. The first thing its personnel faced was the lack of border posts, as the Bulgarians had destroyed most of them during the occupation in order to obliterate the borderline between Bulgaria and Macedonia. The new border posts could be built only after establishing the new borderlines, which would happen after the signing of peace accords. This resulted in inefficient possession of a large part of the borderlines. Staying in improvised shelters, tents, huts and dugouts in various weather conditions represented an additional burden for the members of the Border Troops.

The Gendarmerie was a formation of mixed military-police character responsible for the protection of public safety. In organizational terms it was a military formation, but its use was regulated and controlled by the Ministry of Internal Affairs.

Cooperation of civil authorities, Army, police and Gendarmerie was under the strong influence of local circumstances and traditions and had a different character, intensity and success in implementation.

Initial Response to Paramilitary Activities in the Yugoslav South

In the first years after the First World War, the IMRO tried to renew its presence in Macedonia and increase its influence among the local population. Apart from circulating news about the presence of numerous individual *komitajis*,[5] during the spring and summer of 1919 several clashes with *komitaji chete* occured causing losses on both sides.[6] This is where the Yugoslav intelligence and other official reports differ from IMRO claims. According to the IMRO claims *komitajis* were not present on Yugoslav soil at that point. Those mentioned in reports were actually various outlaws and IMRO *komitajis* who became 'illegal', i. e., rogue and no longer members of the organization. From the IMRO perspective those outlaws had caused enormous damage to the image of the organization primarily because their actions were, in most instances, robberies or kidnapping for ransom. For the IMRO that was quite a big deal, while for the Yugoslav authorities it was all the same.

However, if we look into the IMRO's recent history, these kinds of actions were something familiar and of quite frequent occurrence. Their main purpose was, beside acquiring financial gains, propaganda and creating awareness among the international public of the situation in Macedonia. By the end of the 1890's cases of abduction for ransom of rich dwellers of Macedonia, both Christian and Moslem, as well as foreigners became frequent. In 1897, in the town of Veles, the band of Gotse Delchev kidnapped the son of a local rich Bulgarian. They let the boy go after a ransom of 200 Ottoman pounds was paid. The following year they did the same, this time, in Kruševo with the son of a local rich widow. The ransom was considerably higher—2,500 Ottoman pounds. For the French engineer Chevalier, kidnapped in 1899, *komitajis* demanded 15,000 Ottoman pounds. Although Ottoman authorities initiated military action in order to free the poor man, the ransom eventually had to be paid.[7] The most famous case was the so-called *Stone Affair* when in 1901 IMARO *voivode* Yane Sandanski and Hristo Chernopeev kidnapped American Protestant missionary Ellen Stone. After six

---

[5] VA, r. 4/3, b. 54, f. 11, d. 12/907, Report of the office of Skopje district to the command Vardar divisional district, confidential no. 907 from 2 May 1919, forwarded report of the office of Prespa county to the chief of Bitola district; VA, r. 4/3, b. 54, f. 11, d. 12/85, Report of the office of Bitola district to the command of Bitola divisional district, confidential no. 452 from 7 May 1919, forwarded report of the office of Kruševo county, confidential no. 199; VA, r. 4/3, b. 54, f. 11, d. 12/102, Report of the command of town of Prilep, confidential no. 350 from 23 May 1919. године; VA, r. 4/3, b. 54, f. 11, d. 12/101, Report of the command of Bitola divisional district to the command of Third army district, confidential no. 4680 from 21 May 1919, forwarded report of the command of town of Prilep, confidential no. 338 from 20 May 1919. године; VA, r. 4/3, b. 54, f. 11, d. 12/102, Report of the command of town of Prilep, confidential no. 350 from 23 May 1919.

[6] VA, r. 4/3, b. 54, f. 11, d. 12/106, Report of the office of Skopje county to the command Vardar divisional district, confidential no. 898 from 1 May 1919, forwarded report of the office of Veles county, confidential no. 199; VA, r. 4/3, b. 54, f. 11, d. 12/86, Report of the Head of Bregalnica district to the command of Third army district, confidential no. 505 from 14 May1919, forwarded report of the office of Radoviš county, telegram no. 2135; VA, r. 4/3, b. 54, f. 12, d. 12/129, Report of the command of Third army district to Ministry of Army and Navy, confidential no. 4421 from 31 July 1919, forwarded report of the command of Vardar divisional district, confidential no. 6963 from 27 July 1919 received from head of Kumanovo district, confidential no. 6191 од 21 July 1919.

[7] Nadine Lange-Akhund, *The Macedonian Question 1893–1908, from Western Sources* (Boulder: East European Monographs, 1998) 63–4.

months of the kidnappers avoiding Ottoman pursuits, *The American Missionary Board* paid them 14,000 Ottoman pounds.[8]

However, in 1919 IMRO officials invested some efforts to distance themselves from characters like Mita Sokolarski-Sudzhukareto, Grigor and Mitrush Ciklev, Ivan Yanev-B'rlyo, Stoyan Mishev, Slave Ivanov, Lazar Todorov-Fertiko, and others who committed numerous criminal acts in the Yugoslav parts of Macedonia between 1919 and 1921. In total, some 70–80 *komitajis* from Kratovo, Kočani and Štip areas, in the absence of organized revolutionary work and without political orientation and guidance, decided to act on their own. Additional reasons for this kind of behaviour were their own financial difficulties because they remained without regular income. Their actions made a huge impression upon the inhabitants of Macedonia. Many lost their confidence simply because they witnessed how once-proud revolutionaries became brigands and outlaws.[9]

Future leader of IMRO, Ivan Mikhailov, wrote extensively in his memoirs about the situation in the organization's ranks at that time, and especially on previously mentioned incidents caused by former IMRO activists.[10] Another prominent IMRO leader, Georgi Bazhdarov, also mentioned that these incidents had caused huge concern.[11]

Because the IMRO leadership exhausted all peaceful means 'to bring the outlaws to their senses and persuade them to leave the wrong and dangerous road' they were forced to resort to punishments.[12] For Yugoslav authorities it was practically the same whether perpetrators of the above-mentioned crimes were legal or illegal in the eyes of the IMRO Central Committee. When in 1924 the Belgrade imprint 'Vreme' published an extensive study of Dr. Archibald Reiss, prominent Swiss criminologist and forensic expert in Serbian/Yugoslav service, on different criminal acts committed by IMRO *komitajis* after the Great War, the crimes and misdeeds of both 'legalist' and 'illegals' were mentioned.[13] Reiss's study was

[8] On *Stone Affair* see: Konstantin Pandev, Maya Vaptsarov (eds.), *Aferata 'Mis Stoun'; Spomeni, dokumenti i materiali* (Sofia: Izdatelstvo na Otechestveniya front, 1983); see also: Nadine Lange-Akhund, *The Macedonian Question 1893–1908*, pp. 96–7. The Stone Affair was probably one of the first recorded manifestations of 'Stockholm syndrome', because after her release Ellen Stone gave several conferences in favor of the IMARO.
[9] Zoran Todorovski, *Avtonomističkata VMRO na Todor Aleksandrov 1919–1924*, (Skopje: Makavej, 2013) 94–5.
[10] Ivan Mikhailov, *Spomeni II, Osvoboditelna borba 1919–1924* (Louvain, 1965), 767–73.
[11] Georgi Bazhdarov, *Moite Spomeni*, (Sofia: Inst. B'lgarija-Makedonija, 2001), http://www.promacedonia.org/gb/gb_3_2a.html [last checked 12 December 2016]
[12] Ivan Mikhailov, *Spomeni II, Osvoboditelna borba 1919–1924* (Louvain, 1965), 772.
[13] R. A. Reiss, *La question des comitadjis en Serbie du Sud* (Belgrade: Vreme, 1924). In 1914 the Serbian government invited Reiss to conduct a professional criminal investigation of atrocities committed by the Austro-Hungarian army in their first offensive against Serbia in August 1914. He did it very thoroughly, visiting and investigating actual crime scenes, photographing and documenting sites, interviewing survivors, Austro-Hungarian POW's, and members of the Serbian army. He published a series of articles in *Gazette de Lausanne* where he described in detail the effects of the Austro-Hungarian offensive; on that see: R.A. Reiss, *Report upon the Atrocities committed by the Austro-Hungarian Army during the first Invasion of Serbia*, (London: Simpkin, Marshall, Hamilton, Kent&Co, 1916). For the

published in French with a clear intention to address the international community and draw attention to this problem, but also to blunt the edge of IMRO propaganda. He presented the history of earlier IMRO actions, its current operations, substantiating it with statements of numerous witnesses and victims.

Another activity some of *komitaji* veterans were resolved to was contraband, which along with pillaging and kidnappings also contributed to certain distortion of the romantic image of the Macedonian freedom fighters. Some of those *komitaji* veterans residing in Kyustendil, Gornya Dzhumaya, Petrich and Strumica, as well as in villages by the border, became active in smuggling different goods from the Kingdom of Serbs, Croats and Slovenes. Their experience and knowledge of the terrain proved very useful, especially because immediately after the Great War Yugoslav security forces were not able to properly secure the Bulgarian—Yugoslav border. Besides that, they were well armed and equipped with pack animals. This deal brought them a substantial income, because of shortages and high prices of different goods in Bulgaria.[14]

The intensifying of IMRO actions marked the following year. Protogerov and Alexandrov stood firmly at the head of the organization. The first rumours of the IMRO and its plans began to arrive in March.[15] Army commands in Macedonia seriously approached an expected intensifying of the IMRO activities, suggesting an increase of the number of officers and NCOs, introduction of new weapons like machine-guns, creation of cavalry squads (as rapid response units), and consolidation of all security forces.[16]

A major IMRO offensive began in June 1920. Todor Alexandrov was leading it from his headquarters in the Kratovo Mountains, from where he had intensive correspondence with Bulgaria and with *chete* on the ground. From there, he returned triumphantly to Bulgaria at the beginning of 1921. With this act Alexandrov ensured his right to a place in the Central Committee since, according to the organization's constitution, each of the three members of the Central Committee had to spend six months per year on the ground in Macedonia, otherwise he would lose his position. Alexandrov also proved that he

---

rest of the war he remained in Serbia, maintaining detailed records on subsequent events: the 1915 epidemic of typhoid fever, defeat and withdrawal across Albania, creation of the Salonika front, final breakthrough and victory in 1918. After the Great War he remained in the Kingdom of Serbs, Croats and Slovenes where he continued his career as a criminologist. He died in Belgrade in 1929; more on Reiss see: Zdenko Levental, *Švajcarac na Kajmakčalanu—knjiga o dr Rajsu*, Prosveta, Beograd 1984.

[14] VA, r. 4/3, b. 54, f. 11, d. 12/97, Report of the Ministry of Army to the command of Third army district, confidential no. 25 193 from 15 May 1919, forwarded report of the command Border troops, confidential no. 668 from 29 April 1919.
[15] VA, r. 4/3, b. 58, f. 7, d. 6/24, Report of the delegate of Supreme command to the command of Third army district, confidential no. 1016 from 5 March 1920.
[16] VA, r. 4/3, b. 60, f. 4, d. 12/35, Report of the command of Vardar divisional district to the command of Third army district, confidential no. 2889 from 10 January 1920.

was most popular among the leaders of the organization.[17] It is said that in the summer and fall of the 1920, the IMRO activity on the ground in Macedonia reached a very high level and that by November in the territories between the Yugoslav-Bulgarian border and the left bank of the river Vardar its organization was restored to an extent similar to the period of Ottoman rule. However, on the right bank of the river Vardar the organization could not be restored to its former size, nor could it gain any considerable size.[18] By spring 1921 the IMRO divided the territory of Macedonia, as in Ottoman times, into five revolutionary districts: Bitola, Salonika, Serres, Skopje and Strumica. The last three were organized remarkably, while Salonika and Bitola significantly lagged behind.[19]

Because of the elections for the Yugoslav Constituent Assembly scheduled for November 1920, *chete* extended their stay and work in Macedonia. Unlike previous years when the first signs of autumn would mark the withdrawal of *komitajis* to their winter harbours in Bulgaria, in November and December 1920 the intensity of events did not differ from those of the summer months. In relation to elections (both local and parliamentary) the IMRO planned to reach a political solution in Macedonia through the support to the Communist Party of Yugoslavia. In order to achieve this the intensive involvement of *komitajis* was required. Results of parliamentary elections and the new security situation initiated a careful investigation by the police and military authorities. Earlier suspicions regarding cooperation between IMRO and the communists, the IMRO and the Albanian-Turkish committee were confirmed, as well as the organization's affection towards Stjepan Radić and his Croatian Peasant Party.[20]

After the great electoral success of the communists some representatives of civil authorities advocated the introduction of extraordinary measures such as isolation of the villages that were connected with IMRO, resettlement of villages known as proven IMRO centres, increasing of military forces, the removal of communist officials, organization of the judicial system, increase of funding for intelligence operations, bringing teachers, priests and gendarmes from Serbia, introducing of severe penalties for carrying weapons, organizing of conscription and effective tax collection as the communist agitation was mainly directed against them, and opening of a large number of schools.[21]

---

[17] Decho Dobrinov, 'Todor Aleksandrov i v'zstanovanieto na VMRO sled p'rvata svetovna vojna (1918-1924 g.)'. In *100 godini V'treshna makedono-odrinska revolucionna organizaciya*, (Sofia, Makedonski nauchen institut, 1994), 145–56 here 150.

[18] Krasimir Karakachanov, *VMRO—100 godini borba za Makedoniya*, (Sofia: VMRO-SMD, 1994), 45.

[19] K. Karakachanov, *VMRO—100 godini borba za Makedoniya*, 46.

[20] VA, r. 4/3, b. 58, f. 9, d. 6/133, Report of the commander of Vardar divisional district to the command of Third army district, highly confidential no. 9784 from 9 December 1920.

[21] VA, r. 4/3, b. 58, f. 9, d. 6/136, Report of the command of Third army district to the Ministry of Army and Navy, confidential no. 8175 from 21 December 1920, forwarded report of the chief of Tikveš district to the command of Third army district (no number).

If we take into account the electoral success of the communists who became the fourth party by the number of votes (200,000), the severity of reactions of civil authorities' representatives testifies to the anxiety and feelings of insecurity that prevailed in those days. The communists won 59 out of 415 seats in the Constitutional Assembly. In Macedonia alone they won 15 seats, which was a huge success. Undeveloped Macedonia provided more votes for the communists than more developed regions of the Kingdom of Serbs, Croats and Slovenes such as Croatia and Slovenia.[22] A previous electoral success in August local elections when the communists achieved victory in 37 communities in the Serbian part of the kingdom alone (including the capital Belgrade and the two most important cities Niš and Skopje) caused huge concerns among traditional parties. Communists as bearers and promoters of some IMRO political ideas could be even more dangerous since they would provide legal cover for IMRO political goals.

In areas populated by Albanians, primarily the regions of Kosovo and Metohija, 1919 seemed to look like the calm before the storm. The defeat of Austro—Hungarian Empire, their main sponsor, shattered Albanian hopes for creation of a unified Albanian state in the Balkans. However, the return of Serbian and Montenegrin authorities represented a factor of mobilization among Albanians. In 1918, they founded the Kosovo Committee, which acted as political organizer of the Albanian struggle from abroad. It acted as political motor of Albanian resistance aimed at the unification of all Albanians. Its leaders—Bayram Curri, Hasan Prishtina, Hoxha Kadriu, Zia Dibra—preferred armed struggle. However, the Committee's involvement in events in the Albanian political arena influenced the developments on the ground a great deal. The Committee's main problem was that besides Belgrade as their primary enemy, Tirana politicians proved to be equally opposed to the Committee's ambitions to create a Great Albania.[23] If we compare the Kosovo Committee and the IMRO, IMRO's struggle, beside political manifestations, had clear features of organized paramilitary activism. On the other hand, the Albanian struggle was much more archaic and it was already seen in Albanian political and military revolts against the policies of the Young Turks during the first decade of the 20th century. Proponents of the Albanian struggle were uneducated and predominantly illiterate outlaws—*kachaks*, while within the ranks-and-files of IMRO fighters among simple Macedonian peasants and crafts-men one could encounter well-educated individuals like teachers, army officers, and civil servants. This is especially visible from the fact that many survived

---

[22] Kostadin Paleshutski, *Yugoslavskata komunisticheska partiya i makedonskiyat v'pros, 1919–1945*, (Sofia: BAN, 1985), 59–60; See also: Ivan Mikhailov, *Spomeni II, Osvoboditelna borba 1919–1924* (Louvain, 1965), 125.

[23] Robert C. Austin, 'Greater Albania: Albanian State and the Question of Kosovo, 1912 -2001'. In John R. Lempi and Mark Mazower (eds), *Ideologies and National Identities. The case of Twentieth Century Southeast Europe* (Budapest and New York: CEU Press, 2004), 235–53, here 241.

IMRO *komitajis* and organization leaders wrote some sort of memoirs. Needless to say, IMRO had strong support from Bulgarian intellectuals and academics, not only of those with Macedonian origin. They supported the organization's actions by popularization of its goals through writings, public lectures and addresses. However, this was not the case with both *kachaks* and political activists of the Kosovo Committee. The first remained to become a subject of Yugoslav police or army reports on anti-state activities during the 1920's, while the latter fell one by one as victims of turbulent political circumstances combined with their own choices. Their side of the story for the most part remained unwritten or is visible only through testimonies of their contemporaries and opponents.

As true bearers of the Albanian rebel spirit *kachaks* were a typical Balkan mixture of brigands, freedom fighters and hired guns (*kaçak*—Turkish for outlaw, fugitive, smuggler). They represented a relic of the Ottoman era, more exactly the final decades of its rule over the Balkans, when the Albanian national movement started to gain impetus.[24] Although the Albanians enjoyed a privileged position during the same period, i. e., the reign of Abdul Hamid II (1876–1909)— being exempted from conscription and allowed to bear firearms—from Young Turk revolution onwards *kachaks* began to transform from simple outlaws to freedom fighters. Famous *kachaks* were Azem Bejta from Drenica, Mehmed Kajumi from Lab, Mehmed Fera from Plav, Kera Sadri from Rugovo, Sadik Rama from Đurđevik, Ramadan Shaban from Klina, Ismail Gusinja from Gusinje and Yusuf Veseljaj from Podgora, as well as many others.[25] Their reappearance in the newly founded Kingdom of Serbs, Croats and Slovenes meant they would continue with their struggle, this time politically profiled and with the backing of a concrete political movement—the Kosovo Committee. The Albanian rebellion did not look like a typical insurgency. From time to time it would grow massive; however, in most of the period between 1919 and 1924 it was manifested in actions of guerrilla groups. Another problem was that the guerrilla actions of *kachaks* in Kosovo and Metohija and surrounding areas, aimed against Yugoslav state authorities and justified by political goals, overlapped with simple criminal actions whose main goals were pillaging and blood feuds. Their perpetrators resembled or were identical to *kachaks*. What is more important, their victims in most of the cases were their fellows Albanians.[26] In 1919, after several defeats and considerable losses, instead of open battles with Yugoslav security forces *kachaks* resolved to guerrilla tactics.[27]

---

[24] For more on *kachaks* see: Pavle Dželetović Ivanov, *Kačaci Kosova i Metohije*, (Beograd: Interjupres; Ekkos, 1990); Vladan Jovanović, 'Suzbijanje kačaka na Kosovu i Metohiji 1912–1929', in *Vojnoistorijski glasnik*, 1/2009, 32–55.

[25] Đorđe Borozan, *Velika Albanija, porijeklo, ideje, praksa*, (Beograd: Vojnoistorijski institut Vojske Jugoslavije, 1995) 77.

[26] For more on analyses of criminal activities on Kosovo and Metohija see introduction of: Ljubodrag Dimić and Đorđe Borozan, (eds), *Jugoslovenska država i Albanci. Tom 1* (Beograd: Službeni list SRJ; Arhiv Jugoslavije; Vojno-istorijski institut, 1998), 275—80 and 289–93.

[27] Lj. Dimić and Đ. Borozan, (eds), *Jugoslovenska država i Albanci. Tom 1*, 275—80 and 289–93.

The centre of *kachak* activities was the Drenica region in Kosovo where the Yugoslav Army and Gendarmerie during April and May 1919 fought several smaller battles against *kachaks* strengthened with armed peasants. It is not by coincidence that Drenica became the centre of *kachak* activities. Most of them originated from this area. Also, Drenica is mountainous area dividing Kosovo from Metohija, both of which are more flat and unsuitable for guerrilla warfare. Finally, Drenica was already very active, as were the other parts inhabited by Albanians during several consecutive insurgencies against Young Turks and their policies 1909–1912. How strong were the ties between the Drenica region and Albanian non-acceptance of Yugoslav/Serbian rule was again demonstrated twenty-five years later during the Second World War when, in late 1944/early 1945, Drenica once again became the centre of Albanian rebellion, this time against the restoration of the Yugoslav state carried out by the Communist Party of Yugoslavia and the Yugoslav partisan movement. After engaging insurgents with considerable forces brought from Montenegro, Serbia and Macedonia, Yugoslav partisans managed to crush the insurgency. However, it was achieved with considerable losses, and as a result small guerrilla groups continued with their resistance all the way to 1947.[28] Half a century later in 1998–1999, after

Fig. 4. Band of Filip Buchinski.

Typical *komitaji cheta* or band from 1920's. Its clearly military features, mostly in term of their equipment, represent a visible shift from previous epoch where national costumes were combined with parts of uniform.

© National Library of Serbia (Belgrade), Album of Nikola Zafirović, 262/LjDf.

---

[28] More on Albanian armed resistance after the WWII see in: Dmitar Tasić, 'Albanski oružani otpor uspostavljanju vlasti nove Jugoslavije 1944-1945'. In Zoran Janjetović (ed), *1945.: kraj ili novi početak?* (Beograd: Institut za noviju istoriju Srbije; Muzej žrtava genocida, 2016), 91–106.

more than a decade of peaceful attempts of Kosovar Albanians to secede from Yugoslavia, by creation of Kosovo Liberation Army (KLA) they resorted to weapons. Drenica was again most important stronghold of Albanian insurgents.

However, in terms of security the situation in Macedonia began to complicate from 1919 onwards. The presence of the *komitaji* bands on the ground was more and more visible, and it began to produce serious repercussions. For example, in 1919 and 1920, Reiss noticed thirty-two criminal offenses of IMRO members (kidnappings, murders, massacres, attacks on law enforcement officials, arsons, mutilations, rapes, beatings, theft, blackmail) while by the end of the 1923 the total figure rises to 261. While in 1920 the number of civilians killed in IMRO actions in Macedonia was seven, the following year that number rose to twenty-eight. In 1922, it came to seventy-seven, while in 1923 it jumped to eighty-eight. The number of killed and wounded members of the security forces—Army, Gendarmerie, and Border Troops—kept rising as well. In 1921 it was two, in 1922 it was already twenty-four killed and seven wounded, while in 1923 it was thirty-two killed and twenty-five wounded. The same could be said for IMRO *komita-jis*—while in 1921 only two were reported as killed, in 1922 number rose to eleven killed, four wounded and one captured. Because of the intensity of actions during 1923, there were twenty-three killed and twenty-five wounded *komitaji* fighters.[29]

One thing, however, is striking. It is the level of violence and brutality characterizing most of these incidents. Although they are clearly distinct (kidnappings for ransom, murders, massacres, attacks on law enforcement officials, arsons, mutilations, rapes, beatings, and pillaging) criminal acts committed by IMRO *komitajis* in most cases represented a combination of two or several particular crimes. Murders that occurred on roads, for example, were as a rule followed by mutilation of victims' bodies. Since most of the killings were targeted—victims were either former members of the IMRO, now considered traitors, or distinguished representatives of 'Serbian rule' like village mayors, police officers, heads of districts and counties, priests, teachers, etc—mutilations were signs of warning aimed to intimidate potential 'renegades'. For the same reason, on several occasions, victims were hanged at crossroads. Also, on several occasions, victims were tortured before being executed. Beatings were regular no matter whether the victim was kidnapped for ransom or taken during raids on villages. Arson was used on several occasions, albeit with caution and when *komitajis* felt secure since smoke and fire were signals for the Gendarmerie and Army that something wrong was going on. Also, if kidnappers' demands for ransom could not be fulfilled, the abducted person most certainly would be killed.

---

[29] Reiss R. A., *La question des comitadjis en Serbie du Sud* (Belgrade: Vreme, 1924), 120–45. Annexe—L'activité des comitadjis en Serbie du Sud depuis la fin de la guerre jusqu'à la fin de l'année 1923; For the list of IMRO actions in period 1920—1923 see also: Ivan Mikhailov, *Spomeni, III, Osvoboditelna borba (1924-1934)* (Louvain 1967), 923–31; Mikhailov admits that he has used Reiss's study for his own book.

In relation to the above-mentioned crimes, among several prominent *komitaji voivods* two clearly singled themselves out. One is Georgi V'ndev Goshev, whose area of operation was the southeast of Yugoslav Macedonia, more exactly the vicinity of town of Strumica. V'ndev and his band were responsible for at least thirteen executions or 'punishing' of former IMRO members and representatives of Yugoslav authorities from 1920 until 1923, as well as for a bomb-attack on a coffee shop in Strumica where one person was killed and five others seriously injured.[30] A clear illustration of his methods was the brutal liquidation of Tuše Đorđević, who was mayor of one municipality in Strumica District, and Ibrahim Useinović which took place on 15 July 1922. A police investigation of the crime scene established Đorđević's body to have '18 thrust wounds made by knife, two cut wounds on his head made by sabre, hands and fingers cut off by sabre and scattered around...'. Useinović's body was identically mutilated. During Ottoman rule Đorđević was a *komitaji voivoda* who after the Great War retired and obviously accommodated to new conditions. Useinović on the other hand was a Yugoslav 'confidant'. From the IMRO point of view they both needed to be punished. Demonstrated brutality was considered 'added value' with the clear aim to intimidate locals and force them to continue supporting the IMRO.[31]

The other well-known IMRO member was the controversial Ivan Yanev-B'rlyo, who immediately after the Great War acted rogue but was accepted back into the ranks of the IMRO, where he, together with other *voivode*, like Pancho Mikhailov-Chavdar performed several important actions and assassinations. Most important were the assassination of the Bulgarian Minister of the Interior and Army Alexander Dimitrov in October 1921, and a raid on Kyustendil in December 1922.[32] In terms of paramilitary violence Ivan Yanev-B'rlyo was responsible for one of the two biggest incidents during the period in consideration. Those were massacres in the Macedonian villages of Kadrifakovo on 16 January and Garvan on 3 March 1923. The second massacre came as retaliation for the first. It is very difficult to draw a precise picture of these affairs as well as to precisely determine their causes and actual sequence of events. Both sides—the IMRO and Yugoslav authorities—tend to spin actual facts by diminishing their own responsibility and by exaggerating that of their opponents. Basically, already by the winter of 1922/1923, the IMRO became concerned by the measures Yugoslav authorities had introduced in Macedonia. While new security measures will be mentioned later, one in particular could have threatened the IMRO, and in the long run

---

[30] Dimitar Tyulekov, *Obrecheno rodolyubie. VMRO v Pirinsko 1919–1934* (Blagoevgrad: Univ. Izd. 'Neofit Rilski', 2001), http://www.promacedonia.org/dt/index.html [last checked on 4 November 2016]; More on actions of V'ndev's band see: Ivan Mikhailov, *Spomeni, III, Osvoboditelna borba (1924–1934)* (Louvain 1967), 923–31.

[31] Archive of Yugoslavia (Arhiv Jugoslavije—AJ), Collection 14 Ministry of the Interior of the Kingdom of Yugoslavia (MUP KJ), 14–177–1138, Command of the 3rd Gendarmerie Brigade, Report to the Commissar for South Serbia, no. 3378 from 22 July 1922.

[32] Ivan Mikhailov, *Spomeni, III, Osvoboditelna borba (1924–1934)* (Louvain 1967), 581–3.

endanger the organization's positions. It was the colonization of Macedonia by Serbian settlers from various regions of the Kingdom of Serbs, Croats and Slovenes. Colonization was seen as a tool that would lead to increased Serbian influence and would contribute to the mixing of locals with other parts of the Yugoslav population. Colonization of Yugoslav south (Macedonia and Kosovo and Metohija) was part of a highly complex issue that also involved emigration of Muslim populations (ethnic Turks, ethnic Albanians and Slavic Muslims) to Turkey and redistribution of their land. War veterans and poor farmers from mountainous areas of Montenegro, Bosnia and Herzegovina, Dalmatia, and Lika were encouraged to accept land in Macedonia and Kosovo and Metohija. The state facilitated their transport and provided them with basic necessities. They were settled in colonies on state land or land taken from emigrated Ottoman landowners, though the IMRO claimed that the land had been taken from the local Christians as well.[33] One such colony was Kadrifakovo in Bregalnica County. The band of Ivan B'rlyo, with some twenty to thirty *komitajis*, came to Kadrifakovo on 16 January 1923. Unusually for *komitajis*, they executed this operation during a winter month probably for practical reasons, because in spring, summer or fall locals would be working in the field. Thus, they were all at their homes. *Komitajis* simply forced them out and shot on the spot twenty-three settlers. Several houses and stables were set on fire as well.[34]

The Yugoslav reaction was equally brutal, and it occurred right after the state had introduced new measures against both IMRO *komitajis* and Albanian *kachaks*. The brutality of the reaction can be associated with Dobrica Matković, the new Head of Bregalnica County, whose name in the following years would be connected with different activities and actions against the IMRO in Bregalnica County as well as in Macedonia as a whole. Unlike previous actions this one was executed by regular troops, but in the recognizable paramilitary manner. It is unclear why Matković chose Garvan to execute retaliation; perhaps its dwellers somehow assisted B'rlyo's band before or after the sack of Kadrifakovo, or were associated with it—it will probably remain a mystery. In total, soldiers executed twenty-eight people. The whole affair was conveniently used by IMRO propaganda as a demonstration of how 'Serbs' treat oppressed people of Macedonia.[35]

---

[33] On the colonization of the Yugoslav south between the two world wars see: Vladan Jovanović, 'In Search of Homeland? Muslim Migration from Yugoslavia to Turkey, 1918-1941', *Tokovi istorije*, br. 1–2/2008, Beograd 2008, 56–67; V. Jovanović, 'Land reform and Serbian colonization. Belgrade's problems in interwar Kosovo and Macedonia'. In *East Central Europe*, vol. 42, issue 1 (2015), 87–103; V. Jovanović, *Jugoslovenska država i Južna Srbija 1918-1929 (Makedonija, Sandžak, Kosovo i Metohija u Kraljevini SHS)*, INIS, Beograd 2002; V.Jovanović, *Vardarska banovina 1929-1941*, INIS, Beograd 2011.

[34] Reiss R. A., *La question des comitadjis en Serbie du Sud* (Belgrade: Vreme, 1924), 134. Reiss states that seventeen settlers (men, women and children) were killed while six were wounded. *Komitajis* burned four houses, three stables and took some cattle as well.

[35] *Garvanskata golgota (2 March 1923)*, (Sofia: I. K. na s'yuza na makedonskite emigranti, 1924); see also: Ivan Mikhailov, *Spomeni II, Osvoboditelna borba 1919-1924* (Louvain, 1965), 62–5 and 666–7.

The whole affair represents one of the best examples that paramilitarism and the paramilitary way of behaviour could be easily associated not only with paramilitary formations or organizations but with regular forces as well.[36]

Besides these manifestations of violence, during 1922 one more occurred as well. Although initially not detected as such by Yugoslav authorities, resulted from a clash between *federalist* and *autonomist* IMRO factions. One of the causes for the discontent of Todor Alexandrov, leader of the *autonomist* faction, was the fact that the *federalist* faction began dispatching its own bands to Macedonia. Alexandrov insisted that no band should be allowed to go 'over', as they used to say, without authorization of the organization's Central Committee. As a result of this rivalry the band of Krum Zografov, prominent *federalist* leader, was deliberately betrayed to Yugoslav police who managed to organize a successful action and kill Zografov in a subsequent shoot-out.[37] What followed was a swift and ruthless retaliation executed not against Gendarmes but against peasants from the village of Koševo, in the vicinity of the town of Štip, who denounced Zografov. A group of nine *komitajis* entered this relatively small village (only eighteen households) around 18.00 on 23 August 1922. There, they first captured and then executed two sons of one peasant and a son of another one. Several women that were present could clearly hear the *komitajis* saying: 'Because your fathers, who are responsible for the death of our *voivode*, escaped, we will kill you instead!' After the execution they set on fire nine out of eighteen houses. Although, for their protection, police authorities had issued rifles to those peasants who denounced Zografov, it proved to be insufficient to provide them with safety. Subsequent investigation led to the identification of most of the perpetrators, since they were familiar to the locals. The *komitajis* were dressed in Bulgarian uniforms; they wore Bulgarian hats and army bag packs.[38]

In Kosovo and Metohija several important events occurred during 1920 and they had a crucial influence on further actions of the Kosovo Committee and their agents on the ground—*kachaks*. Yugoslav authorities realized very soon that one of the most important security issues in the Yugoslav South was an enormous quantity of firearms in private possession. Of course, this was directly connected with the Albanian custom of bearing firearms as well as with IMRO organizational rules, which implied distribution of firearms for the creation of village *chetas* that were supposed to assist *komitaji* bands. For obvious reasons these

---

[36] Simmilar cases of regular forces acting in paramilitary fashion occurred during the Irish War for Independence, see: Anne Dolan, 'The British Culture of Paramilitary Violence in the Irish War for Independence'. In Robert Gerwarth, John Horn (eds.), *War in Peace: Paramilitary Violence in Europe after the Great War*, (Oxford and New York: Oxford University Press, 2012), 200–15, here 209.

[37] Zoran Todorovski, *Todor Aleksandrov*, (Skopje: Makavej; Državen arhiv na Republika Makedonija, 2014),178–86.

[38] AJ, MUP KJ 14–177–571, Report of the Head of Bregalnica County to the Commissioner for South Serbia, no. 6300 from 27 August 1922, forwarded report of the Head of Štip District, no. 4146 from 25 August 1922.

quantities were considerably higher among Albanians than Macedonians. During 1919 it occurred that armed locals would regularly assist bands of *kachaks* whenever they encountered Yugoslav security forces. In order to reduce support to *kachaks* they needed to collect all illegal firearms from the locals. The Serbian army already had experiences with confiscation of weapons from Albanians during and after the Balkan Wars. However, in 1912–1913, it was mostly done by Serbian irregulars and these actions were followed by extreme brutality. Brutal methods applied especially by Captain Vojislav Tankosić and his *chetniks* during the disarmament campaign of local Albanians in the Kosovo region became known as 'Tankosić methods'. Needless to say, thanks to their demonstrated brutality Tankosić's detachment was the most efficient during the disarmament campaigns.[39] Nearly 20,000 pieces of firearms were collected that way.[40] After the Great War disarmament campaigns were conducted as well, but with no paramilitaries involved. In 1919 several smaller and limited campaigns were conducted after initial clashes with *kachaks*. In 1920, however, when the Army and Gendarmerie finally overcame the crisis in terms of their actual strength on the ground, more serious campaigns were executed. First action was initiated in March and lasted until June. The territories of Kosovo and Metohija were divided into sectors, which were canvassed thoroughly. In total, some fourteen infantry companies with the same number of guns and machineguns were engaged (approximately one infantry regiment) together with some 1,500 Gendarmes. It resulted in taking around 11,000 pieces of firearms.[41]

However, regardless of the relative success of the above-mentioned action, *kachaks* maintained and even increased their presence on the ground. There were several assaults on Gendarmerie outposts as well as on Serbian villages. Again, Azem Bejta demonstrated his guerrilla skills—he was all over the place but not a single pursuit brought results. In only two days, on 20 May and 21 May, his *kachaks* killed seven Serbian civilians.[42] Within the next two days that number grew to fifteen.[43] The Army and Gendarmerie continued with this game of cat and mouse, and although they had success against bands of lesser-known *kachaks*, the main figures like Sadik Rama or Azem Bejta kept slipping through. At one moment Army representatives demanded that the Gendarmerie take primacy in anti-*kachak* activities, simply because if the Army had been constantly involved

---

[39] Vladimir Ilić, 'Učešće srpskih komita u Kumanovskoj operaciji 1912. godine', In *Vojnoistorijski glasnik*, 1–3/1992, 197–217, here 216.

[40] Vladan Jovanović, 'Suzbijanje kačaka na Kosovu i Metohiji 1912-1929', in *Vojnoistorijski glasnik*, 1/2009, 32–55, here 35.

[41] Ljubodrag Dimić and Đorđe Borozan, (eds), *Jugoslovenska država i Albanci. Tom 2* (Beograd: Službeni list SRJ; Arhiv Jugoslavije; Vojno-istorijski institut, 1998), 582–627; Vladan Jovanović, 'Suzbijanje kačaka na Kosovu i Metohiji 1912-1929', in *Vojnoistorijski glasnik*, 1/2009, 32–55, here 44.

[42] VA, r. 4/3, b. 58, f. 2, d. 1/98, Report of the command of the Kosovo divisional district to the command of the Third Army district, confident no. 1686 from 21 May 1920.

[43] *Jugoslovenska država i Albanci, tom 2*, pp. 682, 684–6.

in that kind of engagement it could not dedicate proper attention to the training of new recruits. Moreover, this resulted in a deterioration of discipline, which threatened to jeopardize the integrity of an already heterogeneous Army.[44]

By the end of 1919 and during 1920 two events that would have serious and far-reaching repercussions on further counterinsurgency or counter-paramilitary activities in the Yugoslav south took place. They influenced the adoption of new strategies and measures and also changed the reality on the ground. The first event was a meeting of sixty-four representatives of Muslim communities— mostly magnates and landlords from Macedonia and Kosovo and Metohija who were interested in reaching a political platform which would protect their interests. The meeting was held in Skopje on 18 December 1919 and on this occasion a political party, Islamic Society for the Defense of Justice (Islam Muhafazai Hukuk Cemiyeti) commonly known as Cemiyet (the Turkish expression for Society)[45] was founded. Initially, the party entered into arrangements with the Radical Party, led by Nikola Pašić, who in return for their support, agreed to preserve their rights as landlords. In a way, this arrangement blunted the Kosovo Committee blade, since Turkish and Albanian landlords possessed huge influence on Albanian commoners.

The second important event was a conference of high military and civil officials organized on 14 June 1920 in the town of Mitrovica, located in the Kosovo and Metohija region. The idea was to meet and discuss the current state of affairs, and design efficient security measures in the region. Alongside the Minister of the Interior Ljubomir Davidović, who chaired the meeting, there were heads of counties (Kosovo, Peć, Prizren, Metohija, Zvečan and Raška), commanders of divisional districts (Kosovo, Vardar and Bitola), the Chief of staff of the Third Army district, and representatives of the Gendarmerie. After detailed analyses of the situation in each county, which revealed that in many cases incompetent local authorities had contributed to the deepening of the crisis, a long list of proposed measures was drafted. Beside obvious points like the increase of the Gendarmerie, they mentioned several different kinds of measures:

- Technical: assignment of new police precincts; reconstruction of old and building of new roads, railroads and bridges; installation of telephone lines between police precincts; increase of number of motorcars;
- Legal: general disarmament; implementation of *Decree on Banditry* from 1906 which allowed introduction of emergency measures such as taking hostages, internment of perpetrator family members, confiscation of property, fining whole villages for criminal acts committed on their

---

[44] VA, r. 4/3, b. 60, f. 5, d. 12/60, Report of the command of Third Army district to the Ministry of Armu and Navy, confidential no. 2323 from 3 June1920.
[45] Robert Elsie, *Historical dictionary of Kosovo*, Scarecrow Press, 2011, p. xxxvi.

territories, bivouacking of Army units at the expense of villages until surrender of perpetrators;

- Practical: colonization of 'non-Albanian' settlers—primarily Montenegrins
  who showed themselves capable of coping with Albanians; stimulation of
  Albanian emigration; maintaining good relations with Albanian elites
  because of their influence; maintaining good relations with Albanian state,
  founding of a special office for policy towards Albanians, issuing firearms
  to loyal elements, termination of recruitment of Albanians who had already
  served in Austro-Hungarian or Bulgarian armed forces;
- Cultural: respecting Albanian peculiarities such as word of honour (besa)
  and internal clan hierarchies, building high schools and specialized schools
  in all towns in the region;
- Administrative: introduction of financial incentives for public servants
  working in these areas.

Taking into account the results of the conference, in a separate memo titled
Memorandum on development and current status of the Albanian question the
commander of the Third Army district pointed out the strong presence of the
'idea of Great Albania'. He also warned that the idea represented the biggest challenge and without success in its neutralization it could cause serious troubles in
the future. The conference itself did not result in immediate response from the
Yugoslav authorities; however, it resulted in a rise of awareness of specific circumstances in the former Ottoman territories. However, many of the suggested
anti-insurgency measures were introduced in the Yugoslav South in the following
years.[46] As for *kachaks*, they remained a constant threat to the Yugoslav state;
however, in the following years their patrons from the Kosovo Committee became
increasingly involved in events in the political scene in Albania, which often led
to reducing the *kachak's* presence in Kosovo and Metohija. Prominent *kachaks*
remained elusive, and although the Army and Gendarmerie in general became
more successful, the fact that Azem Bejta or Sadik Rama managed to slip through
ambushes and roadblocks or escape all pursuits contributed to their growing
popularity among common Albanians. However, after the delineation of the border between Albania and the Kingdom of Serbs, Croats and Slovenes in 1921, a
so-called 'neutral zone' was established in northern Albania on the Albanian side
of the border. Due to the fact that the 'neutral zone' was characterized by the visible absence of Albanian state authorities, it became a safe haven not only for
kachaks but for all dissatisfied elements within Albanian populations in the
Kingdom of Serbs, Croats, and Slovenes. Those were army deserters or others
who wanted to avoid conscription, wanted criminals, simple bandits and robbers.

---

[46] Ljubodrag Dimić and Đorđe Borozan, (eds), *Jugoslovenska država i Albanci. Tom 2* (Beograd:
Službeni list SRJ; Arhiv Jugoslavije; Vojno-istorijski institut, 1998), 725–32.

In most cases it was difficult to determine the boundaries between these groups. As for criminal activities in these areas, because of strict and precise rules related to blood feuds among Albanians the majority of criminal acts were associated with vendetta. In the majority of cases, victims and perpetrators were Albanians. Their mistrust in state institutions responsible for justice and maintaining public order was equally deeply rooted as their blood feud-related customs. Once initiated, the violent spiral of blood feuds led to considerable losses in human lives.[47] The other negative aspect of blood feuds was that it represented the main generator of banditry. Most of those who committed a murder would not wait to be arrested and tried. It was much simpler to become an outlaw. According to the report of the head of Peć County in the Kosovo and Metohija region from July 1922, in his county alone there were 366 outlaws who went rogue just for the purpose of banditry. Also, there were 199 who went rogue just to avoid blood feuds and 457 of those who just wanted to avoid conscription. In twelve months from July 1921 until July 1922, 135 premeditated killings happened, which were, in the vast majority, related to blood feuds.[48] Later on, it proved that those who did not commit serious crimes or became outlaws to escape the vicious circle of vendetta were ready to answer the call of Yugoslav authorities to surrender and return to normal life. Unlike them, those who were steeped in crime or who established some kind of career in Albania did not want to return.[49]

Introduction of Extraordinary Measures

In 1921, after taking into consideration the increase of IMRO activities in Macedonia and security challenges in Kosovo and Metohija, which were not always related to *kachaks* and the Kosovo Committee, the Yugoslav Ministry of the Interior decided to introduce a whole range of new measures and also to establish new offices. Although these measures were announced as temporary, in reality they illustrate the seriousness of the overall situation in the Yugoslav south. As it is commonly known that 'desperate times call for desperate measures', in this particular case, the desperate aspect was hidden behind a legal approach through introduction of new offices, mechanisms, rules of engagement, measures. However, some time was needed to determine if these measures were efficient or not.

[47] Even today many Albanians are falling as victims of blood feuds. According to one estimation between 1999 and 2017 around 1500 homicides were committed in Kosovo and Metohija as results of blood feuds, *Besa*, Al Jazeera Objektiv, broadcasted on 5 January 2017, https://www.youtube.com/watch?v=fMD6PZLjtIA [checked on 21 August 2019].
[48] AJ, MUP KJ 14-177-775, Head of the Peć County, Report to the Commissar for South Serbia, confidential no. 1107 from 17 July 1922.
[49] AJ, MUP KJ 14-177-1142, Command of the 3rd Gendarmerie Brigade, Report to the Commissar for South Serbia, confidential no. 3335 from 24 July 1922.

In order to coordinate the actions of all state actors in the region—Army, Gendarmerie, and local authorities—the Ministry of the Interior founded two new and temporary offices:

- Commissar for Southern Regions;
- Commissar for Sanjak.

The first one was responsible for counties in Macedonia and Kosovo and Metohija, while the latter was responsible for the relatively smaller and to a less extent insecure territory of Sanjak. Initially, Extraordinary Commissar M. Cerović, an official of the Ministry of the Interior, administered both functions during 1921. However, if we look into available documents, he was still operating the 'old' ways, without proper authority or jurisdiction.

When in 1922 they finally introduced new measures and divided two offices the picture looked rather different. Two Commissars were supposed to work in cooperation, maintaining closest relations with local Army units as well as with the Ministry of the Interior in Belgrade. Commissars were responsible for public safety and they had the Gendarmerie, armed loyalist civilians, and so-called 'special formations' at their disposal Commissars were also entitled to ask for military assistance and they were supposed to report regularly to the Ministry of the Interior as well as to heads of counties. On the other hand, local authorities, such as district and county administrations and police officials, were placed under the Commissar's authority in terms of public safety.[50]

In practical terms this action, which would occupy the attention of Yugoslav authorities in the southern regions for the next couple of months, looked like a typical counter-insurgency operation conducted by regular armed forces in recently occupied territories. However, it had a clear distinction in that at the same time it was a 'winning hearts and minds' type of mission. It had to present the Yugoslav state and its authorities as someone who was making the difference after decades of crises and instability. Despite the fact that police, i. e. Gendarmerie, was supposed to play main role in it, measures, mechanisms and rules of engagement had distinctive military characteristics. However, since it took place in territories that had witnessed similar actions for decades, clear paramilitary features marked whole endeavour as well. The first example was distribution of firearms to local Serbian villages, as well as to those with a mixed population (Turkish or Albanian) which proved to be loyal. In return, they were obliged to maintain guards on roads and high ground, to check the identity of all 'strangers' who would come to the village, to report them and if necessary escort them to the nearest Gendarmerie post or local municipality, to help neighbouring

---

[50] AJ, MUP KJ 14–177–93–103, Ministry of the Interior, Kingdom of Serbs, Croats and Slovenes, Department of Public Safety to the Head of Skopje County, No. 9014 from 8 May 1922.

villages if they found themselves under attack, and assist in actions organized against *komitajis* or *kachaks*.[51]

Duties of representatives of local authorities like heads of municipalities, districts and counties as well as Gendarmerie commanders were precisely determined regarding when, how and in what way they should act if confronted with *komitajis* and *kachaks*. Bearing in mind the mistakes committed by civil authorities in previous years, they were instructed to establish and maintain good relations with all citizens, avoid living in separated colonies (because a large number of state officials actually came from other parts of the Kingdom of Serbs, Croats and Slovenes), get acquainted with the local ground in terms of relief, woods, and every potential hiding place, also get acquainted with local inhabitants, primarily as a precondition for establishment of reliable intelligence networks, which proved to be of crucial importance in counter-insurgency operations. A special part was dedicated to so-called 'special formations'. In essence, it was just a different name for good old *chetnik* bands or detachments. Their rules of engagement followed the same pattern of flying or pursuit detachments from the short period of Serbian rule over Macedonia (1913–1915) and the immediate post-Great War years. But, probably to avoid incidents that occurred in 1919 when the detachment of Jovan Babunski was used in anti-IMRO actions, the composition of new 'special formations' was precisely determined. Primarily, they were supposed to consist of gendarmes both active and reserve with a limited number of 'trustworthy men' (in reality *chetnik* veterans)—'in order not to get compromised the personnel must be chosen between the bravest, most honourable and the righteous'. Their composition was limited to fifteen in each detachment whose normal composition went up to fifty. The Instructions made provision for thirteen detachments with around 240 members in total. Worthy of pointing out is that the Instructions mentioned two *chetnik* veterans by name. One was Krsta Kovačević, *voivoda* of Preševo, right hand of Jovan Babunski, and the other was Blaža Nikodijević. Each detachment was assigned a particular territory (county or district). Because gendarmes from precincts could not perform long patrols, the main task of 'special formations' was to patrol and fight *komitaji* incursions and raids of Albanian cattle-rustlers. This had to be done in closest cooperation with local authorities, Gendarmerie posts and army garrisons who were obliged to provide all necessary support to detachments. This support encompassed basic provisions and ammunition as well as additional manpower like gendarmes and village militiamen.[52] One patrol round was supposed to last between four and six weeks. The Instruction is also very precise in terms of rules of engagement. It describes what are the roles of every official engaged in this counter-insurgency operation, how they should react, what their plans should look like, how they

---

[51]   AJ, MUP KJ 14–177–93–103.
[52]   AJ, MUP KJ 14–177–93–103.

should disseminate information regarding the *komitaji* or *kachak* bands, how to reach unity of action of all actors involved. There are also tips on how and when to engage with *komitaji* bands (for example, preferably at dawn after careful deployment of ambushes because if engaged during the day *komitajis* were experts in using the cover of darkness to disengage and withdraw). Each Gendarmerie brigade in the Kingdom of Serbs, Croats and Slovenes had a so-called Training Company where new gendarmes were prepared for their future duties. These companies were foreseen for counter-insurgency actions as well. The Third Brigade of the Gendarmerie stationed in Skopje had to assign its Training Company for counter-insurgency duties as well, but in this particular case it had the role of Rapid Response Unit. If operations against *komitajis* or *kachaks* demanded engagement of additional forces Training Company was first on the list to answer.[53]

Several areas of intensive presence of *komitaji* and *kachak* bands are mentioned, like the area of Maleš in Macedonia, which was used for successful infiltration of *komitaji* bands; Carev Vrh as a favourite location of Todor Alexandrov when he was operating on the Yugoslav side of the border, and the area of Drenica in the Kosovo region as the main location for *kachak* bands. The latter area was supposed to be in the focus of local authorities in the Kosovo region. In order to limit *kachaks'* freedom of movement, special funds were provided for construction of summer Gendarmerie posts as well as for new telephone lines between precincts and centres of local municipalities, districts and counties.[54]

The Army and its units were also given a role in planned operation. However, because of the specifics of its organization and yearly cycle of training activities, the Army was kept as last resort, only if things were to go from bad to worse. During operations, garrisons were obliged to support patrol actions both of the Gendarmerie and 'special forces' with provisions and accommodation. The Army was to maintain a visible presence on the ground through occasional patrols and bivouacking outside of army barracks. Thus, the local population would become aware of the state's strength and determination. Creation and maintenance of efficient intelligence networks—as one of the most important factors in counter-insurgency operations—was mandatory for all above-mentioned officials. However, because the identities of informants had been compromised in the recent past, which resulted in retaliation by the IMRO manifested in torture and brutal executions, officials were instructed to keep informants' identities secret even from their closest associates. In that way they could guarantee success in actions against *komitajis* and *kachaks* and encourage others to enter into similar arrangements with the state authorities.[55]

---

[53] AJ, MUP KJ 14–177–93–103.
[54] AJ, MUP KJ 14–177–93–103.
[55] AJ, MUP KJ 14–177–93–103.

Fig. 5. Vojvoda Dejan.

Little is known about this *chetnik* champion. This photo is dedicated to a friend as a memory of vojvoda Dejan's years as guerrilla fighter. Here we can see full chetnik attire whose details later on was frequently imitated and misused.

(From Zoran Živković's private collection)

It is visible from the available reports that the Commissar for South Serbia began to work in May or June 1922. The new appointee after M. Cerović was Živojin Budimirović, inspector at the Ministry of the Interior. He immediately began to operate following the above-mentioned Instruction, and one of the first actions was the gathering of intelligence data. For that purpose, two special trustees were sent to Bulgaria in mid-June. One of them was former *komitaji* voivoda Kosta Jovanović.[56] After they illegally crossed the border with Bulgaria using traditional *komitaji* routes two agents visited Kyustendil—an important centre of

---

[56] VA, r. 4/3, b. 58, f. 8, d. 6/82, Report of the Ministry of Army and Navy to the Command of Third Army district, confidential no. 8878 from August 3 1920. Kosta Jovanović was a Bulgarian *komitaji* and former sergeant in the Serbian army. During the Great War, after being wounded and captured, Jovanović joined the IMRO. He became a close associate of Todor Alexandrov and as *komitaji* he participated in numerous incidents in occupied Macedonia as well as in quelling the Toplica Uprising in 1917. After the war he showed readiness to put himself at the disposal of the Yugoslav government in exchange for full pardon of his transgressions during the Bulgarian occupation.

IMRO *komitaji* action. After that they went to Sofia where Jovanović's brother joined them. After reporting to the Yugoslav embassy, they returned from Sofia back to the Petrich region, visiting Gornya Dzhumaya, Petrich, Melnik, Radomir and surrounding places, checking the level of *komitaji* activities and presence. It was sort of a risk because someone could recognize Jovanović. They noticed that most of the *komitajis* were still on Bulgarian territory although Alexandrov was in Macedonia with several bands. In four encampments they counted around 8,000—9,000 *komitajis* from the Yugoslav and Greek parts of Macedonia. After a two-week stay they returned, again illegally crossing the border. Their report proved to be useful for the organization of future actions.[57]

Meanwhile, new measures showed the first results. On 29 June the local Gendarmerie, loyal villagers and one flying detachment, after several days of following the band's movements, engaged with the band of Georgi V'ndev who was operating around Strumica. However, because action and shooting began at 18.00, *komitajis* were able to use darkness to disengage and withdraw.[58]

Several days afterward, on 6 July an event occurred in Kratovo district, which could serve as an example of successfully organized pursuit. The local commander of a flying detachment, Captain Stanojlo Stanić, after receiving intel on a *komitaji* band with some twenty members, well hidden in one creek bed, quickly managed to organize the gendarmes of his detachment and several surrounding precincts, inform his superiors to get the necessary approvals from the heads of district and county, and ask for Army support which arrived in the strength of one platoon with two light machineguns. With thirty-three gendarmes and twenty-two soldiers he surrounded the band and assaulted it. In a dynamic pursuit and gunfight, they managed to kill nine, capture one and wound five *komitajis*. Later sweeps resulted in finding three more corpses of killed *komitajis*. The rest of the band escaped across the border. One soldier and one gendarme were killed; two were wounded along with one civilian working in the field near the place of battle.[59]

Undeniably encouraged with the initial successes, but also because reports were mentioning the increased infiltration of *komitaji* bands, Commissar Budimirović organized a new patrol detail for the most troublesome spots—Kumanovo and Bregalnica Counties. The patrol was supposed to last 11 days, starting from 20 July, and a detailed plan was drafted for two combined companies of gendarmes

[57] AJ, MUP KJ 14–177–1031, Command of the 3rd Gendarmerie Brigade, Report to the Commissar for South Serbia, confidential no. 1350 from 4 July 1922.
[58] AJ, MUP KJ 14–177–1034, Command of the 3rd Gendarmerie Brigade, Report to the Commissar for South Serbia, confidential no. 1339 from 12 July 1922.
[59] AJ, 14–177–1045, Command of the 3rd Gendarmerie Brigade, Report to the Commissar for South Serbia, confidential no. 1469 from 17 July 1922; This story was later published on the pages of *Žandarmerijski kalendar* under the title 'Nice example' as educative material for Gendarmerie rank-and-files, *Žandarmerijski kalendar*, godina 1925, pp. 138–40.

Fig. 6. Captured IMRO *comitaji*.

Occasionally, but rarely, after clashes between inserted *komitaji* bands and Yugoslav security forces some of *komitajis* would end up in Yugoslav hands. Hardships of being guerrilla fighter are clearly visible on this *komitaji* face and attire. Those captured *komitajis* who hadn't been associated with crimes would end up serving prison sentences, however they could hope their sentences to be reduced or abolished thanks to the frequent royal pardons throughout the 1920's and 1930's.

© National Library of Serbia (Belgrade), Album of Nikola Zafirović, 261/LjDf.

(each had three platoons), with the necessary number of horses, machineguns, medics and telephones. Each company had around 150 men.[60]

A new success, although on a smaller scale, was recorded on 5 August when a small patrol of two gendarmes and six armed peasants managed to ambush and disperse a band of six *komitajis* near Veles. Two *komitajis* were killed while the remaining four escaped. This ambush was part of a much larger endeavour, which significantly limited freedom of movement for *komitajis* in that area.[61]

---

[60] AJ, MUP KJ 14–177–1049, Command of the 3rd Gendarmerie Brigade, Report to the Commissar for South Serbia, confidential no. 1382 from 7 July 1922.

[61] AJ, MUP KJ 14–177–1081, Command of the 3rd Gendarmerie Brigade, Report to the Commissar for South Serbia, confidential no. 3789 from 10 August 1922.

However, not everyone agreed with these methods. The head of the Ovče Polje district, who, according to his superior, demonstrated extraordinary talent for intelligence work, had an interesting conversation with one of his agents. The agent or trustee, who was very well acquainted with IMRO actions and was considered a Bulgarian national activist, openly doubted the efficiency of the above-mentioned measures, saying that the organization actually wanted Yugoslav security forces to grow tired by constant patrols and staying on the ground. He also said that Yugoslavs should stop hiring Russians as gendarmes because of their behaviour, that they should bring more reliable gendarmes from Serbia as well as strengthen border security. They should also stop issuing weapons to 'loyal' civilians, especially Turks, because they might turn them against Yugoslav forces. He also suggested that families of all those who had escaped to Bulgaria and joined the IMRO should be interned. Instead of futile patrols he suggested that all efforts should be invested into intelligence work and by that he considered providing generous rewards for those individuals who denounced *komitaji* bands. He himself was dissatisfied with the reward he received when he denounced one band; though he promised to denounce another one soon, in return he expected the reward to be much more generous.[62]

How dangerous could be the position of any type of trustee or informant whose identity was revealed is proved by the example of Džemail Jusein, head of a municipality in Nikoman near Štip. He was killed with one of his clerks Serafim Cvetković on 18 August 1922. *Komitajis* ambushed them on a local road. They were dead almost instantly. The body of Jusein was robbed and mutilated as a warning to others because he was the Yugoslav state's official. As such, he denounced more than forty IMRO members who were arrested and tried. He was fully aware of IMRO intentions and despite numerous attempts to hide, they finally managed to find and kill him.[63]

At the same time the Army additionally contributed to the increase of counter-insurgency actions in the period July—September. In order to hamper movement of *komitaji* bands in Bregalnica County additional Army forces were brought in from other divisional districts (five infantry and two artillery battalions and four squadrons of cavalry). Together with the already present forces of the Vardar divisional district they were deployed in three parallel lines beginning from the Yugoslav—Bulgarian border. In total, there were thirty-seven infantry companies, four cavalry squadrons and seven batteries of mountain artillery. Apart from patrolling and looking for IMRO bands their duty was to create a statistical overview of the villages, other dwellings and surrounding terrain but also to 'win the hearts and minds' of the local population by demonstrating high discipline and order.[64]

---

[62] AJ, MUP KJ 14–177–566, Head of the Bregalnica County, Report to the Commissar for South Serbia, confidential no. 621 from 12 July 1922.

[63] AJ, MUP KJ 14–177–587, Head of the Bregalnica County, Report to the Commissar for South Serbia, confidential no. 6110 from 21 August 1922.

[64] AJ, MUP KJ 14–177–1056, Command of the 3rd Gendarmerie Brigade, Report to the Commissar for South Serbia, confidential no. 1519 from 23 July 1922.

However, during 1922, one of the measures mentioned two years before began to be implemented and, it seems, proved to be very efficient. It was the quartering of army units in villages where criminal acts took place or where evidences of *komitaji* or *kachak* activities existed. A whole unit, usually a platoon or company would be deployed in a village, at the villagers' expense, until locals decided to cooperate or denounce the perpetrators. This particular measure evoked the spirit of another extremely violent period of history. Initially, quartering did not bear negative connotations and had been a very common measure until the appearance of mass armies of the Napoleonic era. Instead of staying in encampments, after arriving at a town or other kind of settlement, soldiers would be accommodated in local households. Often soldiers would pay for this service, which provided their hosts with additional income. But quartering became extremely notorious when the administration of Louis XIV, King of France, by the end of seventeenth century began using this method as a tool in the fight against Huguenots in his kingdom. Even before the Edict of Fontainebleau from 1685 proclaimed their religion illegal, Huguenots or Protestants were obliged to accept soldiers assigned to their houses. Because in most instances soldiers were dragoons (mounted infantry), this practice became known as *dragonnades*.[65] This practice was seen as an incentive for the return of heretics to the true faith. Besides economical strain, because Huguenots were supposed to feed both men and their horses, in most cases a whole household was exposed to different kinds of brutalities, which eventually led to the emigration of the entire French Huguenot population. Between 200,000 and 900,000 people left France and went to England, the Netherlands, Switzerland, German protestant states, French Canada and even South Africa. In Macedonian or Kosovar cases, the practice of quartering was subtler because violence and brutalities were out of the question. However, the sheer presence of soldiers, usually young recruits from all regions and nations of the Kingdom of Serbs, Croats and Slovenes, could create a tense situation. Although for Macedonians, as Christians, the harder part was providing soldiers with all necessary provisions, for Albanians, as Muslims, the hardest part was presence of so many young men in vicinity of their women. The only way to avoid it was to cooperate with the authorities. These were the reasons why Yugoslav authorities considered this measure to be so efficient. So, in July 1922 a platoon of soldiers was deployed in the village of Vladimirovo in Maleš District after a group of outlaws, in a probable act of revenge, assaulted the former head of the district Golubović. It happened that during the assault his daughter was killed.[66] After the incident outlaws joined the band of local IMRO *voivode* Stefan Karadzha. A similar thing happened in the Albanian village of Ostrec in Bitola district, where more than ten outlaws and deserters began to terrorize surrounding villages—both

[65] Dragonade, *Vojna enciklopedija*—volume 2, (Belgrade: VIZ 1971), 531.
[66] AJ, MUP KJ 14–177–572, Head of the Bregalnica County, Report to the Commissar for South Serbia, confidential no. 665 from 20 July 1922.

Christian and Muslim. The local head of the district asked for military reinforcements in order to neutralize this group before they compromised the already troubled public safety. In this particular case the deployment of an entire infantry company was demanded so that they could 'enjoy the hospitality of the local villagers'.[67] The efficiency of this measure was visible from the fact that, as soon as the company of 105 soldiers and two officers was deployed to Ostrec on 2 August, two outlaws responsible for murder surrendered as well as four others who had deserted their army units. The murderers were sent to prison while the deserters were returned to their garrisons. With the company's presence law and order returned to Ostrec. However, six outlaws responsible for different murders refused to surrender.[68]

This measure was again requested on 23 September when, a day earlier, after the shootout with the band of Velichko Velyanov-Skopski (*komitaji voivode* who later executed Bulgarian Prime Minister Alexander Stamboliyski in the course of the 1923 June coup d'état) a flying detachment led by Stojče Dobrić, a Bulgarian renegade in Yugoslav service, found the naked corpse of an unknown man totally mutilated by more than forty knife thrusts. That was probably the body of an earlier abducted teacher from the village of Ljubani. Because the village was loyal to the IMRO, well organized, and refused to cooperate in relation to the abduction of their teacher, the command of the Gendarmerie from Skopje requested one company of soldiers to be deployed there until locals begin to cooperate with the Gendarmerie.[69]

In order to increase the presence of 'special formations' on the ground, the Commissar for South Serbia addressed the Ministry of the Army and Navy to provide his office with the necessary number of volunteers willing to participate in actions against the IMRO. He wanted to create an additional twenty detachments with around thirty men in each. The first step was to determine the exact number of volunteers among personnel of the regular army who were ready to invest additional effort and participate in counter-insurgency operations. The response among officers, NCO's and privates was surprisingly high. For 40 officers, 80 NCO's and 420 soldiers positions 144 officers, 308 NCO's and 4926 privates have applied. Although composed of regular troops, more correctly conscripts, and strengthened by gendarmes experienced in local conditions (five in each detachment) their way of operating was basically a copy of counter-insurgency operations conducted by the Bulgarian occupation regime during the Great War when IMRO *komitaji* bands were engaged against Serbian insurgents.

---

[67] AJ, MUP KJ 14–177–566, Head of the Bitola County, Report to the Commissar for South Serbia, confidential no. 15260 from July 1922.
[68] AJ, MUP KJ 14–177–560, Head of the Bitola County, Report to the Commissar for South Serbia, confidential no. 771 from 9 August 1922.
[69] AJ, MUP KJ 14–177–1133, Command of the 3rd Gendarmerie Brigade, Report to the Commissar for South Serbia, confidential no. 2003 from 23 September 1922.

These new detachments were supposed to patrol troubled areas, especially where the presence of the Gendarmerie was low. Their main and only task was locating, pursuing and destroying *komitaji* bands. In order to be highly mobile, the flying detachments were lightly armed. Logistics was minimal; all provisions were requisitioned and paid for on the spot or taken from military depots on the way. Such a high response among regular troops could be explained by the fact that this action would take them out from army barracks and its drill monotony, and because this engagement would bring them financial gains due to the fact that necessary funds were allocated for their *per-diem* costs.[70] *Chetnik* tradition and reputation could also instigate the wish among new generations to try to experience this kind of life. So, by mid-September, twenty new flying detachments were ready to be deployed in Macedonia. A special meeting was organized in Skopje with the participation of the Head of the Public Safety Department of the Ministry of the Interior, Commissar for South Serbia, commander of the Third Gendarmerie Brigade, Chief of Staff of Third Army district and heads of southern counties. They decided that new detachments would be deployed in the following order: five in Kumanovo County; three in Skopje; eight in most troubled Bregalnica County; three in Tikveš and one in Bitola. These detachments were also under the command of the local Gendarmerie, but with the obligation of establishing the closest possible cooperation with local Army commands and district and county offices. Although each detachment was assigned a particular area of operation, once they engaged *komitaji* bands they were instructed to pursue them until complete annihilation regardless of territorial boundaries.[71]

In the following months, a very important change related to state efforts against actions of Bulgarian and Albanian paramilitaries took place. It was supposed to have deep repercussions on the situation in Macedonia and Kosovo and Metohija. In practical terms it was a step back because the office of the Commissar for South Serbia had been disbanded. The main role was given to Dobrica Matković, another official from the Ministry of the Interior. Matković, unlike many people concerned with state affairs, had a loose notion of 'rule of law'. Instead, he had introduced new measures followed by extreme brutality, which would bring memories of Jovan Babunski's engagement three years earlier. However, unlike the typical representative of the 'old school' Babunski, Matković's way of doing things was on a larger scale with multiple agents involved. Although it quickly brought results, the way in which it was achieved in the long run proved to be devastating for stability in the Yugoslav south.

[70] AJ, MUP KJ 14–177–106, Report to Mr Budimirović, inspector in the Ministry of interior from 28 August 1922.
[71] AJ, MUP KJ 14–177–162, Ministry of Interior, Public Safety Department, information for the Commissar for South Serbia, confidential no. 2655 from 12 September 1922.

Organization against Bulgarian Bandits

Security issues that had existed in the Yugoslav south in relation to IMRO *komitaji* action after the Great War contributed to the appearance of a completely new paramilitary organization. Although throughout the period between the two world wars Yugoslav state authorities officially used to express their determination to introduce modern administration based on the rule of law and strong and reliable state institutions, the situation on the ground was actually quite the opposite. Corruption on all levels and a combination between old client-based relations inherited from the Ottomans and new loyalties based exclusively on party affiliation in practical terms prevented or hampered evolution of these territories as well as the whole Kingdom of Serbs, Croats and Slovenes to a modern and stable state. One of the main reasons for such a picture lay in the unwillingness of Serbian political parties, primarily the Radical Party, to relinquish its control over 'South Serbia' to anyone else. For Radical Party officials, the south represented a vast pool of votes as well as a playground for personal enrichment and nothing more. So, it is no wonder that instead of solving the pressing security issues by 'winning hearts and minds' of the locals through the rule of law and strengthening the institutions of a modern state, local officials decided to continue with shady policies more convenient for the unstable Ottoman times than for a European state that clearly expressed, at least on paper, its ambition in favour of modernization.[72]

Year of 1923 in a way represented culmination of IMRO actions in Yugoslav Macedonia. As already mentioned, only band of Georgi V'ndev Goshev was responsible for at least thirteen executions or 'punishing' of former IMRO members and representatives of Yugoslav authorities from 1920 until 1923.[73] However, culmination of IMRO brutality was sack of Kadrifakovo colony in Bregalnica County, which happened on 16 January 1923. As described, band of Ivan B'rlyo executed twenty-three settlers.[74]

Pressed by the everyday growing presence of IMRO *komitajis* and security challenges arising from it, following existing practices, local officials and 'national workers' decided to introduce a completely new paramilitary formation, of course with the approval and assistance of Belgrade. The simplicity of its title *Organization*

---

[72] Already during the first years of Macedonia's existence within the Kingdom of Serbs, Croats and Slovenes the first analyses warned of different misconduct of state officials on all levels—army, police, local autonomy, as well as of wrong practices that could (and eventually did) alienate local indigenous populations. For example, see Archive of Yugoslavia (Arhiv Jugoslavije—AJ), Collection 334 Ministry of Foreign Affairs of the Kingdom of Yugoslavia, 334-8-108-61.

[73] Dimitar Tyulekov, *Obrecheno rodolyubie. VMRO v Pirinsko 1919-1934* (Blagoevgrad: Univ. Izd. 'Neofit Rilski', 2001), http://www.promacedonia.org/dt/index.html [last checked on 4 November 2016]; More on actions of V'ndev's band see: Ivan Mikhailov, *Spomeni, III, Osvoboditelna borba (1924-1934)* (Louvain 1967), 923-31.

[74] Reiss R. A., *La question des comitadjis en Serbie du Sud* (Belgrade: Vreme, 1924),134. Reiss states that seventeen settlers (man, women and children) were killed while six were wounded. *Komitajis* burned four houses, three stables and had taken some cattle as well.

against Bulgarian Bandits clearly described its agenda. However, circumstances related to its founding and later functioning were far from simple and they are still raising controversies. Officially, the organization was founded at a public rally in the town of Štip on 9 September 1923. The rally was organized to express public outrage at the overall security conditions in 'South Serbia' but especially in the so-called Bregalnica region (in fact a county) in East Macedonia (named after the main river in the region—Bregalnica). Bregalnica County and Štip as its administrative centre were well known for intensive activities of IMRO *komitajis* and strong Bulgarian national and church propaganda.[75]

Although the founders of the *Organization against Bulgarian Bandits* wanted to impose an impression of the organization's creation as a spontaneous reaction of the local population, which in despair addressed central state authorities, the actual setting is far more complicated and includes a multitude of agents and influences.

After almost three years of different approaches whose aim was to suppress activities of IMRO *komitajis* in 1923 a crucial personal change took place when the above-mentioned Dobrica Matković was appointed to the position of *veliki župan*[76] of Bregalnica County. He had immediately introduced measures aimed at strengthening Yugoslav security forces in the region, like bringing additional forces of the Gendarmerie and Army and building new precincts.[77]

However, one other event provided Matković with am extremely valuable asset for successful neutralization of *komitaji* incursions. Again, as with other issues related to this example, it did not happen overnight. The summer of 1923 was very dynamic on the Bulgarian side of the border. The IMRO was already, slowly but with great certainty, heading towards internal schism. A series of actions of Todor Alexandrov's *autonomist* faction against their *federalist* rivals resulted in several *federalist* defeats (actions in Nevrokop in October and in Kyustendil in December 1922). Because of that, prominent leaders of the IMRO *federalist* faction such as Stoyan Mishev, Grigor Ciklev, Mita Sokolarski-Sudzhukareto and others were forced to leave Bulgaria and search for refuge in Yugoslavia in May 1923. It was not that they defected only to ask for refuge, on the contrary, they demonstrated willingness to continue fighting, but this time by entering Yugoslav service. However, it seems that this has been already arranged by the Yugoslav intelligence, primarily because its network was able to notice the emerging schism between *autonomist* and *federalist* factions of the IMRO and to react and use it. The first signs of the future rift appeared in autumn 1919 at the time of the

---

[75] *Spomenica proslave dvadesetogodišnjice Bregalničke bitke i desetogodišnjice osnivanja Narodne samoodbrane*, (Štip: [s. n.], 1933).

[76] Title given to heads of counties in the Kingdom of Serbs, Croats and Slovenes, it was similar to prefects in France.

[77] Vladan Jovanović, *Jugoslovenska država i Južna Srbija 1918–1929 (Makedonija, Sandžak i Kosovo i Metohija u Kraljevini SHS)*, (Beograd: INIS, 2002), 193.

Congress of Macedonian Fraternities when a number of disgruntled *komitajis voivode* made an attempt to get in touch with the authorized representatives of the Kingdom of Serbs, Croats and Slovenes in Sofia. Although, as described in the previous chapter, nothing happened it turned the attention of the Yugoslav intelligence towards this issue in the future.

In the following years, the disputes between the two factions continued as well as attempts at reconciliation; however, defection of *federalist komitajis* was a culmination of the conflict of two factions and in a way represented a point of no return. Matković immediately arranged everything with Stoyan Mishev and his associates and already during the summer of 1923 there were five so-called 'flying detachments' roaming through five districts of Bregalnica County—svetonikolski, kočanski, štipski, radoviški and maleševski.[78] Since these detachments operated on their own, practically without control, it is very hard to determine their 'efficiency'. However, if we take in mind the following, it is possible to sketch some kind of a picture of their status and achievements and place it in the broader political and social context. *Federalists* were already in direct confrontation with *autonomists,* however, until May 1923 that was an internal and soluble conflict. Simple people among IMRO supporters in Macedonia were fully aware of this fact and they had already witnessed and heard mutual public proclamations of condemnations. Real shock, however, resulted when they saw former *komitajis* coming to their villages, but this time in Yugoslav service. Some of them were *komitaji* legends, like Stoyan Mishev who used to be a very close associate of Todor Alexandrov. Unlike the Gendarmerie and Army, which had limited possibilities and authorizations for successful struggle against the IMRO, former *komitajis,* also known as *counter-chetniks,* were able to literally dismantle IMRO organization in the Bregalnica County countryside. Their advantages were not only their authorization, experience, freedom of movement, speed, and element of surprise, but a detailed knowledge of IMRO procedures and organizational structure in Macedonia. For them, there were simply no secrets. So, at the time of official creation of the *Organization against Bulgarian Bandits* these flying detachments were already fully operational. Well-known *voivodes* of these *counter-chetniks* detachments were (apart from Stoyan Mishev, Mita Sokolarski and Grigor Ciklev) Vane Arsov, Pano Eftimov, Pano Zhiganski, Sande Pelivanov, Hristo Umlenski, Iliya Pandurski and others.[79] They are described as loyal to the Serbian cause, but it is admitted that the main driving force lying behind their decision to change sides was hatred of Todor Alexandrov and his followers—'it is simply a blood feud, and it is something that closely connects them to the Serbian cause'.[80]

---

[78] V. Jovanović, *Jugoslovenska država i Južna Srbija*, 194.
[79] Nikola Žežov, *Makedonskoto prašanje vo jugoslovensko-bugarskite diplomatski odnosi (1918– 1941)* (Skopje: Univerzitet 'Sv. Kiril i Metodij', 2008), 96.
[80] AJ 334–8–108–12.

However, in order to get broader state and local political support for such developments and to prevent the whole enterprise from acquiring the character of a mercenary endeavour, former *federalist* renegades were simply incorporated into the *Organization against Bulgarian Bandits*. The founder of the organization was Mihajlo Kalamatijević or Kalamatija, a 'simple' merchant from Štip, who had just survived an assassination attempt ordered and executed by the IMRO. The reason for this attempt was very distant from the usual apprehension of revolutionary ideals—Kalamatijević, together with another fellow merchant refused to make a 'donation' to the cause. Because of that he needed to be punished, as later leader of the IMRO Ivan Mikhailov openly admits in his memoirs. Unlike his friend who was killed, Kalamatijević survived and decided to change sides, as often happened in Macedonia.[81] As a direct consequence of this attempt fourteen locals, including five females, were arrested, tried and sentenced as guilty for this affair.[82] The stage had been set and Matković did not miss the opportunity.

In the context of the creation of the *Organization against Bulgarian Bandits* Kalamatijević is portrayed as a leader of simple people who were ready to join forces in the creation of a local militia-like organization. In the official history of the organization, however, there is no mention of IMRO *federalist* renegades and their role. Needless to say, there is no mention of the fact that Kalamatijević, once an active member of the IMRO, at the time of the organization's 10th anniversary in 1933 was a 'respectable' member of the Yugoslav parliament.[83]

Soon after its founding in September 1923 the *Organization against Bulgarian Bandits* began to spread beyond Bregalnica County. Already in May of the following year it was stated that the organization had 10,000 members throughout the eastern parts of Macedonia. While members from towns had to pay modest monthly membership fees, members from villages had to participate only in patrol duties. Each village had two on-duty patrols (6-8 members); one was on duty from dusk until midnight and the other from midnight until dawn. Each district within Bregalnica County had its own branch responsible to the organization's headquarters in Štip.[84]

By the time of its 10th anniversary the organization was spread throughout eastern Macedonia or, as it was called at that time, on the 'left bank of the Vardar River', from Kumanovo in the North to Gevgelija in the South. However, by that time it was no longer known as *Organization against Bulgarian Bandits* but simply as *People's Self-Defence* (Narodna Samoodbrana). It was organized as a volunteer militia and its members were known as militiamen.[85] This new paramilitary

---

[81] Ivan Mikhailov, *Spomeni II, Osvoboditelna borba 1919-1924* (Louvain, 1965), 139.

[82] I. Mikhailov, *Spomeni II, Osvoboditelna borba 1919-1924* (Louvain, 1965), p. 728. Most of them, although sentenced on 15 years, were pardoned after two or three years.

[83] *Spomenica proslave dvadesetogodišnjice Bregalničke bitke i desetogodišnjice osnivanja Narodne samoodbrane*, 30-1.

[84] AJ, 334-8-108-12.

[85] *Spomenica proslave dvadesetogodišnjice Bregalničke bitke i desetogodišnjice osnivanja Narodne samoodbrane*, 31.

Fig. 7. Anti-comitaji volunteers from Kratovo.

Throughout the 1920's brand new paramilitary formation *Organization against Bulgarian Bandits* was steadily increasing its presence in eastern parts of Yugoslav Macedonia. Basic units were village and town volunteer bands. This one is from town of Kratovo. By the early 1930's this organization reached number of 25,000 members.

© National Library of Serbia (Belgrade), Album of Nikola Zafirović, 264/LjDf.

formation continued to have good relations with the Yugoslav security apparatus. For example, only in 1930 the Army distributed some 25,000 rifles to the trustworthy people throughout eastern Macedonia, mostly to the members of *People's Self-Defence*.[86] It practically coincides with the organization's own claim that in 1933 they had some 25,000 militiamen-members 'ready, at any moment, to be deployed whenever they are needed to carry out designated assignment, which is exclusively to pursue, apprehend and annihilate Bulgarian bandits infiltrated into our territory'.[87]

Why and how did this transformation from *Organization against Bulgarian Bandits* to *People's Self-Defence* occur?

Again, as with all other above-mentioned issues, several reasons could be responsible for it. First, this kind of transformation or evolution was needed in order to 'win the hearts and minds' of the locals. Their faith and allegiance to

---

[86]   Mile Bjelajac, *Vojska Kraljevine SHS/Jugoslavije 1922–1935* (Beograd: INIS, 1994), 238.

[87]   *Spomenica proslave dvadesetogodišnjice Bregalničke bitke i desetogodišnjice osnivanja Narodne samoodbrane*, 33.

IMRO was probably shaken by the fact that Bulgaria was defeated, and they again had ended up under Serbian rule. Turbulent events within the IMRO itself also contributed to the appearance of specific notions of uncertainty as well as disappointment. From 1919 locals witnessed many *komitajis* becoming simple brigands and smugglers. The IMRO's own internal disputes and ruthless vendetta campaigns, into which organization had fallen after the assassination of Todor Alexandrov, additionally drew attention from the organization's main goal. The name itself, *People's Self-Defence,* had a somewhat stronger populist sound compared to *Organization against Bulgarian Bandits.* It had a better correlation with the notion which its founders, the Yugoslav state and the organization itself, wanted to achieve—the notion of poor and fed-up people from 'South Serbia' who decided to organize themselves in order to protect their properties and ensure their safety. Also, bearing in mind that in two years after the foundation most of the federalist *komitaji* leaders who defected to the Yugoslav side had fallen either in combat or in assassinations organized and executed by *autonomist* rivals (Mita Sokolarski in July 1924,[88] and Stoyan Mishev and Todor Panitsa in 1925), the founders were free to transform the organization according to their own needs.

However, two measures, which were gradually introduced in the following two years, were crucial for organizational transformation:

1. Intensive participation of Serbian *chetnik* veterans in the organization's operations against IMRO intrusions and field organization;
2. Replacing of local heads of communities and districts with temporarily retired officers as well as with members of the patriotic association *National Defence.*

These measures contributed to the slow transformation of the *Organization against Bulgarian Bandits* into a serious and massive paramilitary organization under the new name of *People's Self-Defence* whose members preferred to call themselves militiamen.

As for the score of *People's Self-Defence* ten-year history of clashes (1923-1933) with IMRO bands it encompasses:

1. 128 *komitajis* killed (those whose bodies were left behind since *komitajis* usually extracted their fallen comrades);
2. 13 *komitajis* wounded and 151 captured alive.
3. Militiamen suffered casualties of 59 servicemen killed and 14 wounded.[89]

---

[88] NBKM, BIA, Collection 841 VMRO, Archival unit no. 1/16–18, Central Committee of the IMRO, no. 777, 2 August 1924; see also Angel Uzunov, *Spomeni* (Skopje: Makavej, 2014), 320.
[89] *Spomenica proslave dvadesetogodišnjice Bregalničke bitke i desetogodišnjice osnivanja Narodne samoodbrane,* 33.

The organization's network and massiveness combined with other improvements in safety in the Yugoslav South probably contributed to limiting the IMRO's room for manoeuvre, forcing them to adopt changes in their methods of further struggle. Mainly, it was visible in a shift from 'old school' *komitaji* action, embodied in intrusions of small bands from Bulgarian territory, towards terrorist actions against representatives of Yugoslav civil and military authorities as well as against 'renegades' and 'traitors'. In the following years these actions, combined with setting explosive devices on railroad communications and random attacks on coffee places and other public institutions, became the main methods of IMRO action on Yugoslav soil.

After losing strongholds in Bulgaria during successful *autonomist* raids on Nevrokop in September and Kyustendil in December 1922, the admittance of prominent *federalists* to Yugoslav service solved the pressing issue of operational bases. On Yugoslav soil they were able to reorganize, use existing IMRO infrastructure, deprive *autonomist* bands of their communication channels and support points, and launch new campaigns of intrusion against *autonomist* centres in Bulgaria. For Yugoslav authorities this turn of the tide was the most desirable, but in long term it only contributed to a prolongation of the conflict, continuation of instability, changes of methods and new causalities on both sides.

Beside its place in efforts to suppress IMRO actions, *Peoples Self-defence* was equally important for imposing and demonstrating the 'Serbian character' of Macedonia as well as keeping these areas under the strict control of the Radical Party. That led to numerous misuses, affairs, cases of corruption, extortions, beatings, and different kinds of physical violence. The real extent of this is difficult to determine primarily because in their parliamentary addresses the opposition representatives would often exaggerate the extent of misuses. A similar thing happened with writings in opposition press, especially coming from Croatian parties and communists. However, Vladan Jovanović rightfully concludes that in 'South Serbia' there was a 'combination of bureaucratic and police repression as result of anti-*komitaji* action'.[90]

In different state frameworks (Ottoman, Serbian, Bulgarian, Yugoslav) average Macedonians spent more than two decades in conditions of constant repression and violence combined with the war years 1912–1918, food shortages, and pandemics of infectious diseases. During the 1920's it happened that the inhabitants of Macedonia were harassed both by members of revolutionary-separatist organization and by those who were supposed to protect them. Although the Yugoslav state invested huge efforts in reconstruction, improvements in public health, agriculture, and education like the creation of a university in Skopje, security issues and follow-up repression overshadowed positive developments that happened during twenty-three years of Yugoslav rule over Macedonia.

---

[90]   V. Jovanović, *Jugoslovenska država i Južna Srbija*, 189–201.

During the following decade the IMRO continued to play an important role in the unstable political circumstances of Macedonia. Every spring, words from Bulgaria were listened to with uncertainty, in expectation of the arrival of *chete*. Illegal crossings continued together with diversions, conflicts, assassinations, kidnappings, ambushes and pursuits. The State had to activate all its resources to address this serious problem. Considerable funds for additional payments to the Gendarmerie, Border Troops, linemen and flying detachments were allocated and spent. These funds were also used for the construction of border posts and fortification of parts of the border zone, as well as for compensation of the families of deceased members of the security forces and for ransoms.[91] Because of the IMRO's continuing presence, resilience and ability to transform and adapt, the Yugoslav military leadership came to an idea in the late 1920's to prepare and execute pre-emptive military strikes that would destroy *komitaji* centres in Petrich, Nevrokop, Gornya Dzhumaya and Kyustendil. Preparation and execution of the plan were given to the Third army district. The development of the plan began in the summer of 1930. In December the plan was approved but never implemented in practice.[92]

According to the official Yugoslav assertions, the total list of IMRO activities in the territory of the Kingdom of Yugoslavia in the period between 1919 and 1934 counted 467 different actions like: *komitaji* intrusion, assassinations, ambushes, kidnappings, planted bombs and other forms of military and terrorist operations. In clashes with *komitajis* 185 law enforcement servicemen—military and police—were killed or wounded, while among the civilian population that number, as always, was slightly higher—253. Among law enforcement servicemen the heaviest burden was carried by the members of the Gendarmerie, of which two officers and seventy gendarmes were killed while forty-one gendarmes were wounded. IMRO losses were considerable as well. During the same period of time, they lost 268 activists: killed, wounded and captured.[93]

As for the *kachaks*, according to the Yugoslav authorities from 1921 to 1924, 316 *kachaks* were killed in fighting and 175 were captured. Unlike *komitajis* who after surrender would often enter Yugoslav service, *kachaks* would rather immigrate to Turkey. Of 626 who surrendered the majority left for Turkey with their families. The year of 1924 represented the peak of *kachak* activity when they reached a number of 1,200 active men. However, in Albania, political leaders of the *kachaks* within the Kosovo Committee ended on the opposite side from Ahmed Zogu, a new and ambitious Albanian leader. During the same year he managed to return to power with Yugoslav support after being deposed by opponents, among whom members of the Kosovo Committee played a prominent role.

[91] AJ, 37 Collection of dr. Milan Stojadinović, 37–22/331–3 (Report in English).
[92] Mile Bjelajac, *Vojska Kraljevine SHS/Jugoslavije*, 238.
[93] AJ, 37 Collection of dr. Milan Stojadinović, 37–22/326 (Report in English).

What followed Ahmed Zogu's return to power in December 1924 was the removal of the Kosovo Committee from the Albanian political scene. It happened at the same time as the death of one of the legendary *kachaks*, Azem Bejta, who was killed in action by Yugoslav security forces. His death in September 1924 practically represented the end of mass and organized paramilitary or guerrilla action of Albanians in the Kingdom of Serbs, Croats and Slovenes.[94]

Inability or unwillingness of the Yugoslav state to consolidate these regions and address different organizational, economical and infrastructural issues after decades of crisis and conflicts was another important factor. After a series of changes of cabinets and mutinies Albania reached a sort of stability after 1924 and Ahmed Zogu's definite coming to power. Bulgaria, on the other hand, until 1925 went through waves of red and white terror while simultaneously the IMRO fell into a spiral of internal clashes between different factions that led to a higher death toll than their causalities suffered in actions on Yugoslav soil. Nevertheless, the IMRO never relinquished its firm grip over the Petrich County, which until the 1934 May coup remained the organization's stronghold and source of manpower and financial income.

The Yugoslav kingdom, however, throughout its existence was not able to reach the point that would guarantee undisturbed development. Frequent changes of cabinets, parliamentary and constitutional crises, as well as a royal dictatorship were all combined with developments in international relations. It was important for the Yugoslav part of the 'Balkan border lands' that overall instability strongly reflected on local conditions. Already after the first Serbian attempt to incorporate these areas, which was interrupted by the outbreak of the First World War, it became obvious that this ambitious effort would encounter many difficulties. In just eight years these areas went from Ottoman rule, through Serbian and Montenegrin military and civilian regimes, Austro-Hungarian and Bulgarian occupation towards unification in the Yugoslav state. Together with annexations of territories, changes of administrations, interruption of existing trading routes, forceful migrations, epidemics of different diseases, deprivations, occupations and implementations of denationalization policies. All the above-mentioned experiences left a collective trauma among the local population. Clashes of political parties and struggles for power on all levels facilitated activities and propaganda of foreign actors embodied in bands of the IMRO and Albanian outlaws. In that way it had a prolonged effect. The response of the authorities was often equally violent where frequent usage of paramilitaries created new cycles in the already existing spiral of violence.

---

[94] Dragi Maliković, *Kačački pokret na Kosovu i Metohiji: 1918–1924*, (Leposavić: Institut za srpsku kulturu; Kosovska Mitrovica: Filozofski fakultet 2005), 300.

V

The Age of *Coups d'état*

The immediate post-Great War period in the Balkans, like elsewhere in Europe, was marked by overall unrest and economic instability, turbulent political changes, followed by outbursts of violence. However, unlike elsewhere in Europe period of crisis in the Balkans lasted nearly two decades and was marked by struggle of Bulgarian, Serbian and Greek organizations over Ottoman Macedonia (1903–1912), the Ilinden Uprising (1903), the Young Turk revolution (1908), the Austro-Hungarian annexation of Bosnia and Hercegovina (1908), several consecutive Albanian insurgencies (1909–1912) and finally by the Balkan Wars 1912–1913 and the First World War.

The end of the war in late 1918 did not mean stepping out from the state of emergency. Again, a series of smaller crises followed one after another. The whole region was in turmoil with internal political instabilities. Greece, for example, continued with war engagement for several years after the signing of armistice and peace accords. This time it was an attempt to fulfill its own maximalist national project—The Grand Idea (η $M\epsilon\gamma\acute{a}\lambda\eta$ $\iota\delta\acute{\epsilon}a$)—an expansion in areas of Asia Minor inhabited by a Greek population. Albania, although it managed to renew its independency, was faced with open hostilities and the continued presence of armed forces of its neighbors hoping to achieve territorial gains at Albania's expense. Bulgaria was facing new territorial losses and the newly founded Kingdom of Serbs, Croats and Slovenes was struggling for international recognition. Needless to say, the economical situation did not work in favor to those actors trying to finally remove their countries from war tracks.

Following the breakthrough on the Salonika front, Austro-Hungarian troops, which held positions in Albania, left the country. However, for simple Albanians one occupation was just replaced with another, this time coming from the Entente. The French remained in Korça in the southeast and in Shkodra in the north. The presence of the newly established armed forces of Kingdom of Serbs, Croats and Slovenes on the so-called demarcation line between the two countries was clear sign of the ambition of another Albanian neighbor to gain territorial concession there. After being granted permission by the Allied Supreme Commander in the Balkans, French General Franchet D'Espèrey, the Serbs/Yugoslavs took control of this so-called strategic border in Albania, which went beyond the borders agreed in 1913. Finally, the Italians, who were the ones especially keen to remain in Albania, did this mostly by occupying several strategic points like the southern port of Vlora and the nearby island of Sasseno. This

Paramilitarism in the Balkans: The Cases of Yugoslavia, Bulgaria, and Albania, 1917–1924. Dmitar Tasić,
Oxford University Press (2020). © Dmitar Tasić.
DOI: 10.1093/oso/9780198858324.001.0001

would secure the Albania within the Italian sphere of influence and simultan-eously serve as a stronghold for future penetration into the Balkans. Although the country was in state of instability marked by the constant struggle between sev-eral different actors and groups, in time, some of them have reached consensus over the question of fundamental national interest. The first point was the expul-sion of all foreign occupation forces from Albanian soil, while the second was the simultaneous creation of a stable government with basic state institutions. The first one was much easier to accomplish while the second goal needed several years for its fulfillment. This process was followed by frequent changes of cab-inets, interference from foreign states and clashes among rival groups.[1]

The situation in the Kingdom of Serbs, Croats and Slovenes was rather differ-ent. Although it might appear like a difficult task to join together nations, lands and regions which culturally and religiously were so diverse, (with different alphabets, currencies, judicial systems and legal practices, land ownership regula-tions, traditions etc.), yet somehow unification was achieved with the help of, among other things, an agreed period of ten years designated for harmonization of different regulations. Prosperous and regulated ex-Austria-Hungarian lands of Slovenia and Croatia were about to enter a new state together with the undevel-oped ex-Ottoman Macedonia and Kosovo regions which under the short Serbian and Montenegrin administration before the Great War hadn't been fully inte-grated. Finally, there was so-called pre-Kumanovo Serbia and Montenegro[2]—the only independent states among Yugoslav regions, which passed through their own specific developments, but by 1918 both devastated by three consecutive wars. However, in terms of political stability the Kingdom of Serbs, Croats and Slovenes during its infancy was never endangered by the prospects of coups or revolutions. Apart from several political assassinations and attempts, mostly per-formed by the communists—one of them even on the Prince Regent himself—there were no other similar incidents.[3] Yes, there where internal disputes between

---

[1] On post WWI Albania see: Robert C. Austin, *Founding a Balkan State; Albanian Experiment with Democracy, 1920–1925* (Toronto: University of Toronto Press, 2012); and Bernd J. Fischer, *King Zog and the Struggle for Stability in Albania*, (Tirana: Albanian Institute for International Studies, 2012). However, apart of the fact that their books are good for creation of chronology of events, their research relies solely on Western sources and memoires. Serbian and Yugoslav sources and literature are com-pletely neglected what often led to bias misinterpretations and wrong conclusions. In wish to some-how prove continuity of Serbian/Yugoslav policies towards Albania these authors fail to support their claims with actual documents. Again media coverage from the 1990's led historians to oversimplify picture of historical event and make crucial mistake by observing events from the past with criteria and perspective of present days. Very useful amendment represents excellent and thorough study of Saša Mišić, *Albanija: prijatelj i protivnik, jugoslovenska politika prema Albaniji: 1924–1927*, (Beograd: Službeni glasnik, 2009). It represents useful resource for filling gaps as well as deconstruction of exist-ing myths and black-white picture of relations between Serbs(Yugoslavs) and Albanians.

[2] Common name for the Serbian and Montenegrin territories before the First Balkan War and first Serbian victory in it achieved on 23 and 24 October 1912 in battle of Kumanovo.

[3] Member of the Communist Party of Yugoslavia, Spasoje Stejić, war veteran and ex-volunteer in Serbian army threw hand grenade on carriage with Prince Regent and Speaker of the Parliament Dr. Ivan Ribar. He missed and after being arrested was sentenced to life imprisonment. Outbreak of the

different political parties, especially in relation to the issue of internal regulation of the state, but they occurred under parliamentary conditions. Troubles in Yugoslav South—infiltrations of IMRO *komitajis* from Bulgaria and their activities there as well as re-occurring Albanian insurrections represented serious challenges for the new state, however they couldn't endanger its stability and integrity simply because the Kingdom of Serbs, Croats and Slovenes managed to position itself within new international relations. It was achieved with French support and with creating a new military alliance with Romania and Czechoslovakia. This alliance, also known as The Little Entente, served as a tool against the restoration of the Habsburgs and was a part of *cordon sanitaire* against the threat of eventual communist expansion coming from Soviet Russia.

During the post-Great War period the overall political situation in Bulgaria, was very complex. Part of it was a decades-old conflict between deeply divided groups within Bulgarian society. During this time, these conflicted standpoints and their promoters began to rally on two opposite sides of the Bulgarian political scene. What made it more complicated was presence of the allied occupation forces, along with the arrival of the organized and motivated 'White' Russian émigrés, with echoes of the Russian revolutions and their aftermath. One of the biggest issues was uncertainty related to Bulgarian obligations after the signing of peace accords.

Now, after the defeat in the First World War or the Second National Catastrophe, as it was commonly known, Bulgaria witnessed the rise to power of the Bulgarian Agrarian National Union (BANU)—a unique and original party which for decades had been advocating the interests of the overwhelming majority within Bulgarian society—the simple peasants. Under the leadership of Alexander Stamboliyski, an uncompromising, charismatic and resolute leader, BANU was slowly but securely ascending to power.

However, Stamboliyski as Bulgarian Prime Minister came in position where he would have to reap what he did not sow, that is, to lead Bulgaria in this difficult times caused by the policies he strongly objected. Stamboliyski and his party had a long history of criticizing official Bulgarian policies created by the so-called 'old parties' like the Liberal, Radical and Peoples parties. The agrarians also criticized political involvement and the attitudes of king Ferdinand. The agrarians strongly objected pre-Balkan Wars military buildup as something directed against the Bulgarian farmers who would be the first to spill their blood in case of war. They also criticized Bulgarian policy related to the Macedonian issue and consequences

WWII brought him freedom which he used, to continue fighting as member of Yugoslav partisans. There, he was able to meet Dr. Ivan Ribar, a man he had almost killed more than twenty years ago. Ribar, following his two sons, also joined partisan forces and after the war again became Speaker of the Parliament—Vladimir Dedijer, *Novi prilozi za biografiju Josipa Broza Tita. 1*, (Zagreb: Mladost, 1980), 89.

of the Second Balkan war. As a result of objections regarding Bulgaria's joining the Central Powers, Stamboliyski was imprisoned during the Great War.

After the war, beside traditional parties, now grouped in so-called Constitutional Bloc, the agrarians got the new rival. It was the newly established Communist Party, which represented the old party of 'narrow' socialists but with its name changed and stronger connections with Soviet Russia. The main reason for agrarian attitudes toward communism was the communist's doctrine regarding the 'changes of the social order in the countryside' which was already in action in Soviet Russia. This is where the two parties came into conflict because Stamboliyski and BANU were very critical towards the Bolshevik's policy of collectivization and communist attitude on peasants as small capitalists and thus the enemy of the revolution.

As for the Bulgarian armed forces, i.e. its officer's and reserve officer's corps it happened that once numerous, proud and elite social group with the collective conviction of special importance and mission for the national cause, after the Great War went through gradual decrease in numbers as one by one units were disbanded and conscription and compulsory service abolished. Discharged officers, reserve officers and NCO's founded a secret *Military League* and the official *Association of Reserve Officers*. Within these organizations they went beyond the usual activities aimed at protection of existential rights and improvement of social status of their members—discharged officers and NCO's who, in order to survive and support their families were forced to find jobs like tutors, taxi-drivers, bell-boys and porters. By continuing everyday life, at the same time feeling humiliated and frustrated, they evolved into well-organized, disciplined and motivated para-military formations ready to step into the action. In their case, the presence of a strong 'culture of defeat' acted as mobilizing factor for future actions, which would lead to the restoration of old regime. Needless to say, that Stamboliyski, because his pre-war open critics targeted army, privileged status of the officer's corps, procurement of modern weapons, and military build-up in general, had a special place in future plans and actions of *Military League*.[4]

Another factor that Stamboliyski had to take in mind were the *komitajis* of the IMRO. The allied artillery barrage at Dobro Polje in September 1918 suddenly interrupted their daydream of Macedonia finally unified with Bulgaria—what followed was a nightmare. Not only that the territory itself was again lost, but waves of refugees, especially from the Aegean or Greek part of Macedonia, started to

---

[4] Detailed analyses of BANU relations with the armed forces, military organizations, left and right political parties and IMRO in: Veselin Yaanchev, *Armiya, obshtestven red i vatreshna sigurnost mezhdu voynite i sled tyaah: 1913–1915, 1918–1923* (Sofia: Universitetsko izdatelstvo 'Sv. Kliment Ohridski', 2014). Although some of the authors interpretations and conclusions could be considered biased or politically coloured (in terms of his somewhat critical attitude towards the BANU and its role and place in modern Bulgarian history) thoroughness of his research and number of facts presented make this study of primal importance.

arrive in Bulgaria dramatically changing the ethnic structure of that region. In the case of Yugoslav or the Vardar part of Macedonia, the story of the immediate post-war situation regarding the refugees was somewhat different. Most of the Vardar Macedonians who during the Great War joined Bulgarian army, where they fought in the ranks of their own 11th Macedonian division, decided to remain in Bulgaria separated from their families. In addition, in Bulgaria there was already significant number of Macedonians who for years used to live there but hadn't lost the connection with their homeland. Finally, the core of the IMRO—its leadership and a never precisely determined number of *komitajis* also decided, or were forced to, remain in Bulgaria. So, how the IMRO attitude toward the BANU government would look like depended on how the new Bulgarian government would address the Macedonian Question. What became obvious during 1919 was that Bulgaria could only expect new territorial losses; not only in the territories it was claiming or had recently kept under its realm—like Macedonia, but also in territories which were its constituent parts. In this case, those were Thrace and several enclaves the on Yugoslav—Bulgarian border. Additional territorial losses would only mean problems for the agrarian government.

Another issue was presence of a well-organized and armed military organization of 'White' Russians who arrived in Bulgaria, as well as to other Balkan countries after the Bolsheviks inflicted the final blow on Crimea in late 1920.

On top of that, there was a considerable military presence of the Entente troops in Bulgaria and a lot of things depended on the local allied commander. Even before the peace agreement was signed, allied troops (mostly French) were conducting actions of collecting weapons from the disbanded Bulgarian army units. Allies were also controlling where they were stored. In August 1920 these duties were handed over to the Inter-allied Military Control Commission.[5]

As a result of the above-mentioned, Stamboliyski and BANU had restricted maneuvering space. A prominent member of the IMRO, Angel Uzunov, summarized the position of the BANU in his memoirs:

"It is well known how and in what manner A. Stamboliyski and his associates came to power. His rule would be longer and more successful if just he and his like-minded were more tactical and comprehensive...Mistakes made by agrarians went one after another...Agrarians entered into conflict with everyone thinking differently: with state administration, with judiciary, with priests, with the army, even with the communists which for long have been their associates..."[6]

---

[5] Veselin Yaanchev, *Armiya, obshtestven red i vatreshna sigurnost mezhdu voynite i sled tyaah: 1913-1915, 1918-1923* (Sofia: Universitetsko izdatelstvo 'Sv. Kliment Ohridski', 2014), 232.

[6] Angel Uzunov, *Spomeni* (Skopje: Makavej, 2014), 269.

In relation to foreign policy, any concession they would make towards their neighbors would automatically create a new enemy within the country. Although the agrarians demonstrated willingness to restore the good relations with the Kingdom of Serbs, Croats and Slovenes and Greece, the general feeling in these two countries was that it was too early for full reconciliation.

The Balkan Wars of 1912 and 1913 resulted in the creation of an independent Albanian state. It was an expected outcome of the Albanian national revival that started in 1878 and the creation of the *Prizren League*.[7] The newly founded state wasn't near the territorial extent that was initially demanded—four European vilayets of the Ottoman Empire (Shkodra, Ioannina, Monastir and Kosovo). At the time of proclamation in 1913, only the territories of Vlora and its hinterland were under the control of those who proclaimed independence. All other territories were still under the control of the Ottoman, Serbian, Montenegrin and Greek troops. In addition, the intervention of the Great Powers brought to Albania a German prince, Wilhelm zu Wied, as its sovereign, although there were numerous candidates.[8] Albanian independence was short lived however, Prince Wilhelm was forced to leave the country the same year he had arrived (1914), while Albania after the outbreak of the Great War, sank into chaos that was ended by the creation of the Macedonian front in 1916. For the rest of the war, Albania was occupied by the Austro-Hungarian Empire and the Entente—Italians and French. And while the Italians deployed substantial forces throughout south Albania, the French allowed the Albanians to establish an autonomous region in the town of Korça which functioned from 1916 until 1918.[9]

Albanian history of overturns after the Great War had been marked by the intensive engagement of a remarkable political figure named Ahmed-bey Zogu. Before Ahmed-bey Zogu managed to restore and reassure his power in December 1924 as Albanian Prime Minister, his country went through several years of its own soul searching marked by political and economic instability caused by inherited backwardness as well as differing views on how Albania should be arranged as a state. Among many distinctive personalities on the Albanian political scene at the time he proved to be the one with better understanding of the spirit of the time in which he had to operate.

So, who was Ahmed-bey Zogu? Born in 1895, a second son of Xhemal-pasha, a chieftain of the central Albanian clan Mati, young Ahmed-bey witnessed the turbulent changes that occurred in South East Europe at the beginning of the 20th century. He stayed for several years in Constantinople as hostage to the Ottoman throne. There he managed to obtain a basic education in the elite Galatasaray High School and Military Academy in Monastir. He was just 16 when in 1911 he

[7] Peter Bartl, *Albanci, od srednjeg veka do danas* (Beograd: CLIO, 2002) 92.
[8] P. Bartl, *Albanci, od srednjeg veka do danas*, 138–48.
[9] P. Bartl, *Albanci, od srednjeg veka do danas*, 178.

was summoned from Constantinople to lead his clan in one of the Albanian uprisings against the Young Turk regime. That is how his political engagement began. During the Balkan Wars he was again leading his clansmen when he witnessed how 'the Ottoman Empire, which for five centuries had been both an oppressor and a protector was finally on the verge of collapse and the Albanians were forcibly extracted from their long Medieval sleep and thrust into the twentieth century'[10]—this statement represents the most accurate description of the beginnings of Albanian independence and Ahmed-bey Zogu's involvement in it.

The chaotic infancy of Albanian statehood had been marked by the introduction of the Protestant Prince Wilhelm zu Wied as Albanian sovereign; and by the huge ambitions of Zogu's uncle, Esad-pasha Toptani.[11] Ahmed-bey skillfully maneuvered between two maintaining his status of the Mati clan chieftain. During a religiously motivated insurgency against Prince Wilhelm in 1914, Ahmed-bey initially supported his cause, however, after realizing how weak his positions were, Ahmed-bey was smart enough to let his short-time sovereign go 'down the drain'. Success of the insurgents made for a confusing Albanian situation and their search for identity and was marked by the hoisting of the Ottoman colors over the port of Durres—the colors of the state which had vanished from the Balkans. Ahmed-bey's maneuverability is visible from the fact that just before the outbreak of the Great War his name could be found on a list of Albanian magnates and important persons financed by the Serbian government. In October 1915, he even visited Belgrade where he met the Serbian Prime Minister Nikola Pašić, however, details of their conversation remain unknown.[12] Nevertheless, during the course of the Great War, Ahmed-bey found himself on the opposite side of his uncle. During the 1915 war campaign in the Balkans, Albania was occupied by both warring sides and was divided. Esad-pasha followed columns of his retreating Serbian allies and went to Greece, while Ahmed-bey joined the Austro-Hungarians who promoted him to the rank of Colonel and gave him the task of recruiting Albanians for their auxiliary units. After witnessing how untrustworthy he was, they 'invited' him to Vienna where he stayed until the end of the war enjoying life and gaining new knowledge and skills. When he returned to Albania in 1919 he was ready to re-engage in the struggle for Albanian independence. He participated in the Congress of Lushnjë in January 1920. Following that, Ahmed-bey Zogu fully demonstrated his political skills obtained through his family legacy, his education and life in Constantinople; and his wartime stay in Vienna. Between 1920 and 1922, he acted as the Minister of Interior and after that as Minister of War. By the end of 1922 he was Prime Minister. He stayed in

---

[10] Bernd J. Fischer, *King Zog and the Struggle for Stability in Albania*, (Tirana: Albanian Institute for International Studies, 2012), 5.

[11] Ahmed-bey mother Sadije was sister of Esad-pasha Toptani.

[12] Saša Mišić, *Albanija: prijatelj i protivnik, jugoslovenska politika prema Albaniji: 1924–1927*, (Beograd: Službeni glasnik, 2009), 25.

power until February 1924 when there was an attempt on his life and after being overthrown in June 1924 he managed to organize a counter-coup and return to power in December.[13]

The complexity of the Albanian political scene, in spite of its overall backwardness and underdevelopment, was a fair representation of the complexity and diversity of Albanian society. After the Great War two major groups appeared on the Albanian political scene—the Progressives and the Democrats. While they were usually referred to as political parties, they represented something more akin to parliamentary factions and interest groups with no strict notion of party membership and allegiance as in modern terms. Transfers to the opposing side were common practice as well as the creation of temporary 'single issue groups'. Although the name suggests otherwise, the Progressives resembled the conservatives. The fact that the former Ottoman feudal lords or beys constituted the core of this group spoke for itself. As for the Democrats, their agenda was appropriate to their name, the transformation of Albania in the modern Western state, however their ambition often encountered the harsh realities of Albanian backwardness and non-familiarity with the institutions of modern democratic states. The Progressives, on the contrary, were fully aware of Albanian realities, however, their slow progress was often considered as conformity or adjustment rather than a sincere wish for reforms. Eqrem-bey Vlora, a prominent member of the Progressives, in his memoirs described why:

"Throughout history only authoritative factor in Albania was its high class, which depending on its position, wealth, and authority had been named as high or low nobility."[14]

In the following years, clashes between the Democrats and the Progressives dictated the dynamics of the Albanian political scene. Other important players in Albania were the different nationalist organizations, most importantly was the Kosovo Committee. Like Bulgaria, where the IMRO essentially became the organization in emigration but with strong influences both on the Bulgarian political scene and in Yugoslav Macedonia, by the end of the Great War in Albania started to operate the Kosovo Committee—an organization founded by Kosovar Albanians whose political leaders like Hasan Prishtina and Bayram Curri, couldn't reconcile with the fact that Kosovo and Metohija ended under Serbian, i.e. Yugoslav rule. Anyone on the Albanian political scene ready to support Kosovar's claims would automatically become an ally, while all others became

[13] Zogu, Ahmet (08.10.1895–09.04.1961)—Robert Elsie, *A Biographical Dictionary of Albanian History*, (London; New York: B. Tauris, 2013), 507.
[14] Ekrem-beg Vlora, *Sekavanjata ot životot. Tom II*, (1921–1925) (Skopje: Fondacija Otvoreno opštestvo, 2015), 185.

bitter enemies. The Kosovo Committee, like the IMRO, with whom at one point they entered into an alliance, was able to have considerable impact on developments both in Albania and the Kingdom of Serbs, Croats and Slovenes. In Albania this was achieved through official politics, parliamentary struggle, coups and rebellions and in the Kingdom of Serbs, Croats and Slovenes, through guerrilla actions of its supporters or *kachaks,* which for several years led the armed resistance of Kosovar Albanians against the Yugoslav state. Another organization that had influence on events on the Albanian political scene in the early 1920's was *Bashkimi* (Unification)—a nationalist association of primarily young students who saw assassination as a legitimate tool of the political struggle. Other groups or associations, with primarily cultural and patriotic agendas, but oriented against domination of Muslim magnates and landowners, were the *Atdheu* (Fatherland), *Vatra* (Hearth), *Ora et Maleve* (Fairy of the Mountains).[15] Finally, however strong was the political influence of the different groups and organizations in Albania, at the end of the day everything depended on how many heavily armed supporters they could rally to the cause. Beside above-mentioned *kachaks* who operated with the Kosovo Committee, the clan militias proved to be equally important, like the Mati clan militia in case of Ahmed Zogu and other northern mountain clans. Other important players were the paramilitary groups from east Albania, for example the so-called 'Dibrans'—from the town of Dibra (Debar in Macedonia), a former administrative center of the area, which after the Great War became part of Kingdom of Serbs, Croats and Slovenes. Some 'Dibrans', like Taf Kazi and Hallil Lleshi used to be lieutenants in the paramilitary organization of Esad-pasha Toptani until Toptani was assassinated in 1920. Kazi and Lleshi, having at their disposal the remainder of Esad-pasha's paramilitary structures (once financed by Yugoslavs as *Battalions of Organized Albanians*) turned into simple mercenaries. Others, like Elez Isufi remained available 'on the market' to anyone willing to provide compensation for his services.[16] All the above-mentioned players participated in the dynamic struggle for stability of their homeland. However, the real power in Albania lay within the so-called *clique*—secret society which resembled to Turkish Committee for Union and Progress. It was a group of politicians, magnates, national workers etc. Its composition used to change according to their needs and goals, which usually was related exclusively to personal enrichment and promotion. Ahmed-bey Zogu skillfully manipulated the *clique* by having it on his side for most of the time between 1920 and 1924.[17]

---

[15] Robert C. Austin, *Founding a Balkan State; Albanian Experiment with Democracy, 1920–1925* (Toronto: University of Toronto Press, 2012), 11.

[16] Isufi Elez (1861–29.12.1961)—Robert Elsie, *A Biographical Dictionary of Albanian History,* (London; New York: B. Tauris, 2013), 215.

[17] Bernd J. Fischer, *King Zog and the Struggle for Stability in Albania,* (Tirana: Albanian Institute for International Studies, 2012), 27–8.

When the war was finally over, Bulgaria also entered a period of overall instability. Economic instability was exacerbated by the political uncertainty. Most state institutions, other than parliament and government, did not function properly. The Army was in turmoil, and the police likewise. Announcements of strikes and demonstration on railroads and mines threatened to paralyze the country. The IMRO continued with incursions across the Yugoslav and Greek borders but at the same time the organization was torn apart by the internal discord followed by armed clashes. The rule that whenever state institutions are in crisis, there exists considerable space, which is almost always taken by non-traditional political players, in this case it was the paramilitaries. As a result, Bulgaria became fertile ground for paramilitarism and paramilitary violence as its final product. Almost every actor on the Bulgarian political scene had a paramilitary structure or was in the process of establishing one—the Constitutional Bloc had the *Military League* and to some extent could count on the military structures of the Russian 'White' émigrés. The Communist had their own secret military organization, the IMRO had their own experienced, battle-hardened and always-ready-for-actions *komitaji* bands and even the BANU was in the process of creating its own paramilitary force, the *Orange Guard*. In that sense the period between 1919 and 1924 represented the 'Golden Era' of Bulgarian paramilitarism. The climax of the Bulgarian paramilitarism was reached with the June coup of 1923, and the assassination of Prime Minister Stamboliyski and subsequent attempt of a communist revolution in September of the same year. However, the political stability of the Bulgarian state remained under question. One of the reasons for this was the continuation of internal clashes within the IMRO and the extreme violence that followed these clashes as well as the IMRO occupation of Petrich County where they practically created and administrated a 'state within the state'.

Despite being devastated by the war, focused on the struggle for the international recognition and regulation of their borders respectively, the Kingdom of Serbs, Croats and Slovenes and Albania showed a strong willingness to overcome the obstacles they encountered after the war. In the Yugoslav case it was much easier taking into account the long democratic and state-building traditions in both ex-Serbian and ex-Austro-Hungarian parts as well as its affiliation to the group of countries that achieved victory in the Great War. During the initial years of Yugoslav existence there were no indications of radical political changes through coups or revolutions marked by the exceptional participation of the paramilitaries. Like elsewhere in contemporary Europe, there was the presence of general fear related to possible subversive activities of communist movement but it was more a fear of the unknown which had already demonstrated its capabilities for the introduction of drastic social changes and international expansion. Nevertheless, political instability of the Kingdom of Serbs, Croats and Slovenes has been epitomized in frequent changes of cabinets, which marked the entire mid-war life of the Yugoslav state. Albania, on the other hand, until 1924, witnessed a short period of instability due to its own economic, infrastructural and institutional underdevelopment, internal divisions and political diversity. After the final coup in 1924 which brought Ahmed-bey back to power, Albania entered period of political stability, at least in terms of frequent changes of cabinets. Again, even the introduction of political stability was connected with paramilitarism. The enterprise of Ahmed-bey return to power represented a combination of actions of Yugoslav-sponsored paramilitaries (in this particular case Russian 'White' émigrés), the Yugoslav regular army (that acted as paramilitaries) and Ahmed-bey loyal clan militias. It had both brought him back to power and sealed the faith of his opposition.

Bulgarian 1923

June Coup d'état

The preparation and the course of the coup was a well-organized and precisely planned and determined endeavor. The coup itself was prepared and designed by (para)military structures of the *Military League* and *Association of Reserve officers* and performed primarily by the Bulgarian army with massive support from members of the above mentioned organizations who acted as 'volunteers'. Subsequent interpretations and controversies over the 9 June coup, however, even today, speak of deep divisions that existed within the Bulgarian society and its political establishment.[18]

The first ideas of putsch started to circulate among *Military League* members after the events in Veliko Turnovo in late 1922 when numerous BANU supporters, organized in *People's Orange Guard,* managed to prevent a political rally of the so-called Constitutional Bloc—a coalition of parties opposing agrarian rule, i.e. the United Peoples Progressive Party, the Democratic Party and the Radical Democratic Party. This rally was not wholly unexpected as for some time the voices of dissent could be heard from the political right looking to initiate a series of 'hammering blows' against the agrarian government. In fact, leaders of the old parties repeatedly expressed their determination to overthrow the agrarian regime. In response to that the agrarians had already taken measures contributing to the radicalization of the political scene. In previous congress, under the initiative of younger activists, the agrarians created a Committee on Peasant Dictatorship to adequately answer any threat imposed by the parties of the right. They had already envisioned the establishment of a 'peasant dictatorship' as an answer to any attempt to overthrow the government.

---

[18] Veselin Yaanchev, *Armiya, obshtestven red i vatreshna sigurnost mezhdu voynite i sled tyaah: 1913–1915, 1918–1923* (Sofia: Universitetsko izdatelstvo 'Sv. Kliment Ohridski', 2014), 390–416.

On 17 September, on their way to a rally at Veliko Turnovo, leaders of the Constitutional Bloc were stopped at a small railway station in Dolni D'bni. Masses of local peasants disarmed the Constitutional Bloc supporters and publicly humiliated their leaders; Andrey Liyapchev, Alexander Malinov, Stoyan Danev, Mikhail Madzharev and others, by shaving off their beards and moustaches. Only the presence of Rayko Daskalov, acting Prime Minister—since Stamboliyski was attending peace talks in Lausanne—saved them. Daskalov was also in the same train going to Veliko Turnovo, to address—ironically, a convention of sugar-beet growers! However, the ordeal of the opposition leaders continued in Veliko Turnovo where they were nearly court martialed and executed. Again Daskalov stepped in and saved them.[19] Meanwhile, the armed supporters of the Constitutional Bloc dispersed. At the same time on 16 September, the IMRO organized an armed action in the town of Nevrokop in pursuit of rivals from the *federalist* faction. However, they also attacked a small, local garrison taking soldiers as prisoners and looted their weapons and equipment. *Federalists*, including one of their leaders Todor Panitsa, managed to leave town under fight.[20] This action represented a serious challenge to the agrarian authorities.

After these incidents a decision was made that would lead to the further (para) militarization of the agrarian *Orange Guard*. A complete new branch of the guard was established consisting of those guard members with horses and it was called the *Agrarian Mounted Guard*. The idea was to have something like the 'flying detachments' that could act as a rapid response unit to any attempt the opposition might launch. Daskalov was named as their commander.[21] Tensions between the agrarians and the opposition continued to rise as in November a referendum was organized related to the proclamation of the *Law for Prosecution of Ministers from three cabinets* responsible for participation in Bulgarian war defeats. Because law was passed with a considerable majority, the opposition became even more determined to overthrow the agrarian regime.

One of the first steps of the conspirators was to conduct a secret survey among the officers of the regular army regarding their willingness to participate in the organization and execution of the coup. The next step was to determine the dates for action and to design an adequate plan. By May 1923, the leadership of the *Military League* has agreed that the coup take place between 25 May and 10 June, with the coup finally happening at 03.00 am on 9 June. The plan ran smoothly throughout Bulgaria when the designated army units supported by 'volunteers' from the *Military League* and *Association of Reserve Officers* took control over the

---

[19] Dimitrina Petrova, *B'lgarskiyat zemedelski naroden s'yuz 1899–1944*, (Sofia: Fond Detelina, 1999), 99–100.

[20] Veselin Yaanchev, *Armiya, obshtestven red i vatreshna sigurnost mezhdu voynite i sled tyaah*, 302–3.

[21] Dimitrina Petrova, *D-r Rajko Daskalov (1886–1923): politik i drzhavnik reformator*, (Stara Zagora: Znanie, 1995), 34.

important state institutions, railway stations, telegraph posts, police stations, and army depots. They disarmed the agrarian *Orange Guard* and arrested their ministers and leading activists. All active army officers that did not support the coup were placed under house arrest.

What made this plan successful, beside military efficiency and precision, was the fact that the conspirators already had a plan in place for political change, i.e. the establishment of a new government. This was to come about under the auspices of the university professor, Alexander Tsankov, who was the leader of the *People's Covenant*, a group of non-party political figures and intellectuals or members of the second echelon of the Constitutional Bloc. Tsankov in fact pushed the conspirators to rush with the preparations and execution of the coup. He established first contact with the *Military League* in 1920 openly asking them to discuss the possibility of military action against the agrarians.[22] The issue that clouded the whole endeavor was the attitude of Tsar Boris III who was introduced to the *League's* intention to execute the coup, in the hope of obtaining his approval for the action, which was a precondition of many *League* members for their participation. However, the Tsar refused to give his opinion on the matter prior the execution of the coup. Tsankov, who obviously didn't suffer from the need for formalities, vividly described the Tsar's position of essentially 'hedging his bets': 'If the coup shows to be successful he will bless you, if not, you will hang.' However, the Tsar eventually acknowledged the new order and decided to sign the necessary instructions and decrees of appointment of the new Prime Minister, which were already on June 9 published in State Gazette thus legalizing paradoxical 'non-constitutional change in the name of return into the constitutional standards'. The Army and the police were immediately purged of pro-agrarian elements, while the 'volunteers' from the *Association of Reserve Officers* preserved public order.[23]

Despite sporadic manifestation of resistance, the coup was executed equally efficiently in the province. Those agrarian leaders who were not in the capital at the time of the coup attempted to organize their supporters. The agrarian Minister of Justice Spas Duparinov tried to alarm the Plovdiv countryside. Another prominent agrarian Alexander Obov managed to gather some 17,000 peasants and lead them in an attempt to take the town of Pleven. Georgi Damianov tried to mobilize the *Orange Guard* around the town of Orkhanie (today's Botevgrad), but although being an experienced leader, since he assisted Daskalov during the Radomir Rebellion, he suffered defeat. Others were also unlucky. Their failures

---

[22] John D. Bell, *Peasants in Power: Alexander Stamboliiski and the Bulgarian Agrarian National Union 1899–1923*, (Princeton: Princeton University Press, 1977), 209.

[23] Veselin Yaanchev, *Armiya, obshtestven red i vatreshna sigurnost mezhdu voynite i sled tyaah*, 395; and John D. Bell, *Paesants in Power. Alexander Stamboliyski and the Bulgarian Agrarian National Union*, 230. In historiography exists general claim that tsar himself was the *spiritus movens* of the whole enterprise.

were as a result of a simple fact that despite their numbers and training (the majority were Great War veterans), the agrarians were poorly armed and they couldn't match the joined forces of the regular army and the *Military League*. All the above-mentioned agrarian officials were apprehended apart from Obov who managed to escape and find refuge in Romania.[24]

Following its own ideological principles, the Communist Party had already on June 9 instructed its members to remain neutral, not to interfere in internal conflict between urban and rural bourgeoisies; and to decline 'any kind of support' to both the old and the new government.[25] Thus the communists essentially facilitated the overthrow of the BANU government. Vasil Kolarov, one of the leaders of the BKP—at that time in Moscow—already on 14 June criticized the official position of his party urging them to assist the agrarians because otherwise the new authorities would consolidate their positions and turn against the communists.[26] As soon as they realized their own shortsightedness already on 23 June, the Executive Committee of Communist International (Comintern) issued a proclamation calling on Bulgarian laborers and peasants to fight against the capitalist administration and for the establishment of a laborer-peasant government.[27] A special section of this call was dedicated to Macedonians who were 'deceived by bourgeois and drawn into bloody conflict'.

No matter how efficient and relatively bloodless the course of the coup was, with only a total count of eighty-nine killed throughout the country, the participation of another mighty actor colored the whole endeavor with well-documented examples of extreme brutality. The IMRO itself was not included in the organization and execution of the coup although it possessed manpower and organizational know-how. The main reason behind such an omission was the fear that their involvement might provoke the reaction of Bulgarian neighbors, primarily Kingdom of Serbs, Croats and Slovenes. However, the IMRO leadership was aware of preparations and when approached by the conspirators they declined the offer calling the whole matter an 'internal Bulgarian affair and act of Bulgarian patriots', adding however, 'we would appreciate more different government which would not prosecute us'.[28]

---

[24] John D. Bell, *Paesants in Power. Alexander Stamboliyski and the Bulgarian Agrarian National Union*, 238.

[25] *Kominternat i Balgariya, tom I, Dokumenti*, (Sofia: Glavno upravlenie na arhivite pri Ministerskiya Syvet, 2005), 75, No. 13, Poziv na CK na BKP k'm selyanite i rabotnicite v Balgriya.

[26] *Kominternat i Balgariya, tom I, Dokumenti*, 77, No. 14, Radiotelegrama na V. Kolarov do CK na BKP otnosno zaetata ot BKP poziciya k'm prevrata na 9 yuni 1923. g.

[27] *Kominternat i Balgariya, tom I, Dokumenti*, 78, No. 16, V'zvaniye na IKKI k'm b'lgarskire rabotnici iselyanite s priziv da se vdignat na borba sreshtu prevratadzhiite i za ustanovyavane na rabotichesko-selsko pravitelstvo.

[28] Zoran Todorovski, *Todor Aleksandrov*, (Skopje: Makavej; Državen arhiv na Republika Makedonija, 2014), 213.

Unlike the *Military League*, the IMRO was already in a state of war with the agrarian regime. The main reasons were strongly related to the Macedonian Question. The fact that leaders of the IMRO, Protogerov and Alexandrov, after the Great War did not intend to give up their activities in Macedonia, did not suit the agrarian regime. Continuation of IMRO incursions across the Yugoslav border would threaten the international position of Bulgaria and deepen the conflict with its neighbors. One of the first encounters between the BANU and the IMRO was in early November 1919 when the action of 'mass arrests of those persons responsible for the catastrophe of Bulgaria' had been initiated. Targets were prominent journalists, General Protogerov, Todor Alexandrov and most of the former ministers.[29] Some sixty people were apprehended according to the provisions of the *Law for trial and punishment of culprits for national catastrophe*.[30] However, the powerlessness of the government became obvious when Alexandrov and Protogerov escaped from prison soon after[31] and the IMRO continued to operate undisturbed. This incident reinforced and confirmed the earlier assumptions that the IMRO had enough power to function effectively without the assistance of the Bulgarian state. Soon after, on 27 November a peace treaty with Bulgaria was signed in Neuilly.[32] In addition to territorial losses, (Dobruja, Thrace and towns Caribrod, Bosilegrad, Strumica), Bulgaria had to reduce its army to 20,000 men, surrender its fleet and agree to pay war reparations. Macedonia was not even mentioned as a disputed territory.[33] The Prime Minister Stamboliyski did not hide his bitterness over the character of peace, whose provisions were very demanding for Bulgarians and Bulgaria in general. His opinion about the terms of peace being difficult and unfair were recorded—especially in terms of territorial guidelines. He also stated how the treaty did not resolve the Balkan problem, but that Bulgaria would take care to responsibly fulfill its provisions.[34]

However, the BANU formed the majority government on 27 May 1920 and new foreign policy objectives were set out:

- exit of Bulgaria from isolation,
- struggle to reduce the amount of war reparations,
- return of Aegean Thrace, or getting a limited exit to the Aegean Sea,
- protection of the Bulgarian national minority in neighboring countries.

[29] VA, r. 4/3, b. 54, f. 13, d. 12/198, Report of the delegate Of Supreme command in Sofia to the command of Third army district from 6 November 1919. (no number).

[30] Zoran Todorovski, *Avtonomistička VMRO na Todor Aleksandrov 1919-1924*, (Skopje: Makavej, 2013), 64.

[31] VA, r. 4/3, b. 56, f. 9, d. 2/275, Report of the delegate of Supreme command in Sofia to the command of Third army district, confidential no. 803 from 29 November 1919.

[32] 'Bugari potpisali', *Politika*, no. 4247 from 28 November 1919, p. 3.

[33] Čedomir Popov, *Od Versaja do Danciga* (Beograd: Službeni list SRJ, 1995), 137.

[34] Vasil Vasilev, *Pravitelstvo na BZNS, VMRO i B'lgaro-Yugoslavskite otnosheniya*, (Sofia: BAN, 1991), 39.

In order to achieve these objectives, they counted on: support of the Great Powers and support from the League of Nations, strengthening the role of democratic forces in the international politics, and strengthening of the international position of Bulgaria with, if possible, the closest bonds with the Kingdom of Serbs, Croats and Slovenes.[35]

Stamboliyski's rapprochement with the IMRO arch-enemy—Serbia (Yugoslavia) and BANU's support of the *federalist* faction of the IMRO were other reasons for the continuation of conflict. The first victim was the Minister of Interior and Army Alexander Dimitrov, who was killed by the notorious *komitaji voivode* Pancho Mikhailov-Chavdar and Ivan Yanev-B'rlyo in October 1921. That was the end of Dimitrov's intensive engagement against the *autonomist* faction. A year earlier, Alexandrov sent him warning letter entitled 'First warning', simply telling him that if he continued to introduce measures against the *autonomist* bands, supports the creation of the *federalist* bands, and assists in their deployment on Yugoslav territory 'he will lose his head'. After Dimitrov's meeting with Yugoslav Prime Minister Nikola Pašić in June 1921 when they agreed that the *komitaji* action represented the apple of discord between two countries and that it had to be stopped, the decision to kill Dimitrov was put into action. However, the death of Dimitrov did not mean the end of the IMRO conflict with the agrarians.[36]

After the incident in Nevrokop, the IMRO showed to be even more insolent when on 4 December 1922 they repeated the Nevrokop scenario, this time in Kyustendil. Although local military and civilian authorities had been aware of the presence of large numbers of IMRO *komitajis* in the vicinity of Kyustendil they didn't do anything to prevent it. A significant, but not precisely determined number of *komitajis* entered the town, interned local garrison and police forces, and after apprehending some ten members of the *federalist* faction, organized their public execution. They also used the opportunity to publicly read the death sentences against several agrarian top officials including Stamboliyski and Daskalov. Although acting-Prime Minister Daskalov dispatched Minister of Army Tomov to suppress the IMRO incursion, Tomov entered into negotiations with the IMRO leader Pancho Mikhailov. Meanwhile, the *Orange Guard* was summoned from northern and central Bulgaria and some 2,000 came to Sofia by special trains. On arrival they went on a rampage against editorial staffs of the opposition press as well as several embassies and they were placed in the army barracks of the Sofia

---

[35] V. Vasilev, *Pravitelstvo na BZNS*, 40.
[36] Z. Todorovski, *Todor Aleksandrov*, 206–207.

garrison. Minister Tomov, instead of quelling the obvious mutiny, returned to Sofia accepting the IMRO demands, which included:

1. A government hand over to the IMRO all of those who participated in plundering in Macedonia and who committed murders of the IMRO activists;
2. A ban on the presence of any Macedonians in Sofia and Kyustendil without permission of the IMRO;
3. Prime Minister to publicly correct his statements made in Belgrade regarding the Macedonian Question, and to terminate provocations against IMRO activists.[37]

Tomov and his detachment left Kyustendil while *komitajis* withdrew across the border to Yugoslav territory. While Tomov considered his action as triumphant all the others saw it as capitulation and what followed was the introduction of military rule in southwest Bulgaria.

Despite agrarian reluctance to use the *Orange Guard* against serious IMRO provocations, their conflict gradually intensified. During the Kyustendil incident, in its well-known dramatic and theatrical style, the IMRO sentenced Stamboliyski and several prominent members of BANU to death. Needless to say, the *komitaji's* tried to execute the sentence even before the coup. The first one to avoid death was Rayko Daskalov when hand grenades were thrown at him while he was leaving National Assembly in December 1922. Stamboliyski himself also avoided death when during the celebration at the National Theatre on February 4 1923 hand grenades were thrown at his box.[38] Because of these attempts, the BANU entered into open war with the IMRO. However, during the spring of 1923 with growing support for their cause, some election success, and the signing of agreements with the Kingdom of Serbs, Croats and Slovenes on security issues, and with Allies on war reparations, the agrarians mistook these signs and they became overconfident. At one point, after watching a parade of a thousand members of the *Agrarian Mounted Guard*, Stamboliyski claimed:

> "Do not think that the government will fall...but believe that Agrarian rule will continue for twenty-five years. Who can overthrow us?"[39]

---

[37] Veselin Yaanchev, *Armiya, obshtestven red i vatreshna sigurnost mezhdu voynite i sled tyaah*, 312–13.

[38] John D. Bell, *Paesants in Power. Alexander Stamboliyski and the Bulgarian Agrarian National Union*, 226.

[39] Cited from John D. Bell, *Paesants in Power. Alexander Stamboliyski and the Bulgarian Agrarian National Union*, 228.

Agrarian rapprochement with the Kingdom of Serbs, Croats and Slovenes resulted in the signing of the *Niš Agreement* on 17 March 1923. According to the *Niš Agreement* Yugoslav security forces were allowed to cross the Bulgarian border in order to suppress actions of the *autonomist* bands. BANU support to the IMRO *federalist* faction also implied another thing which IMRO was very much afraid off and that was losing their stronghold in Pirin Macedonia, i.e. Petrich County. On 10 April, Todor Alexandrov sent a 'last warning' to Prime Minister Stamboliyski telling him that if he dares to send the *federalists* and *Orange Guard* to Pirin Macedonia, Stamboliyski himself, his ministers and associates will be solely responsible for the outcome. A copy of the letter was also sent to all ministers, press, patriotic associations etc. What followed was a series of arrests of prominent Macedonians both from the IMRO and the legal Macedonian associations. And while the agrarian regime was focused on the IMRO and their supporters from the legal Macedonian associations, the *Military League* was able to prepare and execute the coup without disturbance. With such an attitude the IMRO provided a moral justification for the execution of the coup. Although they didn't take part in the technical matters related to the execution, the *autonomist* bands were concentrated in their strongholds in Gornya Dzhumaya, Kyustendil and Petrich in status of combat readiness.[40] In addition, Todor Alexandrov issued orders to village militias in areas under control of the IMRO to be ready to place themselves at the disposal of regular army units guarding the state border in case of action of the 'Serbian kingdom'.[41]

After the 9 June and successful execution of the coup, the IMRO was able to execute their death sentences. And this was done, like many other issues related to the June coup, raising questions that would probably remain unanswered. The conspirators needed several days to apprehend the Prime Minister because unlike the other leading figures of the BANU he was absent from the capital. At the time of the coup he was on his estate, in his birth village Slivovitsa near the town of Pazardzhik. He had several bodyguards and policemen as protection. It is said that he retreated there to work on the draft of Bulgaria's new Constitution—again, a claim that is unconfirmed. One of the leading conspirators, Slaveyko Vasilev, was on 9 June dispatched from Sofia to organize the capture of Stamboliyski. However, they would need four days and a substantial number of troops to force Stamboliyski to surrender. By 13 June, Stamboliyski, after being hunted down, was captured with his brother Vasil and brought back to the estate in Slivovitsa where the final act of his personal drama would play out. There was already a *komitaji* band of *voivod* Velichko Velyanov-Chicheto, better known as Velichko

---

[40] Z. Todorovski, *Todor Aleksandrov*, 210–14.
[41] Dimitar Tyulekov, *Obrecheno rodolyubie. VMRO v Pirinsko 1919–1934* (Blagoevgrad: Univ. Izd. 'Neofit Rilski', 2001), http://www.promacedonia.org/dt/dt1_2.html [last checked on 3 November 2016]

Skopski (he was the IMRO regional commander for Skopje region in the Kingdom of Serbs, Croats and Slovenes). The brothers Stamboliyski were taken to a barn where they were brutally tortured and finally executed by *komitajis* and several army officers. Before execution Stamboliyski was stabbed nearly 60 times, his right hand was cut off, allegedly because it has signed the traitorous *Niš Agreement*. Finally, the corpses of the Stamboliyski brothers were decapitated because their heads were to be presented as trophies. Their bodies were buried on the spot, while their heads were never retrieved. On the wall of the barn where they were tortured, with his own blood, Stamboliyski managed to write the inscription A S 14 June 1923. To conceal the executions, the conspirators reported that Stamboliyski was liberated and taken away by a group of his supporters. In a follow-up report it was stated that he was killed when the group which had liberated him resisted the posse that was sent to apprehend him.[42]

In the aftermath of the coup, police and paramilitaries brutally murdered some twenty notable agrarians and their members of the parliament. With the death of Stamboliyski, the BANU became yet another political movement divided into factions. Some of the IMRO officials, like Georgi Pophristov, weren't overwhelmed with joy when Stamboliyski was executed. On the contrary, he believed that the IMRO was to remain neutral in this instance. The participation of the IMRO in the liquidation of the agrarians after the coup led to the diminishing of the already questionable autonomy of the organization and the intensive interfering of state authorities into the organization's affairs.[43]

The new Prime Minister Tsankov hurried to assure the alarmed Western Allies that his government would adhere to the provisions of the Neuilly peace agreement and re-establish democratic order in Bulgaria.[44] As for the Bulgarian neighbors, the absence of any decisive action against the drastic political changes proved to be assuring for the new-old Bulgarian regime that they were on the right path. During the summer, the agrarians and their leaders that managed to escape the post-coup repression, like Alexander Obov and Constantine Todorov, regrouped in Prague and Belgrade. They got initial support mainly from the local agrarian parties with whom they had a long-established relationship since the late nineteenth century. The Yugoslav agrarians, together with Democratic Party, openly criticized the passive stance of the Yugoslav government stating that tragic outcomes could have been avoided with timely responses as the Yugoslav

[42] Veselin Yaanchev, *Armiya, obshtestven red i vatreshna sigurnost mezhdu voynite i sled tyaah*, 409. and John D. Bell, *Paesants in Power. Alexander Stamboliyski and the Bulgarian Agrarian National Union*, 237–8. Yaanchev, however misses to refer to the details of Stamboliyski brutal death as well as to reasons for such an outcome.

[43] Georgi Pophristov, *Revolyutsionnata borba v' bitolskiya okr'g*, (Sofia: NS OF, 1953), 85.

[44] Robert Gerwarth, *The Vanquished: Why the First World War Failed to End 1917–1923* (London: Allen Lane, 2016), 150.

authorities were already aware of the preparation for the coup for three months prior to its execution.[45]

As for the IMRO, the organization was determined to fulfill its promises. Although Rayko Daskalov, being a Bulgarian ambassador in Czechoslovakia, avoided the misfortune of his comrades during the coup and its immediate aftermath, the IMRO did not lose sight of him. During the summer of 1923 a special assassin was dispatched to Prague by Alexandrov himself and on 26 August a young IMRO member Yordan Tsitsonkov from Macedonian town of Štip assassinated Daskalov. On 27 August Alexandrov issued a circular note to 'All *voivods* in Macedonia' that 'a young idealist' assassinated Daskalov and that IMRO supports its action.[46] To show its appreciation, the organization provided Tsitsonkov with financial aid and his family was taken care of while he was incarcerated.[47] The next one on the 'hit list' was Petko Petkov, the leader of the BANU parliamentary faction, who was assassinated on the first anniversary of Stamboliyski's death.

Despite massive party membership and solid support BANU was overthrown in a coordinated and well-prepared *coup d'état*. While BANU attention was dispersed on several fronts its enemies were able to prepare and organize the coup of 9 June 1923. Without proper organization and military training the *Orange Guard* couldn't match the well organized and experienced *Military League* and IMRO. The spontaneous armed resistance of the agrarians was organized throughout the country and was more of a consequence of their good party organization than of military preparations. Although most of the BANU membership consisted of battle-hardened war veterans they lacked proper training, structure, and rules of engagement. A comparison could be made with the communists and their secret military organization, which although existed from 1919 wasn't able to execute a revolutionary attempt in September 1923. While the Communists were better organized, trained and armed than the agrarian *Orange Guard*, they couldn't withstand the combined forces of the Army, the *Military League*, the IMRO and the 'White' Russians.

September Uprising or Revolution?

Under the circumstances of the prolonged terror after the June coup, the Bulgarian communists decided to abort their neutral stand and join efforts with the remaining agrarians willing to be part of the resistance. Just a couple of months after the coup when, with its passive stance allowed the return to power

---

[45] Srđan Mićić, 'Kraljevina Srba, Hrvata i Slovenaca i planiranje državnog udara u Bugarskoj 1923–1925', In *Vojnoistorijski glasnik*, 1/2014, 203–32, here 207.

[46] NBKM BIA, 405, AJ2, p. 3, IMRO no. 524, 27 August 1923.

[47] Z. Todorovski, *Todor Aleksandrov*, 217.

of the political right, Bulgarian Communist Party (BKP) decided to attempt a revolution. As to how and why this happened may be found in the concept of ideological exclusivity, a characteristic of the international communist movement. Blindly following the theoretical principles, without adapting them to a real-time context, has more than once led to the utter failure of revolutionary endeavors.[48] The Bulgarian case from 1923 was a typical example. Seeing the overall effects of the events surrounding the 9 June coup, the BKP changed its stance and from early August began intensive preparations. Their activities followed several directions:

1. To organize fighting groups, with the tenth acting as the core unit.
2. To collect as much weapons as possible.
3. To try to attract and organize as many members of the Bulgarian armed forces as possible.
4. To attract as much support from other political organizations like BANU as possible.

In total, the Military organization of the BKP numbered between 30,0000 and 40,000 members.[49] However, most members weren't properly armed with firearms. For example, Sofia accounted for some 1,100 members but they had only 400 rifles and fourteen machineguns, and only one of them operational. In total, only several thousand rifles and 30 machineguns were at their disposal. The situation was so serious there was an official motto 'Sell your clothes, your ox or your land and buy yourself some weapons!'[50] The efficient agitation among army personnel was seen as a potential solution to this problem—communist officials were expecting whole army units to change sides and join them which would considerably increase communist odds and armaments. Some 700 reserve officers, members of the BKP, and some 300 of those supporting their ideas and goals were designated to train and organize all those members of the Military organization who didn't have any kind of military training or experience at all. Finally, with the change of their approach, the Bulgarian communists were now counting on the support of representatives of other political options which had direct interest in overthrowing the 9 June regime—like the BANU and the socialists. Only in the wider Sofia region did they manage to attract some 2,000–2,500 members of the BANU to join their Military organization.[51]

---

[48] On revolutionary events in East Central Europe after the First World War, see: Robert Gerwarth, *The Vanquished: Why the First World War Failed to End 1917–1923* (London: Allen Lane, 2016).

[49] Stela Dimitrova, 'Voennata organizatsiya na BKP (t.s.) pri podgotovka na Septemvrisko v'stanie 1923. godina'. In *Voennoistoricheski sbornik*, 1/1990, 45–7.

[50] Stela Dimitrova, "Voennata organizatsiya na BKP (t.s.), 32–49.

[51] Stela Dimitrova, "Voennata organizatsiya na BKP (t.s.). 49.

In an attempt to increase their odds, the BKP tried to win the support of the IMRO or at least to obtain the organization's neutrality. Throughout the summer of 1923 there were intensive negotiations between the BKP and the IMRO. While the left or *federalist* wing of the IMRO fully supported communist intentions, Todor Alexandrov was pretty much clear with the statement in which he said that actual government is also the IMRO government because it is supporting their efforts in struggle for Macedonia. Because of that the IMRO wouldn't allow any kind of change in Bulgaria, neither parliamentarian, nor violent attempts of toppling the government.[52] Nevertheless, the IMRO and the BKP reached some sort of agreement which guaranteed the IMRO's neutrality during the uprising. Condition was that the communist organization from the Petrich region wouldn't take part in the uprising. However, on the eve of the uprising Alexandrov annulled the agreement informing the BKP that in case of the uprising communists would have to fight the IMRO as well.[53]

The Russian 'White' emigrants were also a critical player now. During previous years the BKP organized and performed several actions aimed against their presence in Bulgaria that eventually led to an increase of antagonism between Bulgarian communists and 'White' Russian émigrés. Soviet authorities and their local operators—Bulgarian communists, constantly used the presence of General Wrangel's forces in Bulgaria for different kind of protests. The BANU regime also contributed to the rise of tensions between the 'White' Russians and the Bulgarian state. These incidents became the excuse for the introduction of different measures aimed against civilian and military representatives of Russian community in Bulgaria. The goal was to disband and disarm the military structures of the Russian émigrés as a prelude to their return (expatriation) to Russia. The extent of repressive measures and the participation of infiltrated Soviet agents during events in the town of Svishtov on 6 January 1922 led to official protests coming from France, Romania and several other states. Bulgarian opposition, on the other hand, and some of their Russophile representatives were showing open signs of favoring the Russian community.[54] The BANU's benevolent attitude towards Soviet Russia as well as reforms favoring labor class rose suspicion among Wrangel's forces. This had the knock-on effect of encouraging their approach towards the opposition parties who had already begun preparations to overthrow the agrarian regime in Bulgaria. The publication of certain classified documents related to the mobilization plans of Wrangel's forces in Bulgaria in 1922 caused massive communist demonstrations calling for the disarmament and disbanding of Wrangel's army. The Communists claimed that the presence of an organized

[52] Zoran Todorovski, *Todor Aleksandrov*, (Skopje: Makavej; Državen arhiv na Republika Makedonija, 2014) 219–21.
[53] Z. Todorovski, *Todor Aleksandrov*, 222.
[54] Cvetana Kyoseva, *B'lgariya i ruskata emigraciya: (20-te—50-te godini na XX v.)* (Sofia: Mezhdunar. Cent'r po problemite na malcinstvata i kulturnite vzaimodejstviya, 2002), 50.

and well-armed formation represents a danger for Bulgarian sovereignty. In fact this was true simply because the Bulgarian armed forces had 12,000 armed men while Wrangel's army had 18,000 to 20,000.[55] On 26 March 1922, BANU was forced to introduce measures for disarming Russian officers as well as the suspension of armed sentries in the barracks of Russian units. A ban on bearing arms was introduced and officers were pressed either to immigrate of try to find job in Bulgaria.[56] Suspicion towards the 'White' Russians increased significantly after another set of documents was discovered ordering Russian forces to maintain neutrality in case of conflict between the government and the opposition; and to interfere only if communists and agrarians organized actions against parties of the political right. Although General Wrangel protested and insisted that these documents were forgeries, they caused rising tensions. General Wrangel's declaration of 16 May 1922 claiming that the Russian émigrés in Bulgaria 'are surrounded with hatred and slander' and that the ongoing campaign against his army would force it to take a defensive stand caused another wave of anti-Russian measures aimed at their total demilitarization, dispersion throughout the country and reducing of their overall numbers by forcing them to immigrate or repatriate.[57] Some 130 leading officer were, arrested on spying charges, while 58 others, 35 of whom where Generals, were expatriated. Commands of Russian units were disbanded. Groups of between 50 and 100 men were designated for hard labor in some 59 places in the countryside for minimum wages or no wages at all. Huge quantities of weaponry were apprehended as well. Russian journals were banned and their editors, along with the Russian imperial ambassador, were expatriated.[58]

In addition, intensive unofficial relations between Bulgaria and Soviet Russia led to the establishment of two institutions through which Soviets came in position to target the 'White' emigrants and influence Bulgarian internal and foreign policies. Following the general amnesty for all members of the 'White' movement proclaimed by the Soviet authorities in 1922, Bulgarian and Soviet communists began a secret agitation among Russian émigrés in Bulgaria in favor of repatriation. As a result, the organization named *Union for the Return to Fatherland—Sovnarod* was formed. In a short time they grouped some 4,000 interested for repatriation and that was the ground work for the introduction of the mission of the Soviet Red Cross in October that same year. This mission's work obviously involved more that just the humanitarian aspect. Thanks to the arrival of experts from *CHEKA—All Russian Emergency Commission for Suppressing Counterrevolution and Sabotage* (Всеросийская Чрезвычнайя Комиссия по

[55] Cvetana Kyoseva, *B'lgariya i ruskata emigraciya (20-te—50-te godini na XX v.)*, 51.
[56] Cvetana Kyoseva, *B'lgariya i ruskata emigraciya (20-te—50-te godini na XX v.)*, 51.
[57] Doncho Daskalov, 'Byalata ruska emigratciya v' B'lgariya mezhdu dvete svetovni voiyni' In *Voennoistoricheski sbornik*, 1/1990, 56–75, here 61–5.
[58] Cvetana Kyoseva, *B'lgariya i ruskata emigraciya (20-te—50-te godini na XX v.)*, 55.

борьбе с контрарреволюцией и саботажем—ВЧК or just ЧК) in short period of time *Sovnarod* was transformed from a pro-Soviet to a Soviet organization.[59] According to the records of *Sovnarod* until the 9 June coup in total 9,570 Russians living in Bulgaria opted for repatriation and returned to Russia. The majority of them (some 65 per cent) were Cossacks, who unlike the rest of Russian emigration were simple peasants. Their social status made them much more vulnerable in terms of homesickness and their desire to return to their homeland. After the coup, Tsankov's government cancelled all anti-Russian regulations and terminated all anti-Russian practices including repatriation. All exiled senior Russian officers were invited to return back to Bulgaria.[60] Thus, the stage for later participation of Russian émigrés in suppression of the communist uprising was set.

Meanwhile, the passive stance of the international community provided a perfect opportunity to the new (old) regime to strengthen its position and, in practical terms, to exonerate itself for the violent acts committed during the June coup. After the eradication of the agrarian opposition, a new regime came into power with a focus on the BKP which, because of it political agenda, clearly represented their number one adversary. Due to the efficient intelligence the new regime was able to find out the BKP plans for revolution and to prepare an adequate response. The first act to significantly disrupt the communist commanding structure was mass arrest on 12 September. In most of the cases, those BKP members who were arrested in this preemptive strike were the ones who were prepared and instructed for the uprising. Those who remained were either unprepared for fighting or were not familiar with the plans and procedures.[61] Around 2,000 of the most important members of the party and its military organization were arrested throughout the country.[62] Other thing that had contributed to the failure of the communist enterprise was the absence of cooperation with the remaining agrarians which, although shaken by the coup, still enjoyed massive support in the Bulgarian countryside. It turned out that when escaped agrarian leaders Todorov and Obov heard news about the September uprising rushed to the Kingdom of Serbs, Croats and Slovenes in order to organize their supporters and help the communists but they were too late—the uprising was already quelled.[63]

The IMRO also participated in the September fighting and following its principles organization was fully engaged against the communist uprising in the areas under IMRO control. So, all communist attempts made in areas around Rozlog and Gornya Dzhumaya were quelled. In some places the local IMRO *voivode* put

[59] Lyudmil Spasov, *Vrangelovata armiya v B'lgariya 1919–1923* (Sofia: Univerzitetsko izdatelstvo Sv. Kliment Ohridski, 1999), 166–77.

[60] Doncho Daskalov, 'Byalata ruska emigratciya v' B'lgariya mezhdu dvete svetovni voiyni', 67.

[61] Stela Dimitrova, "Voennata organizatsiya na BKP (t.s.), 49.

[62] Slavi Chak'rov, 'Voennata organizatsiya i podgotovkata na septemvrijskoto v'stanie 1923. g'. In *Septemviyskoto v'stanie 1923 godina—voennite deiystviya*, (Sofia: Ministerstvo na narodnata otbrana, 1973), 9–45, here 43.

[63] S. Mićić, 'Kraljevina Srba, Hrvata i Slovenaca i planiranje državnog udara u Bugarskoj', 208.

local communist officials under their protection preventing unnecessary losses. Elsewhere, there were violent encounters with enormous death tolls. The Communist organization from Gornya Dzhumaya, taking in mind the IMRO warnings, decided to send its members to assist the uprising in Dupnitsa, which was outside of the IMRO 'sphere of interest'. However, after finding out that the uprising in Dupnitsa has already been quelled they decided to return and on their way back communists were ambushed by IMRO bands which killed 100 of the 160 communist insurgents. On several occasions after the uprising Todor Alexandrov made it clear that he always considered 'Bolshevism' to be harmful for the Macedonian national movement and that he would never allow a communist overturn in Bulgaria.[64]

Another group that had an active participation in fights against the communist insurgents was the Russian 'White' emigration in Bulgaria, and they acted as a military component. Unlike in the June events when they stood aside, this time they were more than a natural ally to Tsankov's regime. Russian units participated in the quelling of the uprising in Boychinovci, Vidin, Lom, Stara Zagora, Nova Zagora and other towns in Bulgaria. In 1924 Tsankov's regime officially recognized the merits of the Russian émigrés in quelling of the September uprising. They were rewarded material help as well as with the possibility to apply for Bulgarian citizenship, which was a precondition for entering state service.[65]

Immediately, after the failure of the September revolutionary attempt (Bulgarian communists avoided to use this formulation knowing how international community is sensitive in regard to the 'export of the revolution') followed detailed analyses. Although the BKP already had a well-organized illegal (para)military structure led by the Great War veterans and which was in possession of, maybe not substantial, but considerable amount of weaponry, the fact that they decided to act several months after the 9 June coup lowered their chances for a successful outcome. According to their own later analyses the Communists failed because of the following reasons:

- Government's preemptive strike on 12 September;
- Great number of party representatives were arrested;
- Serious shortage of weaponry;
- Inadequate support and lack of coordination between urban proletariat and peasantry;

[64] Zoran Todorovski, *Todor Aleksandrov*, (Skopje: Makavej; Državen arhiv na Republika Makedonija, 2014) 222–3.

[65] Lyudmil Spasov, *Vrangelovata armiya v B'lgariya 1919–1923* (Sofia: Univerzitetsko izdatelstvo Sv. Kliment Ohridski, 1999), 222. However there were Russian officers who participated in preparation but not the execution of the June coup. Conspirators refused participation of Wrangel's forces from Kingdom of Serbs, Croats and Slovenes simply because the latter reconciled with Stamboliyski—Cvetana Kyoseva, *B'lgariya i ruskata emigraciya (20-te—50-te godini na XX v.)*, 92–89.

- Lack of revolutionary experience among both urban proletariat and peasantry.[66]

The September uprising added a new circle to the spiral of violence in Bulgaria causing between 1,130 and 1,350 deaths during the uprising and in its follow-up liquidations and court sentences.[67] Research conducted by the Museum of Revolutionary Movement in Bulgaria and published in 1972 as monograph-album under the title *Stars in Centuries* (Звезди във вековете) gives a somewhat different balance sheet for the September uprising and its immediate aftermath. This research claims that in total 841 people died during the uprising.[68] This figure differs drastically from the claims of about 5,000 killed in fighting and the follow up repression.

The Communist leaders Georgi Dimitrov and Vasil Kolarov managed to escape to the Kingdom of Serbs, Croats and Slovenes where they encountered a warm welcome because of their anti-war stance and publicly expressed criticism in Bulgarian parliament against measures in occupied Serbia during the Great War. This time the communists established contact and cooperation with the agrarians who were already present there. From autumn 1923 they worked together to organize, prepare and arm as many of their members and supporters on the Yugoslav side of the border as possible. Simultaneously, the Yugoslav international position improved radically after the signing of the Yugoslav-Italian Friendship Pact at the beginning of 1924. The Italians automatically reduced their support to Hungary, Bulgaria and Albania and started negotiating with Belgrade in favor of joint actions.[69] Because of the possible agrarian-communist incursion and the overthrow of Tsankov government with Yugoslav assistance, the political scene became extremely complex. As well as the above-mentioned players, other groups involved included both factions of the IMRO, the Russian émigrés and Yugoslav paramilitaries from the *chetnik* veteran associations as well as from the newly established *Organization against Bulgarian Bandits*. All of 1924 and 1925 was marked with intensive diplomatic and covert activities aimed at fulfillment of this intention. Agrarians and communists wanting to restore their previous position and power while the Yugoslavs were aiming at the neutralization of the IMRO as a main destabilizing factor in Macedonia. However, although the agrarians looked like a natural ally, the Yugoslavs were very suspicious towards the Bulgarian communists because they feared of their association with the banned Communist

---

[66] *Kominternat i Balgariya, tom I, Dokumenti* (Sofia: Glavno upravlenie na arhivite pri Ministerskiya Syvet, 2005), 137, No. 52, Iz rezolyutsiyaata na VI konferentsiya na BKF otnosno prichinite za porazhenieto na Septemvriyskoto vastanie i predstoyashtite zadach na BKP.

[67] Roumen Daskalov, *B'lgarskoto obshtestvo 1878–1939. Tom 1*, (Sofia: Gutenberg, 2005), 245.

[68] See: Muzeii na revolyucionnoto dvizhenie v Balgariya, *Zvezdi v'v vekovete*, Izdatelstvo na Balgarskata komunisticheska partiya, Sofia 1972.

[69] S. Mićić, 'Kraljevina Srba, Hrvata i Slovenaca i planiranje državnog udara u Bugarskoj', 208–9.

Party of Yugoslavia and Soviet Russia. Basically, any weapons handed over to the Bulgarian communists might end up in the hands of the Yugoslav communists. For the same reasons, the Russian 'White' emigration both in Bulgaria and the Kingdom of Serbs, Croats and Slovenes stayed on high alert. Yugoslav/Serbian paramilitaries wanted to strike a decisive blow in the conflict with the IMRO which originated two decades earlier from the days of their rivalry in Ottoman Macedonia. While the *Organization against Bulgarian Bandits*, i.e. its members that used to be associated with *federalist* faction of the IMRO, commonly known as renegades, wanted to use this opportunity to once and for all finish the rivals from the autonomist IMRO and continue with their own agenda. Looking at this constellation of power positions of the new Bulgarian regime under Prime Minister Tsankov has been extremely difficult. Tsankov had to invest huge efforts in order to simultaneously block any agrarian and communist attempt of a coup and try to persuade the IMRO to limit its operations in order not to provoke Yugoslav military intervention. A deep schism within the IMRO that happened after the assassination of Todor Alexandrov in August 1924 contributed to the complexity of the situation. It was in the autumn of 1924 when the final version of a potential intervention, that is a combination of incursion from the Yugoslav territory and a massive uprising in Bulgaria, was drafted and almost executed. Again, it was the paramilitaries who represented the core of the forces envisaged for this action:

- The *federalists* led by Todor Panitsa toward the Petrich region;
- Bands of Yugoslav Macedonians led by Stoyan Mishev from the *Association against Bulgarian bandits* heading towards Kyustendil;
- Bulgarian emigrants strengthened by Serbian *chetniks* under the command of Kosta Pećanac and Ilija Trifunović-Birčanin in direction of Sofia;
- Bulgarian emigrants in the direction of Belogradchik and Vratsa;

Armaments for the action were provided from several sources with more than 20,000 rifles and around 200 artillery pieces from Czechoslovakian army depots, as well as twenty machineguns and 500 pistols from political allies and individuals throughout Europe. With the logistic of the Yugoslav diplomatic network, beside five trucks converted into armored cars, the Bulgarian emigrants even managed to purchase three airplanes. However, due to the conflicts within agrarian emigration, execution of the planned action was postponed as they continued to flee abroad due to the repression to which they have been constantly exposed in Bulgaria.[70]

---

[70] S. Mićić, 'Kraljevina Srba, Hrvata i Slovenaca i planiranje državnog udara u Bugarskoj', 211–19.

Meanwhile, some of the agrarians decided not to wait for the agreed incursion but resolved to conduct their own individual acts of terrorism. On 1 January 1925 there was an attempt on the Prime Minister himself. On 13 February Professor Nikola Milev from Sofia University was assassinated—he was known for his close connections with the IMRO and other Macedonian organizations in Bulgaria. On 14 January, the Chief of the Crimes Department of the Public security Nedelcho Stefanov was killed, on the seventeenth building of the State Customs was sacked while in the Officers Club an explosive device was activated. One of the Balkan rules in terms of political and (para)military activism is that springtime is the time for action. This has even found its place in traditional songs and folklore. Again, the plan for radical overturn of the regime in Bulgaria has been put in place. The plan was presented to the Yugoslav authorities on 15 April where the actual execution date would be 14 June, i.e. second anniversary of Stamboliyski's brutal murder. Again, detailed routes for the incursion into Bulgaria were drafted. It was envisaged that it would take some thirty to forty days for its execution, i.e. interruption of important communications and annihilation of all military and paramilitary formations supporting Tsankov's government. In total, there were six to seven thousands fighters of whom some 3,000 were Serbian *chetniks* and the organizers also counted on the massive support from the Bulgarian peasantry.[71]

However, parallel developments saw the abandonment of these plans almost as simultaneously as they were presented. Firstly, the communists decided to continue their struggle on their own. That led to famous attempt on Tsar Boris's life on 14 April when a combined anarchist-communist group led by Nesho Tumangelov failed to kill the Bulgarian sovereign.[72] Despite the failure the BKP didn't stand down. Continuing its extreme left revolutionary policy led by the semi-autonomous Military organization they planned and executed another attempt at the church Sveta Nedelya in Sofia, just two days later on 16 April 1925. This time they targeted the sovereign and leading politicians and in the bomb explosion 140 people were killed. In retaliation it is estimated between 670 and 860 persons were executed without trial, often after torture. Even after going through the legal procedure however, 179 people were still sentenced to death, some of them *in absentia*.[73] The Bulgarian sovereign avoided this attempt as well as was attending the funeral service of his associates who were killed two days earlier.

The real threat of communist overturn in Bulgaria contributed greatly to the change of attitudes of the Great Powers towards Bulgaria. Despite Yugoslav protests they allowed the temporary increase of the Bulgarian regular army. This

---

[71] S. Mićić, 'Kraljevina Srba, Hrvata i Slovenaca i planiranje državnog udara u Bugarskoj', 224–6.
[72] S. Mićić, 'Kraljevina Srba, Hrvata i Slovenaca i planiranje državnog udara u Bugarskoj', 226–7.
[73] R. Daskalov, *B'lgarskoto obshtestvo 1878–1939*, Tom 1, 245.

measure helped the Bulgarian regime to launch another repressive campaign against the remaining agrarians and communists and thus to reassure its position.

Following their own agenda with the elimination of Petar Chaulev on 23 December 1924 and his successor Todor Panitsa on 8 May 1925, leaders of the *autonomist* wing of the IMRO won a decisive victory over the rival *federalists*. Meanwhile, a new schism within the organization was created after the assassination of Todor Alexandrov when his protégée and new leader of the IMRO, Ivan Mikhailov, unleashed a new wave of terror. Mikhailov's vendetta campaign targeted those whom he considered to be responsible for the death of his mentor—primarily General Alexander Protogerov. From 1924 until 1928, with the assassination of Protogerov, 193 people died in numerous inner-IMRO showdowns, while an additional 225 died after the death of Protogerov.[74] Until 1934, despite internal clashes within the IMRO, there were no attempts of a coup in Bulgaria.

Albanian Teeter

Zogu's Ascent to Power

As previously discussed, the complexity of the Albanian society strongly influenced its political life in the immediate post-Great War years. The overall backwardness of Albania contributed to its somewhat turbulent developments. Several crises, armed rebellions, border incidents, numerous assassinations, attempts of coup, final coup and counter-coup marked the years between 1920–1924. A central figure of this turbulent period was Ahmed-bey Zogu and it represents a period of his gradual takeover and rise to power.

In the summer of 1921, the Albanian government led by Iliyaz Vrioni encountered serious challenges coming from the north Albanian clan of Miriditë. This strong and numerous clan was somehow excluded from Albanian political life. Being Roman Catholics they feared supremacy of the Muslims while closeness to the Kingdom of Serbs, Croats and Slovenes made them perfect tool for the continuation of Yugoslav interferences after the main Yugoslav ally, Esad-pasha Toptani was assassinated and his followers dispersed. The Miriditë chieftain, Mark Gjonmarkaj, although illiterate, proclaimed a republic claiming that the Tirana government was just a tool of Muslim landowners. The Yugoslav Prime Minister and acting Minister of Foreign Affairs Nikola Pašić seized (or created) this opportunity to interfere in Albania once more. Although the Yugoslavs didn't

---

[74] R. Daskalov, *B'lgarskoto obshtestvo 1878–1939*, Tom 1, 246.

recognize the Miriditë Republic, they assisted Mark Gjonmarkaj with finances, weapons, hired members of the General Wrangel's forces, Esad-pasha's former lieutenant Hallil Lleshi, as well as with concrete assistance of the Yugoslav regular forces—especially artillery. As a result, they insurgents managed to hold out until November when they were finally overrun by government's troops led by Ahmed-bey Zogu.[75] Because of the support provided to Mark Gjonmarkaj Albania accused the Yugoslavs by submitting a memo to the League of Nations. In response the League of Nations convicted the Kingdom of Serbs, Croats and Slovenes for conducting an aggressive policy against Albania.[76] Critically, this was used as one of crucial arguments for Zogu after proclaiming a general amnesty to win over the allegiance of the Miriditë leaders. And while Zogu was busy in the north, a coup occurred in Tirana when Aqif-pasha, one of the Regents, forced the Prime Minister Pandeli Evangjeli to resign. After Kazim-bey Koutzoli wasn't able to form the cabinet Aqif-pasha turned to one of the leaders of the Kosovo Committee, Hasan Prishtina. The existing differences between the Kosovo Committee and Zogu (together with several other Albanian politicians) exposed the serious tensions on the Albanian political scene. The main cause for it was different attitude toward the status of territories inhabited by Albanians that remained outside of Albanian state borders—primarily Kosovo and Metohija. Zogu and his associates, especially those from south considered Albania too weak to address this issue at the moment. This attitude made them apostates and betrayers of national interests in the eyes of Kosovars united around the Kosovo Committee. Either way, Zogu used this opportunity to cross the Rubicon under the pretext of non-recognizing the overthrow of Pandeli Evangjeli's cabinet. After just two days in office Prishtina was faced with the overwhelming force of his opponent consisting of regular troops under Zogu's command, militias of Zogu's and Miriditë's clans. Officers and troops were fleeing the capital in order to join Zogu. It turned out, as it often has in Albania, that the possession of respectable armed forces is the only guarantee for the retention of power. After entering Tirana on 12 December 1921 Zogu used the opportunity to strip Kosovars of any possibility enabling them to return to power. Zogu rearranged the political balance by aligning with the northern clansmen and major landowners. Instead of taking the position of Prime Minster he continued to administer the office of the

[75] Further readings: Robert C. Austin, *Founding a Balkan State; Albanian Experiment with Democracy, 1920–1925* (Toronto: University of Toronto Press, 2012), 24–5; Bernd J. Fischer, *King Zog and the Struggle for Stability in Albania*, (Tirana: Albanian Institute for International Studies, 2012), 28–9; Peter Bartl, *Albanci, od srednjeg veka do danas* (Beograd: CLIO, 2002)188–9; Bogumil Hrabak, 'Miriditi između Italijana, arbanaških nacionalista i Srba'.In *Istorija 20. veka*, 1–2/1993, 35–50.

[76] Saša Mišić, *Albanija: prijatelj i protivnik, jugoslovenska politika prema Albaniji: 1924–1927*, (Beograd: Službeni glasnik, 2009), 21–2. In addition, Conference of Ambassadors recognized Albania in its 1913 borders and decided that in case of Albania incapability to preserve its territorial integrity their representatives will recommend Italy to become protector of Albania's interests.

Minister of Interior.[77] Meanwhile, Zogu maintained intensive clandestine contact with official Belgrade who showed willingness to 'support his party' for certain concessions. Yugoslav expectations included the custom union of two states, construction of a railway line between the town of Prizren and the Albanian Adriatic coast, permit for Miriditë leaders to return to Albania, prevention of all propaganda activities coming from Kosovar émigrés and seizure of all Albanian support to anti-Yugoslav elements like the IMRO. By mid-March 1922, both Zogu and the Albanian government agreed to these terms in form of a half public-half secret oral agreement.[78]

At the same time when the Kingdom of Serbs, Croats and Slovenes recognized Albania in March 1922 there was a new challenge to Zogu's authority when the Kosovars, led by Hasan Prishtina and Bayram Curri, backed by northerners and Dibrans unsatisfied by Zogu's policy of general disarmament, assembled a respectable force and started advancing on Tirana. Prime Minister Xhafer-bey Ypi and most of the Government fled the city leaving Zogu on his own. However, with the assistance of the British ambassador Sir Harry Eyres, who persuaded Elez Isufi, one of the Dibran champions, to stand down, Zogu prevailed. The rift between him and his opponents became even deeper as he, in a swift action of retaliation, court martialed those he considered responsible. Many were sentenced to death *in absentia*.[79] After reinstating Xhafer-bey Ypi to the position of Prime Minister Zogu resumed his position of Minister of Interior. However, dissatisfaction with government's achievements, coupled with the fact that the Albanian north wasn't overwhelmed with the current situation where the state was ruled primarily by people from central and southern regions led to the Ypi's dismissal and Zogu's assuming the position of Prime Minister in December 1922.

Despite promises made by Zogu to the Yugoslavs, the Kosovars managed to maintain a strong influence in Albania especially through their presence in the *clique*. The Yugoslavs weren't satisfied with the fact that many *kachaks* from Kosovo and Metohija found refuge in Albania where they received subsidies while some of them were accepted into the ranks of the Gendarmerie. On the other hand, Zogu was seen as traitor who had to be deposed because of his ties with the Kingdom of Serbs, Croats and Slovenes. His adversaries tried to do it in September as well as in November 1922. In September everything ended quickly because Zogu obtained parliamentary support. The second attempt was much more serious with participation of Gendarmerie, numerous army officers, and the Kosovars. This time Zogu's clan militia and younger officers from the province who refused to participate in the plot against the established government saved him. Both times Zogu managed to survive, but not without consequences. He has

[77] Bernd J. Fischer, *King Zog and the Struggle for Stability in Albania*, 31–4.
[78] S. Mišić, *Albanija: prijatelj i protivnik*, 26–30.
[79] Peter Bartl, *Albanci, od srednjeg veka do danas* (Beograd: CLIO, 2002), 191–2.

lost considerable support and after the November events, the *clique* turned from an ally into his adversary. In elections that were held at the end of month he could not obtain a parliamentary majority so he turned for support toward the beys. He became Prime Minister once more, but compromises made with the *clique* included timely rotation on Minister positions. Inefficiency within the government increased causing overall dissatisfaction. On 23 February 1923 Zogu suffered injuries as a consequence from an attempt on his life performed by the member of the *Bashkimi*. He resigned two days later because according to the Albanian traditions he could leave his house only after getting satisfaction. The Cabinet was created by Shefqet-bey Vërlaci, however Zogu remained in control watching how forces opposed to him grew stronger. Opposition against Zogu rallied around Fan Noli, an Orthodox bishop, graduate from Harvard, an already experienced politician, prominent member of the Democrats, but who was somewhat unaware of Albanian political and especially historical realities. This group grew as former dissatisfied Progressives, army officers, conservative Sunni and Bektashi Muslims, Orthodox and Roman Catholics joined it. Former adherents of Esad-pasha joined Zogu's supporters since the man responsible for the attempt on Zogu was *Bashkimi* leader Avni Rustemi, the assassin of Esad-pasha in Paris in 1920.

Discontent with the central government continued to grow. Southerners were still waiting for long-promised land reform, while northerners either suffered from famine or felt betrayed by Tirana because it didn't support their irredentist policy directed against the Kingdom of Serbs, Croats and Slovenes. Zogu, while waiting to recover from his wounds, was already plotting a counterstrike. He asked for support from Belgrade—mostly weapons and money. Belgrade was keen to help but again under certain conditions, such as the elimination of some of the Kosovo Committee leaders. Also, Belgrade didn't want the situation to get out of hand in order to avoid intervention from a third party; in this case it would probably be Italy. Nevertheless, the Yugoslav help never arrived because of a series of events that hastened the downfall of Zogu. First was the murder of two Americans near Kruje on 6 April 1923. This incident caused plenty of speculation that Zogu was involved and it severely damaged the reputation of Albania and its government abroad. Second was the sudden assassination of Avni Rustemi on 20 April. This incident looked like a vendetta because the assassin was one of Esad-pasha's adherents and clients. Whether it was Zogu's reply to Rustemi and *Bashkimi's* attempt on his life earlier or just a typical Albanian vendetta it was to serve as a prelude to further revolutionary events. If Zogu expected that this assassination would cause general unrest allowing him to intervene, he was wrong, it backfired at him.[80]

---

[80] Robert C. Austin in *Founding a Balkan State; Albanian Experiment with Democracy, 1920–1925*, 45; and Bernd J. Fischer in *King Zog and the Struggle for Stability in Albania*, 60; are bringing opposite

Rustemi was proclaimed a national hero and his funeral turned into a massive statement of revolt and discontent. More than forty members of the parliament and several ministers left Tirana demanding Zogu and his government to resign. Zogu addressed the Kingdom of Serbs, Croats and Slovenes, Italy and Great Britain seeking help, but was refused.[81] What followed was something previously seen in recent Albanian history—that anyone with enough resources to gather several thousand armed men had the crucial advantage and could dethrone the ruling regime. Apart from his loyal clansmen from Mati and several of his closest followers Zogu couldn't count on anyone else. On 10 June the combined forces of insurgents entered Tirana. Together with a handful of his supporters and clansmen Zogu left the country and escaped to the Kingdom of Serbs, Croats and Slovenes where he found refuge.

Albania Under Fan Noli

Witnessing Fan Noli's struggle for Albania's admittance into the League of Nation in 1920 the *Manchester Guardian* observed how Noli was:

"…a man who would have been remarkable in any country. An accomplished diplomat, an expert in international affairs, a skillful debater, from the outset he made a deep impression in Geneva. He knocked down his Balkan opponents in a masterly fashion, but always with a broad smile."[82]

Who exactly was Theophan Stylian—Fan Noli?

Looking at his biography, it's fair to say that Fan Noli was a remarkable person for his time. Born in an Albanian-speaking Orthodox village near the important Ottoman town of Edirne, Noli began his political and cultural career following very different tracks from those of his future political rival Ahmed-bey Zogu. After finishing secondary school in Edirne, Noli travelled throughout Eastern Mediterranean working as actor and teacher. In 1906 he emigrated from Egypt to United States where he assumed the career of a clergyman, first as a deacon, and then as a priest. He was the first priest to serve Orthodox liturgy in Albanian. In addition, he was an editor of the Albanian newspaper *Dielli* (The Sun) and

interpretations to this event. While Austin doubts Zogu's involvement, Fischer is more opened to idea it was a part of larger plan to provoke Zogu's intervention.

[81] S. Mišić, *Albanija: prijatelj i protivnik*, 48–1. Yugoslav ambassador in Tirana gave him only third of the amount of money Zogu asked for because he couldn't provide any kind of guarantee, although his offer to annihilate Bayram Curri was rather tempting for Yugoslavs.

[82] Cited from: Robert C. Austin, *Founding a Balkan State; Albanian Experiment with Democracy, 1920–1925*, 18.

founder and leader of the Pan-Albanian *Vatra* (The Hearth) Federation of America. He came to Albania for the first time after the proclamation of independence as: an established leader of the American Albanian community, writer, journalist, and scholar with a degree from Harvard University. During the Great War he remained in USA where in 1919 he was appointed Bishop of the Albanian Orthodox Church in America. He returned to Albania after successfully advocating admittance of Albania to the League of Nations in 1920. Upon his second arrival to Albania he acted as a member of the parliament in front of *Vatra* as well as several months as Minister of Foreign Affairs. He was also consecrated bishop of Korça and metropolitan of Durres.[83]

When he assumed the position of Prime Minister after the June 'revolution', he immediately encountered a notable feature of Albanian political culture—it was much easier to unite different political factions and movements (Progressives, the Kosovars, the military, dissatisfied beys and Shkodrans) around one goal, in this case the Zogu's deposing, than to force them to work together afterwards. It is worth noting that the overturn was achieved with considerably small number of casualties—just twenty-six killed and fifty wounded throughout the country. As soon as Zogu left the country huge differences appeared on the horizon. Noli was determined to introduce Albania into the community of modern states. Within days of his triumphant entry into the capital, Noli announced his 20 points program. It encompassed radical reforms in state ministries, judiciary, military, taxation, local administration, and financial institutions. There were also a call for general disarmament, land reform, punishing and confiscation of property of all those instigated 'fratricide', 'reestablishment of tranquility, order and sovereignty of the law', elimination of feudalism and establishment of democracy, improvement of life and economic conditions for the farmers, security of employment, allowing of foreign investments, introduction of national health service and modern educational system, 'raise the credit and prestige of the state in the outside world', etc.[84] This was a normal, logical, and achievable plan for every other country but Albania. While trying to fulfill his ambitious plan Noli thrust Albania into even deeper turmoil. What began as a craving for democracy ended in a sort of totalitarian personal regime. One by one his points failed to be realized and it all came undone in just six months. Because he came to power through a revolutionary overturn no one recognized his government. Because of the role and presence of the Kosovars, in the Kingdom of Serbs, Croats and Slovenes were very suspicious, although Noli kept the Kosovars out of his cabinet. Everyone abroad refused him for a loan, so state finances were collapsing. A special tribunal was

[83] Noli, Fan (06.01.1882 -13.03.1965)—Robert Elsie, *A Biographical Dictionary of Albanian History*, (London; New York: B. Tauris, 2013), 333.
[84] Robert C. Austin, *Founding a Balkan State; Albanian Experiment with Democracy, 1920–1925*, 59–60.

established to trial those responsible for fratricide. In total, 107 representatives of former regimes—regents, Prime Ministers, ministers, members of the parliament, army and gendarmerie officers, were tried and sentenced. The most serious failing was with land reform, which was essentially illegal as Noli didn't had a mandate from the parliament—and with one stroke he lost support of the Muslim landowners, while the peasants (tenants) couldn't comprehend this concept. Divisions between Muslims and Christians as well as north and south and Gege and Toske started to appear openly. The only political factor Noli could rely on completely was the *Bashkimi*. However, being a radical, uncompromising and violence-friendly organization, the *Bashkimi* contributed to the deepening of existing crisis. Finally, Noli's address to the Soviet Union and the establishment of first contacts with this state raised considerable suspicion not only among Albania's neighbors, but in the international community as well.

Meanwhile, Zogu was welcomed in the Kingdom of Serbs, Croats and Slovenes where he found safe haven and a willingness of his host to assist him in a return to power—naturally on certain conditions. These included the neutralization of the Kosovo Committee, resolution of several border issues, Yugoslav privileged status in future trade agreements, creation of a Yugoslav bank in Albania, procurement of weapons, stimulating Albanian youth to continue education onto Yugoslav universities, etc. The Yugoslavs didn't want to miss an opportunity to be involved in Albanian matters and by doing so achieve certain gains. This is especially true taking into mind that 1924 was one of the most turbulent years on the Yugoslav political scene because of the frequent changes of cabinets (Nikola Pašić was the head of three different cabinets in first six months of 1924), regrouping of parties, splits of coalitions and entire parties, growing Serbo-Croatian differences, and beginning of stronger interference of the Royal court into country political life. Between July and the end of October the Government was headed by Ljubomir Davidović, the leader of the Democratic Party. However, Yugoslav policy towards Albania followed old guidelines that were once upon a time designed by Nikola Pašić. Now instead of Esad-pasha, his nephew Ahmed Zogu played the role of Yugoslav (Serbian) favorite. A plan for a coup included simultaneous incursion of several armed groups from the Yugoslav territory. Beside Zogu's own clansmen and trustees, the Yugoslavs helped in the recruitment (hiring) of fighters among the Kosovar Albanians as well as among former soldiers of General Wrangel's army. In addition, Yugoslavs provided not only their regular troops but artillery as well.[85] All groups were disguised as Albanian irregulars.

The stage for intervention was set; all parties involved just needed the right moment to act. The Yugoslavs did a good job in concealing preparations, but with only two factors that could jeopardize the whole enterprise. One was the weather, because winter was approaching and roads, or lack thereof on the Albanian side

---

[85] S. Mišić, *Albanija: prijatelj i protivnik*, 65–9.

of the border, could slow down the advancement. The second factor was the extent of Yugoslav involvement, an issue that could damage Zogu's reputation among certain groups in Albania. Initially it had been arranged for the Yugoslav troops not to advance too deep into Albanian territory. Zogu and the Yugoslavs used the change of cabinets in the UK as well as Italian (Mussolini's) troubles that came as consequences of murder of social-democrats leader Matteoti to initiate a counter-coup.

The plan was put in action on 17 December. Zogu's forces fought a decisive battle near Peshkopi where the government's troops were strengthened with Dibran irregulars headed by Elez Isufi. This particular episode represents a good illustration of Albanian ways. During the preparations Isufi was approached by Zogu and asked for support, however, he had already given his word and support to Noli. In the course of battle however, Isufi was fatally wounded. After being taken to his house to die in peace his brother-in-law resumed command of his kinsmen, who nearly killed the local army commander for convincing their old leader to fight against Zogu. After that, nearly 900 of them joined Zogu's forces. Zogu's forces were ordered only to disarm and let go free all those resisting. By doing so, they won the sympathies of northerners who rallied around Zogu. He entered Tirana on 24 December without much resistance while government forces melted like snow. Noli, with his leading ministers and politicians rallied in Vlora hoping to organize resistance in the south, however they fled to Italy with the first steamer.[86]

While estimation of Zogu's Albanian forces were between 5,000 and 6,000, the number of hired 'White' Russians is estimated between 130 and 800. They were well-armed with rifles, machineguns and one battery of obsolete guns. After the successful coup they were offered to stay in the Albanian service. Although most of the Russians accepted the offer within several years the majority decided to return to the Kingdom of Serbs, Croats and Slovenes. By the end of 1930's only nineteen were still in Albania.[87]

The immediate aftermath was triumphant. Zogu proclaimed himself 'Supreme commander'.[88] In January 1925 Zogu introduced a presidential system assuming the position of President. The Regency was dissolved and Albania was proclaimed a republic. With this change of the Albanian political system Zogu abandoned stipulations of the Statute of Lushnjë and slowly but surely was paving the way towards the introduction of a monarchy. Meanwhile, in secrecy, away from public scrutiny, Zogu's minions managed to eliminate his political opponents one by

---

[86] Bernd J. Fischer, *King Zog and the Struggle for Stability in Albania*, 71–5.

[87] Miroslav Jovanović, *Ruska emigacija na Balkanu (1920–1940)* (Beograd: Čigoja, 2006) 57–8; Fischer mentions 1,000 Yugoslavs, 1,000 hired Yugoslav Albanians, 500 Mati clan militiamen and some 800 'White' Russians, pp. 69–70.

[88] Ekrem-beg Vlora, *Sekavanjata ot životot. Tom II, (1921–1925)* (Skopje: Fondacija Otvoreno opštestvo, 2015), 237.

one: Zia Dibra, Bayram Curri. Lef Nosi, Luigj Gurakuqi. Some 300 army officers who remained loyal to Noli were discharged from service as well.[89]

And Noli?

He returned to the United States in 1930. Meanwhile, he lived in Italy and travelled to the Soviet Union. Upon his return to the USA he was no longer politically active. He returned to music and in 1938 he graduated with a bachelor degree in music. His attention turned towards history so in 1945 he got his PhD at Boston University with a dissertation on Skanderbeg. He also participated in Albania's obtaining of church independency. In addition, Fan Noli proved to be an excellent translator of Shakespeare and Ibsen. He died in 1965 at the age of 83.[90]

The success of his adversary during the coup of 1924 saw the introduction a new phase of political stability in Albania. Paradoxically, the subsequent gradual introduction of a monarchy and Zogu's assuming the title of 'King of Albanians' in 1928 was well accepted in Albanian society, especially in those parts which maintained the old customs and clan's allegiances. Ahmed-bey Zogu became Zog I King of the Albanians, he ruled until 1939 when he was deposed by Italian military intervention, after which he continued to live in exile as many other European monarchs who lost their thrones in the turmoil of the new global conflict. He died in 1961 at the age of 66.[91]

We have seen how in all above mentioned cases—whether it was a coup or a counter-coup paramilitaries played important roles. Again it showed how in certain moments state couldn't impose usual monopoly of violence, like in the case of Bulgaria before the 1923 June coup. Instead of relying on state institutions ruling regime resolved to creation of another paramilitary formation for which they were certain would serve the purpose and guarantee regime's stay in power. Bulgarian case also showed how good organization together with long tradition of organizing combined with the clear plan of action and determination could guarantee the success of a coup and crush any spontaneous or organized counter-coup. Non-indigenous paramilitaries, such as 'White' Russians in Bulgaria openly participated in suppressing communist revolutionary attempt in September 1923 spicing it with both their own rationale and frustrations.

However, not even good organization could prevent frequent outbursts of violence followed with extreme brutality. It appeared that these crises represented sort of vent for decades of accumulated differences and conflicts. Unlike Albania which after the 1924 sailed into much calmer political waters and which in way finally achieved stability under King Zog, Bulgaria needed a decade more and yet another coup in 1934 to finally overcome post-Great War effects and so many

---

[89] Bernd J. Fischer, *King Zog and the Struggle for Stability in Albania*, 71–5.

[90] Noli, Fan (06.01.1882 -13.03.1965)—Robert Elsie, *A Biographical Dictionary of Albanian History*, (London; New York: B. Tauris, 2013), 333.

[91] Bernd J. Fischer, *King Zog and the Struggle for Stability in Albania*, 303.

entangled rivalries: communist vs. 'White' Russian, old regime vs. agrarians and probably the bloodiest of all—several consecutive conflicts between different factions of IMRO (autonomist vs. federalists and protogerovists vs. michailovists).

For the Yugoslavs, however, paramilitaries proved to be convenient tool in both neutralizing internal opposition (IMRO *komitajis* and Albanian *kachaks*) in Yugoslav south as well as in projecting state power onto neighboring Albania and Bulgaria. In the case of Bulgaria, Serbian *chetniks*, together with IMRO federalist renegades and agrarian/communist émigrés represented perfect combination for an attempt of counter coup which was suppose to simultaneously bring back to power those forces within Bulgarian society that were advocating reconciliation between two nations and assist in neutralizing those actors who were openly anti-Serbian/Yugoslav. The same applied to Albania with only difference that in the case of Ahmed Zogu's counter-coup Russian émigrés were more willing to take part for adequate reward.

VI

Individuals and Organizations

Renegades

Among specific features of modern Balkan paramilitarism, such as intensive political engagement or strong inclination towards guerrilla warfare, the actions of extraordinary and charismatic individuals with strong characters clearly stand out. This, together with the existence of strong personal allegiances between the rank-and-file and their leaders, led to the appearance of several interesting, some would say paradoxical cases of defection or changing sides. As previously mentioned, from their very beginnings the Balkan paramilitaries were led by strong and often charismatic figures. In time, the influence of these sometimes remarkable characters over their followers caused the creation of special ties and personal rather than institutional or organizational allegiances. Sudden changes or simple ruptures within these complicated relations often led to drastic shifts in career paths. In cases of conflicts or schisms within the organizations personal loyalties often proved stronger than organizational rules, regulations or even political agenda. Controversial or mysterious deaths of popular and charismatic leaders often created confusion among their followers or resulted in vicious and violent vendetta campaigns. In the Balkans, even in modern times, loyalties or affiliations are accustomed to follow ancient rules which are more personal than institutional, ideological, religious or even, what might sound paradoxical, national or ethnic. In the turbulent post-Great War years in the Balkans several interesting cases of defection occurred. As stated before, their motivations were different as well as their significance and actual effects on subsequent events and developments.

In the years immediately after the end of the First World War, among many individual examples of defection, two large-scale cases of defection involving local paramilitaries happened, which at the moment led to a significant change in the balance of power on several levels.

Right after the Great War Yugoslav authorities decided to provide assistance to Albanian magnate Esad-pasha Toptani in organizing his supporters. Esad-pasha was the head of a prominent Toptani family, former Ottoman General, and known Serbian ally. When Albania gained its independence in 1913, as one of its prominent figures, Esad-pasha Toptani, after leaving service in the Ottoman army, began political engagement. After the short rule of German Prince Wilhelm zu Weid, Esad-pasha used Serbian support to impose his own regime on Albania.

Paramilitarism in the Balkans: The Cases of Yugoslavia, Bulgaria, and Albania, 1917–1924. Dmitar Tasić, Oxford University Press (2020). © Dmitar Tasić.
DOI: 10.1093/oso/9780198858324.001.0001

However, after initial success, Serbian defeat in autumn 1915 deprived Esad-pasha of his main sponsor, forcing him to go into exile. With some 2,500 followers he joined Allied troops on the Macedonian front where he participated in clashes and the subsequent breakthrough in September 1918. Because Italians, thanks to the permissiveness of their French and British allies, were allowed to occupy most of Albania, Esad-pasha, as a former Albanian Prime Minister and Serbian ally, was prevented from returning to his homeland and continuing his political engagement. Yugoslavs, on the other hand, had their own calculations. Initially they went along with existing Serbian aspirations to execute crucial influence in Albania as well as to achieve territorial concessions, like the sea outlet in the north Albanian littoral and possession of the important north Albanian town of Shkodra. It made them direct rivals to Italian plans of creating their own sphere of influence in the east Adriatic. Post-Great War circumstances and Yugoslav rivalry with Italy were spiced with some new moments. From the Serbian perspective, in a geopolitical sense, Italy replaced Austro-Hungarian Empire as the main obstacle to Serbian expansion towards the Adriatic coast. At the same time, the creation of the Yugoslav state as well as the poor performance of the Italian army during the Great War, in a practical sense, deprived Italians of a great deal of the spoils promised by the London Treaty. On the other hand, the newly created Yugoslav state had to struggle for international recognition and was too weak, both militarily and politically, to openly confront Italy.

Since Albania was a neutral country during the war it officially was not a subject of the Paris Peace Conference. The Great Powers rather considered it as a not entirely constituted state whose prospects needed to be monitored by one of them—in this particular case it was Italy. Within this framework, in order to get the best out of it, Yugoslavs were forced to play an extremely complex game regarding Albania and Albanians in general. In order to keep in check their own Albanian population in Kosovo and Metohija, Montenegro and western Macedonia, Yugoslavs needed to exercise a strong influence among north Albanian highland clans, both Muslim and Roman Catholic, who, being extremely poor but very well armed, were always ready to sell their guns to a higher bidder. Beside a strong military presence on the so-called demarcation line, Yugoslavs had to maintain good relations with Albanian magnates as well because of their considerable political influence. The inability of Esad-pasha Toptani to return to Albania forced him once more to seek for help, this time Yugoslav. In order to help him, as well as to control and use his supporters, during March 1919 Yugoslavs decided to form four so-called *Battalions of Organized Albanians*.[1] Battalions comprised of people loyal to Esad-pasha were led or commanded by his prominent supporters like Hallil Lleshi and Taf Kazi, and were organized, paid and armed by the

---

[1] Božica Slavković: 'Bataljoni organizovanih Arnauta', In *Vojnoistorijski glasnik* 1(2010), 133–56; and Božica Slavković: 'Bataljoni organizovanih Arnauta', In *Vojnoistorijski glasnik* 1(2012), 51–70.

Yugoslav army. Battalions were deployed on the so-called 'demarcation line' or temporary Yugoslav-Albanian border, just in front of Yugoslav troops, serving as a buffer zone between Italian and Yugoslav troops. While battalions represented Esad-pasha's military structure, the so-called 'Esad-pasha's committee' represented his political organization. After settling down in Debar, a small but very important town on the Yugoslav-Albanian border, the committee initiated propaganda and intelligence activities supporting Esad-pasha's cause. These activities depended on Yugoslav financial and material support, Esad-pasha's reputation and already existing allegiances. Unlike the battalions, which were under the control of the army, the committee coordinated its activities with the Yugoslav Ministry of Foreign Affairs.[2] Soon, the first concrete results started to appear. Battalions participated in numerous skirmishes against other Albanian groups financed and organized by Italians. Thus, they were slowly penetrating deeper into Albanian territory, spreading Esad-pasha's influence instead of Yugoslav troops, which otherwise would compromise the whole endeavor. In the eyes of common Albanians Esad-pasha's influence was on the rise for several reasons— he had efficient armed supporters, didn't depend on Yugoslav troops, and his committee was appointing local officials who slowly introduced law and order. Yugoslav troops remained in the rear and thanks to that were spared a multitude of hardships associated with the rough and inhospitable Albanian mountains. For their engagement the members of *Battalions of Organized Albanians* would receive—as monthly allowance—wages in dinars: privates 80, corporals 90, sergeants 130, officers 230 and battalion commanders 330 dinars. They were also entitled to flour and salt and one pair of shoes per month, while officers also were entitled to fodder for their horses.[3] Compared to privates in two other professional Yugoslav military/police formations with similar duties, Border Troops and Gendarmerie, where starting wages of privates were 100 and 200 dinars,[4] 'organized' Albanians actually did quite well if we consider the fact that the majority of them were illiterate and without any kind of education or training.

In the Albanian case, more precisely in the case of Albanian mountain clans, the road to success in terms of recruitment went through their chieftains. Following traditional rules of allegiances, the clansmen were obliged to follow the choices of their chieftains, however, not without conditions. For example, one of Esad-pasha's old followers Shaqir Dema after the Great War didn't want to join Esad's organization because of a simple fact—one of Esad-pasha's battalion

---

[2] Božica Slavković: 'Bataljoni organizovanih Arnauta', In *Vojnoistorijski glasnik* 1(2010), 133–56, here 137–8.

[3] Dragiša Vasić, *Dva meseca u jugoslovenskom Sibiru*, (Beograd: Prosveta 1990), 65.

[4] Službeni vojni list (Military Gazette—SVL), no. 7 from March 23 1919, 152; and SVL, no. 5 from March 5 1919, 78.

commanders Hallil Lleshi used to be his servant. Shaqir Dema's conditions, beside financial compensation and permission for his clansmen to join *Battalions of Organized Albanians*, included the removal of his former servant from Esad-pasha's service. Yugoslav authorities agreed to all Shaqir Dema's terms except the last one but in order to satisfy him they redeployed the troubled man and his battalion further away.[5]

Nevertheless, a number of serious incidents occurred in areas where Albanian battalions were deployed. It is said that many Albanian battalions' rank-and-file signed up just because this kind of engagement provided them with opportunities to continue with illegal activities like smuggling, pillaging, extortion, etc. Then, there were internal Albanian blood feuds and vendetta assassinations where members of Albanian battalions often acted as hired guns.[6] The biggest problem, however, was cattle rustling, whose victims were stockbreeding communities in western Macedonia. Here, on mountain pastures they used to keep thousands of sheep, cows and horses that attracted the attention of their Albanian neighbours across the border. Numerous cases of cattle rustling were often associated with members of 'organized' battalions. And while, because of these irregularities and incidents, the Yugoslav civil authorities in western Macedonia insisted on immediate disbanding of the *Battalions of Organized Albanians*, the Yugoslav army leadership was much more practical. They advocated the continuation of Albanian engagement for several simple reasons:

1. Despite alleged criminal activities, the Albanians were actually protecting Yugoslav troops from getting into contact with Italian rivals.
2. Finances invested in the engagement of Esad-pasha's supporters were considerably smaller than potential damages caused by their actions either as simple brigands or paramilitaries in Italian service, where they would eventually go if dismissed.
3. With their dismissal from Yugoslav service more than a thousand brigands would be unleashed.
4. The position of Esad-pasha in internal Albanian clashes was strengthened by the fact that he had respectable forces at his disposal.

Not only did Yugoslav military officials operating in these areas support further engagement of Albanian irregulars, they also suggested several measures aimed at introducing control mechanisms like registering and keeping detailed registers of

---

[5] Ljubodrag Dimić and Đorđe Borozan, (eds), *Jugoslovenska država i Albanci. Tom 2* (Beograd: Službeni list SRJ; Arhiv Jugoslavije; Vojno-istorijski institut, 1998) 374–5 and 378.

[6] According to the unwritten code that is still valid among Albanian and Montenegrin clansmen in their blood feuds, if someone commits a murder on someone else's behalf the entire blood debt would be transferred to the person who committed the murder. Because of that it often happened that different outlaws could be hired for money to perform vendetta assassinations. The number of 'male heads' they owed to different families often rated their reputation.

each battalion, providing Albanian irregulars with some kind of ID's and intro-ducing liaison officers attached to each battalion.[7] They also suggested strength-ening them by hiring of another thousand men.[8]

Paradoxically, at the same time when Yugoslav authorities invested huge efforts into suppressing actions of Albanian *kachaks* in the region of Kosovo and Metohija, which were politically inspired by the Kosovo Committee and their aim to unite Kosovo and Metohija with Albania, a respectable number of Albanians decided to join Yugoslav service, thus protecting Yugoslav borders and support-ing Yugoslav interests in Albania. Even after the Congress of Lushnjë and creation of the *Committee for National Defence of Albania* in January 1920, when Albanian leaders reached a consensus over the future of their state and denounced the pro-Italian government, the political and military organization of Esad-pasha was still active. However, when in spring of 1920 an insurgency broke out against the Italian troops demanding their complete withdrawal from the country it became obvious that any foreign presence on Albanian soil would be targeted similarly.

By that time Esad-pasha was already in Paris, where he in practical terms hoped he would be able to cash in on his status of Serbian and Entente ally during the Great War and gain support for his return to the Albanian political arena. However, Avni Rustemi assassinated Esad-pasha in June 1920, proclaiming him as traitor to the Albanian national interests. After the assassination of Esad-pasha his supporters started to suffer defeat after defeat and in no time his political option was removed from the Albanian political scene. After death of their ally the Yugoslavs were forced to look for a new agent in Albanian affairs. However, some of the 'organized Albanians' remained in Yugoslav service for at least a year after Esad-pasha's death. Their engagement was terminated when the Yugoslav-Albanian border was regulated in 1921. After dismissal from Yugoslav service the remains of 'organized Albanians' joined different sides struggling for dominance in Albania.

Meanwhile, as predicted, after the Italian withdrawal the Albanians turned their attention towards the Yugoslavs. In August 1920 newly created Albanian armed forces, supported by numerous irregulars, waged offensive actions against Yugoslav troops. Initial Albanian success forced the Yugoslav army command to bring reinforcements of more than twenty additional infantry battalions with air-planes and artillery. Although the Yugoslavs managed to stop the Albanian advance and return them to their previous positions it again showed how difficult it was for any modern regular army to operate on rough mountainous terrain in Albania. Without airplanes and artillery, and also without veterans from the Great War who were hastily summoned, this could have been a major failure.

---

[7] VA, r. 4/3, b. 58, f. 1, d. 3/7, Report of the Command of Third army district to the Ministry of Army and Navy, confidential no. 299 from February 3 1920.
[8] VA, r. 4/3, b. 58, f. 2, d. 1/84, Report of the Command of Bitola division district to the Command of Third army district, confidential no. 34 from 25 February 1920.

Overall Yugoslav casualties during this campaign were huge—more than 700 dead, wounded and captured.[9]

In the case of the Serbian-Bulgarian rivalry over Macedonia several examples of changing sides happened after the Great War as well. Before the Balkan Wars of 1912–1913, individual changes of sides were quite frequent among the confronted rivals—the IMRO and Serbian *chetnik* organizations. These changes were primarily characteristics of simple local (Macedonian) rank-and-file members of both organizations. This was often a sign or proof of the fluidity of their national affiliation or consciousness, which practically and paradoxically coincided with contemporaneous claims of the Serbian geographer Jovan Cvijić. Based upon his extensive research on the Balkan Peninsula, Cvijić was convinced that Macedonian Slavs represented an undeterminable ethnic composition between Serbs and Bulgarians which would, in time, assume either Serb or Bulgarian national affiliation, depending on the final outcome of the struggle over Macedonia.[10] These changes of sides also happened in Aegean Macedonia where several IMRO *voivodes* decided to defect to the Greek side, like the famous Kotha, Vangelis, or Guelev who decided to change sides after having a quarrel with the Head of the local IMRO.[11]

Reasons for changing sides were sometimes much simpler and were related to existential needs, concern for a family's well-being, or essential features of human nature like greed or self-interest. One of the typical examples took place in 1920 when the Yugoslav envoy in Sofia was approached by a certain Kosta Jovanović, Bulgarian *komitaji* and former sergeant in the Serbian army, who, during the Great War, after being wounded and captured, decided to enter Bulgarian service. He became a close associate of Todor Alexandrov and he participated as *komitaji* in numerous incidents in occupied Macedonia as well as in quelling the Toplica Uprising in 1917. After the war he showed readiness to put himself at the disposal of the Yugoslav government in exchange for a full pardon of his transgressions committed during the period of Bulgarian occupation. Another and equally important reason to make such an offer was his wish to end separation from his wife who at the time resided in Skopje.[12] His name appeared in several reports from a later period, and in the end he was able to strike a deal with Yugoslav authorities and return to Skopje. Two years later, in summer 1922 Kosta Jovanović, together with another trustee, was dispatched to Bulgaria for a mission of gathering intelligence data. His knowledge of IMRO organizational structure proved to

---

[9] Mile Bjelajac, 'Vojni faktor i mogućnosti odbrane nacionalnih teritorija 1918-1921', In *Vojnoistorijski glasnik*, 2/1985, 194–222.

[10] Further readings: Jovan Cvijić, *Makedonski Sloveni, promatranja o etnografiji makedonskih Slovena*, (Beograd: Knjžara Geca Kon, 1906).

[11] Nadine Lange-Akhund, *The Macedonian Question 1893–1908, from Western Sources* (Boulder: East European Monographs, 1998) 209–10.

[12] VA, r. 4/3, b. 58, f. 8, d. 6/82, Report of the Ministry of Army and Navy to the Command of Third Army district, confidential no. 8878 from August 3 1920.

be unparalleled. Two agents managed to infiltrate across the border and to return the same way undetected by either Yugoslav or Bulgarian border guards. They also brought valuable data. Jovanović's only concern during this mission was that someone might recognize and denounce him as a renegade.[13]

However, one of the major cases of defection happened after the Great War when an internal clash of two different and in a way opposed concepts occurred within the IMRO—*federalist* and *autonomist*. When at the beginning of the 1920's the two concepts clashed, it represented the final stage of an internal conflict, which had smouldered from the organization's beginning. The conflict was marked by conceptual differences and occasional disagreements and it had already caused the unexplained deaths of several of the organization's champions. The conflict or actually the split from the 1920's was so serious and deep that it was actually never resolved afterwards.

Everything related to this conflict will be much clearer if we observe the circumstances around the beginning of armed struggle for Macedonia. The last decade of the 19th century began with the creation of two organizations whose aim was the liberation of Macedonia from Ottoman rule. Their creation was the second step after the already achieved church and educational autonomy through creation of the Bulgarian Exarchate in 1872. The first organization was the *Internal Macedonian and Adrianople Revolutionary Organization* (IMARO) founded in Salonika in 1893 by several young intellectuals, most of them teachers in Exarchate schools in Macedonia, like Damyan Gruev and Gotse Delchev. Their main goal was actual implementation of Article 23 of the 1878 Treaty of Berlin, which envisaged administrative reforms in European provinces of the Ottoman Empire aimed at acquiring full political autonomy for two regions (Macedonia and Adrianople).[14] The Macedonian emigrants in Bulgaria founded the second organization in 1895, initially named the *Macedonian Committee*. During same year it changed its name to *Supreme Macedonian Committee*. Their agenda, although focused on Macedonia, was a bit aggressive, being influenced by Bulgarian aspirations towards Macedonia as well as by significant participation of Bulgarian army officers (approximately one third of Bulgarian army officers were of Macedonian origin).[15] Immediately after its creation the *Supreme Committee* initiated sending groups of armed men to Macedonia, hoping to instigate an uprising. Their appearance and actions caused serious reprisal against the local Christian population.[16] The two organizations were operating side-by-side from

---

[13] AJ, MUP KJ 14–177–1031, Command of the 3rd Gendarmerie Brigade, Report to the Commissar for South Serbia, confidential no. 1350 from 4 July 1922.

[14] Nadine Akhund—Lange, 'Nationalisme et terrorisme en Macédoine vers 1900'.In *Balkanologie*, Vol IV, no. 2 (2000), 4.

[15] John D. Bell, *Peasants in Power: Alexander Stamboliiski and the Bulgarian Agrarian National Union 1899–1923*, (Princeton: Princeton University Press, 1977), 89.

[16] Nadine Lange-Akhund, *The Macedonian Question 1893–1908, from Western Sources* (Boulder: East European Monographs, 1998) 47–8.

the beginning, maybe not in coordination but in awareness of each other and in regular contact. However, this relation wasn't without differences and misunderstandings which originated from different personalities or conceptual issues like supremacy and leadership.[17] Although both organizations had profited from mutual contacts and cooperation, primarily in terms of military training provided by the members of the *Supreme Committee* or knowledge of local circumstances, which was the specialty of IMARO members, the main difference between the two organizations concerned the final goal of their struggle—the status of Ottoman Macedonia. Simply said, the *Supreme Committee* favoured unification of Macedonia (three *vilajeyts*—Skoplje, Monastir and Salonika) with Bulgaria while the IMARO advocated the political autonomy of Macedonia, which could evolve into independence and end in a federation with other South Slav states.[18] Another issue was the timing of an uprising in Macedonia. On the eve of twentieth century IMARO was opposing a major uprising while the *Supreme Committee* insisted on it. IMARO leaders thought that Macedonians were still poorly armed and not organized enough while for the *Supreme Committee* the uprising represented a perfect opportunity to take leadership in the Macedonian struggle. However, the famous Ilinden Uprising that took place in August 1903 in Macedonia after intensive activities and insistence of the *Supreme Committee* led to Ottoman reprisals causing huge material and human losses. The Ilinden Uprising also led to international intervention and the signing of the Mürzsteg Agreement for the introduction of reforms in Ottoman Macedonia. After the uprising, and especially after the Rila congress of IMARO in 1906 it became even clearer that within the Macedonian national movement there were two streams, the fact that would mark the rest of the organization's history—the Serres group with a somewhat leftist inclination, headed by Yane Sandanski, and Boris Sarafov's group following guidelines of the *Supreme Committee* promoting close ties with Bulgaria. Their conflict was so serious that in 1907 in Sofia, Sandanski's trustee Todor Panitsa killed Boris Sarafov and his associate Ivan Garvanov.[19] Participation of IMARO bands in the Young Turk revolution, where Sandanski with his followers was fully engaged on the side of the Young Turks, additionally deepened the rift with the group closely associated with Bulgarian official circles.[20]

During the Balkan Wars and the First World War both factions supported Bulgarian war efforts. However, the schism was so deep that even Sandanski became a victim of vendetta assassination in 1915. After the war when Alexandrov, Protogerov and Chaulev restored the old organization, now as the IMRO (Adrianople was dropped out), again they had to cope with differences. At the

---

[17] Nadine Lange-Akhund, *The Macedonian Question, 1893–1908*, 51–4.
[18] Nadine Lange-Akhund, *The Macedonian Question, 1893–1908*, 102–15.
[19] Nadine Lange-Akhund, *The Macedonian Question 1893–1908*, 47–8.
[20] Mehmet Hacısalihoğlu, 'Yane Sandanski as political leader in Macedonia in the era of the Young Turks'. In *Cahiers balkaniques*, 40 (2012), *Jeunes-Turcs en Macédonie et en Ionie*, 1–28, here 3.

same time, a faction within the IMRO known as *Serres revolutionary district* under the leadership of Dimo Hadzhidimov, Georgi Skrizhovski, Chudomir Kantadzhiev and other followers of the ideas of Yane Sandanski established the *Provisional branch of the former IMRO* led by Djorche Petrov. Their goal was the autonomy of Macedonia and for that reason they also criticized the *Executive Committee of the Macedonian fraternities* because of their desire to annex Macedonia to Bulgaria.[21] Immediately after the end of war the Serres group, under the initiative of Dimo Hadzhidimov, issued the so-called *Serres Declaration* stating their goals of an autonomous Macedonia and a Balkan federation in which Macedonia would be restored in its geographical framework. The following year Hadzhidimov issued a brochure under the title *Return Towards Autonomy* explaining in detail his vision of a Balkan federation, criticizing Macedonians in Bulgaria and their leaders for undermining the idea of federation with Macedonia as its central part. He finished his political pamphlet with the slogan *Long live the next Switzerland of the Balkans!*[22] Among the members of *Serres revolutionary districts* there was a strong inclination towards the ideas of the political left and in that sense their differences with the official wing of IMRO were obvious. Strongholds of the Serres group were located in the valley of the river Struma, i. e. around the towns of Drama, Kavala and Serres.[23] However, after the Great War these territories were annexed to Greece. Yugoslav military authorities suggested establishment of contact with this group in order to introduce them to Yugoslav goals and to prevent their transfer into the Bolshevik realm.[24] The Serres group actually represented the core of the *federalist* faction which in the early 1920's began to operate through the *Macedonian Emigrant Federative Organization* (MEFO) and *Macedonian Federative Revolutionary Organization* (MFRO). The only difference between these two organizations was that MFRO was resolved on armed struggle for the liberation of Macedonia.[25] Initially, the *autonomist* faction, and especially one of its leaders, Todor Alexandrov, began a campaign against the

---

[21]   Krasimir Karakachanov, *VMRO—100 godini borba za Makedoniya*, (Sofia: VMRO-SMD, 1994), 43.

[22]   Zoran Todorovski, *Avtonomističkata VMRO na Todor Aleksandrov 1919–1924*, (Skopje: Makavej, 2013) 54.

[23]   An explanation of how and why this group acquired a leftist orientation was given by Mary C. Neuburger, *Balkan Smoke: Tobacco and the Making of Modern Bulgaria*, (Ithaca: Cornell University Press 2013), 60–3: the tobacco-growing 'boom' that occurred in the Balkans by the end of 19th century had deep economical and political repercussions in the region. One of them was the beginning of a labor movement among growing numbers of workers in the tobacco processing industry. Interestingly, the major part of tobacco production was in the above-mentioned regions, as was the case with Bulgarian refugees both before and after the Balkan Wars 1912–1913.

[24]   VA, r. 4/3, b. 54, f. 11, d. 12/97, Report of the Ministry of Army to the command Third army district, confidential no. 25 193 from 15 May 1919, forwarded report of the command of the Border troops, confidential no. 668 from 29 April 1919. The precision of the trustee and the accuracy of his analyses are confirmed by future events, one group of activists having actually joined the Bolsheviks (Hadzhidimov, Vlahov, etc) while others made contact with Yugoslav authorities and later entered their service (Mishev, Sokolarski end others).

[25]   Z. Todorovski, *Avtonomističkata VMRO na Todor Aleksandrov*, 56–7.

federalists. He used his favourite institution, i.e. issuing death threats against everyone who was objecting to his methods.

In order to cause confusion within *federalist* faction, during 1921, Alexandrov ordered the executions (in the form of assassinations) of several prominent *federalists*. The first happened on 28 June when Djorche Petrov, a famous and respected member of the old IMRO, and once the closest associate of Gotse Delchev, was assassinated. A couple of months later, in October, Ivan Yanev-B'rlyo, after a successful attempt on Alexander Dimitrov, Bulgarian Minister of the Army and Interior, managed to kill Doncho Angelov, another prominent *federalist*. These assassinations caused the division between the two factions to deepen further.[26] Immediately after these actions some 60-80 *komitajis* with several *voivodes* decided to abandon the ranks of the *autonomists* and join the MFRO. Soon, some of the *federalist* champions established first contacts with the Yugoslav representatives who agreed on three conditions in order for MFRO to continue the struggle against the IMRO:

1. Necessary funds and resources;
2. Permission for *federalist* bands to withdraw if necessary to Yugoslav territory;
3. Full pardon for transgressions committed prior to 1915.

During 1922 Yugoslav authorities already noticed the presence of opposed bands of both *federalist* and *autonomist* factions on Yugoslav soil. Following Alexandrov's order against *federalist* actions, one of the *federalist* bands led by *voivode* Krum Zografov was deliberately betrayed to Yugoslav police forces which managed to organize successful action, eliminate the band and kill Zografov.[27]

Differences between the two factions also attracted the attention of the Bulgarian government led by BANU. In order to suppress activities of the *autonomist* faction, BANU decided to support the *federalists*.[28] However, Alexandrov's answer was swift and ruthless. On 16 October 1922 more than 1,000 *autonomist komitajis* organized successful action against *federalists* in Nevrokop. Another and identically successful action followed on 4 December in Kyustendil—another important IMRO centre.[29] Beside the fact that the *federalist* faction was defeated, what became visible was the incapability and weakness of the BANU regime to diminish the importance of the *autonomists* and fulfil one of the most important

---

[26] Kostadin Paleshutski, *Makedonskiyat v'pros v burzhoazna Jugoslaviya 1918–1941*, (Sofia: BAN, 1983), 119.

[27] Zoran Todorovski, *Todor Aleksandrov*, (Skopje: Makavej; Državen arhiv na Republika Makedonija, 2014) 178–86.

[28] Veselin Yaanchev, *Armiya, obshtestven red i vatreshna sigurnost mezhdu voynite i sled tyaah: 1913–1915, 1918–1923* (Sofia: Universitetsko izdatelstvo 'Sv. Kliment Ohridski', 2014), 299.

[29] Z. Todorovski, *Avtonomističkata VMRO na Todor Aleksandrov*, 54.

conditions for normalization of relations with the Kingdom of Serbs, Croats and Slovenes. For the remaining *federalists* the only solution to avoid total obliteration was to leave Bulgaria and emigrate across the border to the Kingdom of Serbs, Croats and Slovenes. Among the first ones to defect was the prominent *voivode* Iliya Hristov Atanasov-Pandurski who after several clashes with *autonomist* bands specially dispatched to eliminate him and his band, crossed the Yugoslav border on 27 February 1923. After being hunted down for nearly six months, with a price placed on his head, and his family harassed, defection and entry into Yugoslav service was seen as the only solution for survival.[30] A second and larger wave of defection happened in May 1923. It came about as a result of a success-fully conducted operation of Yugoslav intelligence. Several prominent *federalists* leaders: Grigor Ciklev, Stoyan Mishev, and Mita Sokolarski-Sudzhukareto, openly defected and entered Yugoslav service. Together with their followers and trustees they implemented their knowledge and experience in helping Yugoslav author-ities in neutralization of IMRO illegal structures in Yugoslav Macedonia. Already in September that same year several *federalists* 'renegades', as they were referred to in IMRO proclamations, joined a new paramilitary organization established in Macedonia by Yugoslav authorities. Its name, *Organization against Bulgarian Bandits,* clearly testified its agenda. Organization consisted of IMRO 'renegades', Serbian *chetniks*, retired officers, members of the organization *National Defence* and local volunteers. Because of their new status and role, these 'renegades' became yet another enemy on the long IMRO blacklist and were the cause of numerous assassinations and bloody showdowns in the following years.[31] Local IMRO leaders in Macedonia were informed on 15 March 1924 how they should deal with *federalist* 'renegades'.[32]

Although these cases of defection attracted most of the contemporary atten-tion, there were other individual cases as well. Beside the above-mentioned Kosta Jovanović, during 1922 the name of 'Stojče Dobrić, former Bulgarian chetnik' appeared, who was sent from Belgrade on 16 September 1922, with ten men, to Skopje district where he was ordered to track down and kill or capture IMRO *voivode* Velichko Velyanov, nicknamed Chicheto or Skopski.[33] On 22 September they had their first encounter with Velichko and his band.[34]

---

[30] Dimitar Tyulekov *Obrecheno rodolyubie. VMRO v Pirinsko 1919–1934* (Blagoevgrad: Univ. Izd. 'Neofit Rilski', 2001), http://www.promacedonia.org/dt/dt1_2.html [last checked on 31 October 2016]

[31] Z. Todorovski, *Avtonomističkata VMRO na Todor Aleksandrov*, 147.

[32] Natsionalna biblioteka 'Kiril i Metodiy' (NBKM), B'lgarski istoricheski arhiv (BIA), Collection 841 V'treshna makedonska revolutsyiona organizaciya (VMRO), Archival unit no. 1/14, Central Committee of the IMRO, no. 711, 15 March 1924.

[33] AJ, MUP KJ 14–177, Command of the 3rd Gendarmerie Brigade, Report to the Commissar for South Serbia, confidential no. 1947 from 16 September 1922.

[34] AJ, MUP KJ 14–177–1133, Command of the 3rd Gendarmerie Brigade, Report to the Commissar for South Serbia, confidential no. 2003 from 23 September 1922.

There were no doubts that entering Yugoslav service was the only way for these renegades to survive and continue fighting against autonomist rivals. The level of hatred and desire for vengeance was insurance enough for their new sponsors.[35]

In the years to come the *federalist* 'renegades' reversed the tide by initiating operations on the territory of Pirin Macedonia, which also used to be called 'Macedonia under Bulgarian rule'. They interrupted IMRO communications, created *federalist* network, and recruited local supporters. Thanks to this, IMRO had to seriously reconsider its revolutionary methods and adapt to a new reality. Serious efforts were invested in anti-'renegade' actions often followed by violence and extreme brutality.[36] The impact of renegades' defection on IMRO was very deep. One of the famous contemporary IMRO *voivods*, Pancho Mikhailov-Chavdar, assassin of the Minister of the Interior Alexander Dimitrov and one of the leaders during the IMRO action in Kyustendil in December 1922 where he delivered an inspired speech, and who beside audacity possessed literary talent, wrote and published a short story in which he mentioned *federalist* renegades. In a story titled 'Serbians Passed through the Village' he mentioned: 'Serbian *voivods* of bandit *chetas*, the renegades Stoyan Mishev'ich', Grigor Ciklev'ich' and Mite Sudzhukarev'ich'. He also described the actions and alleged brutality committed by the above-mentioned renegades in Serbian service.[37]

Whenever it happened that some of these 'renegades' either died in accidental gunfights with some IMRO band in the Macedonian countryside or were assassinated in carefully prepared actions, their deaths would cause huge and colourful bursts of satisfaction in the ranks of the IMRO. Already in March 1924, Todor Alexandrov was proud to announce the award *IMRO Organizational Badge with Red Flags* to Cvetan Spasov, an IMRO *komitaji* from Kumanovo, who together with his band managed to liquidate the 'renegade' Mina Stanković who had been 'terrorizing' IMRO supporters in the Kumanovo region during the previous months.[38]

Real outbursts of euphoria were caused by a successful murder attempt on one of the leading 'renegades,' Mita Sokolarski-Sudzhukareto, which took place on market day in Vinica, in Kočani district on 30 July 1924. The official IMRO proclamation and description of his death did not omit to characterize him as a murderer and plunderer who, from 1919 until 1921, under the leadership of another two 'renegades,' Stoyan Mishev and Slave Ivanov, killed and pillaged many

[35] AJ 334–8–108–12. For example, Grigor Ciklev publicly expressed the wish to become a 'good subject,' similar to his brother who had already been in Serbian service and earned respect as an army sergeant. Although the author of this report openly qualifies Ciklev's statement as 'potential comedy,' he could be trusted, bearing in mind the circumstances that led to his entering Yugoslav service.

[36] Dimitar Tyulekov, *Obrecheno rodolyubie. VMRO v Pirinsko 1919–1934* (Blagoevgrad: Univ. Izd. 'Neofit Rilski', 2001), http://www.promacedonia.org/dt/dt2_4.html [last checked on 31 October 2016]

[37] 'Srbite minaha prez seloto' in Pancho Mikhailov, *V' stranata na s'lzite*, (Sofia, 1924), 14.

[38] NBKM, BIA, Collection 841 VMRO, Archival unit no. 1, Central Committee of the IMRO, no. 709, 10 March 1924.

'Bulgarians, Vlachs and Turks' in Macedonia. According to the same proclamation, Sokolarski and other federalists had been at the full disposal of the agrarian
regime from 1921, which was 'plotting with the Serbs to eliminate IMRO leadership'. From 1923 Sokolarski became a 'mercenary of King Alexander and Pašić'.
The assassination of Sokolarski was executed by four *komitajis* disguised as simple
peasants. They were armed with revolvers and hand grenades. Sokolarski was
killed with eight shots. A hand grenade, which was thrown at him, wounded several innocent bystanders. For their bravery and success, the assassins were
awarded with the *IMRO Organizational Badge with Red Flags* as well as with new
revolvers and 5,000 Bulgarian levas and 300 Yugoslav dinars each. Sokolarski was
described as the 'fastest, boldest, ... and most dangerous of traitorous bandits'.[39]

An equally important federalist leader, now a member of the *Organization
against Bulgarian Bandits*, Stoyan Mishev was killed in Štip on 30 December 1924.
His assassin was 21-year-old Kiril Grigorov, a poor Macedonian refugee who
wanted to become a member of IMRO by performing an act of outstanding bravery. Although he initially managed to escape, Grigorov was captured near the
Bulgarian border. He was tried and sentenced to death. Together with other
IMRO assassins with similar faiths, like Yordan Tsitsonkov or Mara Buneva, the
organization celebrated Grigorov as an ultimate hero and martyr.[40]

Another prominent 'renegade', Iliya Pandurski, fell victim to a carefully
planned assassination in the summer of 1925. After causing so many troubles
with his strong and organized *cheta* of nearly 60 *komitajis,* Pandurski came into
the focus of the new IMRO leader Ivan Mikhailov. The first measure was to seize
and confiscate all Pandurski's property. The next one was the execution of a plan
that envisaged infiltration of *komitaji* into Pandurski's band who would use the
first opportunity to kill him. That role was given to Hristo Vangelov Stoev a.k.a
Risto Derizhabo. He was accepted into Pandurski's *cheta* after he allegedly committed the murder of one prominent IMRO leader. As planned, he used the
opportunity to kill Iliya Pandurski. The IMRO press praised Stoev as an ultimate
hero who killed the 'renowned apostate who sold himself to the Serbs'.[41]

As in the case of agrarians after the 9 June coup, *federalists* also started to fall
victim to assassinations which the IMRO organized abroad. In May 1925 in the
Viennese Burgtheater, Mencha Karnicheva assassinated Todor Panitsa, one of the
leading *federalists*. This former *komitaji* and close associate of Yane Sandanski and
Todor Alexandrov (Panitsa organized his prison break in 1919) after 1924 moved

---

[39] NBKM, BIA, Collection 841 VMRO, Archival unit no. 1/16–18, Central Committee of the
IMRO, no. 777, 2 August 1924; see also Angel Uzunov, *Spomeni* (Skopje: Makavej, 2014), 320;
Yugoslav press described in detail whole affair praising Sokolarski and other renegades. Sokolarski
was qualified as 'our voivode'. *Vreme*, 6 August 1924, 'Ubistvo našeg vojvode Mite Sokolarskog', p. 3.

[40] Ivan Mikhailov, *Spomeni, III, Osvoboditelna borba (1924–1934)* (Louvain 1967), 147–55.

[41] Dimitar Tyulekov, *Obrecheno rodolyubie. VMRO v Pirinsko 1919–1934* (Blagoevgrad: Univ. Izd.
'Neofit Rilski', 2001), http://www.promacedonia.org/dt/dt2_4.html [last checked on 31 October 2016]

to Vienna where the *federalists* had established their headquarters. There he participated in the creation of a new organization called IMRO (United) that continued to follow the federalist program but in closest relations with the Comintern.[42] Mencha Karnicheva was acquitted and upon return to Bulgaria she married Ivan Mikhailov, the new leader of the IMRO.[43] Meanwhile, the *federalists* continued their gradual transfer toward communism.

In practical terms the arrival of *federalist* 'renegades' in Macedonia and their entrance into Yugoslav service marked a new stage in the evolution of Balkan paramilitarism. Slowly but clearly, the age of small, armed bands roaming Macedonian villages, gathering and organizing their supporters was coming to an end. However, it cannot be said that there was a single reason for this change. More likely, it can be attributed to the combination of several factors. In the following years measures like the creation of *Organization against Bulgarian Bandits* contributed to a serious reduction of manoeuvrable space for the IMRO and its *komitajis*. Despite the fact that most of the leading 'renegades' were killed, their successors and their bands were partly responsible for the specific 'reverse of the tide' in relation to *komitaji* intrusions on Yugoslav territory in the following years. From 1924 onwards, they organized numerous infiltrations across the Bulgarian borders, causing major disruption of the IMRO infrastructure in Petrich County.[44]

Besides that, the Yugoslav state invested huge efforts in pacifying areas of Macedonia and Kosovo and Metohija. A network of new Gendarmerie precincts was created and additional forces were brought in like 2,000 additional Gendarmes, as well as 1,200 for the single task of protecting the Skopje-Salonika railway. Border Troops were strengthened in number as well, while parts of the borderline with Bulgaria were fortified with new border posts, bunkers and obstacles. Additional funds were allocated for intelligence operations as well as for *chetnik* detachments.[45] An important part of these efforts was the *Organization against Bulgarian Bandits*, which was, in the following years, carefully transformed into another massive paramilitary organization under the name of *People's Self-Defence* with a membership of nearly 25,000 throughout eastern Macedonia.

The massive presence of the Gendarmerie and regular army in Macedonia, together with 'classic' paramilitary formations, forced IMRO *komitajis* to new approaches and a change of style. Disguise became an imperative, so when operating on Macedonian soil after 1925 *komitaji* bands rarely appeared in their

---

[42] On IMRO (United) see: Ivan Katardžiev (ed.), *VMRO (Obedineta): dokumenti i materijali. I i II*, (Skopje: Institut za nacionalna istorija, 1992); and *70 godini VMRO (Obedineta) 1925-1995: Conference proceedings*, (Skopje: Institut za nacionalna istorija, 1998).

[43] See: Mencha K'rnicheva, *Zashto ubih Todor Panitsa?* (Sofia: VMRO—SMD, 1993).

[44] Dimitar Tyulekov, *Obrecheno rodolyubie. VMRO v Pirinsko 1919-1934*, http://www.promacedonia.org/dt/dt2_4.html [last checked on 31 October 2016]

[45] Archive of Yugoslavia (Arhiv Jugoslavije—AJ), Collection 37 Milan Stojadinović, 22/331-333.

traditional outfit. In order to ease their movements, they either wore civilian clothes both from countryside and towns or uniforms of the Yugoslav army and Gendarmerie. Long beards and bandoliers became features from some old photographs, while rifles were replaced with much lighter revolvers and hand grenades. However, another event of 1924 contributed to the organizational and doctrinal changes within the IMRO. The sudden and unexpected assassination of Todor Alexandrov which occurred in August while he was heading to attend a meeting of the Serres revolutionary district also marked the end of the classical *komitaji* period. The charismatic personality of Alexandrov was soon replaced by the indistinguishable figure of Ivan Mikhailov—a revolutionary-bureaucrat. Instead of Alexandrov, a typical representative of old school, who drew his popularity from sharing hazards and risks with other common *komitajis* roaming Macedonian villages and avoiding Yugoslav posses, the new leader of the IMRO was a typical office style suit-up activist with no previous experience in guerrilla warfare. Although Mikhailov used to pose in full *komitaji* outfit he never became a classical *voivode*. Internal frictions and clashes between opposing groups within the IMRO additionally influenced the shift toward political terrorism rather than guerrilla warfare. However, how strong the legacy of *komitaji* action was became obvious during the last months of the Second World War when the security apparatus of the newly established Yugoslav communist regime in Macedonia reported the appearance of several IMRO *komitaji* veterans who utilized the existing security vacuum to give the last vent to their passion. They continued to appear in Macedonia until the early 1950's when they definitely left the historical scene.[46]

Life Trajectories of some of the Balkans Paramilitaries

Stanislav Krakov (Kragujevac, 1895—Geneva, 1968), the famous and controversial Serbian and Yugoslav intellectual, once used his own example to describe how changes that often happened in one's life in the Balkans could appear to be so drastic. Summarizing his life, this multi-talented personality and incredibly prolific writer, war veteran, movie director, journalist, and in one moment even paramilitary, said:

[46] Military Archive Belgrade (Vojni arhiv—VA), Arhiv Vojnobezbednosne agencije (Archive of the Military Security Agency—AVBA), file 4—3.2.06, Terrorism, banditry, banditism 1947–1954, Report on outlaw bands for February 1947 from the II Department of the 5th Army headquarters to the 5th Army Department of Counterintelligence, confidential no. 68 from 13 March 1947; Military Archive Belgrade (Vojni arhiv—VA), Yugoslav People's Army (Jugoslovenska Narodna Armija -JNA), Command of the Corps of National Defence of Yugoslavia and Border Troops of Yugoslavia (KNOJ i GJJ), no. 3718–14, Numerical strenghth of 'bandits' during 1948; VA, JNA, Command of the KNOJ and GJJ, no. 3705–5, Operative history of the Corps of National Defence of Yugoslavia and Border Troops of Yugoslavia for 1949. Overview of the annihilation of bands in Yugoslav interior.

"I had a chance to dine with several kings, yet I was lucky when I was able to roast a handful of corn over a nearly extinguished fire. For hundreds of meters I walked over a horrifying bridge made of human cadavers and horse carcasses turned into a thick and muddy mass, without touching the ground, yet I was carried as a victor on hands of cheering maidens through the street covered with flowers. I knew personally and was introduced to many heads of states and mighty dictators, yet I had the opportunity to meet their rivals and even hangmen...

Once I was a player in a game of baccarat in Caen and Deauville with multimillionaire Blumenthal and former Portuguese king Manuel, yet again later I played poker in the prison 'casino Bourbaki' with the burglar Jeanot, one *Vietminh* agent and one Belgian homosexual with one lump of sugar as a stake.

Two towns in my own country proclaimed me their honorary citizen with fanfare and under flags and flowers, one even named its main street after me, while a couple of years later I had to hide in distant mountain houses under a false name, occupation and nationality.

One of the encyclopaedias in my country noted me as the "great war hero", yet another new master while conquering the place of my residency named me "enemy of the people".

I was decorated with 18 decorations, half of them in peace, half during wartime. Three times I've been sentenced to death."[47]

Krakov's father Sigismund was a Polish immigrant who became a doctor in the Serbian army. His mother Persida was the sister of three prominent Serbian officers: Colonel Božidar and Generals Milutin and Milan Nedić (during WWII the latter was the head of the Serbian quisling regime). Krakov was also close to Dimitrije Ljotić, the leader of the Yugoslav extreme right movement Zbor. His controversy actually comes from his ties with the above-mentioned people as well as from his opposition to Yugoslav Communists who tried to erase him and his work from public memory. Krakov's life was dynamic and adventurous and represented an inexhaustible source for his literary opus. When he was a teenager, he joined Serbian paramilitaries during the Balkan Wars. After the wars he enlisted in the Military Academy. Krakov participated in all the major events of WWI. After the war he served in the Royal Guards and was sent on a mission to north Albania. He resigned his commission and became a journalist for several leading Yugoslav newspapers. He also graduated from the Belgrade Faculty of Law. He married Ivanka Ivanić, a dentist, poet and novelist, daughter of Milica Mihajlović, the first female dentist in Serbia. Between the wars he published numerous

---

[47] Stanislav Krakov, *Život čoveka na Balkanu*, (Beograd: Naš dom; Lausanne: L'Age d'Homme, 2006), 12.

stories, travelogues, reviews, criticim, essays. His best works are the novels 'Kroz buru' ('Through the Storm', 1921) and 'Krila' ('Wings', 1922) (one of the best Serbian anti-war novels), the travel work 'Kroz Južnu Srbiju' ('Across South Serbia', 1926), war memoirs, Naše poslednje pobede' ('Our Last Victories', 1928), historical pieces 'Plamen četništva' ('Blaze of Chetniks', 1930) and the monograph 'General Milan Nedić I-II' published in 1968. The manuscript of his novel 'Čovek koji je izgubio prošlost' ('The Man Who Lost his Past') was lost in the Balkan vortex. Fragments from his autobigraphy were published under the title 'Život čoveka na Balkanu' ('The Life of the Man in the Balkans'). Krakov became famous for his movie 'Za čast Otadžbine' ('For the Honor of the Fatherland', 1930) as well several documentaries which were lost during the Second World War. During his stay in immigration he was not politically active.

The dynamics of the historical development in the Balkans in the first half of the twentieth century has undoubtedly left deep traces in the lives of different paramilitaries that were active during that period, not only of simple rank-and-file but of organization's leaders and prominent members as well. However, through both their actions and writings some of them have actually left a strong personal influence on the above-mentioned dynamics. As their personalities grew stronger, equally strong was their influence, not only on their comrades but on their broader surrounding as well. Beside active political engagement, their lives were filled with violence committed not only against their rivals and adversaries but against their own comrades as well.

In terms of motivation for joining the paramilitary organizations the situation in the Balkans after the Great War was slightly different than elsewhere in Europe. In European states like Austria, Germany, and Hungary, joining was motivated differently according to age and war record. While older paramilitaries were strongly influenced by the defeat they had suffered and the wish to maintain a way of life resembling that of the army, with its camaraderie and *esprit de corps*, younger ones were actually frustrated by the fact that when they reached the age that would allow them to join the war effort, the war had already ended. In Latvia, Lithuania and Estonia, joining the local paramilitaries was mostly motivated by nationalism and the need to protect their newly founded states. In the Balkans, paramilitaries came out from the war in already functioning and active organizations, which, with minor adaptations to new circumstances, continued to operate as earlier.

Some of the motifs, which stood behind their decisions to make such a drastic change in their lives, were an integral part of the local folklore for generations. Taking the rifle and going into mountains, where one would find a 'band of brothers' and embrace it as a new family is the *leitmotif* of hundreds of folk songs all over the Balkans. Sometimes it was because of unrequited love, personal tragedy or desire to prove one's manhood. In several instances joining paramilitary groups was motivated by the wish to contribute to the organization's mission more directly, in person and with long-term effects. For example, some of the prominent paramilitaries, although they had been educated to become teachers, decided to swap classrooms, blackboards and chalk with mountains and repeating rifles. Typical examples were Todor Alexandrov and Jovan Babunski. The first was one of the most popular leaders of the IMRO and at one moment member of the organization's Central Committee. The other is one of the best-known leaders of Serbian *chetniks* in Ottoman Macedonia.

Some were motivated by national ideals and they showed readiness to make the ultimate sacrifice like Vasilije Trbić, an Austro-Hungarian Serb, who started his career as a monastic novice and who, after spending several years among *chetniks,* decided to settle in Macedonia where he found a new home and got married, and where he remained to live long after he had 'hung up his rifle on a peg'. In addition, after the Great War, Trbić ventured into politics and was elected several times as MP in his constituency in the Macedonian town of Prilep.

Others were career officers who wanted to contribute to the greater cause with their own set of particular skills like Bulgarian Colonel Peter D'rvingov, a person with incredible organizational skills, a talented writer and military historian who was at one moment organizing and conducting brutal reprisals against Toplica

Fig. 8. Elementary school in Macedonian village Omorani named after Jovan Babunski.

Naming of state institutions such as schools after national heroes included Serbian paramilitaries as well. This one in named after Jovan Babunski and in a way represented interesting homage to his never destined profession as a teacher.

© National Library of Serbia (Belgrade), Album *Chetnik Movement,* AF 175.

insurgents, while at the other was hiding in Bulgarian mountains identically to his previous victims, in order to avoid arrest and trial for his transgressions. Besides being an officer and prominent *komitaji* leader before the Great War, D'rvingov lived to be admitted as a member of the Bulgarian Academy of Sciences. For some of them the career of paramilitary became a matter of memories like in the case of Serbian Colonel Pavle Blažarić. As young Captain during the Macedonian years before the Balkan Wars of 1912–1913 he was the Chief of *chetnik* Mountain Headquarters. During the Balkan Wars he continued his paramilitary engagement by leading one of Serbia's *chetnik* detachments. However, during and after the Great War he remained officer of the regular army and ended his career in that status. He died in 1947 at the age of 69.[48] Others swapped green mountains, forests and rifles for parliament benches like Dragutin Jovanović-Lune or the already mentioned Vasilije Trbić and Puniša Račić. Another ex-paramilitary, Sreten Vukosavljević, beside being elected as MP was simultaneously actively engaged in the colonization process of the south Yugoslav regions and managed to became a prolific author of many contributions in the field of agrarian sociology, which eventually brought him a part-time lectureship at the Belgrade Faculty of Law. After the Second World War Vukosavljević reached the position of a Minister in socialist Yugoslavia as well as memberships in several academies and a position in a research institute.[49]

Several former *chetniks* remained active in mid-war period, such as Kosta Milovanović-Pećanac, one of the legendary *chetniks* from the years of Serbian *chetnik* action in Macedonia, and one of the leaders of the Toplica Uprising in 1917—the only uprising in occupied Europe during the Great War. He continued with his career as a paramilitary, but this time as head of the *chetnik* veteran association *Association of Chetniks* from 1932 until 1944.[50] An identical case was Ilija Trifunović-Birčanin, another legendary *chetnik* from the years of Serbian *chetnik* action in Macedonia who was severely wounded in 1916 during the fighting on the Macedonian front. Both as a veteran and war invalid he was active as head of the *Association of Chetniks* till 1932 when he passed his leadership to Pećanac, while he took over the leadership of the patriotic association *National Defence*.[51] Both Pećanac and Birčanian ended their careers during the Second World War. Pećanac became the leader of a quisling paramilitary formation and was brutally executed in 1944 by a rival organization's death squad, while Birčanian died of natural causes as a refugee in the Italian-occupied Dalmatian town of Split.

---

[48] Pavle Blažarić, *Memoari*, (Leposavić: Institut za srpsku kulturu, 2007).

[49] For the most complete biography of Sreten Vukosavljević see: Momčilo Isić, Milovan Mitrović, Dobrilo Aranitović, *Život i delo Sretena Vukosavljevića 1881–1960* (Beograd: Službeni glasnik, 2012).

[50] For the most complete biography of Kosta Pećanac see: Momčilo Pavlović, Božica Mladenović, *Kosta Milovanović-Pećanac 1878–1944*, (Beograd: Institut za savremenu istoriju, Beograd 2006); See also: Kosta Milovanović—Pećanac, *Dnevnik Koste Milovanovića—Pećanca: od 1916. do 1918*, (Beograd: Istorijski institute SANU 1998).

[51] John Paul Newman, *Yugoslavia in the Shadow of War. Veterans and the Limits of State Building 1903–1945* (Cambridge: Cambridge University Press, 2015)107.

Others experienced drastic turns in their career paths like Mustafa Golubić, a Bosnian Muslim who, first as a member of *Young Bosnia*, and afterward the *Black Hand*, participated in the Balkan Wars of 1912–1913 and the Great War. After the war, being disappointed with the destiny of his patron, the *Black Hand* leader Colonel Dragutin Dimitrijević-Apis, Golubić made a drastic turn by joining the Communist movement and subsequently becoming a highly positioned operative of the Comintern. Throughout the mid-war period he lived in exile while his personality was surrounded with a wreath of legends. During the occupation of Yugoslavia in WWII he was arrested by the Gestapo and shot.[52] Similar life path was one of Božin Simić, first Yugoslav ambassador in Turkey after the Second World War, although his biography references are even more fragmented and shrouded in mystery than those of his comrade Golubić. He was one of the officers' conspirators responsible for the overthrow of Obrenović royal dynasty in 1903 *coup d'état*. As member of the *Black Hand* and officer of Serbian Border Troops just before the Balkan wars 1912–1913 he was responsible for the infiltration of Serbian *chetniks* on Ottoman territory. During the Balkan wars he was commander of one *chetnik* detachment.[53] During the Great War he continued with his military career. However, in course of the final showdown with the *Black Hand*, on staged Salonika trial in 1917, as many others Božin Simić was sentenced to prison sentence. Because he was sentenced *in absentia* (he was in Russia organizing Yugoslav volunteers) he decided not to return to Salonika and face the indictment. Instead, he remained in Russia where he eventually joined the Bolsheviks. After Russia he went to France. He returned to Yugoslavia in 1936 where he was immediately sent to prison, but was pardoned and fully exonerated after just two days.[54] He remained in close contact with few remaining comrades from the *Black Hand* and period of *chetnik* action.[55] Simić played important role during the process of establishment of diplomatic relations between Yugoslavia and Soviet Union in 1940. He was also very active during turbulent events around the *coup d'état* in March 1941 when after official signing of an agreement with the Axes, group of pro-British officers on 27 March deposed Yugoslav government Simić advocated

---

[52] There is no biography of Mustafa Golubić; however, Bosnian writer Sead Trhulj, intrigued by Golubić's vibrant personality, wrote a play in the mid-80's, *Mustafa Golubić, čovjek konspiracije* (with commentaries) which was re-published in 2007; see: Sead Trhulj, *Mustafa Golubić, čovjek konspiracije*, (Sarajevo: Zalihica, 2007). However, Trhulj acted as historian because in the introduction to his play he actually gathered all relevant secondary sources, mostly extracts from memoirs of different Yugoslav Communist Party officials who had opportunities to encounter Golubić in the mid-war years. In that sense his life path can be partly reconstructed although many blanks, which are still stirring up the spirits, need to be filled. See also: Dragan Bakić, 'Apis's Men: The Black Hand Conspirtors after the Great War'. In *Balcanica*, XLVI (2015), 219–39.

[53] Milić Milićević, 'Četnička akcija neposredno pre objave i tokom prvih dana srpsko-turskog rata 1912. godine'. In *Prvi balkanski rat 1912/1913. godine: društveni i civilizacijski smisao. Knj. 1,* (Niš: Filozofski fakultet, 2013), 221–34, here p 231.

[54] Vasilije Trbić, *Memoari. II,* (Beograd: Kultura 1996)187–8.

[55] Dragan Bakić, 'Apis's Men: The Black Hand Conspirators after the Great War', *Balcanica* XLVI (2015) 219–39.

reaching an agreement with Soviet Union, which would ease Yugoslav unfavorable situation of total encirclement by the Axes. Agreement was reached in Moscow, however to late to make a change. Official signing happened on 6 April, in Simić's presence, the same day when Axes invaded Yugoslavia. Simić himself mentioned several times that during the small night reception after the signing of agreement he broke out in a cold sweat when Stalin while shaking his hand just said: 'Yes, the black hand'. After the war he returned to Yugoslavia where he entered state service and served as ambassador. He died in 1966 in the age of eighty-five.[56]

Among many prominent IMRO *komitajis* the career paths of several are clearly distinguishable. Pancho Mikhailov-Chavdar, apart from being very active in 'classical' *komitaji* action, demonstrated literary talent. His beginnings do not differ from those of other IMRO activists. He was born in 1891 in the Macedonian town of Štip, at that time a part of the Ottoman Empire. He finished Pedagogical School in Skopje and served as a teacher before he decided to join the Bulgarian army as a volunteer in 1912. After the Second Balkan War 1913 he remained in Bulgaria where he attended school for reserve officers. During the Great War he fought in the Bulgarian army as a company commander. After the war Mikhailov became an accountant in a coalmine in Pernik. In 1921 he joined the IMRO and was assigned as area *voivode* for Kočani district.[57] He became well known after several actions and gunfights with Yugoslav security forces. However, his name became known for his participation in the assassination of the Bulgarian Minister of Interior and Army Alexander Dimitrov in 1921. Dimitrov was placed on the IMRO blacklist for his engagement in reconciliation with the Kingdom of Serbs, Croats and Slovenes.[58] Another of Mikhailov's triumphs was the anti-federalist intrusion and occupation of Kyustendil by the IMRO in December 1922. Parallel to his paramilitary engagement he wrote and published a collection of short stories, *In the Country of Tears*.[59] He also collected and edited an anthology of folk poems from Macedonia.[60] However, soon afterward his situation drastically changed and from a popular poet-revolutionary Mikhailov ended up dead, executed by his fellow *komitajis*. According to Ivan Mikhailov's memoirs Pancho was sentenced to death because of his immoral behaviour concerning females—a thing highly punishable by IMRO rules. Both on the ground in Macedonia as well

---

[56] 'Božin Simić sa sto lica', Večernje novosti, 27 March 2016 http://www.novosti.rs/vesti/naslovna/drustvo/aktuelno.290.html:597571-Bozin-Simic-sa-sto-lica

[57] Cocho V. Bilyarski, 'Okupiraneto na Kyustendil prez 1922 g. ot chetite na VMRO, komandvani ot Kochanskiya voivoda Pancho Mikhailov i shtipskiya voivoda Iovan B'rlyo' http://www.sitebulgari-zaedno.com/index.php?option=com_content&view=article&id=314:-1922-&catid=29:2010-04-24-09-14-13&Itemid=61 [last cheked on 29 August 2019]

[58] Zoran Todorovski, *Todor Aleksandrov*, (Skopje: Makavej; Državen arhiv na Republika Makedonija, 2014) 206–7.

[59] Pancho Mikhailov, *V' stranata na s'lzite*, (Sofia, 1924).

[60] Pancho Mikhailov (ed.), *B'lgarski narodni pesni ot Makedoniya*, (Sofia: Shtipskoto blagotvorno bratstvo v' Sofia, 1924).

as during breaks in Bulgaria he was constantly in pursuit of female company despite the fact that he was married. Often, he requested the company of young peasant girls, some of them close relatives of members of his own band.[61] The Central Committee of the IMRO issued a Communiqué on his execution on 15 June 1925.[62]

On the other hand, Dimitar Vlahov, one of the prominent members of the left-wing federalist faction of the IMRO (although he was not active in the paramilitary aspect of the organization's activities), after a short career in IMRO (United), joined the Communist Party of Yugoslavia. Vlahov, who after the Young Turk revolution became a member of the Ottoman parliament, lived long enough to be elected Speaker of the Yugoslav Parliament after the Second World War.[63]

The career paths of several Albanian paramilitaries fit the overall picture. However, because most of them didn't possess adequate education and in general they weren't 'men of the pen' we only have rough sketches of their lives, obtained through fragments of memoirs of their contemporaries. For example, Eqrem-bey Vlora in his memoirs mentions the colourful personality of Taf Kazi, one of the so-called 'Dibrans', describing him as 'one of the typical leaders of mercenaries from Debar...although he was loyal and devoted to anyone he served at the moment, in his career as mercenary he used to frequently change his master'. Initially Kazi was one of the lieutenants of Esad-pasha Toptani, in whose service he was awarded with some properties. He was commander of one of his battalions in the turbulent years of 1920–1921. On one occasion Taf Kazi and his associates sacked and set ablaze the stronghold of Ahmed-bey Zogu in the Mati region. However, that didn't prevent him from entering Zogu's service in 1924–1925 and 'bargaining' for new properties and privileges. It is said that he was smart enough to retire on time and enjoy his spoils: 'In his life he fought, won and finally distanced himself from "bargains"'.[64] Another mercenary leader among the 'Dibrans' was Hallil Lleshi. As Kazi he joined the service of Esad-pasha Toptani to whose political platform he remained loyal even after Esad-pasha's assassination in Paris in 1920. With his battalion Lleshi proved his valour numerous times. He was described as a typical proud Albanian who possessed something medieval, chivalrous, and romantic:

[61] Ivan Mikhailov, Spomeni, III, Osvoboditelna borba (1924–1934) (Louvain 1967), 577–80.
[62] Cocho V. Bilyarski, 'Okupiraneto na Kyustendil prez 1922 g.' http://www.sitebulgarizaedno.com/index.php?option=com_content&view=article&id=314:-1922-&catid=29:2010-04-24-09-14-13&Itemid=61 [last cheked on 29 August 2019]
[63] Mary C. Neuburger, Balkan Smoke: Tobacco and the Making of Modern Bulgaria, (Ithaca: Cornell University Press 2013), 67.
[64] Ekrem-beg Vlora, Sekavanjata ot životot. Tom II, (1921–1925) (Skopje: Fondacija Otvoreno opštestvo, 2015), 239.

"He wasn't submissive, he didn't flatter and when his eyes would start to glow angrily it resembled burning villages, blood feuds, and mutilated bodies, the usual picture of Albania during the last eleven years....He wasn't of high intelligence, but he had a natural gift for soldiering. During combat he used to lead by his personal example, he used to punish mercilessly, he would deploy his troops and command like an experienced soldier, he used to assess situations quickly and correctly".[65]

Unlike Taf Kazi, whose final years were peaceful and prosperous, Lleshi died in June 1924 in a gunfight with assassins hired to kill him. Like in some story from the conquest of the American Wild West, Lleshi, armed only with his revolver, managed to kill all his assailants before he died from multiple wounds.[66]

The same thing happened with Elez Isufi who, for decades, successfully stayed on the Albanian political 'market', moving between Ottomans, Serbs, Austrians, different Albanian magnates and political movements. He earned considerable wealth as well as allegiances; however, during the 1920's he found himself on the opposite side of Ahmed-bey Zogu and his ascent to power. Despite the fact that he participated in a coup attempt against Zogu in 1922, and the overthrow of Zogu's regime in 1924, Zogu's agents approached Elez Isufi during preparation for a counter-coup with an offer to join Zogu's endeavour to return to power. This time he remained determined against all odds and refused Zogu's generous offers. In December that same year he was defending an important position between the Yugoslav border and the Albanian capital with his clansmen. After being severely wounded Isufi died holding to his vow.[67]

Unlike the 'Dibrans', another kind of Albanian paramilitaries were *kachaks*, usually associated with the region of Kosovo and Metohija. Their beginnings are associated with the last days of Ottoman rule over the Balkans; however, they continued to be active during Serbian/Yugoslav rule as bearers of the Albanian rebel spirit. Among many different characters representing a mixture of outlaws, rebels and 'guns for hire' the name of Azem Bejta-Galica clearly distinguish itself. Closely associated with the Kosovo Committee, he headed *kachak* groups from the rebellious Kosovo region of Drenica for several years. Atypically for Albanian circumstances, his wife Shote (a.k.a. Qerime Radisheva) followed him and used to fight by his side. Azem Bejta successfully challenged Yugoslav authorities, avoiding all pursuits and ambushes. His death in 1924 marked the end of the

[65] Milosav Jelić, *Albanija, zapisi o ljudima i dogaðajima*, (Beograd: Geca Kon, 1933), 19.
[66] M. Jelić, *Albanija, zapisi o ljudima i dogaðajima*, 19.
[67] Isufi Elez (1861–29.12.1961)—Robert Elsie, *A Biographical Dictionary of Albanian History*, (London; New York: B. Tauris, 2013), 215; and Milosav Jelić, *Albanija, zapisi o ljudima i dogaðajima*, 22–5 and 89.

kachak age. His wife continued with rebellious activities for several more years when she finally withdrew to Albania.[68] Another example of an Albanian paramilitary was Bayram Curri, one of the Kosovo Committee founders and champions, who was described as a politician and guerrilla fighter. Although not originally a *kachak* he was closely associated with them. Initially an officer in the Ottoman army, Curri embraced the idea of an Albanian national movement. He participated in several uprisings against Ottoman as well as against Serbian and Yugoslav rule later. During the Great War, together with Hasan Prishtina he supported the Central Powers. After the war he settled in Albania, taking an active part in the state-building process. Curri led newly founded Albanian forces in

Fig. 9. Vasilije Trbić.

His very long life (1882–1961) was marked by extreme activism where his years as a Serbian paramilitary in Ottoman Macedonia represent just piece in remarkable puzzle. He was monk who broke his vows, paramilitary, farmer, mayor, MP, a political prisoner, intelligence operative etc. Unlike many other Serbian paramilitaries of that time he wrote extensive memoirs in which he, although manifested tendency to overestimate significance of his exploits, gave valuable and exceptionally colorful and exciting description of his life and time in which he lived.

© National Library of Serbia (Belgrade), Album *Chetnik Movement*, AF 175.

---

[68] Galica Azem (12.1889–25.07.1924) and Galica Shote (1895–01.07.1927.)—Robert Elsie, *A Biographical Dictionary of Albanian History*, (London; New York: B. Tauris, 2013), 160.

actions against Esad-pasha's followers. He also participated in clashes with Yugoslav forces. The uncompromising policies of the Kosovo Committee determined him an opponent to the policies of Ahmed-bey Zogu, and Curri was active in all attempts to overthrow him. At the end, he supported the short-lived revolutionary experiment of Fan Noli. However, Zogu's return to power in December 1924 sealed Curri's fate. A price was put on his head and in just a matter of weeks he was located, surrounded and killed on 29 March 1925 in north Albania near the town which today carries his name.[69]

Interestingly, those ex-paramilitaries who survived the turbulent times of the first half of the twentieth century managed to reach old age. In that sense their energy and resilience acted as a barrier against the difficulties and hardships in which most of them lived. Wars and their consequences, physical strains, deprivations, life in outdoor conditions on the edge of famine, years spent in exile, and the personal losses they suffered seemed like could not influence or reduce their energy and determination. They were all members of the same generation, born by the end of the 1870's and the beginning of the 1880's. Petar D'rvingov (born in 1876) died in 1958 in Sofia at the age of 82. Vasilije Trbić (born in 1881) lived until 1962 when he died at age 81. Sreten Vukosavljević (born in 1881) managed to live until the 1960 when he died at the age of 79. Božin Simić (born in 1881) died in 1966 at the age of 85, while Dimitar Vlahov (born in 1878) lived until 1953 when he died at the age of 75. Ivan Mihailov, the last leader of the IMRO, although he belonged to the next generation (born in 1896), reached the age of 94. He died in 1990.

International Networks

Another aspect of post-Great War engagement of the Balkan paramilitaries and their respective movements was building and maintaining international networks. In this particular case these networks weren't solely reserved for paramilitary movements and organizations but for political parties and movements as well. The main reason for that was redistribution of power that emerged as a consequence of the turbulent changes during and after the First World War. In the Balkans, as elsewhere in Europe, several distinctive groups of states had emerged from the ruins of old empires whose main characteristics depended on their post-war status and ability to recover and cash in their wartime status and engagement.

Since the world was clearly divided into those who were defeated and those who were victorious, all future activities were seen as preparations for the rematch

---

[69] Curri Bayram Bey (1862–29.03.1925)—Robert Elsie, *A Biographical Dictionary of Albanian History*, (London; New York: B. Tauris, 2013), 93.

whose main goal was a major revision of existing peace treaties[70] While Serbian paramilitaries considered their mission as fulfilled, they were actually satisfied to continue operating closely attached to the state structures, enjoying state support in order to defend and strengthen their legacy. For Bulgarians from the IMRO and Kosovar Albanians from the Kosovo Committee, continuation of the struggle was the only option. The only change was how and with whose assistance and support it could be done. The logical solution was to go along the lines 'the enemy of my enemy is my ally'. It practically meant that any successful anti-Yugoslav action or activity aimed at destabilization of the Kingdom of Serbs, Croats and Slovenes would assist the IMRO's and Kosovo Committee's ongoing operations on Yugoslav soil.

Already during 1919 the IMRO established the first contacts with Italian representatives in Bulgaria. Besides establishing contacts and cooperation with actors on the Bulgarian political scene, such as opposition parties and the Military League, one of the important items of the old-new IMRO political agenda in the new political circumstances, was establishing cooperation with foreign actors as well, both state and non-state. Italy already proved to be a strong Yugoslav opponent primarily because of the fact that creation of the Yugoslav state practically deprived Italy of a good deal of war spoils once promised to her. Instead of becoming the sole power on the Adriatic, in place of Austro-Hungarian Empire, Italy got a new neighbour, although not that large and strong, but with respectable armed forces and good relations with other Great Powers, primarily France. The Kingdom of Serbs, Croats and Slovenes, beside cultivating strong anti-Italian feelings that existed in Dalmatia and Slovenia, was able to execute a strong influence on the substantial South Slav minority in Italy, as well as to block or at least make difficult any Italian attempt to increase its influence in Albania. The first major Italian anti-Yugoslav interference was during the so-called Christmas Revolt in Montenegro (7 January 1919) when the supporters of conditional unification of Serbia and Montenegro, or so-called *Greens,* using Italian assistance attempted to take the Montenegrin capital Cetinje. The *Greens,* led by exiled Montenegrin King Nikola Petrović didn't agree with the decision of the Grand National Assembly of the Serbian Nation in Montenegro, which from 24 until 29 November convened in Podgorica (also known as the Podgorica Assembly), to unite Montenegro with Serbia and to overthrow the dynasty of Petrović-Njegoš. The *Greens,* who arrived in Montenegro with Italian help, clashed with the so-called *Whites* or supporters of unconditional unification. The *Greens* were defeated and dispersed with many of them arrested. The rest of them withdrew to Italy where they enjoyed Italian hospitality and support in a camp near the town of Gaeta. From there they were

---

[70] On post-Great War developments in Europe see: Robert Gerwarth, *The Vanquished: Why the First World War Failed to End 1917–1923* (London: Allen Lane, 2016).

occasionally infiltrated to Montenegro until 1921, when Italy suspended further assistance to King Nikola's cause.[71]

A hostile Italian attitude was also visible from the fact that throughout 1919 Yugoslav military authorities in Macedonia were constantly drawing attention to the impudent behaviour of Italian soldiers stationed in Macedonia, primarily as operatives on telephone-stations. They also carried IMRO mails and messages and transported *komitajis* in their vehicles. Italian, as well as French and Greek troops stayed in Macedonia for nearly a year after the end of war securing important communications that were used for supplying allied contingents dispersed from Hungary to Salonika and from Albania to Constantinople.[72]

The first official contact between IMRO and Italian representatives in Bulgaria was established already in March 1919, when three members of the IMRO Central Committee—Protogerov, Alexandrov and Chaulev—met with the Italian military attaché Lieutenant-Colonel Lodi. The Italians promised arms and ammunition in return for full-scale *komitaji* actions in Macedonia. Thus, the Kingdom of Serbs, Croats and Slovenes would be destabilized in the middle of the struggle for international recognition. The Bulgarian government was also involved because Italians promised that they would raise the question of Macedonia at the on-going Paris Peace Conference. The Italian offer seemed very attractive, especially if we bear in mind that IMRO organization in the western parts of Macedonia, or right bank of the river Vardar, was still undeveloped, primarily because it was very hard and dangerous for IMRO bands to travel all the way from Bulgaria across Macedonia, which was filled with different army, police and paramilitary units. With Italian assistance, the IMRO would establish its bases in Albania from where it would be much easier to infiltrate, bring weapons and organize their supporters. With Italian funds it became much easier to recruit and pay new *komitajis*. Finally, two emissaries of the IMRO Executive Committee, Ljubomir Miletich and Nikola Milev, went to Rome, where they, after meetings with representatives of the Italian General Staff and Ministry of Foreign Affairs, made an agreement for the 'initiation of *Komitaji* action in Serbian Macedonia so

---

[71] On Montenegro at the end of Great War and in the immediate post-war period, see: Novica Rakočević, *Crna Gora u Prvom svetskom ratu 1914–1918* (Cetinje: Obod, 1969); Radoslav Raspopović, 'Montenegro' In *1914–1918-online. International Encyclopedia of the First World War*, Daniel, Ute…[et al.] (eds.), (Berlin: Freie Universität Berlin), 2014-10-08. DOI: 10.15463/ie1418.10243; Srdja Pavlović, *Balkan Anschluss; The Annexation of Montenegro and Creation of a Common South Slav State*, (West Lafayette: Purdue University Press, 2008); *Greens* are the consequence of a complex story of unification and creation of Yugoslav state and specifics of Monetenegrin identity. This complex story also include facts that: the most of the *Greens*, together with their leaders, were pardoned and given various poistions in following years; and that during the Second World War both groups have reached consesus over the most important issues that resulted in full collaboration with Italian ocupation regime. Although some of the remaining *Greens* have continued their resistance throughout the 1920's, here we cannot find elements of the classical Balkan paramilitarism.

[72] Dmitar Tasić, *Rat posle rata, Vojska Kraljevine Srba, Hrvata i Slovenaca na Kosovu i Metohiji i u Makedoniji: 1918–1920*, (Beograd: Utopija, 2008), 101–3.

that the consolidation of Yugoslavia would be prevented and also for the initiation of struggle in Bulgaria with the aim of overthrowing the Stamboliyski's government'. Beside six million Italian liras, IMRO emissaries got promises of
material help as well as Italian diplomatic support in dealing with the Great
Powers.[73] The change of regime in Italy which happened in 1922 didn't affect
cooperation with IMRO and it continued along established guidelines. However,
when in 1924 the Kingdom of Serbs, Croats and Slovenes and fascist Italy reached
one of the agreements that relaxed tensed relations between two neighbours,
Italian support to the IMRO had to be reduced.

Besides Italy, in the immediate post-Great War years a logical IMRO ally was
the Kosovo Committee. Although founded much later than IMRO, the Kosovo
Committee, in the personalities of its leaders like Hasan Prishtina and Bayram
Curri, was a successor to the already alive and active movement whose initial goal
was emancipation and liberation from Ottoman rule. After the Balkan Wars of
1912–1913 and the Great War, in new political surroundings with an already
existing independent Albanian state, Kosovar Albanians and their political leaders couldn't accept the fact that Kosovo and Metohija ended up under Serbian,
i. e. Yugoslav rule. Again, it was the logic 'the enemy of my enemy is my ally' that
brought together the Kosovo Committee and IMRO. Albanian—IMRO cooperation proved to be efficient during the so-called Debar-Ohrid Uprising in
September 1913, when the IMRO, after the end of the Second Balkan War, con-
sternated by the fact that most of Macedonia ended up under Serbian and Greek
rule, organized a revolt. Their action was followed by a strong incursion of
Albanian irregulars in the region of the border town Debar. Although the uprising was initially successful, Serbian military and local *chetnik* detachments managed to quell the revolt.[74]

Right after the Great War the Kosovo Committee was able to exercise a considerable impact on developments both in Albania and the Kingdom of Serbs, Croats
and Slovenes. In Albania it was through official politics, parliamentary struggle,
coups and rebellions and in the Kingdom of Serbs, Croats and Slovenes through
guerrilla actions of its supporters or *kachaks* which for several years led the armed
resistance of Kosovar Albanians against the Yugoslav state.

In November 1920, the IMRO and Kosovo Committee signed an agreement
defining the spheres of interests of the two organizations as well as organizing
some practical issues. In reality, the Albanians recognized IMRO claims over
Macedonia.[75] Another important issue was the organization of bases for IMRO

[73] Zoran Todorovski, *Avtonomističkata VMRO na Todor Aleksandrov 1919–1924*, (Skopje: Makavej,
2013) 87–9.
[74] *Ohridskoto—debarskoto septemvrisko vostanie od 1913 godina/Kryengritja e shtatorit në ohër e
Diber ë vitit 1913*, (Skopje: Institut za nacionalna istorija/Instituti historisë *nacionale*, 2014).
[75] Kostadin Paleshutski, *Makedonskiyat v'pros v burzhoazna Jugoslaviya 1918–1941*, (Sofia: BAN,
1983), 116–17.

komitajis on Albanian soil from which they could infiltrate Yugoslav territory or where they could find refuge after successful actions.[76] Needless to say, this this arrangement proved to be very useful for the IMRO because its bands operating in west Macedonia were now exempted from the dangerous and tiresome withdrawal to Bulgaria, risking annihilation by numerically superior Yugoslav security forces.

Although on the ground there was no intensive collaboration between the two movements, the IMRO continued to enjoy the hospitality of some Albanians before and after incursions in Macedonia.[77]

According to the words of Ivan Mikhailov 'among other nations in Yugoslavia the Macedonian struggle had most sympathy among Croats'.[78] In particular, it was visible in attitudes of the Croat (Republican) Peasant Party and its leader Stjepan Radić. From the beginning Radić, as a republican, was against the unification with Serbia. During the first years, despite overwhelming support among Croatian peasantry, his party boycotted parliamentary sessions because he refused to pledge allegiance to the crown. In his speeches and writings, he often supported the IMRO cause. One of the IMRO leaders, Todor Alexandrov, was in correspondence with Radić. The other one, Alexander Protogerov once even met Radić. However, the main distinction was Radić's pacifism and political culture of parliamentarism embodied in his readiness for compromise. In one of his letters to Alexandrov Radić clearly said: 'I am very sorry because you still haven't realized that pacifism is my policy, not merely my tactics.' According to Radić, any concrete cooperation between the two movements was possible only if the IMRO were to abandon its revolutionary practices and adopt legal means of political struggle.[79] Contrarily, Alexandrov was determined that the only possible way to communicate with the Serbian regime was 'with rifle, bayonet and hand grenade'.[80] When in 1924 Radić and his party returned to parliamentary benches, dropping 'Republican' from the name of their party, and entering government, the situation changed, but not drastically. Although there was a sense of disappointment on the part of Alexandrov, he continued to show his respect towards Radić and his political legacy. Likewise, when Alexandrov was assassinated in September 1924, several Croatian newspapers issued obituaries praising his revolutionary spirit and determination.[81] However, the true cooperation between IMRO and Croatian political representatives would happen several years later.

---

[76] Ivan Mikhailov, *Spomeni II, Osvoboditelna borba 1919–1924* (Louvain, 1965), 159–60.
[77] Georgi Pophristov, *Revolyutsionnata borba v' bitolskiya okr'g*, (Sofia: NS OF, 1953) 89. See also: Petar Shandanov, *Bogatstvo mi e svobodata; Spomeni*, (Sofia: Izdatelstvo 'Gutenberg', 2010), 118.
[78] Ivan Mikhailov, *Spomeni II*, 165–6.
[79] Kostadin Paleshutski, *Makedonskiyat v'pros v burzhoazna Jugoslaviya 1918–1941*, (Sofia: BAN, 1983), 145–6.
[80] Ivan Mikhailov, *Spomeni II*, 313–17.
[81] Zoran Todorovski, *Todor Aleksandrov*, (Skopje: Makavej; Državen arhiv na Republika Makedonija, 2014) 325–6.

After the assassination of several leaders of the Croatian Peasant Party during the parliamentary session in June 1928, including Stjepan Radić, due to the political instability in January 1929 King Alexander Karađorđević decided to introduce a royal dictatorship and to suspend the constitution. As a result, one of the leaders of the nationalist Croatian Party of Right, Ante Pavelić, left Yugoslavia and in exile founded an extremist movement under the name Croatian Ustashe (ustaša— insurgent in Serbo-Croat).[82] Already in April 1929 he visited Sofia where he met IMRO leader Ivan Mikhailov.[83] From that moment onwards the two movements acted in close cooperation. The IMRO was able to transfer its revolutionary know-how to the inexperienced *ustashe*, which eventually led to the assassination of the Yugoslav King Alexander in October 1934 in Marseilles during his official visit to France. In a joint action of *ustashe* and IMRO, Mikhailov's personal driver and bodyguard Vlado Chernozemski managed to kill the Yugoslav sovereign.[84]

Almost simultaneously the IMRO, *ustashe*, and Kosovo Committee, according to Mikhailov, managed to draft an agreement, similar to those from 1920, which regulated future relations between the three states that would emerge from the remains of Yugoslavia—Great Albania, Croatia and Macedonia. It supposedly happened in 1933 when the Kosovo Committee was already banished from Albania and when its leader Hasan Prishtina visited Bulgaria and had a meeting with Ivan Mikhailov. However, in August 1933, Prishtina was assassinated in Salonika where he lived in exile. The assassin was probably Zogu's agent, although everything appeared like a blood feud.[85]

As for Mikhailov and Pavelić, close cooperation between the two leaders evolved into a close friendship. During the Second World War, Ivan Mikhailov, already in exile from which he would never return, lived in Zagreb as a personal guest of Ante Pavelić.

Relations that the IMRO had established with other anti-Yugoslav movements or revisionist states in the 1920's weren't kept secret; on the contrary, they were used as an argument for attracting new members and as a proof of the organization's strength. Of course, the terminology and approach were adapted to *komitajis* usual

---

[82] On Pavelić and ustashe see more in: Bogdan Krizman, *Ante Pavelić i ustaše*, (Zagreb: Globus, 1978).

[83] Ličina Đorđe, Vavić Milorad, Pavlovski Jovan, *Andrija Artuković, Vjekoslav Luburić, Xhaver Deva, Vančo Mihailov* (Zagreb: Centar za informacije i publicitet, 1985); See also: Đorđe Vasiljević, *Zavera protiv Srbije: VMRO Vanče Mihajlova*, (Beograd: Politika, 1991).

[84] On assassination of King Alexander see: Branko Petranović, *Jugoslavije 1918–1988. I*, (Beograd: Nolit, 1988), 210–12; Nikola Žežov, 'VMRO i atentatot vrz jugoslovenskiot kral Aleksandar Karageorgevik', 'VMRO i atentatot vrz jugoslovenskiot kral Aleksandar Karageorgevik'. In *Godišen zbornik na Filozofskiot fakultetot na Univerzitetot 'Sv. Kiril i Metodij', Kniga 60* (Skopje: 2007), 333–47. Dmitar Tasić, 'The Assassination of King Alexander: The Swan Song of the Internal Macedonian Revolutionary Organization'. In *Donau, Tijdschrift over Zuidost-Europa*, 2008/2, 2008, 31–9; Mitre Stamenov, *Atentat't v Marsiliya: Vlado Chernozemski. Zhivot otdaden na Makedoniya*, (Sofia: VMRO— SMD, 1993). http://www.promacedonia.org/ms/ms_index.html [last checked 8 November 2014].

[85] Ivan Mikhailov, *Spomeni, III, Osvoboditelna borba (1924–1934)* (Louvain 1967), 601–3.

audience—Macedonian peasantry. In July 1922, in his deposition, after surrender to Yugoslav authorities, IMRO *komitaji* Gligor Todorov Petrov, among other things related to IMRO field organization, confidants, secret routes, meetings, and assassination plans, mentioned something else as well. After arrival in villages or at secret gatherings, *voivode* Georgi V'ndev, into whose band Petrov was drafted, in his speeches to peasants would regularly underline that 'Bulgaria is ally to Albania, Italy, Hungary, Montenegro and Germany, that they should not be afraid because Bulgaria is a small country, and everything that the committee has done is done in an agreement with the above-mentioned states, as well as with Turkey'.[86]

However, relations between Balkan paramilitaries, in this particular case the IMRO, and the international communist movement after the Great War were far more complex and dynamic than any of the relations with the above-mentioned movements, parties or states. The appearance of the communist ideology and emergence of Soviet Russia after the turbulent revolutionary years had global significance. Global communism became a force that needed to be taken into account in most European countries. The examples of Germany, Bavaria, Hungary and Austria showed that the export of revolution was possible and that it could make a serious impact on local political developments. Balkan nations were by no means an exception to this rule. As elsewhere in Europe, international participants of revolutionary events in Russia started to return to Bulgaria and the newly created Kingdom of Serbs, Croats and Slovenes, bringing new ideas and experiences, although only part of them came with the particular task of organizing and preparing local communist parties for future action. As already said, the complexity of the political and ideological situation in these two countries was increased because parallel with ex-revolutionaries, waves of their former adversaries from the ranks of 'White' Russians begin to arrive as well, bringing their own visions, hopes, frustrations and political agendas.

The first case of IMRO support to a Balkan communist organization occurred in 1920 during the campaign and elections for the Constitutional Assembly of the Kingdom of Serbs, Croats and Slovenes. Simple and practical political calculations led the IMRO leadership to decide to give support to the Communist Party of Yugoslavia (KPJ). According to later interpretations of Ivan Mikhailov, the IMRO would benefit from the success of any opposition party since the establishment of a genuine Macedonian political party in the Kingdom of Serbs, Croats and Slovenes, which would protect Macedonian interests, was not allowed.[87] In IMRO they believed that the transformation of the Kingdom of Serbs, Croats and Slovenes into a federal state, as a step toward the final secession of Macedonia, could be reached through the forthcoming parliamentary elections for the

[86] AJ, MUP KJ 14–177–1040, Report of the Command of the Third Gendarmerie Brigade to the Commissioner for South Serbia, confident no. 1443 July 18 1922 in Skopje.
[87] Ivan Mikhailov, *Spomeni II*, 124–5.

Constitution Assembly, which had been scheduled for 23 November 1920. Thus, the advocates of decentralization would be introduced to the Assembly, among whom members of the KPJ clearly stood out (together with Croatian and other opposition representatives).[88]

Unlike the situation in the spring and summer when, according to reports of the heads of districts and counties and certain garrison commanders, IMRO activity could not be noticed, in the autumn it was very intense. In early October 1920, activities of the IMRO were described as 'very lively and energetic.' High hopes were placed on the upcoming parliamentary elections because IMRO activists hoped that by supporting communists they would be able to introduce their supporters into the parliament. Also, disobedience, distrust and isolation started to appear among peasants in remote mountain villages. The response of conscripts was very poor, while elections for village majors and members of township councils were boycotted.[89]

Due to the elections for the Constitution Assembly, *chete* and IMRO activists extended their stay on Macedonian soil. Unlike previous years when the first signs of autumn marked the withdrawal of *komitajis* to their winter safe haven in Bulgaria, the intensity of events in November and December 1920 did not differ from some of the summer months. The IMRO plan to reach a political solution in Macedonia through the support to the KPJ demanded intensive involvement of *komitajis*. During their stay in villages *komitajis* openly demanded from the peasant voters, under threat of death, that they vote for the communists because their election victory could mean ending the Serbian rule in Macedonia. While campaigning for the communists, *komitajis* used to move around freely in military uniforms, in full gear, with rifles, Bulgarian caps, bandoliers and bombs.[90]

The results of parliamentary elections and the new security situation initiated a careful investigation by the police and military authorities. It was found that in the area of Veles the IMRO had increased its presence before the election.[91] Also, it was found that in addition to promotional material, *komitajis* brought weapons from Bulgaria that were supposed to be distributed among locals for the uprising in case of destabilizing of the Kingdom of Serbs, Croats and Slovenes.[92] Earlier

[88] The Belgrade newspaper *Politika* reported that in communities where communists won the majority of votes in local elections their local leaders were close to the IMRO and used their influence, wealth and connections to hamper activities of the Gendarmerie, see: 'Bugaraši u Maćedoniji', *Politika*, no. 4474 from 6 October 1920. *p.* 2.

[89] VA, r. 4/3, b. 61, f. 8, d. 3/81, Report of the command of Vardar divisional district to the command of Third army district, confidential no. 8461 from 11 October 1920.

[90] VA, r. 4/3, b. 58, f. 9, d. 6/136, Report of the command of Third army district to the Ministry of Army and Navy, confidential no. 8174 from 19 December 1920. Also see, 'Akcija "makedonstvujuščih"', *Politika*, no. 4346 from 18 December 1920.

[91] VA, r. 4/3, b. 58, f. 9, d. 6/133, Report of the commander of Vardar divisional district to the command of Third army district, highly confidential no. 238 from 14 December 1920.

[92] VA, r. 4/3, b. 58, f. 9, d. 6/141, Report of the commander of town of Kratovo to the command of Vardar divisional district, confidential no. 24 from 16 December 1920, forwarded report of the office of Kumanovo district (no number).

suspicions regarding cooperation of IMRO and the communists, and IMRO and the Albanian-Turkish committee had been confirmed, as well the organization's affection towards Stjepan Radić and his party.[93]

After the great electoral success of the communists some representatives of civil authorities advocated the introduction of extraordinary measures such as isolation of the villages that were connected with IMRO; resettlement of villages known as proven IMRO centres; increase of military forces; removal of communist officials; reorganization of the judicial system; increase of funding for intelligence operations; bringing teachers, priests and gendarmes from Serbia; introduction of severe penalties for carrying weapons; making conscription and collection of taxes more efficient because the communist agitation was mainly directed against these two issues, and opening of a large number of schools.[94]

As already mentioned by winning 200,000 votes communists became the fourth strongest party in the kingdom (communists won fifty-nine mandates in the Constitutional Assembly of a total of 415). In Macedonia alone they won fifteen mandates, which was a huge success. If we consider that much more developed regions of the Kingdom of Serbs, Croats and Slovenes, with numerous labourers, among whom the Marxist ideology was rooted and the communist party already present, gave proportionally fewer representatives than rural and industrially undeveloped Macedonia, the picture of the effects of IMRO involvement becomes clearer.[95] Previous electoral success in local elections in August when communist had won in thirty-seven communities in the Serbian part of the kingdom alone (including the capital Belgrade and the two most important cities Niš and Skopje) already caused huge concern.[96] Of course, the excuse was a concern for state interests, because communists in possible coalitions could play a decisive role in resolving important issues, like reorganization of the state. Needless to say, the Hungarian and German examples resonated in the Balkans, especially in the Kingdom of Serbs, Croats and Slovenes. In the southern parts of the Kingdom of Serbs, Croats and Slovenes, communists as bearers and promoters of some IMRO political ideas could be even more dangerous.

IMRO support to KPJ during the 1920 elections represented just the first act in extremely complex relations between the IMRO and the international communist movement. Meanwhile in Bulgaria the local communist party continued to thrive, becoming stronger every day. Unlike in the Kingdom of Serbs, Croats and

[93] VA, r. 4/3, b. 58, f. 9, d. 6/133, Report of the commander of Vardar divisional district to the command of Third army district, highly confidential no. 9784 from 9 December 1920.
[94] VA, r. 4/3, b. 58, f. 9, d. 6/136, Report of the command of Third army district to the Ministry of Army and Navy, confidential no. 8175 from 21 December 1920, forwarded report of the head of Tikveš district to the command of Third army district (no number).
[95] Kostadin Paleshutski, *Yugoslavskata komunisticheska partiya i makedonskiyat v'pros, 1919–1945*, (Sofia: BAN, 1985), 59–60; See also: Ivan Mikhailov, *Spomeni II, Osvoboditelna borba 1919–1924* (Louvain, 1965), 125.
[96] Branko Petranović, *Jugoslavije 1918–1988. I*, (Beograd: Nolit, 1988), 107 and 113.

Slovenes where the 1921 ban practically eliminated communists from the polit-ical theatre, in Bulgaria communists became a movement whose strength had to be taken into account. The complexity of IMRO relations with communism also included the roles and influences of BANU, old parties grouped in the Constitutional Bloc, 'White' Russians, as well as the presence of different pro-Soviet and Soviet organizations. However, a special place belonged to the conflict between the already mentioned *autonomist* and *federalist* factions of the IMRO where, among the latter—as it appeared—Bolshevik ideology found fertile ground. This would have serious consequences at several levels in the future. Bulgarian communists, on several occasions, tried to achieve, if not support, at least a neutral stand of the IMRO in their revolutionary plans. However, the IMRO had its own calculations, which included multiple agents and components, especially after another setback caused by the establishment of Yugoslav and Greek rule over Macedonia. Involvement of the *autonomist* IMRO in the turbu-lent events of 1923, first the coup of 9 June and then the September revolution, where it demonstrated both passive and active support for the Bulgarian political right, showed IMRO's willingness to support only political options which would allow the organization to continue its struggle for the liberation of Macedonia. Agrarians and their post-Great War rapprochement with the Kingdom of Serbs, Croats and Slovenes directly endangered IMRO infrastructure and future plans. With communists it was pretty much the same, with the important distinction that they were supported by Soviet Russia. In both cases the IMRO (*autonomist*) acted in order to prevent the change of the status quo, i. e. change or end of their semi-autonomous rule over Petrich County—their stronghold, source of income and reservoir of new recruits needed for the continuation of struggle. However, the events of 1923 didn't prevent another avenue of approach, which happened under the pretext of unifying Macedonian revolutionaries, i. e. *autonomist* and *federalist* factions. This time, a new and increasingly strong actor on the inter-national scene stood behind this action. It was the Comintern or 'Centre of the global revolution'. No matter how interpretations of the causes and consequences of this process differ between contemporaries and especially between Bulgarian and Macedonian historians,[97] what happened was that after several rounds of negotiations agreement was reached. On one side there were Alexandrov and Protogerov from the *autonomist* faction, together with Chaulev who acted as member of the IMRO Central Committee but who, together with Dimitar Vlahov, was strongly inclined toward reaching an agreement On the other side there were Filip Atanasovski and Slave Ivanov from the *federalist* faction (actually MFRO). The place for negotiations was Vienna, and everything was done through medi-ation of the Comintern representative Solomon Goldstein-Cherski. Several

---

[97] See: Lenina Žila, *Vienska 'stapica': Istorija na pregovorite megu SSSR i VMRO na Todor Aleksandrov*, (Skopje: Institut po nacionalna istorija, 2014).

agreements were signed during April and May. The climax was reached in the May Declaration. Alexandrov did not sign it personally but he authorized Protogerov and Chaulev. Basically, the two organizations agreed to reconcile and continue their struggle for a free Macedonia as part of a larger Balkan federation under the patronage of Soviet Russia.[98]

How did it happen that less than a year after the dramatic summer of 1923, the IMRO, in a practical sense, made such a radical shift?

In the clouds of *post festum* interpretations that are shrouding this important event lays basic instincts of survival and the wish for continuation of the struggle no matter the changed circumstances. For paramilitaries from the IMRO their struggle became the essence of their life, some of them had been active more than twenty or thirty years. However, the fact that the organization became closely associated with the Bulgarian state began to take its toll. When Alexandrov realized that his signature, although authorized, would deepen the organization's confrontation with Tsankov's regime he immediately wanted to postpone publication of the Manifest as long as possible. Basically, IMRO was depending on, if not support, then at least tolerance, of the Bulgarian state. When in March 1923 Tsankov initiated a campaign of mass arrests of Macedonian activists from both legal and illegal organizations, like the *Ilinden Organization*, Macedonian fraternities and the IMRO, everything appeared to be similar to the actions of BANU year before. The main reason was, again, the wish of the Bulgarian regime to make rapprochement with IMRO's archenemy—the Kingdom of Serbs, Croats and Slovenes. This time it was because the Bulgarian international position was weakened after the Kingdom of Serbs, Croats and Slovenes and Mussolini's Italy had reached an agreement. This meant an immediate seizure of all Italian support to Bulgaria's, and automatically IMRO's, cause. It seems also that there was strong bottom-up pressure on IMRO leadership caused by the anxiety of the young rank-and-file to get involved, a feature that was very present in Central European paramilitary organizations after the Great War where new generations, that didn't have an opportunity to participate in the war, demonstrated excessive zeal in order to compensate for their lack of experience. Also, because the IMRO and above-mentioned legal associations proved to be a safe haven for members of the Bulgarian Communist Party after the

---

[98] Zoran Todorovski, *Todor Aleksandrov*, (Skopje: Makavej; Državen arhiv na Republika Makedonija, 2014) 227–52; On the role of Chaulev see: Katerina Todorovska, *Petar Čaulev*, (Skopje: Univerzitet 'Sv. Kiril i Metodij', Filozofski fakultet, 2014), 183–96; For interpretations of Bulgarian historiography prior to the democratic changes of 1990's see: Kostadin Paleshutski, *Makedonskiyat v'pros v burzhoazna Jugoslaviya 1918–1941*, (Sofia: BAN, 1983), 151–70; Mikhailov in his memoirs did everything to diminish or avoid Alexandrov's participation in the negotiations and signing. Instead, he blamed Chaulev, for his evident inclination towards the political left, and connections with Soviet representatives. Unlike Mikhailov, Shandanov gave a detailed account of events after the affair and Alexandrov's attitudes, see Petar Shandanov, *Bogatstvo mi e svobodata; Spomeni*, (Sofia: Izdatelstvo 'Gutenberg', 2010), 154–72; Same is with Uzunov, see Angel Uzunov, *Spomeni*, (Skopje: Makavej, 2014), 290–324.

September revolution, there was also a new wave of movement towards the political left (the first one consisting of *federalists*).[99] Thus, Alexandrov got into an awkward position; he was realizing that if the IMRO didn't continue with its classic *komitaji* style they might lose connection with Macedonia and their supporters on the ground. Time was passing by, things began to change, from day to day it became increasingly difficult to infiltrate bands and keep them on the ground. The biggest obstacles were not the Army and Gendarmerie but their former comrades in arms, now in Yugoslav service. Animosity was so strong that sometimes *autonomists* were not able to see the bigger picture because they were predominantly focused on annihilation of the *federalists*. One of the points of the Declaration was seizure of all activities aimed against the *federalist* bands—that was something Alexandrov was not willing to comply with. Alexandrov was well aware of the importance of 'going over', i.e. to Macedonia, remaining there, doing business as usual, showing himself to the locals, solving their internal problems, inspiring them to resist. However, to do that they needed Bulgaria as a safe haven, which would come into question if IMRO got into an open conflict with Tsankov's regime. When Vlahov and Chaulev, despite Alexandrov's and Protogerov's urging not do so, published the Declaration in the first issue of *Balkan Federation* (*Federation balkanique*) published in Vienna in summer 1924, two leaders of the IMRO decided to publicly withdraw their signatures. What followed was the continuation of the extermination war between the two factions, not only in Bulgaria and Macedonia but throughout Europe as well. The assassination of Alexandrov on 31 August threw the organization into another schism also marked by brutal showdowns and numerous killings. It marked, in a way, the beginning of a new phase for the IMRO.

Existence of plenitude of unique, remarkable and often charismatic figures was common feature among all Balkan paramilitaries during the investigated period. Previous decades of struggle besides maintaining their respective organizations active gave birth to such a remarkable individual. Also, they have significantly shaped their personalities. Dynamic years of Macedonian struggle 1903–1908, Albanian revolts 1909–1912, the Balkan Wars 1912–1913, and the Great War made these individuals and organizations resilient and adaptable. By the end of the Great War active Balkan paramilitaries were in their late thirties to early forties, an age which was traditionally considered as 'the best years' of someone's life. Years of this kind of activism contributed to building of strong personal ties and allegiances. In their cases also happened that the chances of drastic shifts grew proportionally with the extent of their commitment or personal sacrifice. Changing attitudes or sides represented usual outcomes of serious differences that often resulted in open conflicts and schisms within the organizations. Strong,

---

[99] Kostadin Paleshutski, *Makedonskiyat v'pros v burzhoazna Jugoslaviya 1918–1941*, (Sofia: BAN, 1983), 151–70.

intolerant, violent and uncompromising personalities of organizations' leaders and prominent members were usually the reason for such outcomes. In addition, the phenomenon of renegades was a normal companion of Balkan paramilitarism from its earliest phases. The seriousness of internal conflicts often led to the temporary paralyses of organizations' normal functioning. Also, internal conflicts and follow up vendetta campaigns were extremely violent and bloody. IMRO represented the most drastic example, where internal disputes had been a characteristic from the organization's earliest stages. Appearance of renegades was visible example of above-mentioned drastic shifts. Even if they changed their uniforms for suits and ties and Macedonian mountains for parliamentary chambers some of the Balkan paramilitaries never abandoned violent ethos and particular way of behaviour—the most drastic example of that was shootout in Yugoslav parliament in 1928.

However, post-Great War changes led to the appearance of two confronted worlds—those who were victorious and those vanquished. The Balkans was not exception. Strong desire for revision of the Versailles order influenced some of the paramilitary organizations or movements in the Balkans to forge new alliances. While in the previous times they were either self-sufficient or partly (in some cases completely) depended on state support, after the Great War Balkan paramilitaries went beyond national borders following simple logic 'enemy of my enemy is my natural ally'. This was especially visible in Yugoslav case where anti-Yugoslav/Serbian movements started to cooperate simultaneously seeking for support from states, such as Italy or international organizations such as the Comintern who both were interested in destabilizing Yugoslavia. Some of these alliances proved to be efficient and long lasting, such as the alliance between IMRO and Croatian *ustashe,* while others were short-lived despite time and efforts invested, such as the never fully achieved alliance between communists and IMRO.

VII
Legacies

In decades that followed events presented in this study, the dynamics of political changes in the region actually demonstrated to what extent Balkan paramilitary traditions, i.e. paramilitary culture, is deeply imbedded in local milieu. Throughout the period between the two global conflicts, the turbulent and violent Second World War; and its immediate aftermath, paramilitarism remained to be present. Another specificity manifested during and after the Second World War, which in the Balkan case went along the strong connection between paramilitarism and guerrilla warfare, is the non-existence of clear boundaries between military and paramilitary, between regular and irregular warfare; and between kinds of behavior which are supposed to be characteristic to each of them respectfully. In addition, fifty years later, the violent and bloody dissolution of Yugoslavia was marked by the resurrection of paramilitary violence as well, but on a larger scale and with some new moments.

The paramilitaries in Yugoslavia, Bulgaria and Albania followed somewhat different paths after 1924. In Yugoslavia they continued to operate but mostly as veteran associations with limited influence on political developments. In Bulgaria, however, IMRO continued to have a strong influence in everyday political life. After the assassination of Todor Alexandrov in 1924, Alexander Protogerov and former Alexandrov's secretary, Ivan Mikhailov continued to lead the organization jointly until a new conflict broke out causing another schism within the organization. The cause was a revenge campaign initiated by Ivan Mikhailov against those he considered responsible for the death of his mentor. After the assassination of Protogerov in 1928, Mikhailov seized all power. Despite sometimes intensive and bloody showdowns between different factions, IMRO still managed to control Petrich region in the Bulgarian southwest making it a 'state within the state'. The organization also continued to operate on Yugoslav territory by spreading propaganda and infiltrating bands. Because of the intensity of these activities General Staff of the Yugoslav armed forces created an emergency plan for the secret military intervention aimed at destruction of *komitaji* centers on Bulgarian territory.[1] However, by the end of the 1920's IMRO *komitajis* changed their methods moving towards individual terrorist actions. The main reason for that were changes in organization of security in Yugoslav Macedonia that practically disabled

---

[1] Mile Bjelajac, *Vojska Kraljevine SHS/Jugoslavije 1922–1935* (Beograd: INIS, 1994), 238–9.

Paramilitarism in the Balkans: The Cases of Yugoslavia, Bulgaria, and Albania, 1917–1924. Dmitar Tasić,
Oxford University Press (2020). © Dmitar Tasić.
DOI: 10.1093/oso/9780198858324.001.0001

movements of armed bands, as well as the fact that Mikhailov wasn't inclined toward the traditional methods primarily because he was never actively involved in classical *komitaji* action. Unlike his mentor, who used to draw his authority from active presence on the ground as simple *komitaji*, Mikhailov was a typical example of a bureaucrat revolutionary. However, the greatest IMRO action—assassination of Yugoslav King Alexander 1934 in Marseilles—happened when IMRO was already banned in Bulgaria, with its leader forced to immigrate and never to return. On the other hand, Mikhailov managed to maintain and improve already created connections with other anti-Yugoslav actors, like Croatian opposition and Italy. After the introduction of King Alexander's royal dictatorship in 1929, instead of Croatian opposition from HSS, IMRO got a new ally—Croatian extremists *ustashe* and their leader Ante Pavelić. Thanks to the IMRO, whose members managed to efficiently transfer their experience and 'know-how' to their allies, *ustashe* were able to master the required skills for continuation of their struggle. As a result of close friendship created in those years between two leaders Mikhailov stayed in Zagreb throughout the Second World War as Pavelić's personal guest.

In Albania, Ahmed Zogu, after returning to power and proclaiming himself president of Albania, invested huge efforts in crushing every kind of opposition coming from political organizations like Kosovo Committee or mutinous mountain clans from the north. Pursuing his agenda aimed at creating political stability, he practically managed to de-paramilitarize Albanian society. Other reasons included his fears of vendetta as well as his mistrust in clan's militias, including his own Matti clan militia. However, despite the recommendations coming from foreign advisers, the goal of de-paramilitarization has been achieved simply by militarization, that is, increasing the strength of regular army and Gendarmerie. By 1928 nearly half of the national budget was spent on military expenditures. In 1928, strength of the regular army grew to 11,000 compared to 8,000 at the end of 1925. In order to sustain his plans Zogu became increasingly dependent on Italy. In 1928 he proclaimed himself as King of Albanians. It was *de iure* acknowledgement of his *de facto* status. He also changed his name from Ahmed Zogu to King Zog. Nevertheless, ancient rules of Leka Dukagjini were still in force and it is said that, thanks to his efforts in crushing opposition, by the 1928 Zogu already had as many as 600 blood feuds on his hands. Unwillingly and unconsciously, even as a sovereign, Zog and his ministers continued to follow old practices by carrying revolvers at every possible occasion.[2] Although Zog's reliance on Italy brought him a powerful ally, its grip in time became stronger leading to the 1939 invasion, occupation and incorporation of Albania into Mussolini's fascist empire. It happened that in 1941 Albania, under Mussolini's regime was finally united with all

[2] Bernd J. Fischer, *King Zog and the Struggle for Stability in Albania*, (Tirana: Albanian Institute for International Studies, 2012), 118–24.

Balkan regions inhabited by Albanians after the collapse and dismemberment of Kingdom of Yugoslavia. However, in reality, it was a puppet-state, which in 1944, after Italian capitulation and after Nazi Germany took care of it, vanished together with its protectors. During that period, Albanians continued to fill the ranks of different military and paramilitary formations struggling for different ideologies and political agendas, again giving their rifles to highest bidder. King Zog would never return to his country. From exile, he observed how his fatherland under the communist regime of Enver Hoxha became one of the most isolated countries in the world.

The Second World War marked a series of huge changes in the region for the local paramilitaries. While some simply continued to operate in new circumstances, like veteran organization *Chetnik Association* of Kosta Milovanović-Pećanac, others appeared to more easily embrace the existing traditions of paramilitarism experiencing a metamorphosis from political to paramilitary movements and militias. In Yugoslavia, typical examples were the transformation of Yugoslav National Movement Zbor (Jugoslovenski nacionalni pokret Zbor) to *Serbian Volunteers Corps* (Srpski dobrovoljački korpus—SDK), as well as the transformation of numerous organizations of the Russian White émigrés residing in Serbia into *Russian Protection Corps* (Ruski zaštitni korpus—RZK). In Bulgaria, expanded with occupied Yugoslav Macedonia and Greek Thrace, there appeared resistance movements following existing traditions of active resistance and guerrilla warfare, led predominantly by local communists. However, in dealing with local resistance, the Bulgarian Army and Gendarmerie continued to rely on already proven practices from previous war, i.e. usage of auxiliary forces known as *Counter-chetnik* squads. In the course of the war, several new organizations appeared in Albania as well. They did not represent paramilitary movements *per se*, but rather something between political movements and militias. Those were *National Front* (Bali Kombëtar), *Second Prizren League*, and *Legality*.

Some aspect of paramilitary tradition like the inclination towards guerrilla warfare proved to be crucial during the Second World War in the Balkans both in organization of the armed resistance against the Axes as well as in the counterinsurgency measures performed by the Axes and local collaboration regimes. The same happened in the years that followed the Second World War when radical political changes occurred as a result of the Soviet dominance over the Eastern Europe. The reshaping of the Balkan political map according to the Yalta agreement included intensive implementation of counterinsurgency measures against various military and political actors that opposed the establishment of envisaged political systems. In all three countries, for several years after the war, existed an armed resistance of different intensity—they were either the remnants of already existing resistance movements and collaboration regimes, as in Yugoslavia and Albania, or they appeared as resistance against the rapid 'sovietisation' of postwar society and political scene as in Bulgaria. In all three countries, communists eliminated traditional democratic parties and movements from everyday political life and for some of their supporters, armed resistance was considered as the only solution. For some of those who kept on fighting, the legacy of 'old Balkan paramilitaries' represented a useful propaganda tool as well as a valuable resource of experience that could help them successfully prolong their struggle. However, their opponents had the same opinion and they also used this legacy in organizing counter-insurgency measures.

The most recent events where paramilitarism played an important role are related to the violent dissolution of the Yugoslav state during the last decade of twentieth century. All sides in this confusing conflict relied on the services of different paramilitary groups, either self-organized or under the strong control of state actors like the army, police, secret services or even political parties and movements. Again, the legacy of paramilitarism proved to be alive and strong. It is somewhat confusing how newer generations have witnessed or even better performed the resurrection of paramiltarism and paramilitary violence despite the fact that more than fifty years has passed since communist dictatorship tried to suppress all aspects of paramilitarism. Nevertheless, immediately after the war broke out in 1991 on all sides numerous guard, volunteer, or *chetnik* detachments and squads appeared with authentic uniforms, symbols, and mottos. Needless to say, the majority of perpetrators of some of the most brutal atrocities in the Balkans recent history were members of different paramilitary units.

Between World Wars

In Yugoslavia, former *chetniks* continued to be active through different associations. Due to the political crisis of 1924-1925, a split occurred in the *Chetnik Association* when Puniša Račić managed to withdraw the majority of organization membership into a new *Association of Serbian Chetniks 'Petar Mrkonjić'* (Udruženje srpskih četnika Petar Mrkonjić—Petar Mrkonjić was pseudonym of King Peter I Karađorđević when he was participant in Herzegovina Uprising in 1875). Račić's decision was motivated by the fact that the Democratic Party leadership, traditional sponsor and supporter of Serbian *chetniks*, decided to join efforts with the Croatian Peasant Party (Hrvatska seljačka stranka - HSS). For Račić, this represented the ultimate treason in favor of separatism and antinational policy so he decided to leave the organization and create his own. Opposite to pro-Yugoslav *Chetnik Association,* led by Ilija Trifunović-Birčanin, Račić's association was clearly Serbian and it became closely associated with People's Radical Party (Narodna radikalna stranka—NRS).[3] While *Chetnik*

[3] John Paul Newman, *Yugoslavia in the Shadow of War. Veterans and the Limits of State Building 1903–1945* (Cambridge: Cambridge University Press, 2015), 105–6.

Association managed to maintain it's independent position, Račić's organization in time transformed into the NRS party militia. The Yugoslav agenda was abandoned for the sake of protection of Serbian national interests. What was peculiar with Račić's unique personality was that he acted in the same manner regardless of the context. Typical features of 'violent Dinarod' paired with acquired paramilitary behavior and war experiences marked his acts in the mountains of 'South Serbia' as well as in parliament chambers in Belgrade. As John Paul Newman has commented for Račić, 'politics was a mere continuation of war by other means and political opponents were not looked upon as part of loyal opposition whose differences could be worked through in the state's national institutions, rather they were to be dealt with in the same manner as the Ottomans, the Habsburgs, or the Bulgarians during the war.'[4] Gunshots fired by Račić during the parliamentary session on 20 June 1928, aimed at the representatives of HSS, represented the final act of the existing political crisis. After being pounded by a series of qualifications and personal insults, Račić, being offended by the representatives of the opposition who mocked the Serbian sacrifice during the Great War, responded in the only way familiar to him. He pulled out his gun and killed Pavle Radić (nephew of the HSS leader Stjepan Radić,) and Đura Basariček. Stjepan Radić and Ivan Pernar and Ivan Granđa were wounded. Due to the severity of his wounds and diabetes, Stjepan Radić died two months later. Račić's shots served as an introduction into King Alexander Royal dictatorship, which was declared on 6 January 1929.

After Račić who was tried and sentenced, the new leader of *Chetnik Association* became Ilija Trifunović-Birčanin (1930–1932), a *chetnik* veteran from the Macedonian years and Great War, who lost his arm in 1916 during the battle of Kajmakčalan as a member of *Volunteer Detachment* that fought under command of Vojin Popović—Vojvoda Vuk, another legendary *chetnik* leader. Birčanin relinquished the position to Kosta Milovanović-Pećanac in 1932 so that he could focus on managing the patriotic association *National Defence* (Narodna odbrana). Pećanac remained head of *Chetnik Association* until the outbreak of the Second World War and the German attack on Yugoslavia in April 1941.

By the end of the 1920's, IMRO presence in Yugoslavia witnessed a decrease in the number of actions and incidents mostly due to the improvements in police work and overall stability. Instead of infiltration of numerous bands, IMRO introduced actions of individuals targeting representatives of civil and military authorities. Meanwhile, in Bulgaria IMRO continued with bloody internal disputes of different factions marked by showdowns and assassinations. However, while Sofia boulevards and coffee places witnessed many gunfights, in Bulgaria's southwest, i.e. so called Petrich County, IMRO ruled almost without interference from the

---

[4] J.P. Newman, *Yugoslavia in the Shadow of War*, 107.

Fig. 10. Chetnik celebration in 1930.

Following Serbian tradition Chetnik Association adopted church holiday of Meeting of the Lord as its "Slava" or patron saint. On that day in 1804 gathered Serbian leaders and champions decided to initiate uprising against the Ottoman rule. In 1930 survived chetniks, their families and followers gathered in Belgrade's Hotel Imperial to celebrate their patron saint.

© National Library of Serbia (Belgrade), Album Chetnik Movement, AF 175.

central state authorities. Decisions of 1925 congress of IMRO, the first one after the death of IMRO legend Todor Alexandrov, clearly stated the importance of Petrich County or 'Macedonia under Bulgarian rule' for IMRO revolutionary activities. The organization continued with introducing and developing their own (para)military, judicial and financial institutions aimed at further strengthening and making the organization less dependent on external factors. Despite friction within the organization, in five districts of this region, IMRO created bodies with precisely determined *komitaji* formations and militia encompassing all able-bodied men in the region. During the crisis, which emerged after the Sveta Nedelya attempt, special patrols were roaming the region and town streets (latter discreetly armed only with revolvers) in order to prevent any action of communist and 'communist sandanists' (*federalists*).[5] The organization was procuring armaments from various sources, including secret shipments from army depots. The first test happened in October 1925 when a border incident evolved into a full-scale invasion of the Greek regular forces. *Komitaji* of the IMRO, together with village militiamen, provided crucial assistance to border guards and regular army in

---

[5] Dimitar Tyulekov, *Obrecheno rodolyubie. VMRO v Pirinsko 1919–1934* (Blagoevgrad: Univ. Izd. 'Neofit Rilski', 2001), http://www.promacedonia.org/dt/dt2_1.html [last checked on 4 November 2016]

Fig. 11. Revealing of the monument to Vojin Popović-Vojvoda Vuk in Belgrade 1936.

One of the most famous if not the most famous Serbian chetnik champion Major Vojin Popović beter known as Vojvoda Vuk had to wait twenty years to receive proper place for his monument. Monument was solemnly revealed on 23 October on one of the most beautiful squares in Belgrade.

(From Zoran Živković's private collection)

preventing Greek advancement. IMRO successfully mobilized and deployed some 4,000 armed men who stood their ground. This proved to be an efficient way of maintaining a respectable force, so that in 1926 the organization had 1,651 local *komitajis* and 8,709 able-bodied militiamen on-site, the approximate number which they managed to maintain throughout the 1920's.[6]

During 1925 IMRO began with enforcing its own revolutionary institutions of justice, a process that caused a new wave of violence, colored with well-known brutality. What was then envisaged for IMRO infrastructure and members in Yugoslav and Greek and parts of Macedonia, was now implemented in Bulgaria, i.e. the Petrich region. A peculiar fact emerged, the IMRO completely ignored official state and its judicial and legal institutions. In three different cases, it resulted in arrests, investigations, trials, sentencing and brutal executions without state interference. In the first of these instances, the D'bnitsa affair, (named after village in vicinity of town of Nevrokop) in May-June 1925, 300 people were arrested under suspicion of conspiring with the *federalist* wing of IMRO. For forty days the special IMRO judicial committee investigated them. This affair resulted in the sentencing and execution of an undetermined number of accused—some estimated between forty-nine and 'more than 100'. The IMRO Central Committee approved all the sentencing. Investigations were marked by extreme brutality, embodied in torture, while executions were performed by firing squads, clubbing to death, hanging in public spaces and on crossroads as warning to all conspiring against IMRO. Several of the accused after been beaten were thrown into fires and burned alive. After the ban of the IMRO in 1934, the D'bnitsa affair resulted in numerous investigations, often ideologically driven, aimed towards ascertaining the truth.[7]

Similar events happened in the villages of Gradevo near Bansko in July, but this time IMRO action was directed against local communists. With the approval of police and military authorities communist groups were apprehended. Following previous practice, they were accused of conspiracy 'with already infiltrated groups from Serbia' to sabotage railways, roads and bridges. After trial, thirteen prisoners were sentenced to death while fourteen were beaten, fined and then released. Here, local *komitajis* acted as executioners. In the village of Krupnik and several surrounding villages, near Simitli, the IMRO acted against associates of the notable renegade Iliya Pandurski. Again, it resulted in the torture and humiliation of those apprehended. Of ten apprehended and sentenced to death, one was pardoned while nine were executed. Post-mortems performed in September 1934

---

[6] D. Tyulekov, *Obrecheno rodolyubie. VMRO v Pirinsko 1919–1934*, http://www.promacedonia.org/dt/dt2_4.html [last checked on 4 November 2016]

[7] D. Tyulekov, *Obrecheno rodolyubie. VMRO v Pirinsko 1919–1934*, http://www.promacedonia.org/dt/dt2_2.html [last checked on 4 November 2016]

showed that no firearms were used for execution but knives and other sharp objects as well as ropes and belts for the purpose of strangulation.[8]

Another feature used that underlined the IMRO's firm grip over the Petrich County, was a parallel taxation system aimed at financing organizations needs and activities. Because of the significant, if not total drop of revenues from the two parts of Macedonia 'occupied' by Greeks and Serbs—the organization was forced to reorganize its finances. Originally, IMRO was financed from multiple sources like donations, membership fees, fines, 'revenues obtained by the force of firearms' etc. Money was needed for salaries, food, family support, procurement of armaments and ammunitions, official trips and per-diem costs, office supplies and publishing costs. In the new circumstances in which the organization entered after the Great War, other sources of finances were found in sales tax on tobacco— which was the number one crop in the region. In addition, almost every transaction related to logging, live stock trading, exporting goods to 'Serbia and Greece', property sales, hunting, sales of alcohol, etc., was subjected to IMRO taxation. One special tribute envisaged for wealthy individuals was colorfully named 'Macedonian patriotic tribute'—a subtle name for extortion or racketeering. Usually it was assessed on an annual basis according to the individual's solvency. Revenue services were well organized including audit and control because, being completely illegal, it often was subject to different forms of embezzlement. These practices brought the appearance of paid revolutionaries, alternative bureaucracy and new relations characterized by servile behavior, which eventually led to the depersonalization of the whole IMRO.[9] Another important source of income for the organization during its rule over Petrich County was opium. Macedonian opium from both Yugoslav and Bulgarian parts of Macedonia was known for its high quality. Because of numerous irregularities and low purchase prices significant quantities of opium used to end up in illegal facilities where they were used for production of heroin, which afterwards used to easily find its ways to demanding American markets.[10]

For years this area continued to look like a state within the state, however it seems that the official Bulgarian state couldn't keep turning a blind eye indefinitely. Almost autonomous rule of indigenous paramilitary movement in one of Bulgarian counties was accompanied by abuses and 'mafia'-like behavior. This caused the local population to submit numerous complaints to the central state authorities. In 1929, during the congress of patriotic association *Homeland*

[8] D. Tyulekov, *Obrecheno rodolyubie. VMRO v Pirinsko 1919–1934*, http://www.promacedonia. org/dt/dt2_2.html [last checked on 4 November 2016]
[9] D. Tyulekov, *Obrecheno rodolyubie. VMRO v Pirinsko 1919–1934*, http://www.promacedonia. org/dt/dt2_3.html [last checked on 4 November 2016]
[10] Vladan Jovanović, 'Rađanje balkanske Kolumbije'. In *Peščanik* https://pescanik.net/radanje-bal-kanske-kolumbije/ [last checked on 11 November 2016]; see also Vladan Jovanović, 'Makedonski opi-jum: o finansijskim i političkim razmerama fenomena (1918-1941)'. In *Godišnjak za društvenu istoriju*, XVI/3, 2009, 69–79.

Protection (Rodna zashtita), in his address made on 7 October, leader of the association General Shkoynov unequivocally pointed out the significance of IMRO but also addressed the alarming situation in the country caused by conflicts within the organization:

"It was not enough that our nation is divided on multitude of hostile parties, on top of that a schism WAS ALLOWED within organization fighting for clearly national cause – IMRO. We have never interfered in its affairs nor we want to. We can only convey our comradely warning that schism within this organization and its self-annihilation is just helping our enemies. We as Bulgarians are begging them for reasoning and tolerance. In the same time we cannot omit mentioning ongoing illegal activities in Petrich and Nevrokop regions where innocent people and our members are being intimidated, abducted and murdered. They are not going to remain unpunished because our patient is not limitless and abovementioned people, because there is no authority to protect them, will adhere to the law of self-protection. That's why we constantly demand IMRO to adhere to the interests of Bulgaria, to respect its sovereignty, and obey its laws. If they refuse to do so Bulgarian government should perform its lawful role and make them obey its laws. If government can't do that THAN FOR THE PURPOSE OF PRESERVING NATIONAL SOVEREIGNTY SOMEONE ELSE WILL COME WHO CAN AND MUST DO IT."[11]

On 19 May 1934, the officer's movement *Zveno* performed yet another successful *coup d'état* in the turbulent history of mid-war Bulgaria. One of their goals (stated under point no. 14) was 'restoring the authority of the state over the entire territory of the country'. Very quickly it became clear to whom this point was related. The most important issue for the new regime became complete disarmament of the organization in Petrich region. Although there were no serious clashes, in several months IMRO spine was literally broken. Most of its leaders were interned while Ivan Mikhailov fled the country never to return. With the help of several Mikhailov's inner-IMRO opponents, like Petar Shandanov, the organization was successfully disarmed and its infrastructure dismantled.[12]

According to the leader of *Zveno* and the new Prime Minister Kimon Georgiev's parliamentary address on 12 July 1934 only in IMRO central office safe in Sofia some 50 millions levs have been confiscated. He also said:

"Let us turn our attention towards one of the darkest and scandalous episodes of our recent history. Remember the time when certain groups and individuals

[11] AJ, MUP KJ, 14–29/410.
[12] D. Tyulekov, *Obrecheno rodolyubie. VMRO v Pirinsko 1919–1934*, http://www.promacedonia. org/dt/dt3_4.html [last checked on 4 November 2016]

placed themselves well above the state authority and its laws. In entire counties state sovereignty existed only on paper. There were moments when entire foreign affairs of our country were dealing with different border incidents. Government of 19 May established state sovereignty throughout the territory of our Kingdom through annihilation of IMRO and through return of Petrich County under the state rule. Numerous changes in administration occurred while organization's weaponry has been confiscated. To general astonishment it counted 10.938 rifles, 767 hand grenades, 637 revolvers, 47 machineguns, 15 sub-machineguns, three mortars and 701.388 rounds."[13]

On the other hand, one of the typical features of he Balkan paramilitaries—strong inclination towards guerrilla warfare managed to found its place within official military doctrines and practices. It happened that between two world wars experiences gained through performances of irregular detachments attracted attention of both Bulgarian and Yugoslav militaries.

By the end of the 1920's an official doctrine of *chetnik* warfare has been introduced into the Yugoslav Royal Army and Navy, under the name *Instruction for Chetnik Warfare* (Uput za četničko ratovanje).[14] With this *Instruction* Yugoslav armed forces for the first time firmly stepped in what used to be a feud of different paramilitary groups and secret organizations, in this case *The Black Hand*, which for years had exclusive right on organization of guerilla warfare. As for the *Instruction* itself, it represents a detailed list of actions and rules on how guerilla action should be organized and conducted.

However, by the end of the 1930's attitudes in Yugoslav military related to *chetnik* or guerilla warfare reached completely new level. In 1940, with the creation of seven *Chetnik battalions*, Yugoslav military performed the final act of appropriating the legacy of the Serbian *chetniks*. These battalions were designed as special units and their rules of engagement envisaged performance of guerrilla warfare. Again, a legacy of the old *chetniks* was invoked, this time not only in doctrine but also in visual identity and their name. It provided firm foundation for construction of genuine tradition. *Chetniks* uniforms and insignia clearly reflected it. Stylized hats, coats and the famous *Skull with crossed bones* were introduced as their official emblems.[15]

However, the creation and existence of *Chetnik battalions* couldn't remain outside of internal Yugoslav disputes. Because of the objections of Croatian politicians claiming that term *chetnik* clearly signals Great Serbianism, Yugoslav

[13] AJ, Stojadinović, 37–22/323.
[14] *Uput za četničko ratovanje*, (Beograd: Ministarstvo vojske i mornarice, 1929). According to the existing procedures Instruction was introduced after the suggestion of General Staff and under the special order from the Minister of Army and Navy.
[15] Aleksandar Životić, 'Jurišne (četničke) jedinice vojske Kraljevine Jugoslavije 1940-1941', In *Vojnoistorijski glasnik*, 1–2/2003, 44–65, here 53–4.

military was compelled to change their name from *Chetnik* to *Assault battalions*.[16] Under this name they participated in the so-called April War of 1941 when the Axes invaded Yugoslavia. However, little is known about *Assault battalion's* performance during this short conflict.

In Bulgaria in the immediate after-war period the legacy of irregular warfare, an important segment of paramiltarism, remained firmly in the hands of the IMRO. Existing manuals and instructions continued to be in use, such as *Rules for Volunteers Bands which will Operate in Macedonia and Thrace during the War for Liberation* (Правилникь за Доброволските чети койито ще действат во Македония и Одрин вь Ослободителана воына)[17] designed by three prominent IMRO members, all of them active army officers: Lieutenant Colonels Alexander Protogerov and Major Petar D'rvingov just before the beginning of First Balkan War (on 17th September 1912). Short and precise, this instruction continued to be used by Bulgarian guerrilla detachments in subsequent war conflicts as well.

Bulgarian military temporarily turned its attention towards other issues. As a result of the stipulation of Neuilly peace agreement and abolishment of compulsory military service and introduction of a small professional army little was done in regard of the doctrines and regulations related to irregular warfare. However in the mid 1930's occurred a renewal of Bulgarian armed forces based on a traditional model with compulsory military service. One of the new regulations was *Rules of engagement during the quelling of conflicts, insurgencies and pursuits of bandit gangs* (Упьтване за действие на войските при потушаване на размирици, въръжени въстания и при преследване на разбойнически банди).[18] The other one was *Rules of engagement for coordinated actions between civil authorities and the army in time of peace* (Правилникь за съдействието което войска дава на гражданските власти вь мирно време), which represented amended regulations issued under the same name in 1900.[19] These two regulations were more related to counterinsurgency tactics than classical guerrilla warfare. This, however, proved to be valuable during the Bulgarian occupation of Yugoslav and Greek territories in the course of the Second World War where Bulgarian occupation forces were faced with massive resistance.

[16] A. Životić, 'Jurišne jedinice', 47.
[17] *Pravilnik' za dobrovolskite cheti kojito shte dejstvat vo Makedoniya i Odrin v' Osloboditelana voyna*, published in: *Nacionalen centr' po voenna istoriya, Nacionalnoosvoboditelnite borbi na b'lagirite ot Makedoniya i Odrinska Trakiya prez Balkanskata voyna (1912–1915)*, (Sofia: Izdatelstvoto na Ministerstvo na otbranata Sv. Georgij Pobedonosec, 1994).
[18] *Up'tvane za deistvie na vojskite pri potushavane na razmirici, v'r'zheni vystaniJa i pri presledvane na razbojnicheski bandi*, (Sofia: Ministerstvo na voinata, 1935).
[19] *Pravilnik' za s'deistvieto koeto voiska dava na grazhdankite vlasti v' mirno vreme*, (Sofia: Ministerstvo na voinata, 1936).

Second World War and Paramilitaries in the Balkans: Between Resistance, Collaboration, Revolutions, Counterrevolutions and Civil Wars

The strong inclination towards the guerilla warfare clearly manifested itself in a series of mass uprisings that broke out in Yugoslav territory during 1941. Whether they were result of spontaneous resistance against genocide as in Croatia and Bosnia and Herzegovina, or occupation as in Montenegro, Serbia, Slovenia and Macedonia, or they were result of precisely organized and coordinated actions of political movement which had plans for state restoration (uprising organized by *chetnik* movement of Draža Mihailović) or overall change of social order and relations (uprisings organized by Communist Party of Yugoslavia) all of them were marked by performance of guerilla warfare, at least in their initial stages.

As in most parts of Europe, beginning of the Second World War in the Balkans was marked by the swift victories of the Axes, occupation and subsequent appearance of resistance. Resistance itself depended on several factors including:

- Occupation policies and measures;
- Local traditions;
- Level of social and cultural development.

In addition, a critical factor was how the occupiers—Germans, Italians, Hungarians, and Bulgarians or regimes of newly created satellite states, in Yugoslav case it was Independent State of Croatia—reacted to the appearance of armed resistance.

Participation of paramilitaries in these events is a complex issue and is something which literally 'comes with the territory' when talking about the Balkans.

What did the Balkans look like after the April of 1941?

The Yugoslav and Greek defeat provided the perfect opportunity for the large-scale revision of the existing order and territorial possessions in the Balkans. The Third Reich, practically, was in a position to almost completely satisfy the existing aspirations of its satellites, clear losers in previous war—like Hungary and Bulgaria, or losers in victory—like Italy. Looking from the north, Slovenia was divided between Germans and Italians with some of its smaller parts directly annexed to Italy and the Third Reich. On April 10 1941 in Zagreb, *ustashe* have officially proclaimed Independent State of Croatia—consisting of Croatia, Bosnia and Herzegovina and a region of Srem. However, large parts of Dalmatia and its islands were handed over to Italy, finally satisfying its long existing desire to rule over the whole of the Adriatic. In addition, Italy was given the right to occupy Montenegro, birth country of Italian Queen. Hungarians were awarded with regions of Prekomurje, Međimurje, Bačka and Baranja. The Italian puppet-state Albania was extended with Yugoslav territories populated with Albanians—Kosovo and

Metohija, western Macedonia and southeast parts of Montenegro. Thus the Great Albania was officially created. East parts of Macedonia and south Serbia were handed over to Bulgarians.[20]

Greece was divided in three occupational zones. Germans having taken Athens, Salonika, island of Crete with several Aegean islands as well as the very sensitive border area with Turkey. Bulgarians was given Thrace, with parts of Greek Macedonia. Italians were granted the rest of the Greek territories.[21]

From a German perspective, Serbia was seen as 'society of conspirators', full of secret societies like *Black* and *White Hands* which used to instigate unrest in neighboring countries. This is where the 'Austrian' component of Hitler's character and deeply imbedded prejudices clearly manifested. As an additional punishment for 'traitorous behavior', besides being deprived of some of it territories, Serbia was placed under the direct occupation regime of the Third Reich.[22]

As a rule, on each of these territories had harsh measures of denationalization and economical exploitation were introduced. Several thousands of Slovenes were expatriated to Serbia. In addition, Serbs that were colonized in mid-war period were forced to leave Hungarian, Bulgarian and Albanian zones. From personal and practical reasons Germans were particularly keen to take over the control of important mining and industrial facilities as well as to fully implement the policy of 'Final solution'.

By the end of April following German practices and indigenous racial ideology in Independent State of Croatia initiated large-scale genocide against Serbs, Jews and Gypsies (Roma). Genocide against the Serbs in particular was manifested on several levels through ethnic cleansing where some of the population were forced to immigrate to Serbia or Italian zones, some were sent to concentration camps or killed in mass executions on the spot, while others were forcefully converted to Catholicism.[23] This quickly led to the appearance of resistance among Serbs in Bosnia and Herzegovina which already in June completely paralyzed several counties.

In Serbia, the first signs of resistance were expressed by the members of the Yugoslav army who escaped being taken as PoW's. One group of them gathered in the village of Ravna Gora in west Serbia where on May 13 they proclaimed the beginning of an uprising. The head of the group was Colonel Dragoslav-Draža Mihailović. This group began with organizing units all over west and central Serbia. They decided to attract the masses with something that was familiar to the locals—tradition of the *chetniks*. And they had success from several reasons. Firstly, it appealed on the notion of freshly suffered embarrassing defeat from the

---

[20] Branko Petranović, *Jugoslavije 1918–1988. II*, (Beograd: Nolit, 1988), 26–31.
[21] Richard Clogg, *A Concize History of Greece*, 2nd ed. (Cambridge: Cambridge University Press, 2002), 123–4.
[22] B. Petranović, *Istorija Jugoslavije II*, 26–31.
[23] B. Petranović, *Istorija Jugoslavije II*, 43.

same enemy whom they have defeated in previous war. Secondly, the region itself was the heartland of Serbian independence from where struggle for independence and unification had started in the early 19th century. Finally, Yugoslav's King Peter II, Yugoslav Royal government and a small army and air force contingent, managed to escape and place himself under the protection of the United Kingdom—at that moment the only country remaining to fight the Axes. In time that followed, Mihailović managed to establish contact with the Yugoslav Royal government in exile and to extend his organization and influence beyond Serbia. King and government promoted him to the rank of General and proclaimed him as Minister of Army while his forces were named as *Yugoslav Army in the Fatherland*. However, despite all of this, until the final end, his forces remained known as *chetniks*—a clear sign of how strong the legacy was that they invoked. Insisting on *chetnik's* legacy was most visible in terms of their visual identity. *Chetniks* used to appear in outfits that were combinations of Yugoslav military uniform and local national costumes. Most known *chetnik's* hallmarks were long hairs and beards. Beside Yugoslav Royal Army insignia, like colors and cockades, equally present were black *Chetnik* banners with *Skull and crossed bones* and inscriptions *With trust in God for the King and Country* or *Liberty or Death*.[24] However, other aspects of *chetnik* tradition, like brutal liquidation of traitors, spies and supporters of political opponents, contributed largely to its alienation among the common folk. Needless to say, these cases have been extensively used by contemporary, anti-*chetnik* propaganda.[25]

Although Yugoslav by name, the *chetnik* organization was limited to territories inhabited by Serbs (Serbia, Montenegro, Bosnia and Herzegovina, Lika and Dalmatia), but there were a few exceptions like Slovenia where pro-Yugoslav sentiments were still strong, and in parts of west Macedonia where Serbian *chetnik* action used to be very much alive in the past.[26]

However, connections of Mihailović *chetnik's* with traditional Serbian paramilitarism existed strictly in terms of its legacy and visual identity. For him and his followers these traditions merely represented a convenient source to attach themselves to—useful for attracting supporters and maintaining a presence among the

---

[24] For years after the Second World War, particulary in Yugoslav regions with Serbian majority, long beard was considered as clear sign of specific political affiliation, and although was not prohibited by the law it could cause to those wearing it lot of troubles.

[25] 'To put someone under the letter Z' was common expression used for those designated to be physically eliminated by cutting of their throat (in Serbian—*zaklati*). This kind of capital punishment was widely used by all factions during the struggle over Macedonia before the Great War, its main purpose was to set up an example and intimidate weavers and potential treators.

[26] Aleksandar Simonovski, 'Učestvoto i dejnosta na Milivoj Trbić-Vojče vo Ravnogorsko dviženje vo Makedonija (1942-1944)'. In *Glasnik na Institut za nacionalna istorija*, godina 58, br. 1–2, 2014, 131–41. Thanks to reputation and legacy of his father Vasilije Trbić, well-known leader of Serbian *chetnik* action in Ottoman Macedonia, Milivoj Trbić was able to organize his group and maintain presence in Macedonia under Bulgarian occupation until much stronger forces of the People's Liberation Movement led by communists defeated him.

common people. His organization, structure of units, terminology, chain of command, and officer's ranks had characteristics of traditional military organization firmly associated with existing state organization and its ruling ideology. Being a career officer, Mihailović was well aware of the existing doctrines for guerilla warfare and their implementation, especially in the terms of eventual reprisals against civilians—what actually was strong and very much alive memory of the Great War and Austro-Hungarian and Bulgarian brutal response to Serbian resistance.

On the other hand their adversaries, a partisan movement led by Yugoslav communists, did not have doubts in relation to how they should fight and what was their final goal. Yugoslav communists resolved to armed resistance, however on somewhat different foundations than Mihailović's royalists. Communist preparations for the mass uprising started to intensify after the 22 June 1941 when Germans initiated the invasion of the Soviet Union. Although Yugoslav communist's allegiance lay elsewhere, i.e. in Moscow, through their actions they demonstrated a patriotism that hasn't been their characteristic in the mid-war period. Instead of destroying the Yugoslav state, which were the initial plans of the Comintern, during the war they worked very actively on its restoration, naturally on new socialist and federal foundations aimed to reconcile existing national disputes as well as to recognize Macedonian and Montenegrin nations. The Communist Party's pre-war status as one of the main anti-state movements, its growing power and support beyond Serb populated areas, introduction of new local authorities as first step in an on-going revolution, taking of power and change of social system, contributed largely in the specific mobilization of forces which considered communists as a greater evil than the German and Italian occupiers. These forces belonged to the predominantly conservative, nationalist and pro-fascist political structures of which some were involved in the organizing of the paramilitary structures. Thus, the stage for civil war was set-up.

As in Yugoslavia and Albania, following existing traditions and influences of external factors, armed resistance also appeared in Greece. Again, as in Yugoslavia and Albania, there occurred a political split that eventualy led to the civil war. The first organization that appeared in September 1941 was *Front for National Liberation* (EAM) together with its military component *National Liberation Army* (ELAS) with some 60,000 fighters. Although the majority of EAM and ELAS fighters were not members of the communist party, the communists actually had the strongest influence on these two organizations. The second organization was The *National Republican Hellenic Alliance* (EDES) and it encompassed members of non-communist poltical orientation. Both organizations waged guerrilla warfare aganist the occupiers through raids resulting in reprisals against the civilian population.[27] In Greece, however, civil war lasted untill 1949.

---

[27] R. Clogg, *A Concize History of Greece*, 128–34.

Yugoslav partisans, i.e. members of *People's Liberation Movement* (Narodnooslobodilački pokret—NOP) evolved into an organized and conventional armed force primarily by the gradual transformation and massing of a movement that initially had strong guerilla and revolutionary features. From its early stages doctrine of guerilla warfare was its integral part. Although, on the local level indigenous traditions of guerrilla warfare existed, the doctrine of organizing and use of partisan units was based on principles that were developed and taught elsewhere, more precisely in the Soviet Union—in schools and education and training institutions of Comintern and Soviet military and security structures. Their main goal was the training of non-Soviet cadres for the organization of socialist revolutions in their own countries. Although, the Communist Party of Yugoslavia has organized and initiated an uprising against occupiers, its main goal was a change of the social system. These efforts encountered firm objections from representatives of the legitimate state authorities and social system—the *Yugoslav Army in the Fatherland* and its leader General Mihailović, leading a whole country into a bloody civil war. However, for Yugoslav as well as for all other communists' worldwide, civil war was considered an inseparable part of the socialist revolution and they had invested huge efforts in preparation and training of their cadres for performance of special assignments—like diversions, the making of IED's (improvised explosion devices) and assassinations.[28] In strictly military terms partisan movement prevailed because, opposite to its adversaries, it did not have formal limitations in the implementation of guerrilla warfare principles, mainly in relations toward the civilian population as potential targets of enemy reprisals.

It sounds paradoxically that although Yugoslav partisans performed the same kind of guerilla warfare widely present in the Balkans, they represented a formal discontinuity with traditions of *chetniks* and *chetnik* warfare. Some of the reasons for this include:

1. The opposing side in the civil war, the *chetniks*, represented themselves as true successors of *chetnik* tradition demonstrating this claim through names and visual appearance (*Skull with crossed bones* cockades, beards, fur-hats, knives, mixture of army uniforms and national clothes, black banners and inscriptions *Liberty or death*).
2. Through deliberate actions of partisan leadership the Soviet organizational influence has been widely spread out.

---

[28] More on guerrilla warfare trainning of Yugoslav Communists cadres, see in: Aleksey Timofeyev, 'Vojne i bezbednosne strukture SSSR u pripremi partizanskog ratovanja do početka Drugog svetskog rata', *Vojnoistorijski glasnik* 2/2008, 36–52; Aleksey Timofeyev, '"Partija građanskog rata": Pripreme kadrova Kominterne za izvođenje partizanskog rata i revolucije', *Vojnoistorijski glasnik* 1/2009, 56–77; and, Aleksey Timofeyev, 'Sovjetska uloga u školovanju i pripremi jugoslovenskog partizanskog kadra do početka Drugog svetskog rata', *Vojnoistorijski glasnik* 2/2009, 55–77.

It came out that partisans, like the *chetnik's*, used to perform the same basic principles of guerilla warfare so deeply imbedded in local military traditions. However, its ideological-political context completely overshadowed the historical reality, military traditions and arts-of-war, and in the final instance led to a formal breaking away from an authentic and rich military tradition.

While nominally both the partisans and Mihailović *chetnik's* were fighting the Axes, only the partisans could be considered the warring party. Mihailović *chetnik's*, with a few exceptions, mostly remained locally oriented, maintaining their organization, waiting for a solution to happen on other fronts. By the end of 1941, the Germans managed to neutralize the uprising in Serbia with several military operations against the partisans and *chetniks* and by enforcing brutal reprisals against the civilian population (ratio was execution of 100 civilians for one German soldier killed). These actions essentially pacified the Mihailović organization, forcing him and his headquarters to leave Serbia and to settle down in the Italian occupation zone in northern Montenegro. After suffering several defeats the partisan forces also moved out of Serbia but unlike the *chetniks* they went to Bosnia and Herzegovina. The majority of remaining Mihailović's forces in Serbia went through the process of so-called legalization, i.e. joining the formations of quisling regime led by General Milan Nedić.[29]

In Bosnia, the partisans initiated mobile warfare, forming new units and so-called liberated territories, maneuvering on the line that separated German and Italian occupation zones. Here, the complexity of the civil war in Yugoslavia during the Second World War had reached new levels. Those were the territories of the Independent State of Croatia where the local Serb population already rose up in May 1941. Here, partisans, beside Germans and Italians had a new enemy—the army of a newly established Independent State of Croatia. Although a major part of it consisted of a Croatian Home Guard, its most trustful and ardent part were *ustashe*, a military component of Croatian extremist emigration. Unlike the Home Guard that was organized on traditional conscription, *ustashe* were primarily volunteers. Their role and organization was almost identical to those of Mussolini's Black shirts or Hitler's SS. Beside participation in conventional warfare, *ustashe* were also responsible for the implementation of genocide policies against the Serbs, Jews and Roma, as members of death squads or concentration camps personnel. Additionally, in Bosnian part of the Independent State of Croatia, local Muslims beside joining ustashe en masse were allowed to form their own militias.

Depending on geographical circumstances, the extent of the collaboration of *chetnik* forces was different. In zones occupied by Italians it has reached levels of written agreement which precisely arranged the creation and obligation of *Milizia*

[29] Đoko Slijepćević, *Jugoslavija uoči i za vreme Drugog svetskog rata*, (Minhen: Iskra, 1978), 315–20.

volontaria anticommunista (Anti-communist Voluntary Militia—MVAC) official name of the local *chetnik* units that used to successfully assist action of the Italian army directed against the partisan forces.[30]

The same happened in Albania where Albanian communists also initiated guerrilla warfare against Italian forces and later against German forces, as well as against nationalist organizations and their paramilitary structures such as *National Front* (Bali Kombëtar). National Front was a nationalist organization, formed in 1942 in northern Albania. It soon became well-established in Kosovo and Metohija as well. Although its leadership continued to rely on western allies—primarily Great Britain, this was just another collaborationist organization sponsored, at first, by Italians and than by Germany. Its main foe were partisan movements in Albania and Yugoslavia, primarily because they were bearers of communist ideology, as well as because Yugoslavs endangered fulfilment of their main political goal—creation of Great Albania.[31] From 1943 and the capitulation of Italy in territories of Kosovo and Metohija another Albanian nationalist organization started to operate—the *Second Prizren League*. It also pursued the goal for a Great Albania but this time with strong support from Berlin.[32] Among its members, Germans initiated the recruitment of personnel for their auxiliary units like *vulnetars, Kosova regiment* and 21 SS division *Skanderbeg*. After the German retreat from the Balkans in the fall of 1944, a substantial number of former members of these groups remained on the ground continuing to fight.

While from the beginning Mihailović *chetnik's* and *National Front* in Albania had been considered as resistance movements, on a local level, they entered into open collaboration—initially with Italians and then with the Germans. Instead of Axes, in time, their main enemy became the local communist movements.

As for other paramilitary organizations that appeared during the course of the Second World War, anti-communism became their *raison d'etre*. The first organization was commonly named *Chetniks* of Kosta Milovanović-Pećanac as opposed to *Chetniks* of Draža Mihailović. Pećanac was the leader of mid-war *Chetnik Association*—a veteran organization and in practical terms the only true heir of Serbian paramilitary tradition. His traumatic experience of resistance during the Great War and the Toplica Uprising where the actions of insurgents caused serious reprisals of the Austro-Hungarian and especially Bulgarian occupation forces and their irregulars influenced his later political attitude to a great extent. After the German occupation in April 1941 he used the existing network of *Chetnik Association* in Serbia to organize his supporters. While his stronghold was in southeast Serbia, it had limited influence elsewhere. Initially he objected to

[30] Dragan S. Nenezić, *Jugoslovenske oblasti pod Italijom 1941–1943* (Beograd: Vojnoistorijski institut Vojske Jugoslavije, 1999), 118.

[31] *Vojna enciklopedija*, tom 1, Bali Kombetar, 441.

[32] B. Petranović, *Istorija Jugoslavije II*, 272.

both Mihailović and communist's actions that resulted in German reprisals. For him everything resembled too much like events from the Great War when he, although being an official representative of Serbian Supreme Command, was overruled by several over-zealous promoters of armed resistance that eventually caused huge civilian causalities. Therefore in 1941 Pećanac placed himself into the service of the Serbian quisling regime headed by General Milan Nedić who had similar views on the matter. In addition, Pećanac also maintained contact with the German Gestapo. During the course of war he used to fight not only against the partisans but also against the Albanian irregulars in northern Kosovo who often initiated raids against local Serbs. However in 1944, together with his most trusted associates, he decided to join Mihailović and his movement, but he was tricked and brutally executed by Mihailović's death squad.[33]

The *Yugoslav National Movement Zbor* (zbor is Serbian for *assembly* or *gathering*) was a small, but well organized political party of the extreme right that promoted the abandonment of traditional democratic institutions and the introduction of the corporate state system. The party was led by a charismatic and proliferate political writer Dimitrije Ljotić who was also a lawyer, reserve officer and war veteran. Beside the corporate state *Zbor* promoted the Yugoslav idea, as well as the ideas of eastern Christianity and anti-communism. However, its influence on the Yugoslav political scene was relatively small. Right after the occupation in 1941 the organization disbanded itself. However, by September 1941, they started with the enlistment of volunteers aimed at assisting General Milan Nedić's quisling regime in the struggle against the mass uprising in Serbia. These enlisted volunteers, around 3–4,000, had been organized in a paramilitary unit called the *Serbian Volunteers Corps* (Srpski dobrovoljački korpus—SDK) and were headed by Ljotić himself. As Pećanac had previously done, Ljotić and his SDK entered the service of the Serbian quisling regime and proved to be most trustful and disciplined unit in numerous clashes against communists. In one moment they were organized in five infantry regiments and one artillery battalion. Until the end of the war and their own bitter end volunteers managed to maintain their structure. In 1944 under strong pressure of advancing forces of the Red Army and Yugoslav partisans, SDK managed to leave Serbia and with German assistance, regroup in Slovenia together with other Serbian and Slovenian collaborationist's forces. While their leader Ljotić died in a car accident in April 1945, the volunteers managed, despite heavy clashes with advancing forces of Yugoslav partisans, to withdraw to Austrian territory where they surrendered to the British forces. However, the Britons handed most of them back over to the Yugoslav partisans. There, in the Slovenian mountains the volunteers were brutally executed together with the captured *chetniks* and *Slovenian Home Guard*.[34]

---

[33] Đ. Slijepčević, *Jugoslavija uoči i za vreme Drugog svetskog rata*, 312–14.
[34] Đ. Slijepčević, *Jugoslavija uoči i za vreme Drugog svetskog rata*, 320–6.

The third paramilitary organization that was created in occupied Serbia was the *Russian Protection Corps* (Ruski zaštitni korpus—RZK). The RZK consisted of Russian émigrés or their descendants living in Serbia and was founded by Germans in autumn 1941 with the simple task of fighting partisan insurgents in occupied Serbia. The Germans named them *Russian Protection Unit* (Russische Schutzgruppe) and assigned them to protect important mines, railroads and industrial facilities in occupied Serbia. In that sense the RZK was more auxiliary unit than a simple paramilitary formation. In the beginning, RZK counted some 1,500 members and their number continued to grow thanks to the Russian volunteers coming from all parts of the Balkans as well as to Soviet PoW's who also volunteered. By the 1944 the RZK was fighting partisans in Serbia and together with other quisling formations like SDK and Pećanac *chetniks* was deployed on the river Drina in order to prevent partisan incursion from Bosnia. At that time RZK had five regiments with 11,197 soldiers. By the end of 1944 they got the opportunity to fight their main foe—the Red Army itself, which in the course of offensive operations in Romania entered Serbia from the east. After suffering several defeats the RZK withdrew from Serbia along with the German troops. Most of them managed to reach Austria and surrender to the Western allies. From a final count of 17,090 soldiers that passed through the ranks of RZK during the period 1941–1945, 6,709 were listed as causalities (dead, seriously wounded, or missing in action).[35]

In the case of Serbia's 'White' émigrés several factors contributed to their successful engagement on the side of the Axes. As noted earlier, Russian émigrés upon arrival in the Kingdom of Serbs, Croats and Slovenes experienced favorable living conditions compared to other countries where they had settled after the revolution and civil war. By 1924 the number of Russians in the Kingdom of Serbs, Croats and Slovenes reached 42,000. Due to continuing emigration, as well as a return to the Soviet Union this number was reduced to around 25,000 in the years just before the outbreak of the Second World War; nevertheless, it was still the largest number in whole of southeast Europe.[36] In Yugoslavia they enjoyed the personal patronage of the Yugoslav king and Patriarch of Serbian Orthodox Church. They kept their political and military organization almost intact as their political affiliation towards the political right, which was to be expected since they came from Russia as opponent of changes that have radically transformed their homeland. Another factor was the Yugoslav policy of anti-communism and refusal to establish a diplomatic relationship with the 'first country of socialism'. So, when in the summer of 1941 Yugoslav communists initiated their way of

[35] Aleksey Timofeyev, *Crveni i beli; ruski uticaji na događaje u Jugoslaviji 1941–1945*, Beograd: Ukronija, 2014) 43–5.
[36] Miroslav Jovanović, *Doseljavanje ruskih izbeglica u Kraljevinu SHS 1919–1924*, (Beograd: Stubovi kulture, 1996), 96.

resistance, which meant simultaneously carrying out drastic changes to the political system, Russian émigrés found themselves in a familiar position between civil war and Red terror. Rather than assaulting German occupation forces, partisans started raids against centers of local authorities destroying community records, registers and archives. In addition, following the pattern already seen in the course of the Bolshevik revolution, one of their targets became prominent members of the Russian community in Serbia, which at that time accounted for 20,000 members. According to the estimations of the Russian community in Serbia some 300 of their members (in majority of cases with their whole families) were brutally liquidated by communist *Death squads* during summer months of 1941. After these events some of the Russians in the Serbian province organized their own units and together with local German forces repelled attacks of communist guerrilla detachments. That resulted in the decision of the German command in Serbia to form the RZK.[37]

While not a topic under discussion in this study, it is worth mentioning that some of the 'White' Russians went even further in their affiliation with the German occupiers. Under the auspices of *Wehrmacht's* rival—the Waffen SS, in 1942, initially a battalion and afterwards a whole SS regiment named *Vareg* had been formed. It consisted of the extreme members of RZK and the Russian emigrant community in Serbia. They were deployed in several Serbian towns in so called companies of auxiliary police *Hilfe Polizei*—a.k.a *HiPo*, with the task to fight the partisans. Parts of these units had gone through special training and were sent to the Eastern front. Meanwhile, new members coming from the ranks of Soviet PoW's additionally strengthened the unit. They reached their final composition of some 2,500 men and received an official name, *First special SS Regiment Vareg* (Sonderregiment SS I 'Varäger') in Slovenia in late 1944. While in Slovenia, the regiment participated in fights against the local partisans. After the final surrender of the Axes forces in May 1945 in Slovenia, partisans liquidated part of *Vareg* fighters together with other captured Serbian and Slovenian quisling and anti-communist units. Others managed to surrender to the Western allies who allowed Russian émigrés to leave for South America while former Soviet soldiers were handed over back to the Soviets.[38]

Paramilitaries and Paramilitarism in the Balkans after the Second World War

Huge political changes that appeared in the Balkans during and after the Second World War led to the establishment of communist regimes in all Balkan countries

---

[37] A. Timofeyev, *Crveni i beli; ruski uticaji na događaje u Jugoslaviji 1941–1945*, 37–9.
[38] A. Timofeyev, *Crveni i beli; ruski uticaji na događaje u Jugoslaviji 1941–1945*, 45–6.

except Greece and Turkey. However, the existence of genuine political traditions and culture in Yugoslavia, Romania, Bulgaria and Albania resulted in the appearance of a different kind of resistance, including an armed one, which, with or without foreign aid, existed till the early 50's. The just initiated Cold War added additional complexity to the matter because from the western countries point of view anti-communist movements and organizations were considered as a convenient ally in destabilizing the newly established communist regimes and Soviet supremacy in the region. Although in all above-mentioned countries traditional political parties and movements continued with their activities, in years that followed, one by one, they have all been eliminated from the political scene by using combinations of different brutal methods. For all non-communists in the Balkans the question arose; how to continue the struggle against communist oppression? Some of their supporters continued the political struggle either by joining existing paramilitary formations or movements as in Yugoslavia and Albania, or by creating isolated armed groups sometimes invoking traditions of the old Balkan paramilitaries and irregulars as in Bulgaria where the IMRO represented an obvious example.

In Albania, local nationalists and monarchists were considered a main enemy to Enver Hoxha's regime. Their groups were still active, especially in mountainous north Albania where additional problems for the new regime were attitudes of the local clansmen.[39] From summer 1945, in Yugoslavia, a newly established regime led by Josip Broz—Tito, initiated a large-scale campaign against remnants of former adversaries: Mihailović *chetniks*, Croatian *ustashes*, *Slovenian Home Guard*, and Albanian *balists*. In Bulgaria events in their political theatre led to the appearance of resistance that was manifested through legal and illegal organizing and struggle.[40]

In Yugoslavia, for example, there was no unified anti-communist resistance, even so, most of the post-war anti-communist guerrilla fighters like Croatian *ustashe* and Albanian *balists* beside being anti-communist were anti-Yugoslav as well. Although in period May-June 1945 the majority of them was either liquidated or managed to escape and surrender to the Western Allies, some 12,000 of *chetniks, ustashes, Slovenian Home Guards* and *balists* remained on Yugoslav soil.[41] Their communist opponents had huge advantages like a clear political platform, determination, organization, strong propaganda and a security apparatus.

---

[39]   Peter Bartl, *Albanci, od srednjeg veka do danas* (Beograd: CLIO, 2002) 233.

[40]   Dinyu Sharlanov, *Goryanite. Koi sa te?* (Sofia: Prostranstvo & Forma 1999), 10.

[41]   *Razvoj oružanih snaga SFRJ 1945-1985. Savezni sekretarijat za narodnu odbranu I*, (Beograd: VIZ, 1990), 34; Actuall approximate number of anti-communist guerrilla fighters in Yugoslavia in July 1945 was 14.834 (9.693 *chetniks*, 3121 *crusaders*, 650 *Slovenian Home Guard* and 1370 *balists*): VA, JNA, k. 46, f. 3, red. br. 1/1, Pregled odmetničkih bandi za vreme od oslobođenja do 31. jula 1946. g, MNO FNRJ Generalštab Jugoslovenske armije, II Odeljenje, str. pov. 452 od 09.10.1946. godine.

Their self-confidence and arrogance was visible from the simplification and joint denominator of their adversaries—they were all simply named as bandits.

In Slovenia, one part of the anti-communists forces ogranized themselves into so-called *King Matijaž Army* invoking the mythical story of an old king sleeping under the mountain waiting to be awoken and bring freedom to his people. Members of *King Matijaž Army* fought against the communists hoping for the decisive intervention of Western Allies that would overthrow the communist regime, restore democracy and join Yugoslavia to the community of free nations.[42] From September 1945, Yugoslav political emigration that operated within the *National Committee of Kingdom of Yugoslavia* also supported the activities of *King Matijaž Army*, under the full knowledge and support of the Western Allies.[43] Compared to the other anti-communist groups they enjoyed the support of western intelligence agencies on Austrian soil from where they infiltrated Yugoslav territory. Up until 1949 and the Yugoslav conflict with the Soviet Union they enjoyed the support of the American CIC (Counter Intelligence Corps) and British FSS (Field Security Service).[44] Unlike other Yugoslav anti-communist groups members of *King Matijaž Army* even managed to publish newspapers.[45] While they operated on Yugoslav territory they had been equiped with radios and from several radio stations located in Austria they were also able to broadcast radio-programes.[46]

King Matijaž Army was specific to Slovenia. Its actions remained pretty much unknown to the rest of the Yugoslav population due to the strict control of the information imposed by the communist regime. Members of the *King Matijaž Army* were die-hard anti-communists. Their actions were directed towards the new authorities and ideology, however in time these actions became just pillaging raids. In their appearance they resembled the Serbian *chetniks*, they wore uniforms of the Yugoslav Royal Army and *chetnik* cockades, thus becoming another paramilitary group inspired by the *chetnik* legacy.[47]

Compared with other anti-communist forces Mihailović *chetniks* had been the most numerous. Their presence was strongest in Bosnia and Herzegovina, west Serbia, Sanjak and the border area between Serbia, Montenegro, Bosnia and Herzegovina and to a lesser extent in parts of Croatia (Lika, Dalmatia and Slavonia) and Macedonia. Unlike others, their leader, General Mihailović decided

[42] Martin Premk, *Matjaževa vojska 1945–1950* (Ljubljana: Društvo piscev zgodovine NOB Slovenije, 2005), 180.
[43] M. Premk, *Matjaževa vojska*, 107.
[44] Martin Premk, *Matjaževa vojska*, 108. After Tito-Stalin conflict in 1948 socialist Yugoslavia was seen as convenient ally in struggle against the USSR and its satellites primarily because it was considered as an example for East European countries for possible way to break up with Soviet Union.
[45] M. Premk, *Matjaževa vojska*, 260.
[46] M. Premk, *Matjaževa vojska*, 114. Those were radio-stations 'Ravna Gora', 'Triglav', 'Radio Ljubljana', 'Svoboda ili smrt', 'Združena Slovenija', 'Slobodna seljačka Hrvatska', 'Radio Sava'.
[47] M. Premk, *Matjaževa vojska*, 161–76.

to stay in Yugoslavia and to continue fighting. His example was followed by several prominent *chetnik* commanders as well.[48] However, the capturing of Mihailović in March 1946, his subsequent trial and final execution in July same year inflicted a heavy blow to his movement.[49]

Unlike other movements, the real influence of the *chetniks* did not correspond with their overall numbers. *Chetnik* groups used to operate on familiar grounds among well-known people, but they were not interconnected and they did not enjoy the support that the Croatian *crusaders* had within the Roman-Catholic clergy. Similar to *Slovenian King Matijaž Army*, *chetniks* also hoped for a decisive intervention from the Western allies.

In Yugoslav territories inhabited by an Albanian national minority—Kosovo and Metohija, west Macedonia and to a lesser extent Montenegro operated Albanian anti-communist and nationalist groups who were commonly known as *balists*. Balists used to be associated with the *National Front* organization. While the members of *National Front* remained active after the Second World War, so too did the members of other nationalist organizations—*Second Prizren League* and organization *Legality* comprising of few remaining supportes of exiled King Zog. Also, there were Albanians that used to serve in Italian, Bulgarian and German auxiliary forces or in SS units, such as 21 SS division *Skanderbeg*.[50] However, *balists* at that time more resembled simple outlaws than members of a paramilitary movement with a clear political agenda. Their political influence was minimal because they and their potential audience were predominantly illiterate and uneducated. Their position was made more difficult because this time, unlike during the past, Yugoslavia and Albania shared common ideology and politycal system. Interestingly, in their appearance and way of operating they evoked the legacy of *kachaks*.

If we take into consideration factors such as: number, teritorial distribution, internal organization, support, propaganda and political actions, the greatest influence in the Balkans was achieved by the so-called *crusaders* (križari). This romantic title actually served as rallying point for the ex-members of the armed forces of the Independent State of Croatia and its political structures, primarily *ustashe*. *Crusaders* were very active in Croatia and Bosnia and Herzegovina. They operated under the slogan "'All for Christ against the Communists'". Unlike the Independent State of Croatia which mannaged to attract and mobilize *en masse*

---

[48] VA, AVBA, 1–3.2.06, Terorizam, odmetništvo, banditizam 1944 i 1945, Obaveštajni odsek Štaba 4. divizije 1. jugoslovenske armije, Pregled četničkih bandi na teritoriji 4. divizije za mjesec novembar 1945. g, str. pov. br. 90 od 25.11.1945. godine.

[49] Kosta Nikolić, Bojan Dimitrijević, 'Zarobljavanje i streljanje generala Dragoljuba Mihailovića 1946. godine – Nova saznanja o arhivskoj građi', *Istorija 20. veka*, 2/2009, 9–20. Nikola Milovanović, *Kroz tajni arhiv UDBE*, (Beograd: Sloboda, 1974); Tamara Nikčević, *Goli otoci Jova Kapičića* (Podgorica: Daily press, 2009), 100.

[50] Đorđe Borozan, *Velika Albanija, porijeklo, ideje, praksa*, (Beograd: Vojnoistorijski institut Vojske Jugoslavije, 1995), 360–9.

Muslims from Bosnia and Herzegovina, the political influence of the *crusaders* on local Muslims was almost non-existent.[51] Like all other anti-communist movements in Yugoslavia, *crusaders* also placed their hopes on the intervention of the Western Allies. Despite the fact that their leadership was annihilated or in exile, (similar to the *chetniks)* due to the strong support of Roman Catholic clergy the *crusadres* continued to operate and effect strong propaganda influence among the Croatian population. While most of the *chetniks* groups acted autonomously, without contact and exchange of information, and Slovenians were completely dependent on logistics from abroad, the *crusaders* enjoyed all the advantages coming from the centuries old infrasturcture of the Roman Catholic church. It provided them with almost everything, starting from basic needs like refuge, hideouts, and provisions, all away to communicating messages, printing and distribution of propaganda material and influencing the common people during the Sunday services sermons. Because of this support, as well as a benevolent attitude towards the Independent State of Croatia in general, participation in genocide against Serbs, Jews and Gypsies, participation in forceful conversion of Serbs or indifference towards the genocide in the Independent State of Croatia, many Roman Catholic priests were prosecuted by the new authorities.[52] One of the counts of the indictment against the Aloisius Stepinac, the Archbishop of Zagreb and Head of the Roman Catholic church in Croatia was providing help and support for one group of the *crusaders*.[53]

Some of the *ustashe* leaders that managed to evade capture, gathered in Austria and Italy, where already during 1946 under the command of Ante Pavelić himself, started to operate as the *Croatian People's Board* (Hrvatski narodni odbor—HNO). This board became representative of Croatian political emigration and organizer of the anti-communist resistance in Yugoslav territories inhabited by Croats.[54]

As in the case of Slovenian anti-communist emigration there was a considerable level of cooperation between *ustashe* and Anglo-American secret services, but to what extent and for what purposes it remained unknown. However, it was accepted that just about everyone tried to fit into the western projections within the context of the expected showdown with communism. After the Yugoslav split

---

[51] On post WWII anti-communist resistance in Croatia see: Zdenko Radelić, *Križari. Gerila u Hrvatskoj 1945-1950*, (Zagreb: Hrvatski institut za povijest, Dom i svijet, 2002).
[52] On attitudes of Roman Catholic church in Croatia and communist authorities measures against it, see: Dragoljub R. Živojinović, *Vatikan, katolička crkva i jugoslovenska vlast 1941-1958*, (Beograd: Prosveta, Tersit, 1994).
[53] D. Živojinović, *Vatikan, katolička crkva i jugoslovenska vlast*, pp. 203–4. Basically, archbishop Stepinac, as most other Roman Catholic clergy in Yugoslavia, was prosecuted because of his opposition to communist regime. However, the core of the indictment represented connections of Roman Catholic clergy with Indenpendent State of Croatia and involvement in its functioning and commited crimes.
[54] Z. Radelić, *Križari. Gerila u Hrvatskoj*, 45.

with Stalin in 1948, it became obvious that Western powers wouldn't back someone whose main goal was the destruction of the Yugoslav state. Instead, for the
purposes of destabilizating the monolith communist block they would provide
every possible to support the Yugoslav communist 'renegades'.[55]

Other than these four groups already discussed, it is also worth mentioning the
members of the IMRO who, right after the Second World War, started to show up
in regions of east Macedonia. Despite the fact that they represented an historical
legacy of almost exotic past they couldn't make any real difference since the
Yugoslav security apparatus invested huge efforts in the elimination of all
enemies.

After they settled in fammiliar surroundings, among supporters, friends and
relatives, all anti-communists groups and movements initiated different armed
actions including assaults on representatives of local authorities, party members,
and demobilized war veterans. Regularily they raided centres of local communities and agricultural cooperatives because they were symbols of the new regime
and depots of different provisions. As a rule they avoided engaging with larger
military units. Instead, most of their actions like ambushes or raids were executed
during night time. Their targets were messengers, smaller army and militia
patrols, vehicles like buses and cars. In order to faciliate their movements they
often used seized army or militia uniforms. Groups usually had up to 15–20 fighters, their activities used to have highest intensity from spring untill autumn. Their
usual hideouts were mountain cottages, caves, dugouts, inaccessible woods, lonely
farms etc. In case of accidental encounters with army and militia forces they
almost aways tried to avoid conflict. Suicide was often the last resort of surrounded anti-communist fighters. Some of them used to be extremely brutal
esspecially towards their helpers and supporters traditionaly called *yataks*
(Turkish for shelter or secret hideout offered to law-ofenders) who showed signs
of wavering or betrayal.[56]

Yugoslav security forces, again following the Balkan traditions of counter-
insurgency or anti-guerrilla warfare, adapted operating mode of their adversaries.
Usual actions were ambushes, patrols, pursuits, roadblocks etc. In time, the most
efficient way proved to be an infiltration of agents within the enemy groups.[57]
Some of the leading figures of the anti-communist groups in Yugoslavia were captured using these methods. General Mihailović was captured in early 1946 after
infiltration of an agent into the group of Nikola Kalabić who was one of the most
trusted associates of Mihailović and commander of well known *chetnik* unit

[55] Z. Radelić, *Križari. Gerila u Hrvatskoj*, 51.
[56] VA, JNA, Komanda KNOJ i GJJ, Inv. br. 3705–1, Istorijat jedinica KNOJ-a, Taktika bande.
[57] VA, JNA, Komanda KNOJ i GJJ, Inv. br. 3705–1, Istorijat jedinica KNOJ-a, Taktika naših
jedinica.

called *Mountain Guard*. Kalabić was first captured and afterwards compelled to cooperate and reveal the whereabouts of his commander.[58]

Using the same methodology during 1947 and 1948 the Yugoslav security apparatus in Croatia captured several prominent leaders of *crusaders*. The *crusaders* operation under the code name *10 April* (day of official proclamation of Indenpendent State of Croatia in 1941) aimed at organizing en-masse anti-communist resistance was suppresed by the operation of the Yugoslav state security operation under the code name *Gvardijan*. Before they were able to finalize their mission, agents of the state security succesfully infiltrated *crusader's* routes and network of supporters. In the course of this action, some 96 crusaders and their supporters were apprehended while another 200 were investigated. In total, 91 were trialed and most of those were sentenced to death.[59]

Although anti-communist resistance in Bulgaria after the Second World War could not be described entirely as paramilitary, it certainly corresponds with traditional notion of paramilitarism in the Balkans whose main feature is strong inclination towards irregular or guerrilla warfare.[60] This lies in contrast to Yugoslavia, where post-war anti-communist resistance and its paramilitary features represented a continuation of activities of already existing anti-communist and anti-Yugoslav groups and movements. Appearance of anti-communist resistance in Bulgaria, had somewhat different origins. These origins could be traced back to the peculiarities of Bulgarian internal politics in period betwen the two world wars as well as in participation in Second World War on the side of Axes. Unlike its neighbors Yugoslavia, Greece and Romania, Bulgaria did not witness intensive destruction or suffer high human causalities. In addition, there were no Bulgarian troops on the Eastern front and Bulgaria never declared war on the Soviet Union.[61] In fact due to the exploitation of occupied regions in Yugoslavia and Greece, Bulgaria even experienced some economic growth. Although armed resistance existed it never reached the level of anti-fascist struggle and number of

[58] On action that led to the capturing of General Mihajlović, see: Kosta Nikolić, Bojan Dimitrijević, 'Zarobljavanje i streljanje generala Dragoljuba Mihailovića 1946. godine – Nova saznanja o arhivskoj građi', *Istorija 20. veka*, 2/2009, 9–20. Nikola Milovanović, *Kroz tajni arhiv UDBE*, (Beograd: Sloboda, 1974); Tamara Nikčević, *Goli otoci Jova Kapičića* (Podgorica: Daily press, 2009), 100.

[59] Z. Radelić, *Križari ; Gerila u Hrvatskoj*, 115–21.

[60] More on post-WWII anti-communist resistance in Yugoslavia and Bulgaria see in: Dmitar Tasić, 'Violence as Cause and Consequence: Comparisons of Anti-Communist Armed Resistance in Yugoslavia and Bulgaria after the Second World War'. In *CAS Working Paper Series*, No. 10/2018, 1–36, https://www.ceeol.com/search/journal-detail?id=659

[61] Ekaterina Nikova, 'Sledvoennoto nasilie: balgaro-gratski paraleli'. In *Balkanite Modernizatsiya, identichnosti, idei. Sbornik v chest na prof. Nadya Danova*. (Sofia: Institut za balkanistika s Cent'r po trakologiya, 2011), 482–501, here 483. In total some 10.000 Bulgarians lost their lives during the Second World War. From that number some 1.700 died in allied bombings while about the same number died in an 'anti-fascist struggle'.

participants as in Yugoslavia, Greece and Albania.[62] Resistance was led by the *Fatherland Front* (Otechestveni front)—a coalition of several political parties and movements, each different—communists, social-democrats, radical factions of BANU, as well members of the movement *Zveno*.[63] Following a great offensive by the Red Army towards the southeast in the Summer of 1944 and its approach towards the Bulgarian border caused political crisis that *Fatherland Front* used for its own advantage—they carried out a *coup d'etat* on 9 September 1944 and seized all power.[64]

However, changes that occured in Bulgaria foreshadowed a turbulent and extremely violent period. The systematic approach of the elimination of political opponents performed by the new authorities and accompanying repression contributed to the introduction of a totalitarian regime.[65] This, then, led to the appearance of an armed resistance since all other ways of demonstrating political discordance and diversity were blocked and doomed to fail.

There were two periods of anti-communist resistance in Bulgaria:

1. From 1945 till 1949 as a result of the simultaneously carried out terror against representatives of the former regime and the gradual elimination and discrediting of partners within the *Fatherland Front*.

2. After 1949, new groups willing to fight for changes appeared. This was caused by, among other things, irregularities and misconduct of local authorities and was supported through the clandestine operations of intelligence agencies of the Western countries.[66]

In Bulgaria, the first ten days after the coup d'état of September 9, 1944 when the *Fatherland Front* came to power,[67] saw a wave of terror against those who were considered enemies of the new regime and of 'the people' in general. The majority of those killed were civil servants, policemen, lawyers, teachers, and prominent

---

[62] Ekaterina Nikova, 'Sledvoennoto nasilie: balgaro-gratski paraleli', 497. Some 8.000 Bulgarian partisans enjoyed support of some 20.000 supporters.

[63] Ekaterina Nikova, 'Sledvoennoto nasilie: balgaro-gratski paraleli', 494.

[64] Ričard Dž. Krempton, *Balkan posle Drugog svetskog rata*, (Beograd: CLIO, 2003), 82–3. While communist party before the 1944 had only 9.000 members, by the end of January 1945 its membership grew to 250.000. Bulgarian agrarians, although divided in several factions, with 750.000 party members and 230.000 members of its youth section represented the strongest political movement. Socialdemocrats traditionaly enjoyed support of Bulgarian inteligentsia while *Zveno* enjoyed support within the army and anti-monarchist intelectuals.

[65] Some authors questioned attitude that ruled till 1989 and political changes that Bulgaria was the only state in the East block that peacefully and unquestioningly has accepted introduction of communist regime, see: Ivaylo Znepolski (ed.) *NRB ot nachaloto do na kraya*, (Sofia: Ciela, 2011) 169.

[66] Dinyu Sharlanov, *Goryanite. Koi sa te?* (Sofia: Prostranstvo & Forma 1999), 10.

[67] On the September 9 coup, see the extensive study by Alexander Vezenkov, *9 septemvri 1944 g.* (Sofia: Institut za izsledvane na blizkoto minalo and Ciela, 2014).

citizens close to the former regime.[68] Additionally, *People's Tribunal* was founded in October 1944 and by April 1945 of 11,122 accused, 2,730 had been sentenced to death, 1,514 were cleared of all charges while the rest—regents, kings advisers, members of the parliament, politicians, senior civil servants—were sentenced to serve prison time.[69]

From spring 1945, organized groups or individuals that were commonly named as *goryani* (men from the mountains or hills) started to appear all over Bulgaria. This rebellion was spontaneous, it came about without instigation from abroad, neither from Bulgarian émigrés nor a specific country.[70] Aditionally, anarchists, former members of the *Union of the Bulgarian National Legionaries* (Bulgarian extreme right) and other nationalists founded new groups.[71] Beside mass repression, two other reasons for 'going to the mountains' were land collect-ivisation and attempts to 'create' a Macedonian nation. These reasons were con-sidered as 'mechanisms' that unleashed the resistance.[72] In most cases *goryani* were middle-age men with families. They were very diverse concerning their ideology: they comprised of anarchists, disappointed communists, nationalists, and fascists, etc.[73] Beside *legionaries* there were members of the nationalist asso-ciation *Father Paisiy* as well as members of the IMRO i.e. its Ivan Mikhailov fac-tion. The last group brought to the whole endeavour a romantic notion of 'tradition', because they relied on the rich heritage of the IMRO *komitajis*. Bulgarian anti-communist resistance represented a mixture of ideologically and structurally different groups. The fact they were so diverse made it difficult to coordinate their actions.[74]

However, the *goryani* could not exist without support. As elsewhere in the Balkans these supporters were named as *yataks*. They were mostly *goryani* friends and relatives but also members of the former parties and their networks—like BANU and IMRO. They provided them with basic necessities like food and shel-ter and carried their messages. In a way, the State and party authorities were in

---

[68] Ekaterina Nikova, 'Sledvoennoto nasilie: balgaro-gratski paraleli', 492. It is said that 25,000 to 30,000 people were killed throughout Bulgaria without trial in supposedly spontaneous actions. Vezenkov, however, challenges these figures and argues that the total number of those killed, either randomly or after trial by the People's Tribunal, was considerably smaller—less than 7,000, see Vezenkov, *9 septemvri*, 365–7.

[69] Ekaterina Nikova, 'Sledvoennoto nasilie: balgaro-gratski paraleli', 493.

[70] D. Sharlanov, *Goryanite. Koi sa te?*, 15.

[71] *Goryanite. Sbornik dokumenti, tom 1 (1944–1949)*, (Sofia: Glavno upravlenie na arhivite pri min-isterskiya savet 2001), Document no. 4,15–21.

[72] Roger D. Petersen, *Resistance and Rebelion: Lessons from Easter Europe*, (Cambridge: Cambridge University Press, 2001), 7–15.

[73] *NRB ot nachaloto do na kraya*, 171.

[74] *NRB ot nachaloto do na kraya*, 171–2. It is estimated that during the first period of organizing, their numbers grew from 173 in 1945 to 780 by the end of 1948. In total during that period there were some 1,800 *goryani*. The second period was marked by the enlargement of their overall number of groups and their composition. During 1950 there were 1,520 *goryani* while during 1952–1953 Bulgarian secret services counted 3,130.

more fear of the organized and mass networks of the *yataks* than from the bands of *goryani* that operated in the mountains.[75]

From 1949, aside from the existing groups within Bulgaria, new bands that had been organized by Bulgarian political emigration, with the wholehearted assistance of the Western intelligence services—primarily American—started to be infiltrated across Bulgarian borders. These groups also proved to be diversive because within Bulgarian political emigration operated 12 different political parties, factions and youth organization. Again, the strongest group were the agrarians and the IMRO (Ivan Mikhailov).[76]

An important factor in supporting these different armed groups and their actions was the Bulgarian radio station named 'Goryanin' which broadcast programs from Greece between 1951 and 1962. Needless to say that it was done with the full backing of the US intelligence comunity. Its operations was a major headache to the Bulgarian State Security not just because they broadcast anti-communist programs but also sent out encoded messages and instructions to the *goryani* bands through its transmissions.[77]

The Bulgarian state invested considerable efforts to supress the anti-communist activities of the *goryani*, especially the armed groups—these efforts were similar to those in the other East European countries.[78]

The primary instigator of this suppression was the Ministry of Interior, more specifically its Main Directorate of People's Militia.[79] Their preferred and most efficient tactics proved to be the infiltration of agents into the *goryani* groups and that method was extensively used since 1948. Infiltration was the first step of so-called *processing*. The first signs of results after the *processing* of a typical *goryani* band would come after 7 to 8 months of intensive intelligence data gathering and mapping of the movements and patterns of the group's behavior.[80] These methods

---

[75] *NRB ot nachaloto do na kraya*, 173. Precise number of *yataks* is impossible to determine but according to some reports there were approximately 7,000 confirmed (registered) *goryani*, and between 40,000 and 50,.000 *yataks* (showing a ratio of 1:5 or 6)

[76] D. Sharlanov, *Goryanite. Koi sa te?*,151–2. According to Bulgarian State Security in 1951 Bulgarian political emigrants used to reside in Turkey (863), Greece (551), Yugoslavia (688), Italy (282), France (88) and elsewhere (213).

[77] D. Sharlanov, *Goryanite. Koi sa te?*, 167–70.

[78] *NKVD-MVD SSSR v bor'be s banditizmom i vooruzhennym natsionalisticheskim podpol'yem na Zapadnoy Ukraine, v Zapadnoy Belorussii i Pribaltike (1939-1956),*(Moskva: Ob"yedinennaya redaktsiya MVD Rossii, 2008). 7; All away to the mid-1950's Soviet security apparatus continued to fight against nationalist movements in regions that have been annexed to Soviet Union before the June 22 1941: Ukraine, west Belarus, Lithuania, Latvia and Estonia. In three Baltic states from 1941–1950 there were 3426 armed assaults in which 5155 Soviet officials were killed. In the same period Soviet security forces (primarily Internal army of the NKVD) have annihilated 878 armed groups killing 575 and wounding 878 insurgents. In west Ukraine these action were even more intensed. In period 1945–1953 Ukranian nationalist performed 14.424 actions. In total from 1945 till 1955 some 17,000 people were killed in their actions. See also: *Istoricheskiy opyt primeneniya vnutrenih voysk v bor'be s bandoformirovaniyaami v 1920-1950-e gg. Voenno-istoricheskiy trud*, (Moskva: Federal'nayaa sluzhba voysk nacional'noy gvardii Rossiyskoy federacii 'Na boevom postu', 2017).

[79] *Goryanite. tom 1 (1944-1949)*, Document no. 5, 22–3.

[80] *NRB ot nachaloto do na kraya*, 173–4; *Goryanite. tom 1 (1944-1949)*, Document no. 8, 26–30.

followed the strong Soviet influences and experiences of the Soviet NKVD in fighting their own opponents in the Baltic States and Ukraine.[81] However, there were occasions where the infiltrated agents joined the groups they were supposed to neutralize, and in that case conventional methods needed to be applied like roadblocks, patrols, ambushes, and pursuits. This happened in the case of IMRO group led by Gerasim Todorov in vicinity of Sveti Vrach (todays Sandanski). They enjoyed wide support and managed to survive until early 1948 when the group was destroyed. Its leader, following the old ways of the IMRO *voivods* refused to surrender and committed suicide.[82]

New methods of suppression like dislocation (internment) of *goryani* family members were also applied.[83] By 1953 the complex mechanism of repressive measures against families and households of so-called 'traitors of the homeland' was fully developed. If they had knowledge of their relative's activities and failed to report them, they were prosecuted as accomplices. Their properties were confiscated; they would be stripped of their civil rights and sent to labor camps for a period of seven years. Their children would be taken from them and sent to state schools and schools for the cadres of the Ministry of the Interior.[84] Partly because of that in time activities of armed *goryani* bands came to a halt.

Inventing Traditions: Paramilitarism and the 'Wars of the Yugoslav Succession'

Long after the Second World War was over, Balkan paramilitary traditions looked like a feature from a distant past whose actors can be seen only in the movies of ideologically controlled national cinematography. In all three states Albania, Bulgaria and Yugoslavia different types of communist regimes were introduced. The Albanian regime was considered the most oppressive and isolated, while the Yugoslav regime was seen as the most liberal. Bulgaria was somewhere in the middle, having a communist regime with strong national features. In all three cases different paramilitary organizations and movements from respective national histories were stigmatized by the use of an existing ideologically constructed vocabulary: like reactionary, counter-revolutionary, fascist, quisling etc.

---

[81] Roger D. Petersen, *Resistance and Rebellion: Lessons from Easter Europe.* (Cambridge: Cambridge University Press, 2001), 19–20.

[82] Dmitar Tasić, 'Violence as Cause and Consequence: Comparisons of Anti-Communist Armed Resistance in Yugoslavia and Bulgaria after the Second World War'. In *CAS Working Paper Series*, No. 10/2018, 1–36, here 29, https://www.ceeol.com/search/journal-detail?id=659

[83] *Goryanite. tom 1 (1944–1949)*, Document no. 9, 30–2. By 1949 around 1,153 families with 6,734 members were dislocated from the southern border regions to northern Bulgaria.

[84] *Goryanite. tom 11 (1949–1956), (1949–1956)* (Sofia: Glavno upravlenie na arhivite pri ministerskiya savet 2010) Document no. 169, 558–60. By the end of 1953, primarily from the border regions, 3,920 such families with 17,790 members had been dislocated.

It's also worth noting that some of these movements continued to operate abroad. In the Yugoslav case, they were all considered and labeled as 'enemy emigration'. Most of them continued to act through different propaganda activities like radio broadcasts, publications and public protests, however in several cases some of them (primarily the *ustashe*) organized terrorist attacks on Yugoslav diplomatic, economic and cultural representations and offices as well as attempts at incursion of several armed groups with the aim of instigating an uprising. The most famous incursion occurred in the summer 1972 when 19 members of *Croatian Revolutionary Brotherhood* (Hrvatsko revolucionarno bratstvo—HRB), a paramilitary organization of Croat émigrés, tried to instigate an uprising on mountain Raduša in central Bosnia. The Yugoslav police and the army annihilated the group in a joint action with 15 of its members killed in combat and the remaining four captured. Three of those captured were tried and sentenced to death. Only Ludvig Pavlović survived because his death sentence was replaced by a twenty years prison sentence. In 1991 when Yugoslavia was sliding towards its demise he was pardoned and he immediately joined the paramilitary group of Bosnian Croats only to be killed under mysterious circumstances that same year. Several paramilitary units of Bosnian Croats during the war in Bosnia and Herzegovina were named after him.[85]

Following a seismic shift in the political landscape by the end of the 1980's and the fall of the Berlin Wall, repercussions in the Balkans were strongly felt. However, the 'hot peace of the Cold War', at least in the Balkans, was ended by yet another series of bloody wars that, with small breaks, lasted almost a decade. While in Albania and Bulgaria communist regimes collapsed without barely a drop of blood, in the Yugoslav case happened the worst possible scenario of the violent dissolution of a complex multinational and multi-confessional state. The political and economical crisis which Yugoslavia was plunged into after the death of its leader, Josip Broz–Tito in 1980, created an environment ripe for the reoccurrence of suppressed inner-Yugoslav national and religious antagonisms and differences. The awakening of nationalism and parochial perceptions of Yugoslav federal units leaderships contributed to the enhancement of the existing economical and internal constitutional crisis. Even today, over-simplification and omissions of a deeper analysis of the origins of the Yugoslav crisis are contributing to a prolonging of the nationalist discourse in existing scholarship.

---

[85] See: Đorđe Ličina, *Dvadeseti čovjek*, (Zagreb: Centar za informacije i publicitet, 1979). Although this book represents typical example of popular publications widely present in socialist Yugoslavia where authors (by rule closely connected with secret services) were given rights and partially info's to wright contribution on some controversial event by weaving fact and fiction, in terms of basic information and chronological context and lack of relevant documents they could be considered as reliable. Book was used for a screenplay for a TV series filmed in 1985.

In relation to the main subject of this study, the so-called 'Wars of the Yugoslav succession', were marked by yet another revival of violence and brutality and also, the revival of paramilitarism:

"It is noteworthy that paramilitary groups perpetrated the most ferocious war crimes and they were responsible for the most of the attacks against the civilian population. They arrested civilians and mercilessly killed them. They committed wide scale looting and wantonly destroyed houses, institutions, cultural monuments in various towns and villages. In so doing, they contributed to the massive expulsion of unwanted elements of the population. If we consider that these atrocities were the main component of ethnic cleansing, it can be fairly said that the paramilitaries were not some exceptional and subsidiary elements of the Yugoslav wars, but the most important feature of them."[86]

In the Yugoslav case happened that the overall instability, statehoods in flux, quasi-elites and their inadequacy for the challenging times led to yet another revival of paramilitarism.[87] Its traditions and legacies were used to create numerous paramilitary units and organizations in Croatia, Bosnia and Herzegovina and Serbia.[88] For example, in Croatia among several smaller paramilitary organizations one that clearly distinguished itself was *Croatian Defense Forces* (Hrvatske odbrambene snage—HOS). This unit was organized by the pro-fascist *Croatian Party of Right* (Hrvatska stranka prava). At one point during the war it had merged with Croatian regular forces but was still active in Bosnia and Herzegovina acting alongside local Croatian forces of the Croatian Council of Defense—HVO (Hrvatsko vijeće odbrane). Although not openly, the HOS used to rely on the visual identity of Croatian *ustashe*.

Before they created their own armed forces, rebel Serbs from the Republic of Serbian Krajina (Republika Srpska Krajina—RSK), with the help of the Serbian State Security, created a paramilitary unit popularly called *Knindže* (combination of two words, Knin—capital of RSK and ninja—Japanese assassins) which participated in several early battles against the Croatian forces.

---

[86] Tetsuya Sahara, 'The Contemporary Paramilitary Phenomenon and the Yugoslav Wars for Succession'. In Marković, Predrag J., Momčilo Pavlović, Tetsuya Sahara (eds.), *Guerrilla in the Balkans. Freedom fighters, Rebels or bandits—Researching the Guerrilla and Paramilitary Forces in the Balkans,* (Tokyo: Meiji University; Belgrade: Institut za savremenu istoriju, 2007), 13–19, here 14. For valuable analysis of paramilitary phenomenon, Balkan mentalities and guerrilla warfare traditions see also: Xavier Bougarel, 'Yugoslav Wars: "The Revenge of the Countryside" Between Sociological reality and Nationalist Myth' In *East European Quarterly* XXXIII, No. 2, June 1999, 157–75.

[87] James Horncastle, 'Unfamiliar Connection: Special Forces and Paramilitaries in the Former Yugoslavia', In *Special Operations Journal* 2/2016, 12–21, here 15–18.

[88] Dejan Anastasijević, 'Kratka istorija paravojnih jedinica u jugoslovenskim ratovima 1991–1995: Grabljive zveri i otrovne bube' In YU Historija, http://www.yuhistorija.com/serbian/ratovi_91_99_ txt01c9.html [last checked 24 August 2019]. According to UN Group of experts' research in 1994 there were 55 Serbian paramilitry groups, 14 Bosniak and 13 Croatian.

In the initial stages of war in Bosnia and Herzegovina, local Muslims relied on a paramilitary unit popularly called the *Green berets* (Zelene beretke). Its name referred to the Islamic sacred color as well to US Green berets. *Green berets* were volunteers close to the Party of Democratic Action (Stranka demokratske akcije—SDA) which was a political organization led by Alija Izetbegović, a Bosnian Muslim politician and former Yugoslav dissident. After the creation of the Army of Bosnia and Herzegovina, *Green berets* were incorporated into their ranks.

At the same time within Serbian national boundaries paramilitary units started to pop up like mushrooms after the rain. Until recently topic of different conemporary paramilitary organizations and units was primarily covered by journalists,[89] some of them, like Dejan Anastasijević, beside writing in Serbian and international press even appeared as witnesses during the trials at International Tribunal for the former Yugoslavia (ICTY). By the rule, after journalists have already 'spent' particular topic academia slowly steps in and, again by the rule, starts to correct and enrich often too simplified image. Contemporary paramilitarism is not different and it already became subject of research.[90]

In the Serbian case, paramilitarism was revived through the creation and actions of numerous armed groups. Those that distinguished themselves had formal affiliation to different organizations, primarily political parties and secret services or both. There were other groups as well, mostly self-organized. In the cases Army of RSK (VRSK) and Army of Serbian Republic (VRS) (Serbian part of Bosnia and Herzegovina) most of the 'non-affiliated' groups were slowly incorporated into the regular forces during the 1990's. Some of them were allowed to keep their insignia and specific traditions like *Wolves from Vučijak* (Vukovi sa Vučijaka).

Again, as it was the case at the beginning of 20th century, Albanians, more correctly Kosovar Albanians, were the last to join the wave of the rekindled Balkan paramilitarism. Before the wars of 1990's, Kosovar Albanians had been for years engaged in a political struggle aimed at secession from the Yugoslav federation through occasional violent outbursts in street demonstrations and public protests. But it was in 1994 when they created the *Kosovo Liberation Army* (Ushtria Çlirimtare e Kosovës—UÇK) organization that later on would initiate armed struggle.[91] The Kosovo Liberation Army used to evoke traditions of the *Prizren League* and Albanian insurgencies against Ottoman, Serbian and Yugoslav rule.[92]

---

[89] *Jedinica*, documentary by Filip Švarm (Beograd: Vreme film; B92), https://www.youtube.com/watch?v=U_NUBuciOkQ [last checked 25 August 2019].

[90] Utrecht University is currently conducting project on contemporary paramilitarism in Turkey, Serbia and Syria, see https://paramilitarism.org/. I am grateful to PhD candidate Iva Vukušić for sharing some of her research. Within this project she is working on case study of Serbia, which is in the same time her PhD thesis.

[91] Henry H. Perritt Jr, *Kosovo Liberation Army: The inside Story of an Insurgency,* (Urbana and Chicago: University of Illinois Press, 2008), 8.

[92] H. H. Perritt Jr, *Kosovo Liberation Army*, 20–24.

In Serbia's case these troubled years were marked by general paramilitarization which was visible not only in the above-mentioned groups, but also in the transformation of some of the state institutions such as the Police and Customs. Serbian police officials were given army ranks including the highest one of General, police equipment was improved (anti-riot gear, armored vehicles, etc), and both officers and rank-and-file members received new army-like camouflage uniforms. The same thing occurred within the Federal Directorate of Customs.[93] It looked like the whole of society was passing through a process of 'paramilitarization' in terms of weakening and compromising the traditional state institutions such as the armed forces, police, judiciary, revenue, customs etc. and introducing new (actually historic) mechanisms of client based relations, interest groups, contraband, racketeering, and other aspects of pre-state organizations and a gray economy.

Certain paramilitary units were sponsored and organized by Serbian political parties arriving from the political right. Their justification for such a decision lay in the supposed mistrust of the Yugoslav People's Army (Jugoslovenska narodna armija—JNA) the only regular armed force in former Yugoslavia, which according to the belief of the above-mentioned Serbian political parties was still following communist and Yugoslav agendas without taking into consideration the actual needs and national interest of the Serbian people.[94] In the same time the nucleus of the Serbian political right—a small party known as Serbian National Renewal (Srpska narodna obnova—SNO) became the founder of numerous paramilitary formations as well. Because of strong and dominant personalities among its founders; like Mirko Jović, a former basketball player and small entrepreneur and the charismatic Vuk Drašković—a dissident writer and one of the organizers of first anti-communist demonstrations in Belgrade in March 1991, the SNO went through several splits that eventually led to the creation of a number of political parties. One was Serbian Movement of Renewal (Srpski pokret obnove— SPO), founded by Vuk Drašković while another was Vojislav Šešelj's Serbian Chetnik Movement (Srpski četnički pokret) that grew into Serbian Radical Party (Srpska radikalna stranka—SRS). Splits within the party led to splits within its paramilitary structure and so two paramilitary formations were associated with the SNO. One was the *White Eagles* (Beli orlovi) and the other was *Dušan the*

---

[93] It is said that during one official reception on the occasion of Police Force Memorial Day a certain newly appointed police General addressed (under the influence of alcohol) several guests from the armed forces saying that at that moment police only needed its own air force to become more powerful than the Army.

[94] These claims were true to a certain extent because JNA proved to be the most persistent political actor in preserving the Josip Broz Tito cult of personality as well as opponent of introduction of multi-party and democratic political system. In addition, political structures within the JNA, actually army section of the once ruling *Union of the Yugoslav Communists—SKJ* (Savez komunista Jugoslavije) created new party called *Union of the Communists—Movement for Yugoslavia* SKPJ (Savez komunista— pokret za Jugoslaviju).

Mighty (Dušan Silni—a popular name of a medieval Serbian Emperor). Also, several *chetnik* groups were organized under the patronage of Vojislav Šešelj's SRS in both Croatia and Bosnia and Herzegovina.

One of the paramilitary formations associated with a political party that clearly stood out was the *Serbian Guard* (Srpska garda). Behind this formation was SPO, which provided the unit with the majority of its rank-and-file members. *Serbian Guard* was led by a high-profile Belgrade criminal, Đorđe Božović-Giška and a private entrepreneur named Branislav Matić-Beli. However, both died in the summer 1991. Matić was assassinated in front of his house in Belgrade, while Božović was killed during the fights around town of Gospić in Croatia where his *Serbian Guard* was deployed to assist the Krajina Serbs. Their deaths were used as propaganda to further mystify and encourage conspiracy theories surrounding the Serbian State Security campaign against the SPO and its leadership.

Among different paramilitary formations a special place belongs to *Serbian Volunteers Guard* (Srpska dobrovoljačka garda) whose founder and leader was Željko Ražnatović–Arkan. Arkan belonged to the world of Yugoslav and later the Serbian underground long before he got involved in organizing a paramilitary unit. He is known for committing many burglaries in different Western countries and arranging several prison breaks as well. However, it seems that the important part of the puzzle was his close connection with the former Yugoslav and afterwards Serbian secret services (State Security Service—Služba državne bezbednosti SDB). Allegedly he enjoyed the protection of the state security structures due to the favors that he has done abroad. He was also one of the leaders of the supporters of the Red Star Belgrade football club. These supporters were in fact hooligans and represented the core of his paramilitary unit when it was founded in the fall of 1990. His connection with the Serbian state security structures was more than obvious because they were the main provider of units' armaments and equipment. The unit was also known as *Arkan's Tigers* (Arkanovi Tigrovi). From 1991 until 1995, Arkan and his unit participated in many battles in Croatia and Bosnia and Herzegovina. *Serbian Volunteers Guard* enjoyed substantial media coverage, they issued adverts in newspapers and broadcast several video clips while Arkan himself was a guest in political and entertainment talk shows. Invocation of Serbian military, but not paramilitary, traditions was visible in Arkan's frequent appearances in exact replica of the Serbian Field Marshal uniform from the First World War and also with the introduction of his own unit decorations. However, in 1997 Arkan was indicted by the ICTY for numerous crimes against humanity, participation in ethnic cleansing, breaches of the Geneva Convention and violations of the laws and customs of war.

What set Arkan's *Serbian Volunteers Guard* apart from other cases of paramilitary organizing in Serbia during the 1990's was that in one moment paramilitary formation ended creating political party known as Party of Serbian Unity (Stranka srpskog jedinstva). This party eventually participated in parliamentary elections and even managed to win several parliament seats. Some of its leading figures continued to be very active in Serbian political life even after the Željko Ražnatović–Arkan was assassinated in 2000. Some members of his unit had dynamic career paths, like Borislav Pelević who at one time was a Serbian presidential candidate, or Zvezdan Jovanović whose career went from simple locksmith to the rank of police Lieutenant Colonel. In 2003 Jovanović went on to fire the sniper shots that killed Serbian Prime Minister Zoran Đinđić. Another one of those shady characters was Milorad Luković Ulemek, better known as Legija. Being a problematic youth in Belgrade, he joined the French Foreign Legion where he stayed for 6 years before deserting its ranks to join *Arkan's Tigers*. He distinguished himself as member of Arkan's unit and eventually became a commander of another paramilitary unit, again organized by the Serbian State Security.

Within this case of the 'Wars of the Yugoslav succession' we can find typical examples of these invented traditions used by different characters and actors, from romantic and patriotic ones, to the shady ones affiliated to the worlds of organized crime and the local secret services. In case of the Serbian paramilitaries, their wish to attract public attention and support resulted in their insisting on the visual identity of the Serbian paramilitaries from previous epochs. However, in nearly all cases, it was marked by extreme kitsch and distaste.

The war records of most of the paramilitary groups on all warring sides during the violent 1990's were filled with violent acts, atrocities, pillaging, contraband, ethnic cleansing, and mass executions. Paradoxically, throughout the war conflicts in Croatia and Bosnia and Herzegovina, existing criminal and secret services networks created during the Yugoslav era continued to be active for the benefit of all sides involved. Contraband of arms and munitions, fuel and cigarettes was firmly in hand of those groups and their patrons. The same occurred after the wars when these networks facilitated the continuation of criminal activities, this time upping the ante to include drug trafficking.

A typical example of a paramilitary formation which was formed by non-military structures, primarily the secret services, was the *Unit for Special Operations* (Jedinica za specijalne operacije—JSO). Also known as simply *The Unit*, it operated within the SDB.[95] It was created in 1996 by merging the remnants of Arkan's *Serbian Volunteers Guard* and the already existing Serbian state security special unit, which operated under the command of Franko Simatović during the 1990's.[96] The new unit, now under the command of Milorad Luković Ulemek,

---

[95] After the dissolution of federal state in Serbia secret services continued to operate as usual within the Ministry of interior which was divided on two departments: Department of Public Security and Department of State Security.

[96] Franko Simatković—Frenki and his superior Jovica Stanišić, head of the SDB (1991–1998) were both indicted by ICTY. They were charged and trialed with persecution, murder, deportation and inhumane acts.

a.k.a. Legija, was the epitome of Serbian paramilitarism of the 1990's, not only by its composition but primarily by its deeds committed during war and peace. This time they started to operate together with one of the Serbian drug-trafficking clans, the so-called *Zemun clan* (named after Zemun, a suburb of Belgrade). Their deeds included kidnappings, drug trafficking, racketeering, arson, intimidation, extortion and political assassinations—all under the state patronage and with major funds provided for the unit's armament, equipment and provisions. They were responsible for the kidnapping of several Serbian businessmen and celebrities,[97] and also organized the assassinations of leaders and members of rival criminal organizations.

In terms of politically motivated violence the JSO and its patrons from state security structures were responsible for the assault on Vuk Drašković, the leader of the SPO, in October 1999 when four prominent party members were killed. The assault was carried out by a truck that collided directly with the column of vehicles of the SPO riding to a party rally. One year after that incident, in June 2000, there was another attempt on Drašković life in Budva, Montenegro, where he was shot at and lightly wounded. In August of the same year, members of the JSO abducted and murdered the Serbian politician, Ivan Stambolić who was seen as possible candidate for the united opposition against the regime of Slobodan Milošević. Stambolić was abducted, murdered and buried in a secret location which would only be revealed three years later during the course of another investigation. All those responsible for the above mentioned crimes were tried and sentenced.

Milorad Luković Ulemek's personality featured an inclination towards a specific kind of violent behavior. He relied on a mix of different traditions and often combined the legacies of political extremism. He earned his nickname—Legija—because of the time he served in the French Foreign Legion where he reached the rank of Sergeant. His new assignment as commander of the JSO was followed by the introduction of the Legion's training techniques and practices together with marching drills and salutes. The nickname of the JSO base *Stoltz* (German for Pride) near the town of Kula in Vojvodina clearly speaks of another kind of inclination. What began as a boyish fascination and obsession with shiny uniforms, salutes, unique marching songs and style, ended in the creation of death squads, which operated alongside a drug-trafficking clan.

The climax of the engagement of this specific Paramilitary Crime Inc. was reached in March 2003 with the assassination of Serbian Prime Minister Zoran Đinđić. The JSO member Zvezdan Jovanović fired sniper shots that killed the Serbian Prime Minister while he was entering a government building. After the introduction of martial law and intensive police actions, the assassins were

---

[97] See: Mile Novaković, *Otmice Zemunskog klana*, (Beograd: Novosti, 2013). Total income of ransoms was estimated around 20 millions Euros.

apprehended, tried and sentenced. It was during this investigation when the true extent of their criminal enterprise was revealed. However, the political background of the assassination of the Serbian Prime Minister and its inspirers remain unknown. The JSO was rapidly disbanded and some of their members were allowed to join the Army or Gendarmerie. However, in the years that followed, former members of the JSO were often connected to the activities of organized crime not only in the Balkans but elsewhere in the world.

Another paramilitary unit, however, became epitome of violent wars of the 1990's. It was *Scorpions* (Škorpioni) the unit, which similar to JSO, was under the control of Serbian State Security. Members of this unit participated in mass executions, of which especially infamous was brutal liquidation of six Bosnian Muslims in the aftermath of Srebrenica events in July 1995. Existence of this recording resulted in arrest of the perpetrators, trial and sentences—first in Serbia related to the 1990's wars.[98] *Scorpions* were also associated with another massacre; in town of Podujevo in Kosovo region on 28 march 1999. This time victims were civilians, fourteen of them—seven women and seven children. This case also ended up in Serbian court with perpetrators tried and sentenced.[99]

While the story of the development of Serbian paramilitarism in the 1990's clearly collaborates the existing claims that the undeveloped and dysfunctional state institutions actually provided a perfect maneuvering space for the paramilitaries. In this particular case, with pursuit of their own political agendas they also contributed to the growth of the European and Global criminal networks. They did it to such an extent that in the end it became questionable what their political aim was after all. It appears that extreme nationalism was just a convenient disguise for lucrative criminal activities. This became even more obvious when after the end of bloody wars in former Yugoslavia, from time to time, names of the Serbian paramilitaries started to appear in newspapers and TV news headlines describing cases of criminal activities such as armed robberies, drug-trafficking, human-trafficking, and murders. Similarly, almost 20 years after the end of the war in Bosnia and Hercegovina, information on activities of the secret paramilitary unit called *Larks* (Ševe), closely associated with the security structures of Bosnia and Herzegovina, started to appear. Not only that during the war they

---

[98] Dejan Anastasijević, 'Kratka istorija paravojnih jedinica u jugoslovenskim ratovima 1991–1995'; More on the massacre and subsequent trial see: Iva Vukušić, 'Nineteen Minutes of Horror: Insights from the Scorpions Execution Video', In *Genocide Studies and Prevention: An International Journal*, Volume 12/2018, Images and Collective Violence: Function, Use and Memory, Issue 2, 35–53. https://scholarcommons.usf.edu/gsp/vol12/iss2/5/ [Last checked on 24 August 2019]; and, Ivan Zverzhanovski, 'Watching War Crimes: The Srebrenica Video and the Serbian Attitudes to the 1995 Srebrenica Massacre'. In *Southeast European and Black Sea Studies*, 7, no. 3 (2007),—*Dark Histories, Brighter Futures? The Balkans and Black Sea Region—European Union Frontiers, War Crimes and Confronting the Past*, 417–30.

[99] For the crime in Podujevo, see: https://www.b92.net/info/vesti/index.php?yyyy=2009&mm=06&dd=18&nav_category=64&nav_id=366737 [Last checked 24 August 2019]

were responsible for the liquidation of PoW's and sniping during the siege of Sarajevo, when lot of civilians lost their lives, but were also responsible for the liquidation of rival individuals and groups within the Bosnian political and security structures. According to the subsequent testimonies, they continued with similar actions throughout the 20-year post-war period.[100]

Like in so many other cases before, the visual identity of the traditional paramilitaries represented a useful tool for attracting public attention and securing new membership. As noted, violence and brutality against the combatants and the civilians was an integral part of Balkan paramilitarism. Violent acts were committed not only against the enemy but against all those who were perceived as a threat to the existing visions and plans. So while old Serbian, Bulgarian and Albanian paramilitaries from the time of the Macedonian struggle, the Balkan Wars and the First World War looked like ascetic figures committed to the fulfillment of a national idea, the modern paramilitaries in their acts and appearance more resembled the members of the South American drug cartels. This point is demonstrating the discontinuity of the traditions of paramilitarism in the Balkans but also serves to warn the future generations of its strong legacy.

---

[100] On *Larks* see: https://bnn.ba/vijesti/spisak-seva-kako-su-formirane-ko-im-je-naredivao-i-koga-su-ubijale-0 (Checked on 1 September 2019); Edin Garaplija, bivši pripadnik DB BiH i AID https://www.youtube.com/watch?v=wegGZXHRT4k (Checked on 1 September 2016).

Conclusion: Balkan Paramilitaries

Unlike the millions of mobilized on the eve of the Great War all over the world, for the most of Serbian, Bulgarian and Albanian paramilitaries violence, destruction, brutality and displacement were already integral parts of their lives. Again, while most of the world became relieved by the fact that war has ended for the most of Balkan paramilitaries 11 November 1918 was just another day among 365 others. For some of them peace didn't mean achievement of their goals and fulfillment of existing political agendas. For those who started struggling around 1903, post-Great War years were just continuation of already very long engagement. Actually, the experiences gained during their 'Macedonian years' were merely enriched with their participation in combats during the two Balkan Wars of 1912–1913 and the Great War.

On-going conflicts between different Balkan paramilitaries became open and even more brutal during the course of the Great War. The Toplica Uprising in 1917 in occupied Serbia was the typical example of a brutal encounter of old adversaries. Not only did the Bulgarian army engage *komitaji* squads for the purpose of quelling the uprising, but also two leading representatives of Bulgarian occupation authorities responsible for this task, General Alexander Protogerov and Colonel Petar D'rvingov, were at the same time IMRO high officials. Although they were career officers, their acts and their consequences—mass reprisals and war crimes against the civilian population actually corresponded to the paramilitary way of behaviour. In addition, leading authorities of one non-Balkan participant of the Toplica Uprising—Austro-Hungarian Empire—became very quickly aware of the advantages that the engagement of local paramilitaries could provide. Because of that, Austro-Hungarians used to regularly hire Albanian irregulars both for the frontline duties on the rough and demanding Albanian front as well as for the anti-insurgent actions in south Serbia.

However, after the war Serbian chetniks were crippled because of the annihilation of their powerful sponsor—secret organization *Black Hand* and the death of its leader Colonel Dragutin-Dimitrijević Apis in 1917. While after the Great War some resolved to civilian life organized in veteran associations commemorating important events from chetnik's rich history others continued fighting as volunteers in the service of new Yugoslav state against its old as well as new foes.

IMRO *komitajis*, although shaken by the Bulgarian military defeat and *Second national catastrophe*, kept the core of its organization untouched and opted for continuation of struggle in new political circumstances. They adapted, becoming

Paramilitarism in the Balkans: The Cases of Yugoslavia, Bulgaria, and Albania, 1917–1924. Dmitar Tasić,
Oxford University Press (2020). © Dmitar Tasić.
DOI: 10.1093/oso/9780198858324.001.0001

aware of the changes and their significance for the development of their struggle. IMRO as an organization recovered remarkably quickly, simultaneously adjusting to the new circumstances, immediately finding new sponsors, supporters and allies. Its leaders and their enormously strong personalities, readiness for self-sacrifice and personal examples they used to set inspired many exiled and deprived Macedonians to continue with the struggle either as *komitajis* or simply by financially supporting the organization.

Following practice from war years some Albanian paramilitaries continued to provide their services to various sides in conflict—to Albanian government or its opponents, while others led by the Kosovo Committee entered into several years long conflict with Yugoslav authorities hoping to secede territories inhabited with Albanians and unify them with Albanian state.

Newcomers to the Balkans, Russian émigrés and ex-participants in revolutionary events in Russia added some new shades on an already complex picture of the post-Great War Balkans. While first struggled to maintain their internal structure and autonomy, both military and political, for some future battles against the Bolsheviks, second, now integral part of new Communist parties hoped to perform identical transformation of their nations societies as they did or contributed to in Soviet Russia.

All Balkan states after the Great War needed several years to consolidate and address different organizational, economical and infrastructural issues. After series of changes of cabinets, mutinies and overthrows Albania managed to reach fragile stability after 1924 and Ahmed Zogu's definite coming to power. Yugoslav kingdom throughout its existence wasn't able to reach the point that would guarantee undisturbed development. Frequent changes of cabinets, parliamentary and constitutional crises, differences (national, religious, legal, etc) between countries regions, and ever-present national questions, as well as royal dictatorship were all combined with developments in international relations. What was important for the Yugoslav part of 'Balkan border lands' is that overall political and economical instability strongly reflected on local conditions. Already after the Second Balkan War 1913 and first Serbian attempt to incorporate these areas, which was interrupted by the outbreak of First World War, it became obvious that this ambitious effort would encounter many difficulties. In just eight years these areas went from Ottoman rule, through Serbian and Montenegrin military and civilian regimes, Austro-Hungarian and Bulgarian occupation, towards the unification in Yugoslav state. Wars, annexations of territories, changes of administrations, interruption of existing trading routes, forceful migrations, epidemic of different diseases, deprivations, occupations and implementations of denationalization policies and all sorts of violence—all above mentioned experiences left collective trauma among local population of whom nearly half were not enthused at all by the fact that they had become Serbian or Montenegrin subjects. Human losses and the level of destruction in the Balkan war theatre speak in favour of those claiming that the

Great War was a total war. The Yugoslav state was here faced not only with destroyed towns and communications, impoverished rural areas suffering from lack of basic provisions, decimated draught and pack animals, and poor levels of hygiene, but also with political instability and serious security issues. Additionally, after the Great War clashes of political parties and struggle for power on all levels only facilitated activities of different paramilitaries, both state and non-state. Similar to Ottoman times Yugoslav Macedonia, as well as Sanjak and Kosovo and Metohija witnessed activities of various paramilitaries.

Defeat that Bulgaria suffered contributed to serious political changes visible in rise of BANU and its charismatic leader Alexander Stamboliyski. However, old political structures, army and especially IMRO were constantly blocking Stamboliyski's efforts envisaged to improve Bulgarian position in international relations as well as to stabilize country's economy. Despite majority in parliament and huge support among Bulgarian peasantry BANU could not execute control over the important state institutions like police and army forcing agrarian leadership to create yet another paramilitary formation—the *Orange Guard*. However, at the end, BANU's opponents proved to be stronger.

The real importance and efficiency of the paramilitaries in the Balkans could be clearly seen from several examples of performed and attempted coups. In Bulgaria, the coup of 9 June 1923 demonstrated how the well-organized broad alliance of political actors, with clear ideological determination and a precise plan of action, could operate together and literally annul the developments of previous years. Existing culture of defeat or actual unwillingness to reconcile with the traumatic experiences became the driving force behind the conspirators and their actions. However, without officers, both active and discharged from service, organized within a secret *League*, the success of the coup was doubtful. Their *esprit de corps* proved to be stronger than allegiance to the legally elected government. Another factor—the IMRO—contributed to the successful outcome of the coup. Level of violence they demonstrated was proportional to their frustrations with the agrarian regime and its readiness to sacrifice the IMRO so that the agreement with the Kingdom of Serbs, Croats and Slovenes could be implemented. The mutilation of the Prime Minister Stamboliyski's body—the cutting off of his hands and head by certain *komitaji* leaders—brought in memories from the times of *komitaji* action in Ottoman Macedonia and the violent methods used by rival organizations in order to punish traitors and renegades and intimidated opponents. The post-coup period was marked by new cycle of violence, which in following years caused numerous violent deaths through executions without trials and in political assassinations.

After the 1923 coup IMRO began with rampage by sending new bands and assassins to Yugoslav Macedonia but it also felt into series of internal clashes in which many members lost their lives. With the government's silent consent IMRO also took control over the Petrich County in southwest making it 'state within the state'.

Unlike in Bulgaria, where the period of several years after the Great War represented the 'golden age of Bulgarian paramilitarism', traditional Balkan style paramilitaries in Serbia were already leaving the historical scene. One of the reasons was their participation in the Great War and the serious casualties they suffered. Unlike the IMRO, which despite the casualties suffered could still count on several thousands of experienced *komitajis*, the remaining number of Serbian *chetniks* was just several hundreds. Another reason was the distrust and suspiciousness of new Yugoslav civil and military authorities coming from the history of paramilitaries' previous engagements, their behaviour and the effects of their actions. Another reason that raised suspicion was the paramilitaries association with the *Black Hand* and its legacy. Several examples of *chetnik* engagement immediately after the war actually justified authorities's fears. Nevertheless, in the following period *chetniks* continued to be engaged but strictly within the Gendarmerie and its structures, thus becoming fully dependent on the state and its resources. In addition, this tendency led to the creation of a completely new state-controlled paramilitary organization in Yugoslav Macedonia, initially called the *Organization against Bulgarian Bandits*, which in several years evolved into the *People's Self-Defence*, a massive and well-armed militia-like organization established by the local political opportunists whose core encompassed former *chetniks*, retired officers, members of *National Defence* and IMRO renegades.

Another aspect of the post-Great War engagement of the Balkan paramilitaries was building and maintaining international networks. Since their world was clearly divided into those who were defeated and those who were victorious, all future activities were seen as preparation for the rematch as an introduction of major revisions to the existing peace accords. While Serbian paramilitaries considered their mission fulfilled, they were actually satisfied to continue operating within state-arranged conditions and support, so that they could defend and strengthen their legacy. For Bulgarians and Kosovar Albanians from the Kosovo Committee, continuation of the struggle was the only option. The only change was how and with whose assistance it could be done. The logical solution was to go along the line 'the enemy of my enemy is my ally'. It practically meant that any successful anti-Yugoslav action or activity aimed at destabilization of the Yugoslav state would facilitate IMRO and Kosovo Committee operations on Yugoslav soil. By acting in this manner, despite ideological and political differences, IMRO was able to establish contacts with the Kosovo Committee, Mussolini's Italy, Montenegrin separatists, and Stjepan Radić's HSS. Finally, even the headquarters of 'World's Revolution', the mighty Comintern, entered into serious negotiation with the IMRO leadership in order to obtain its cooperation in realizing the project of the Balkan federation. However, the relations that IMRO established with the Croatian political representatives proved to be lasting and very close. Their contacts and cooperation radicalized when IMRO established contacts and cooperation with the *ustashe*—Croatian extreme-right movement. Through this cooperation the *ustashe* grew into a powerful organization. The first generation of *ustashe* fighters were trained by the prominent *komitaji* instructors. Their joint effort, and at the same time 'swan song' of the IMRO was the assassination of Yugoslav King Alexander and French Minister of foreign affairs Louis Bartou on 9 October 1934 in Marseilles, France.

Despite the fact that already by the end of 1920's Balkan paramilitarism started to fade away, its legacy was still present. In Yugoslavia the paramilitaries maintained their presence through veterans' associations, however, in practical terms the legacy of paramilitarism, i. e. its relation to the rich traditions of guerrilla warfare was completely taken over by the armed forces through adoption and regulation of guerrilla warfare doctrine and subsequent formation of special units, which happened on the eve of the Second World War.

However, the outbreak of the Second World War contributed to another revival of paramilitarism in the Balkans. Not only did some traditional players, like the *Chetnik Association*, renew their activities, but new ones appeared as well. For some of them, such as General Draža Mihailović's royalist resistance movement, the legacy of the Serbian paramilitaries was a convenient tool for attracting popular support. Mostly because of that, throughout the whole period of their existence they were simply called *Chetniks*. The legacy of Balkan paramilitarism, and especially the aspect of guerrilla warfare, was so strong that its pattern was embraced by some political movements, like the extreme right political movement Zbor in occupied Serbia, which with German help, reorganized itself on military foundation into the *Serbian Volunteers Corps* with the sole purpose of fighting the communists. The newly arrived Russian émigrés faced with the continuation of civil war imposed on them through the actions of Yugoslav communists did the same and grouped themselves into the *Russian Protection Corps*. Some of them brought their anticommunism to a new level by joining SS troops and by participating in fights against the Red Army on the Eastern front.

On the other hand, Yugoslav communists demonstrated their full revolutionary and military potential after the German invasion of the Soviet Union on 22 June 1941. Years of illegal struggle, skills and knowledge obtained in Comintern international schools, and participation of some of their members in the Spanish Civil War provided them with the necessary tools for organizing successful guerrilla warfare. The cases of Albanian and Bulgarian communists were almost identical because they also organized fighting units. The readiness and willingness of Balkan communists to drastically change the political landscapes of their countries through revolutionary actions represented the main cause of civil wars in their countries respectively. In Bulgaria however, there was no civil war but rather a post-war wave of ideologically and politically motivated violence directed against the representatives of the political system that existed between the First and Second World War. The violence performed during this period actually resulted in the appearance of anti-communist resistance throughout Bulgaria. Again, the existing traditions of paramilitary organizing and guerrilla warfare contributed to the appearance of armed groups coming from a wide range of movements and parties which were present in the Bulgarian political theatre. The struggle against the *Bolshevization* of their country represented a joint denominator for former pro-fascist Legionaries, members of the nationalist union 'Paisiy Hilendarski', agrarians and members of the IMRO who to the whole enterprise brought in the charm of the once vibrant and restless *komitajis*. Although they belonged to several different political groups, the common feature was their name—*goryani* or people from the mountains. Meanwhile, beside spontaneously organized resistance new groups appeared as well. They were organized, financed and prepared in neighbouring countries by the Western intelligence agencies. In the new Cold War context these new *goryani* were considered as a valuable asset for the destabilization of Bulgarian communist regime. Following Soviet experiences and instructions, the Bulgarian security apparatus invested huge efforts in the eradication of *goryani*.

Compared to the Bulgarian example, the Yugoslav situation looked more like a continuation of war because despite the fact that many members of former royalist, anti-communist and anti-Yugoslav movements, armed groups and organizations managed to defect across the border, a considerable number of them still remained on the ground. The most numerous one, *chetniks*, soon became decapitated when their leader General Draža Mihailović was captured and subsequently tried, sentenced and executed. The *ustashe*, although smaller in number, were better organized and supported primarily by the Roman Catholic church and its infrastructure. Slovenian royalists continued to exercise a limited political influence by occasional incursions from Austrian territory. Albanian *balists*, after being heavily defeated in the last months of the Second World War, continued to operate, but more like simple outlaws than a serious political movement, almost like the ancient *kachaks*. Joint efforts of the Yugoslav army, militia and Soviet-like organized internal army led to a gradual but definite cessation of the activities of their opponents. However, unlike in the Bulgarian case where Western intelligence agencies continued to support and sponsor the activities of Bulgarian anti-communist opposition throughout the 1950's, Yugoslav anti-communists lost this kind of support already by the end of 1948. The main reason for this was the Yugoslav split with the Soviets, at the time seen as an unexpected gift for Western powers. In a drastic change of policies, support provided to the rebellious Yugoslav regime became a convenient means for the destabilization of the Eastern bloc, where the Yugoslav example could be followed by other Soviet satellites.

The 'hot peace of the Cold War', at least in the Balkans, was ended by yet another series of bloody wars that with interruptions lasted almost a decade. Overall instability, statehoods in flux, newly created quasi-elites and their inadequacy for the challenging times led to another revival of paramilitarism. To say that during the 1990's Wars of Yugoslav Succession on all sides appeared many paramilitary formations could be seen as understatement. Better term would be booming or resurgence of the Balkan paramilitarism. Except in Slovenia all sides in period of 1991–1999, and even further if we conclude this period with return of the Yugoslav forces in Demilitarized Land Zone and subsequent short war in Northern Macedonia in 2001, were relying on paramilitaries. However, in this particular case we can locate typical examples of invented traditions where different characters and actors, from romantic and patriotic to the shady ones, affiliated with the realms of organized crime and local secret services, (mis)used existing legacies of *chetniks, ustashe, kachaks* or *balists*.

In the case of Croatian and Bosnian forces paramilitaries served as embryo of their regular armed forces. In cases of Croatian and Bosnian Serbs, that is their state formations RSK and Serbian Republic happened that parallel with appearance of many paramilitary formations their regular armed forces VRSK and VRS were created by simple transformation of local units of former JNA that were left behind after its final departure from these territories in 1992. While both above-mentioned Serbian armies tried and to great extent managed to incorporate most of the indigenous paramilitary formations, they were not able to do the same with those formations with close ties with Serbian state security apparatus. This is the point where several important questions rise up. Were these formations, such as *Arkan's Tigers, Red berets* or *Scorpions* merely a tool for destabilisation of Serbian neighbours: Croatia and Bosnia and Herzegovina? (more correctly neighbours of Federal Republic of Yugoslavia—SRJ) Or were they for Serbia's regime in the same time powerful tool of support as well as control over Croatian and Bosnian Serbs and their actions? In simplified views on Yugoslav crisis this is often neglected. Truth is probably somewhere in the middle but there is also a question to what extent Bosnia and Croatia in the time of their international recognition were states in full meaning of that word? Was premature international recognition of Slovenia, Croatia and Bosnia aimed as mean of support or they were designed as a blow in series of blows that would end the existence of Yugoslav state? This and many other questions are already stirring up spirits among historians dealing with the violent dissolution of Yugoslavia during the 1990's. Resurgence of paramilitarism is an integral part of it and it speaks of strong legacies of classic Balkan paramilitarism and of its potential to appear again and again with similar outcomes despite different historical, political and ideological contexts.

Works Cited

Archival Collections

Serbia

Archives of Yugoslavia
  - 14 Ministry of the Interior of the Kingdom of Yugoslavia
  - 37 Milan Stojadinović
  - 334 Ministry of Foreign affairs of the Kingdom of Yugoslavia
Military Archives
  - Command of the Third Army District
  - Military Security Agency
  - Yugoslav People's Army

Bulgaria

National Library 'Kiril i Metodiy'—Bulgarian Historical Archive
  - 405 Todor Alexandrov Poprushev
  - 841 Internal Macedonian Revolutionary Organization

Newspapers and periodicals

Politika, Vreme, Večernje novosti, Žandarmerijski kalendar, Službeni vojni list

Printed primary sources

Dimić, Ljubodrag and Đorđe Borozan, (eds), *Jugoslovenska država i Albanci. Tom 1* (Beograd: Službeni list SRJ; Arhiv Jugoslavije; Vojno-istorijski institut, 1998).

Dimić, Ljubodrag and Đorđe Borozan, (eds), *Jugoslovenska država i Albanci. Tom 2* (Beograd: Službeni list SRJ; Arhiv Jugoslavije; Vojno-istorijski institut, 1998).

General Staff of the Yugoslav Royal Army, *Veliki rat Srbije za oslobođenje i ujedinjenje Srba, Hrvata i Slovenaca 1914–1918*, (Beograd: Glavni đeneralštab 1937).

Grozeya, Nedyalka et al. (eds), *Goryanite: sbornik dokumenti. Tom I, (1944–1949)* (Sofia: Glavno upravlenie na arhivite pri ministerskiya savet 2001).

Grozeya, Nedyalka amd Bugarcheva, Elena (eds), *Goryanite: sbornik dokumenti. Tom 1I, (1949–1956)* (Sofia: Glavno upravlenie na arhivite pri ministerskiya savet 2010).

Katardžiev, Ivan (ed), *VMRO (Obedineta): dokumenti i materijali. I i II*, (Skopje: Institut za nacionalna istorija, 1992).

Revyakina, Luiza et al. (eds), *Kominternat i Balgariya. Tom I, Dokumenti*, (Sofia: Glavno upravlenie na arhivite pri Ministerskiya Syvet, 2005).

Bibliography

Anastasijević, Dejan, 'Kratka istorija paravojnih jedinica u jugoslovenskim ratovima 1991–1995: Grabljive zveri i otrovne bube'. In YU *Historija, http://www.yuhistorija.com/serbian/ratovi_91_99_txt01c9.html*

Anatol'evich Martsenvuk, Yuroy, et al., *Istoricheskiy opyt primeneniya vnutrenih voysk v bor'be s bandoformirovaniyaami v 1920–1950-e gg. Voenno-istoricheskiy trud* (Moskva: Federal'nayaa sluzhba voysk nacional'noy gvardii Rossiyskoy federacii, 'Na boevom postu', 2017).

Austin, Robert C, 'Greater Albania: Albanian State and the Question of Kosovo, 1912–2001'. In John R. Lempi and Mark Mazower (eds), *Ideologies and National Identities. The case of Twenty Century Southeast Europe* (Budapest and New York: CEU Press, 2004), 235–53.

Austin, Robert C., *Founding a Balkan State; Albanian Experiment with Democracy, 1920–1925* (Toronto: University of Toronto Press, 2012).

Bagni, Bruno, 'Lemnos, l'île aux Cosaques'. In *Cahiers du Monde russe*, Vol. 50, No. 1, *Écrits personnels. Russie XVIIIe–XXe siècles*, (Janvier–mars 2009), 187–230.

Bakić, Dragan, 'Apis's Men: The Black Hand Conspirators after the Great War'. In *Balcanica*, XLVI (2015), 219–39.

Bartl, Peter, *Albanci, od srednjeg veka do danas* (Beograd: CLIO, 2002).

Bartov, Omer and Eric D. Weitz (eds), *Shatterzone of Empires: Coexistence and Violence in the German, Habsburg, Russian and Ottoman Borderlands* (Bloomington: Indiana University Press: 2013).

Bazhdarov, Georgi, *Moite Spomeni*, (Sofia: Inst. B'lgarija-Makedonija, 2001) http://www.promacedonia.org/gb/index.html

Bell, John D., *Peasants in Power: Alexander Stamboliiski and the Bulgarian Agrarian National Union 1899–1923*, (Princeton: Princeton University Press, 1977).

Besa, Al Jazeera Objektiv, broadcasted on 5 January 2017, https://www.youtube.com/watch?v=fMD6PZLjtIA

Bilyarski, Cocho V., 'Okupiraneto na Kyustendil prez 1922 g. ot chetite na VMRO, komandvani ot Kochanskiya voivoda Pancho Mikhailov i shtipskiya voivoda Iovan B'rlyo' http://www.sitebulgarizaedno.com/index.php?option=com_content&view=article&id=314:-1922-&catid=29:2010-04-24-09-14-13&Itemid=61

Biondich, Mark, *The Balkans: Revolution, War, and Political Violence since 1878* (Oxford: Oxford University Press, 2011).

Bjelajac, Mile, 'Vojni faktor i mogućnosti odbrane nacionalnih teritorija 1918–1921' In *Vojnoistorijski glasnik*, 2/1985, 195–222.

Bjelajac, Mile, *Vojska Kraljevine SHS/Jugoslavije 1922–1935* (Beograd: INIS, 1994).

Blažarić, Pavle, *Memoari*, (Leposavić: Institut za srpsku kulturu, 2007).

Blumi, Isa, 'An Honorable Break from *Besa*: Reorienting Violence in the Late Ottoman Mediterranean' In *European Journal of Turkish Studies* 18 (2014), *(Hi)stories of Honor in Ottoman Society*, 1–19.

Bogićević, Vojislav, *Sarajevski atentat. Stenogram Glavne rasprave protiv Gavrila Principa i drugova*, (Sarajevo: Državni arhiv NR Bosne i Hercegovine, 1954).

Borozan, Đorđe, *Velika Albanija, porijeklo, ideje, praksa*, (Beograd: Vojnoistorijski institut Vojske Jugoslavije, 1995).

Bougarel, Xavier, 'Yugoslav Wars: 'The Revenge of the Countryside' Between Sociological reality and Nationalist Myth' In *East European Quarterly* XXXIII, No. 2, June 1999, 157–75.

Brunnbauer, Ulf,' "Bold and Pure Highlanders" Mountains and National imagination in the Balkans', In Predrag J. Marković, Tetsuya Sahara, Momčilo Pavlović (eds), *Guerrilla in the Balkans/Gerila na Balkanu*, (Belgrade: Institut za savremenu istoriju; Tokyo: Meiji University, 2007), 31–56.

Brunnbauer, Ulf and Robert Pichler, 'Mountains as "lieux de mémoire": Highland values and the nation-building in the Balkans', *Balkanologie* 6 (1–2), 2002, 77–100.

Čepreganov, Todor, et al., *Makedonskiot identitet niz istorijata*, (Skopje: Institut za nacionalna istorija, 2010).

Chak'rov, Slavi, 'Voennata organizatsiya i podgotovkata na septemvrijskoto v'stanie 1923. g'. In *Septemviyskoto v'stanie 1923 godina—voennite deiystviya*, (Sofia: Ministerstvo na narodnata otbrana, 1973), 9–45.

Chaulev, Peter, *Skipniya*, (Carigrad': Tip. L. Babok' i S-v'ya Galata, ul Kamondo 8, 1924).

Clogg, Richard, *A Concize History of Greece*, 2nd ed. (Cambridge: Cambridge University Press, 2002).

Crampton, Richard J., *Aleksandur Stamboliiski: Bulgaria*, (Chicago: University of Chicago Press and Haus Publishing, 2009).

Crampton, Richard J., *Bulgaria*, (Oxford and New York: Oxford University Press, 2007).

Cvetkovska, Nadežda, *Makedonskoto prašanje vo jugoslovenskiot paralament među dvete svetski vojni*, (Skopje: Institut za nacionalna istorija, 2000).

Cvijić, Jovan, *Makedonski Sloveni, promatranja o etnografiji makedonskih Slovena*, (Beograd: Knjžara Geca Kon, 1906).

Cvijić, Jovan, *O balkanskim psihološkim tipovima* (Beograd: Prosveta, 2014).

Daskalov, Doncho, 'Byalata ruska emigratciya v' B'lgariya mezhdu dvete svetovni voiyni' In *Voennoistoricheski sbornik*, 1/1990, 56–75.

Daskalov, Roumen, *B'lgarskoto obshtestvo 1878–1939. Tom 1*, (Sofia: Gutenberg, 2005).

Dedijer, Vladimir, *Novi prilozi za biografiju Josipa Broza Tita. 1*, (Zagreb: Mladost, 1980).

Dimitrova, Stela. 'Voennata organizatsiya na BKP (t.s.) pri podgotovka na Septemvrisko v'stanie 1923. godina'. In *Voennoistoricheski sbornik*, 1/1990, 45–7.

Dobrinov, Decho, 'Todor Aleksandrov i v'zstanovanieto na VMRO sled p'rvata svetovna vojna (1918–1924 g.)'. In *100 godini V'treshna makedono-odrinska revolucionna organizaciya*, Makedonski nauchen institut, (1994), 145–56.

Dolan, Anne, 'The British Culture of Paramilitary Violence in the Irish War for Independence'. In Robert Gerwarth, John Horn (eds.), *War in Peace: Paramilitary Violence in Europe after the Great War*, (Oxford and New York: Oxford University Press, 2012), 200–15.

Đurišić, Mitar, *Prvi Balkanski rat 1912–1913: (Operacije crnogorske vojske)*, (Beograd: Istorijski institut Jugoslovenske narodne armije, 1960).

Dželetović Ivanov, Pavle, *Kačaci Kosova i Metohije*, (Beograd: Interjupres; Ekkos, 1990).

Dzhonev, Angel, *Pogrom't v Bosilegradsko 16–17 may 1917. g*, (Kyustendil: Faber, 2016).

Elsie, Robert, *A Biographical Dictionary of Albanian History*, (London; New York: B. Tauris, 2013).

Elsie, Robert, *Historical dictionary of Kosovo*, 2nd edition (Lanham; Toronto; Plymouth Scarecrow Press, 2011).

Edin Garaplija, bivši pripadnik DB BiH i AID https://www.youtube.com/watch?v=weg GZXHRT4k *Encyclopedia Britannica*

Executive Committee of the Macedonian Brotherhoods, *Garvanskata golgota (2 March 1923)*, (Sofia: I. K. na s'yuza na makedonskite emigranti, 1924).

Fischer, Bernd J., 'The Balkan Wars and Creation of Albanian Independence'. In, James Pettifier and Tom Buchanan (eds) *War in the Balkans; Conflict and Diplomacy before World War I*. (London: I.B. Tauris 2016).

Fischer, Bernd J., *King Zog and the Struggle for Stability in Albania*, (Tirana: Albanian Institute for International Studies, 2012).

Fromkin, David, 'Dimitrios Returns: Macedonia and the Balkan Question in the Shadow of History'. In: *World Policy Journal*, Vol. 10, No. 2 (Summer, 1993), 67–71.

Gerwarth, Robert and John Horn (eds), *War in Peace; Paramilitary Violence after the Great War*, (Oxford: Oxford University Press, 2012).

Gerwarth, Robert and John Horn, 'Paramilitarism in Europe after the Great War; An Introduction'. In Robert Gerwarth, John Horn, (eds.) *War in Peace; Paramilitary Violence in Europe after the Great War*, (Oxford: Oxford University Press, 2012), 1–18.

Gorgiev, Dragi et al. (eds), *Ohridskoto—debarskoto septemvrisko vostanie od 1913 godina/ Kryengritja e shtatorit në ohër e Diber ë vitit 1913*, (Skopje: Institut za nacionalna istorija/ Instituti historisë *nacionale*, 2014).

Grishina, R. P. (ed), *Makedoniya—Problemy istorii i kul'tury*, (Moskva: Institut slavyano-vedeniya, Rossiyskaya Akademiya Nauk, 1999).

Hacısalihoğlu, Mehmet, 'Yane Sandanski as political leader in Macedonia in the era of the Young Turks'. In *Cahiers balkaniques*, 40 (2012), *Jeunes-Turcs en Macédonie et en Ionie*, 1–28.

Hadži-Vasiljević, Jovan, *Spomenica Jovana S Babunskog*, ([S. l.]: Udruženje rezervnih oficira i obveznika činovničkog reda, 1921).

Hall, Richard 'War in the Balkans'. In: 1914–1918-online. International Encyclopedia of the First World War, Daniel ... [et al.](eds.) (Berlin:Freie Universität Berlin) 2014-10-08. DOI: http://dx.doi.org/10.15463/ie1418.10163.

Horn, John and Alan, Kramer, *German Atrocities 1914, A History of Denial* (New Haven: Yale University Press; 2001).

Horncastle, James, 'Unfamiliar Connection: Special Forces and Paramilitaries in the Former Yugoslavia' in *Special Operations Journal* 2/2016, 12–21.

Housden, Martin, 'White Russians Crossing the Black Sea: Fridtjof Nansen, Constantinople and the First Modern Repatriation of Refugees Displaced by Civil Conflict, 1922–23' In *The Slavonic and East European Review*, Vol. 88, No. 3 (July 2010), 495–524.

Hrabak, Bogumil, 'Miriditi između Italijana, arbanaških nacionalista i Srba'.In *Istorija 20. veka*, 1–2/1993, 35–50.

Ilić, Vladimir, 'Učešće srpskih komita u Kumanovskoj operaciji 1912. godine', In *Vojnoistorijski glasnik*, 1–3/1992, 197–217.

Ilić, Vladimir, *Srpska četnička akcija 1903–1912*, (Beograd: Ecolibri, 2006).

Isić, Momčilo, Mitrović, Milovan and Aranitović, Dobrilo, *Život i delo Sretena Vukosavljevića 1881–1960* (Beograd: Službeni glasnik, 2012).

Ivanović, Drago, *Razvoj oružanih snaga SFRJ 1945–1985. Savezni sekretarijat za narodnu odbranu I*, (Beograd: VIZ, 1990).

Jedinica, documentary by Filip Švarm (Beograd: Vreme film; B92) https://www.youtube.com/watch?v=U_NUBuciOkQ

Jelavich, Charles and Barbara, *The Establishment of Balkan National States 1804–1920* (Seattle; London: University of Washington Press, 1977).

Jelić, Milosav, *Albanija, zapisi o ljudima i događajima*, (Beograd: Geca Kon, 1933).

Jelić, Milosav, 'U mrtvome gradu'. In *Letopis Juga*, (Beograd, 1930).

Jevđević, Dobrosav, *Sarajevski zaverenici, Vidovdan 1914.*, (Beograd: Familet, 2002).

Jovanović, Miroslav, *Doseljavanje ruskih izbeglica u Kraljevinu SHS 1919–1924*, (Beograd: Stubovi kulture, 1996).

Jovanović, Miroslav, *Ruska emigracija na Balkanu (1920–1940)* (Beograd: Čigoja, 2006).

Jovanović, Vladan, 'Land reform and Serbian colonization. Belgrade's problems in interwar Kosovo and Macedonia'. In *East Central Europe*, vol. 42, issue 1 (2015), 87–103.

Jovanović, Vladan, 'In Search of Homeland? Muslim Migration from Yugoslavia to Turkey, 1918–1941'. In *Tokovi istorije*, br. 1–2/2008, 56–67.

Jovanović, Vladan 'Makedonski opijum: o finansijskim i političkim razmerama fenomena (1918–1941)'. In *Godišnjak za društvenu istoriju*, XVI/3, 2009, 69–79.

Jovanović, Vladan 'Rađanje balkanske Kolumbije'. In *Peščanik* https://pescanik.net/radanje-balkanske-kolumbije/

Jovanović, Vladan, 'Suzbijanje kačaka na Kosovu i Metohiji 1912–1929', in *Vojnoistorijski glasnik*, 1/2009, 32–55.

Jovanović, Vladan, *Jugoslovenska država i Južna Srbija 1918–1929 (Makedonija, Sandžak i Kosovo i Metohija u Kraljevini SHS)*, (Beograd: INIS, 2002).

Jovanović, Vladan, *Slike jedne neuspele integracije: Kosovo, Makedonija, Srbija, Jugoslavija*, (Beograd: Fabrika knjiga; Peščanik, 2014).

Jovanović, Vladan, *Vardarska banovina: 1929–1941*, (Beograd: INIS, 2011).

K'rnicheva, Mencha, *Zashto ubih Todor Panitsa?* (Sofia: VMRO—SMD, 1993).

Karakachanov, Krasimir, *VMRO—100 godini borba za Makedoniya*, (Sofia: VMRO-SMD, 1994).

Katardžiev, Ivan, *Makedonsko nacionalno pitanje 1919–1930*, (Zagreb: Globus, 1983).

Kecojević, Dragiša I., *Valandovski pokolj 20. marta 1915 godine*, (Skoplje: D. Kecojević, 2005).

Krakov, Stanislav, *Plamen četništva* (Beograd: Vreme, 1930).

Krakov, Stanislav, *Život čoveka na Balkanu*, (Beograd: Naš dom; Lausanne: L'Age d'Homme, 2006).

Krempton, Ričard Dž., *Balkan posle Drugog svetskog rata*, (Beograd: CLIO, 2003).

Krizman, Bogdan, *Ante Pavelić i ustaše*, (Zagreb: Globus, 1978).

Kyoseva, Cvetana, *B'lgariya i ruskata emigraciya: (20-te–50-te godini na XX v.)* (Sofia: Mezhdunar. Cent'r po problemite na malcinstvata i kulturnite vzaimodejstviya, 2002).

Lange-Akhund, Nadine, 'Nationalisme et terrorisme en Macédoine vers 1900'. In *Balkanologie*, Vol IV, no. 2 (2000), 1–11.

Lange-Akhund, Nadine, *The Macedonian Question. 1893–1908, from Western Sources* (Boulder: East European Monographs, 1998).

Lazarević, Milutin, *Drugi Balkanski rat*,(Beograd: Vojno delo, 1955).

Lekić, Dragan R. (ed), *Drugi pešadijski puk 'Knjaz Mihailo'—Gvozdeni puk u oslobodilačkim ratovima: 1912–1918*, (Prokuplje: Istorijski arhiv Toplice, 2014).

Lekić, Radoje, *Toplički vitezovi—nosioci Karađorđeve zvezde sa mačevima iz Topličkog okruga*, (Prokuplje: Biblioteka Narodnog muzeja Toplice u Prokuplju, 2013).

Levental, Zdenko, *Švajcarac na Kajmakčalanu—knjiga o dr Rajsu*, (Beograd: Prosveta, 1984).

Ličina, Đorđe, Milorad Vavić and Jovan Pavlovski, *Andrija Artuković, Vjekoslav Luburić, Xhaver Deva, Vančo Mihailov*, (Zagreb: Centar za informacije i publicitet, 1985).

Ličina, Đorđe, *Dvadeseti čovjek* (Zagreb: Centar za informacije i publicitet, 1979).

MacMillan, Margaret, *Peacemakers. The Paris Conference of 1919 and Its Attempt to End War*, (London: John Murray, 2002).

Maliković, Dragi, *Kačački pokret na Kosovu i Metohiji: 1918–1924*, (Leposavić: Institut za srpsku kulturu; Kosovska Mitrovica: Filozofski fakultet 2005).

Maljcev, Denis Aleksandrovič, 'Ruske jedinice u Francuskoj i na Solunskom frontu tokom Prvog svetskog rata'. In *Prvi svetski rat i balkanski čvor: Zbornik radova*, (Beograd: Institut za savremenu istoriju, 2014), 477–88.

Marić, Ljubomir, 'Valandovski zločin i njegove žrtve'. In *Ratnik*, IV (1930), 19–31.

Marić, Ljubomir, 'Moravska divizija II poziva u ratu 1912. i 1913. godine' In *Ratnik* IV/1924.

Micić, Milan, *Srpsko dobrovoljačko pitanje u Velikom ratu: (1918–1914)*, (Novo Miloševo: Banatski kulturni centar; Beograd: RTS, 2014).

Mićić, Srđan, 'Kraljevina Srba, Hrvata i Slovenaca i planiranje državnog udara u Bugarskoj 1923–1925', In *Vojnoistorijski glasnik*, 1/2014, 203–32.

Mikhailov, Ivan, *Spomeni II, Osvoboditelna borba 1919–1924* (Louvain, 1965).

Mikhailov, Ivan, *Spomeni, III, Osvoboditelna borba (1924–1934)* (Louvain 1967).

Mikhailov, Pancho (ed), *B'lgarski narodni pesni ot Makedoniya*, (Sofia: Shtipskoto blagotvorno bratstvo v' Sofia, 1924).

Mikhailov, Pancho, *V' stranata na s'lzite*, (Sofia, 1924).

Milićević, Milić, 'Četnička akcija neposredno pre objave i tokom prvih dana srpsko-turskog rata 1912. godine'. In *Prvi balkanski rat 1912/1913. godine: društveni i civilizacijski smisao. Knj. 1*, (Niš: Filozofski fakultet, 2013), 221–34.

Miloradović, Goran, *Karantin za ideje; Logori za izolaciju 'sumnjivih elemenata' u Kraljevini Srba, Hrvata i Slovenaca: 1919–1922*, (Beograd: Institut za savremenu istoriju, 2004).

Milovanović, Nikola, *Kroz tajni arhiv UDBE*, (Beograd: Sloboda, 1974).

Milovanović—Pećanac, Kosta, *Dnevnik Koste Milovanovića—Pećanca: od 1916. do 1918*, (Beograd: Istorijski institute SANU 1998).

Minchev, Dimitre, *Participation of the Population of Macedonia in the First World War: 1914–1918*, (Sofia: Voenno Izdatelstvo, 2004).

Mišić, Saša, *Albanija: prijatelj i protivnik, jugoslovenska politika prema Albaniji: 1924–1927*, (Beograd: Službeni glasnik, 2009).

Mitrović, Andrej, *Serbia's Great War: 1914–1918*, (London: Hurst&Company, 2007).

Mitrović, Andrej, *Ustaničke borbe u Srbiji: 1916–1918*, (Beograd: SKZ, 1987).

Mladenović, Božica B. and Miroslav D. Pešić,'Prvi balkanski rat u memoarma Pavla Blažarića'. In: *Prvi balkanski rat 1912/1913. godine: društveni i civilizacijski smisao. Knj. 1*, (Niš: Filozofski fakultet, 2013), 287–300.

le Moal, Frédéric, *La Serbie: du martyre à la victoire, 1914–1918*, (Paris: Saint-Cloud, 2008).

Muzeii na revolyucionnoto dvizhenie v Balgariya, *Zvezdi v'v vekovete*, (Sofia: Izdatelstvo na Balgarskata komunisticheska partiya, 1972).

Nenezić, Dragan S., *Jugoslovenske oblasti pod Italijom 1941–1943* (Beograd: Vojnoistorijski institut Vojske Jugoslavije, 1999).

Neuburger, Mary C., *Balkan Smoke: Tobacco and the Making of Modern Bulgaria*, (Ithaca: Cornell University Press 2013).

Newman, John Paul, 'The Origins, Attributes, and Legacies of Paramilitary Violence in the Balkans'. In Gerwarth, Robert, John Horn (eds.), *War in Peace; Paramilitary Violence in Europe after the Great War*, (Oxsford: Oxford University Press, 2012), 145–62.

Newman, John Paul, *Yugoslavia in the Shadow of War. Veterans and the Limits of State Building 1903–1945* (Cambridge: Cambridge University Press, 2015).

Nikčević, Tamara, *Goli otoci Jova Kapičića* (Podgorica: Daily press, 2009).

Nikolić, Kosta and Dimitrijević, Bojan, 'Zarobljavanje i streljanje generala Dragoljuba Mihailovića 1946. godine – Nova saznanja o arhivskoj građi' in *Istorija 20. veka*, 2/2009, 9–20.

Nikova, Ekaterina, 'Sledvoennoto nasilie: balgaro-gratski paraleli'. In *Balkanite Modernizatsiya, identichnosti, idei. Sbornik v chest na prof. Nadya Danova*. (Sofia: Institut za balkanistika s Cent'r po trakologija, 2011), 482–501.

Novaković, Mile, *Otmice Zemunskog klana*, (Beograd: Novosti, 2013).

Paleshutski, Kostadin, *Jugoslavskata komunisticheska partiya i makedonskiyat v'pros, 1919-1945*, (Sofia: BAN, 1985). http://www.promacedonia.org/kp_ju/kp_ju_sydyr.html.

Paleshutski, Kostadin, *Makedonskiyat v'pros v burzhoazna Jugoslaviya 1918-1941*, (Sofia: BAN, 1983).

Paleshutski, Kostadin, *Makedonskoto osvoboditelno dvizhenie 1924-1934*, (Sofia: Akademichno izdatelstvo, Prof. Marin Drinov', 1998).

Paleshutski, Kostadin, *Makedonskoto osvoboditelno dvizhenie sled P'rvata svetovna vojna: (1918-1924)* (Sofia: BAN, 1993).

Panayotov, Panayot, *B'lgaro savetski otnosheniya i vr'zki: 1917-1923* (Sofia: Darzhavno izdatelstvo nauka i izkustvo, 1982).

Pandev, Konstantin and Vaptsarov, Maya (eds), *Aferata 'Mis Stoun'; Spomeni, dokumenti i materiali* (Sofia: Izdatelstvo na Otechestveniya front, 1983).

Pavlović, Momčilo and Mladenović, Božica, *Kosta Milovanović-Pećanac: 1878-1944*, (Beograd: Institut za savremenu istoriju, 2006).

Pavlović, Srdja, *Balkan Anschluss; The Annexation of Montenegro and Creation of a Common South Slav State*, (West Lafayette: Purdue University Press, 2008).

Pavlović, Živko, *Bitka na Jadru avgusta 1914. godine*, (Beograd: Grafički zavod 'Makarije', 1924).

Pavlowitch, Steven K., *A History of the Balkans 1804-1945*, (New York and London: Longman, 1999).

Perritt Jr, Henry H., *Kosovo Liberation Army: The inside Story of an Insurgency*, (Urbana and Chicago: University of Illinois Press, 2008).

Petersen, Roger D., *Resistance and Rebelion: Lessons from Easter Europe*, (Cambridge: Cambridge University Press, 2001).

Petranović, Branko, *Istorija Jugoslavije 1918-1988. I* (Beograd: Nolit, 1988).

Petranović, Branko, *Istorija Jugoslavije 1918-1988. II* (Beograd: Nolit, 1988).

Petreska, Darinka et al. (eds), *70 godini VMRO (Obedineta) 1925-1995: Conference proceedings*, (Skopje: Institut za nacionalna istorija, 1998).

Petrova, Dimitrina, *B'lgarskiyat zemedelski naroden s'yuz 1899-1944*, (Sofia: Fond Detelina, 1999).

Petrova, Dimitrina, *D-r Rajko Daskalov (1886-1923): politik i drzhavnik reformator*, (Stara Zagora: Znanie, 1995).

Pisari, Milovan, 'Gušenje Topličkog ustanka: VMRO na čelu represije'. In *Vojnoistorijski glasnik* 2 (2011), 28-41.

Pollman, Ferenc, 'Albanian irregulars in the Austro-Hungarian army during World War I'. In Raugh, Harold E. Jr (ed): *Regular and Irregular Warfare: Experiences of Historical and Contemporary Armed Conflicts* (Belgrade: Institute for Strategic Research 2012), 63-8.

Pollman, Ferenz, 'Austro-Hungarian atrocities against Serbians during WWI (Šabac, 17 August 1914)'. In: *Prvi svetski rat i Balkan—90 godina kasnije: tematski zbornik radova*, (Beograd: Institut za strategijska istraživanja 2010), 135-41.

Pophristov, Georgi, *Revolyutsionnata borba v' bitolskiya okr'g*, (Sofia: NS OF, 1953).

Popov, Čedomir, *Od Versaja do Danciga* (Beograd: Službeni list SRJ, 1995).

'Pravilnik' za dobrovolskite cheti kojito shte dejstvat vo Makedoniya i Odrin v' Osloboditelana voyna'. In: *Nacionalen centr' po voenna istoriya, Nacionalnoosvoboditelnite borbi na b'lagirite ot Makedoniya i Odrinska Trakiya prez Balkanskata voyna (1912-1915)*, (Sofia: Ministerstvo na otbranata Sv. Georgii Pobedonosec, 1994).

Pravilnik' za s'deistvieto koeto voiska dava na grazhdanskite vlasti v' mirno vreme, (Sofia: Ministerstvo na voinata, 1936).

Premk, Martin, *Matjaževa vojska 1945–1950* (Ljubljana: Društvo piscev zgodovine NOB Slovenije, 2005).

'Presuda za zločin u Podujevu' (Portal B92, 18. June 2009). https://www.b92.net/info/vesti/index.php?yyyy=2009&mm=06&dd=18&nav_category=64&nav_id=366737

Princip, Gavrilo, *Princip o sebi* (Zagreb: Jugoslovenska knjiga, 1926).

Radelić, Zdenko, *Križari. Gerila u Hrvatskoj 1945–1950* (Zagreb: Hrvatski institut za povijest, Dom i svijet, 2002).

Radev, Simeon, *Ranni spomeni* (Sofia: Strelec 1994).

Rakočević, Novica, *Crna Gora u Prvom svetskom ratu 1914–1918* (Cetinje: Obod, 1969).

Raspopović, Radoslav 'Montenegro' In *1914–1918-online. International Encyclopedia of the First World War*, Daniel, Ute…[et al.] (eds.), (Berlin: Freie Universität Berlin), 2014–10–08. DOI: 10.15463/ie1418.10243.

Reiss, R. A., *La question des comitadjis en Serbie du Sud* (Belgrade: Vreme, 1924).

Reiss, Rodolphe Archibald, *Report upon the Atrocities committed by the Austro-Hungarian Army during the first Invasion of Serbia*, (London: Simpkin, Marshall, Hamilton, Kent&Co, 1916).

Ristović, Milan 'Occupation during and after the War (South East Europe)'. In *1914–1918-online. International Encyclopedia of the First World War*, Daniel, Ute…[et al.] (eds.), (Berlin: Freie Universität Berlin), 2014–10–08. **DOI**: http://dx.doi.org/10.15463/ie1418.10481.

Robert Gerwarth, *The Vanquished: Why the First World War Failed to End 1917–1923* (London: Allen Lane, 2016).

Rossos, Andrew, *Macedonia and the Macedonians: A History*, (Stanford: Hoover Institution Press, Stanford University, 2008).

Sahara, Tetsuya, 'The Contemporary Paramilitary Phenomenon and the Yugoslav Wars for Succession'. In Marković, Predrag J., Momčilo Pavlović, Tetsuya Sahara (eds.), *Guerrilla in the Balkans. Freedom fighters, Rebels or bandits – Researching the Guerrilla and Paramilitary Forces in the Balkans,* (Tokyo: Meiji University; Belgrade: Institut za savremenu istoriju, 2007), 13–19.

Šaljić, Jovana D.'Muslimani u oslobođenju Srbije 1912/1913: od mita do stvarnosti'. In *Prvi balkanski rat 1912/1913. godine: društveni i civilizacijski smisao Knj. 1* (Niš: Filozofski fakultet, 2013), 325–39.

Samoodbrana, Narodna, *Spomenica proslave dvadesetogodišnjice Bregalničke bitke i desetogodišnjice osnivanja Narodne samoodbrane* (Štip: [s. n.], 1933).

Scheer, Tamara, 'Forces and Force. Austria-Hungary's occupation regime in Serbia during the First World War' In *Prvi svetski rat i Balkan – 90 godina kasnije: tematski zbornik radova* (Beograd: Institut za strategijska istraživanja 2010), 161–79.

Schindler, John, 'Disaster on the Drina; The Austro-Hungarian army in Serbia 1914'. In *War in History* 9/2, 2002, 159–95.

'Sefer Halilović i Munir Alibabić O Ševama ratno specijalnoj jedinici DB' https://www.youtube.com/watch?v=GX2YWbE5Vak

Shandanov, Peter, *Bogatstvo mi e svobodata; Spomeni*, (Sofia: Izdatelstvo 'Gutenberg', 2010).

Sharlanov, Dinyu, *Goryanite. Koi sa te?* (Sofia: Prostranstvo & Forma 1999).

Simonovski, Aleksandar, 'Učestvoto i dejnosta na Milivoj Trbić-Vojče vo Ravnogorsko dviženje vo Makedonija (1942–1944)'. In *Glasnik na Institut za nacionalna istorija*, godina 58, br. 1–2, 2014, 131–41.

Skendi, Stavro, *The Albanian National Awakening 1878–1912* (Princeton, NJ: Princeton University Press, 1967).

Slavković, Božica, 'Bataljoni organizovanih Arnauta'. In *Vojnoistorijski glasnik* 1(2010), 133–56.

Slavković, Božica, 'Bataljoni organizovanih Arnauta' in *Vojnoistorijski glasnik* 1(2012), 51–70.

Slijepćević, Đoko, *Jugoslavija uoči i za vreme Drugog svetskog rata* (Minhen: Iskra, 1978).

Spasov, Lyudmil, *Vrangelovata armiya v B'lgariya 1919–1923* (Sofia: Univerzitetsko izdatelstvo Sv. Kliment Ohridski, 1999).

Sretenović, Stanislav and Danilo Šarenac (eds.), 'Srpski zarobljenici Centralnih sila' In *Leksikon Prvog svetskog rata u Srbiji*, (Beograd: Institut za savremenu istoriju; Društvo istoričara Srbije 'Stojan Novaković', 2015), 388–91.

Stamenov, Mitre, *Atentat't v Marsiliya: Vlado Chernozemski. Zhivot otdaden na Makedoniya*, (Sofia: VMRO—SMD, 1993). http://www.promacedonia.org/ms/ms_index.html

Stanojević, Saša, 'U slavu Gvozdenog puka – svečanosti povodom otkrivanja spomenika Topličanima palim u Oslobodilačkim ratovima i žrtvama Topličkog ustanka u Prokuplju 1934'. In Dragan R. Lekić (ed), *Drugi pešadijski puk 'Knjaz Mihailo' – Gvozdeni puk u oslobodilačkim ratovima 1912–1918*, (Prokuplje: Istorijski arhiv Toplice, 2014), 151–9.

Stojančević, Vladimir et al., *Istorija srpskog naroda.V-1*, (Beograd: SKZ, 1994).

Tasić, Dmitar, 'Između slave i optužbe – Kosta Milovanović Pećanac 1919'. In *Istorija 20. veka*, 2/2007, 2007, 119–24.

Tasić, Dmitar, 'Leteći odred Jovana Babunskog u sprečavanju komitske akcije VMRO 1919. godine'. In *Vojnoistorijski glasnik* 1–2/2006, 79–92.

Tasić, Dmitar, 'Repeating Phenomenon: Balkan Wars and Irregulars'. In Catherine Horel (ed), *Les guerres balkaniques (1912–1913): conflits, enjeux, mémoires* (Bruxelles: Peter Lang, 2014), 25–36.

Tasić, Dmitar, 'The Assassination of King Alexander: The Swan Song of the Internal Macedonian Revolutionary Organization'. In *Donau, Tijdschrift over Zuidost-Europa*, 2008/2, 2008, 31–9.

Tasić, Dmitar, 'Violence as Cause and Consequence: Comparisons of Anti-Communist Armed Resistance in Yugoslavia and Bulgaria after the Second World War'. In *CAS Working Paper Series*, No. 10/2018, 1–36. https://www.ceeol.com/search/article-detail?id=703533

Tasić, Dmitar, 'Albanski oružani otpor uspostavljanju vlasti nove Jugoslavije 1944–1945'. In Zoran Janjetović (ed), *1945.: kraj ili novi početak?* (Beograd: Institut za noviju istoriju Srbije; Muzej žrtava genocida, 2016), 91–106.

Tasić, Dmitar, *Rat posle rata, Vojska Kraljevine Srba, Hrvata i Slovenaca na Kosovu i Metohiji i u Makedoniji: 1918–1920*, (Beograd: Utopija, 2008).

Tasić, Dmitar, 'Pecanac, Kosta'. *1914–1918-online. International Encyclopedia of the First World War*, Daniel, Ute... [et al.] (eds.), (Berlin: Freie Universität Berlin), 2014-10-08. DOI: http://dx.doi.org/10.15463/ie1418.10112.

Tasić, Dmitar, 'Warfare 1914–1918 (South East Europe)'. In: *1914–1918-online. International Encyclopedia of the First World War*, Daniel, Ute... [et al.] (eds.), (Berlin: Freie Universität Berlin), 2014-10-08. DOI: http://dx.doi.org/10.15463/ie1418.10366.

Timofeyev, Aleksey Yurevich, 'Serbskie chetniki nakanune i v hode Balkanskih voin: social'nii fenomen, nacional'naya tradiciya i voennaya taktika' In *Modernizaciya vs. voina—Chelovek na Balkanah nakanune i vo vremya Balkanskih voin (1912–1913)*, (Moskva: 2012), 102–22.

Timofeyev, Aleksey, *Crveni i beli; ruski uticaji na događaje u Jugoslaviji 1941–1945*, (Beograd: Ukronija, 2014).

Timofeyev, Aleksey, 'Partija građanskog rata': Pripreme kadrova Kominterne za izvođenje partizanskog rata i revolucije'. In *Vojnoistorijski glasnik* 1/2009, 56–77.

Timofeyev, Aleksey, 'Sovjetska uloga u školovanju i pripremi jugoslovenskog partizanskog kadra do početka Drugog svetskog rata'. In *Vojnoistorijski glasnik* 2/2009, 55–77.

Timofeyev, Aleksey, 'Vojne i bezbednosne strukture SSSR u pripremi partizanskog ratovanja do početka Drugog svetskog rata'. In *Vojnoistorijski glasnik* 2/2008, 36–52.

Todorovska, Katerina, *Petar Čaulev*, (Skopje: Univerzitet 'Sv. Kiril i Metodij', Filozofski fakultet, 2014).

Todorovski, Zoran, *Avtonomističkata VMRO na Todor Aleksandrov 1919–1924*, (Skopje: Makavej, 2013).

Todorovski, Zoran, *Todor Aleksandrov*, (Skopje: Makavej; Državen arhiv na Republika Makedonija, 2014).

Tomac, Petar, *Vojna istorija* (Beograd: VIZ JNA, 1959).

Tourkantonis, G. et al,, *A Concise History of the Balkan Wars 1912–1913*, (Athens: Army History Directorate, 1998).

Trbić, Vasilije *Memoari. I*, Kultura, Beograd 1996.

Trbić, Vasilije *Memoari. II*, Kultura, Beograd 1996.

Trhulj, Sead, *Mustafa Golubić, čovjek konspiracije*, (Sarajevo: Zalihica, 2007).

Trifunović-Birčanin, Ilija, *Trnovitim stazama*, (Beograd: Štamparija Glavnog saveza srpskih zemljoradničkih zadruga, 1933).

Trumpener, Ulrich, 'Turkey's War'. In *The Oxford illustrated History of the First World War* (Oxford: Oxford University Press, 2014).

Tyulekov, Dimitar, *Obrecheno rodolyubie. VMRO v Pirinsko 1919–1934* (Blagoevgrad: Univ. Izd. 'Neofit Rilski', 2001), http://www.promacedonia.org/dt/index.html

Up'tvane za deistvie na vojskite pri potushavane na razmirici, v'r'zheni vystanija i pri presledvane na razbojnicheski bandi, (Sofia: Ministerstvo na voinata, 1935).

Uput za četničko ratovanje, (Beograd: Ministarstvo vojske i mornarice, 1929).

Uzunov, Angel, *Spomeni* (Skopje: Makavej, 2014).

Vasić, Dragiša, *Dva meseca u jugoslovenskom Sibiru*, (Beograd: Prosveta, 1990).

Vasilev, Vasil, *Pravitelstvo na BZNS, VMRO i B'lgaro-Yugoslavskite otnosheniya*, (Sofia: B'lgarskata akademija na naukite, 1991).

Vasiljević, Đorđe, *Zavera protiv Srbije: VMRO Vanče Mihajlova*, (Beograd: Politika, 1991).

Veljanovski, Novica et al.m *Makedonija vo dvaesettiot vekot*, (Skopje: Institut za nacionalna istorija, 2003).

Vezenkov, Aleksandar, *9 septemvri 1944 g.* (Sofia: Institut za izsledvane na blizkoto minalo and Ciela, 2014).

Vickers, Miranda, *The Albanians: a modern history* (London: Tauris, 1995).

Vishnyakov, Yaroslav Valeriyanovich 'Balkanskie voini 1912–1913.gg i organizaciya "Chernaya ruka"'. In *Modernizaciya vs. voina—Chelovek na Balkanah nakanune i vo vremya Balkanskih voin (1912–1913)* (Moskva, 2012).

Vladimirtsev, N (ed.), *NKVD-MVD SSSR v bor'be s banditizmom i vooruzhennym natsionalisticheskim podpol'yem na Zapadnoy Ukraine, v Zapadnoy Belorussii i Pribaltike (1939–1956)*, (Moskva: Ob'yedinennaya redaktsiya MVD Rossii, 2008).

Vlora, Ekrem-beg, *Sekavanjata ot životot. Tom II*, (1921–1925) (Skopje: Fondacija Otvoreno opštestvo, 2015).

'*Vojna enciklopedija*', (Beograd: VIZ, 1970).

Vukušić, Iva, 'Nineteen Minutes of Horror: Insights from the Scorpions Execution Video'. In *Genocide Studies and Prevention: An International Journal*, Vol. 12/2018, Images and Collective Violence: Function, Use and Memory, Issue 2, 35–53. https://scholarcommons.usf.edu/gsp/vol12/iss2/5/

Vulkov, Martin and Dimitar Grigorov, 'The Toplice Uprising'. In *The First World War and its impact on the Balkans and Eurasia, 17–18 September 2013*, Sofia University, PAPERS, 5. http://www.viaevrasia.com/documents/D.Grigorov%20M.Valkov%20THE%20TOPLICE%20UPRISING%20.pdf

Yaanchev, Veselin, *Armiya, obshtestven red i vatreshna sigurnost mezhdu voynite i sled tyaah: 1913–1915, 1918–1923* (Sofia: Universitetsko izdatelstvo 'Sv. Kliment Ohridski', 2014).

Žežov, Nikola, 'VMRO i atentatot vrz jugoslovenskiot kral Aleksandar Karageorgevik'. In *Godišen zbornik na Filozofskiot fakultetot na Univerzitetot 'Sv. Kiril i Metodij', Kniga 60* (Skopje: 2007), 333–47.

Žežov, Nikola, *Makedonskoto prašanje vo jugoslovensko-bugarskite diplomatski odnosi (1918–1941)* (Skopje: Univerzitet 'Sv. Kiril i Metodij', 2008).

Žila, Lenina, *Vienska 'stapica': Istorija na pregovorite megu SSSR i VMRO na Todor Aleksandrov,* (Skopje: Institut po nacionalna istorija, 2014).

Živojinović, Dragoljub R., *Vatikan, katolička crkva i jugoslovenska vlast 1941–1958,* (Beograd: Prosveta; Tersit, 1994).

Životić, Aleksandar, 'Jurišne (četničke) jedinice vojske Kraljevine Jugoslavije 1940–1941'. In *Vojnoistorijski glasnik*, 1–2/2003, 44–65.

Ivaylo Znepolski (ed.), *NRB ot nachaloto do na kraya,* (Sofia: Ciela, 2011).

Zverzhanovski, Ivan, 'Watching War Crimes: The Srebrenica Video and the Serbian Attitudes to the 1995 Srebrenica Massacre'. In *Southeast European and Black Sea Studies,* 7, no. 3 (2007), *Dark Histories, Brighter Futures? The Balkans and Black Sea Region—European Union Frontiers, War Crimes and Confronting the Past,* 417–30.

Index